EVOLUTION IN THE COURTROOM

A REFERENCE GUIDE

EVOLUTION IN THE COURTROOM

A REFERENCE GUIDE

Randy Moore

A B C ⬥ C L I O

Santa Barbara, California   Denver, Colorado   Oxford, England

Library of Congress Cataloging-in-Publication Data

Moore, Randy.
    Evolution in the courtroom : a reference guide / Randy Moore.
        p. cm.
Includes bibliographical references.
    ISBN 1-57607-420-X (hardcover : acid-free paper); ISBN 1-57607-421-8
(e-book)
    1. Evolution—Study and teaching—Law and legislation—United
States—History. 2. Creationism—Study and teaching—Law and
legislation—United States—History. I. Title.
    KF4208.5.S34 M66 2001
    344.73'077—dc21

                                    2001005295

06 05 04 03 02 01   10 9 8 7 6 5 4 3 2 1

This book is also available on the World Wide Web as an e-book.
Visit abc-clio.com for details.

ABC-CLIO, Inc.
130 Cremona Drive, P.O. Box 1911
Santa Barbara, California 93116-1911

This book is printed on acid-free paper ∞.

Manufactured in the United States of America

This book is for Richelle, Emily, Dylan, and Hannah.

CONTENTS

Randy Moore (right) and Susan Epperson (of Epperson v. Arkansas*). (Courtesy of Randy Moore)*

PREFACE

In the nineteenth century, virtually everyone agreed that science and religion were different aspects of the one plan of the one God. Most educated Christians accepted the claim of Irish prelate James Ussher that life's creation had occurred as recently as 4004 B.C. Similarly, English science was morally grounded in Christian and Hebrew Scriptures, and the purpose of the famed Royal Society of London was to glorify God and improve man's life. Everything had a fixed, preordained station in life, and nature was viewed as a harmonious, benevolent, and nearly perfect world. The special creation of life and the divinely ordered harmony of nature were widely accepted views of sectarian religion as well as science.

Evolution-based explanations of life's diversity had been proposed but rejected. The most famous of these explanations was Jean-Baptiste Lamarck's inheritability of acquired traits. All of the other explanations, such as the upward, progressive changes proposed in 1844 by Robert Chambers in his popular book *Vestiges of the Natural History of Creation*, were teleological and relied on metaphysical events to attain predetermined conclusions. None of these theories had withstood scientific scrutiny.

The publication of Charles Darwin's *On the Origin of Species* in 1859 changed everything. Darwin argued that organisms are not perfectly adapted and that natural selection updates organisms by tailoring them to their environment. Organisms that appear to be "perfect" are merely the latest stages of evolution resulting from the endless competition associated with getting ahead.

Darwin challenged claims of special creation, eliminated the requirement of purpose for humanity (other than the production of fertile offspring), and replaced the claims of a benign and perfectly designed world with one based on an amoral and brutal struggle for existence. This challenged the moral and social aims of science, for in Darwin's world, science no longer depended on miracles.

Overwhelming evidence indicates that organisms—humans included—evolve. Nevertheless, large percentages of people want to either replace or supplement the teaching of evolution with the biblical story of creation. To many of these people, the acceptance of evolution undermines biblical doctrine and salvation. This clash of views has produced a long and lively controversy.

This book discusses the legal history of the evolution/creationism controversy. I've presented this history in a variety of ways:

Court cases: Chapters 1–7 summarize the most influential court cases associated with the controversy. Although some of these cases are well known (e.g., the Scopes "Monkey Trial"), other influential cases remain relatively unknown.

Biographies: Chapter 8 presents biographies of the key people who have been involved in the evolution/creationism controversy. Who were the people associated with the major events in the controversy? When did they live? What did they say? What did they do?

Chronology: Chapter 9 presents a chronology of the controversy. Here you'll find a timeline describing the major (and a few merely curious) events associated with the controversy, as well as how they relate to other important events in biology. As you'll see, most of the events associated with the evolution/creationism controversy have occurred outside of the legal system.

Documents: Here you'll find excerpts from the major court decisions associated with the controversy.

I hope you enjoy this book.

Randy Moore
April 2001

ACKNOWLEDGMENTS

I'm grateful to many people for their help in preparing this book. Richard Cornelius critiqued my ideas and graciously gave me access to photographs in the archives of Bryan College. Similarly, Susan Epperson gave me access to her personal records; both Susan and Don Aguillard discussed their court cases with me and provided helpful feedback. Finally, Kevin Downing, Susan McRory, and Liz Kincaid have been supportive, helpful, and forgiving editors. Without these and other people, this book would have been delayed considerably and not been as good. Thanks.

I also thank the National Association of Biology Teachers for allowing me to use in this book portions of articles that appeared in the *American Biology Teacher*.

ACRONYMS

AAAS	American Association for the Advancement of Science
AAUP	American Association of University Professors
AAUW	American Association of University Women
ACLU	American Civil Liberties Union
AEA	Arkansas Education Association
AFT	American Federation of Teachers
AIBS	American Institute for Biological Sciences
ASA	American Scientific Affiliation
BBC	British Broadcasting Corporation
BSCS	Biological Sciences Curriculum Study
CAVE	Citizens for Another Voice in America
CRS	Creation Research Society
CSRC	Creation Science Research Center
FLAG	Family Life, America, and God
HB	House Bill
ICLU	Indiana Civil Liberties Union
ICR	Institute for Creation Research
MACOS	Man: A Course of Study
NABT	National Association of Biology Teachers
NAS	National Academy of Science
NRC	National Research Council
NSF	National Science Foundation
NSTA	National Science Teachers Association
SB	Senate Bill

EVOLUTION IN THE COURTROOM

A REFERENCE GUIDE

IN THE BEGINNING . . .

*No mention of religion, the only basis for morality; not a suggestion of
a sense of responsibility to God—nothing but cold, clammy materialism! Darwinism transforms the Bible into a story book and reduces
Christ to man's level. It gives him an ape for an ancestor on his
mother's side at least and, as many evolutionists believe, on his Father's side also. The instructor [of evolution] gives the student a new
family tree millions of years long . . . and then sets him adrift, with infinite capacity for good or evil, but with no light to guide him, no
compass to direct him, and no chart of the sea of life!*
—William Jennings Bryan, 1922

*We must, however, acknowledge, as it seems to me, that man with all
his noble qualities . . . still bears in his bodily frame the indelible
stamp of his lowly origin.*
—Charles Darwin

*There is a war going on in society—a very real battle . . . but we must
wake up to the fact that, at the foundation level, it's really creation
versus evolution.*
—Ken Ham, 1987

Although evolution is the unifying theme for understanding life and "one of
the best documented, most compelling and exciting concepts in all of science" (Gould 1983), it has repeatedly been challenged—not by new discoveries, but by a group of people collectively called "creationists." Despite
the overwhelming evidence supporting evolution (see Prelli 1989; Hays
1983; Scott 1997; and references therein), creationism remains an overwhelmingly popular belief (e.g., Sinclair and Pendarvis 1998; Monsour
1997). For example, Raymond Eve and Francis Harrold (1991) estimate
that "over a quarter—and perhaps as many as half—of the nation's high
school students get educations shaped by creationist influence." Interestingly, creationism is popular with science teachers and educators; many
school board presidents and almost half of the science teachers in the United
States support including creationism in the classroom (Affannato 1986). A
poll conducted in March 2000 reported that 79 percent of educators back
creationism in schools (Glanz 2000). Nationally, only 57 percent of science
teachers consider evolution to be a unifying theme in biology, and almost
half of all science teachers believe that there is as much evidence for cre-

THE ORIGIN OF SPECIES

BY MEANS OF NATURAL SELECTION,

OR THE

PRESERVATION OF FAVOURED RACES IN THE STRUGGLE FOR LIFE.

BY CHARLES DARWIN, M.A.,

FELLOW OF THE ROYAL, GEOLOGICAL, LINNÆAN, ETC., SOCIETIES;
AUTHOR OF ' JOURNAL OF RESEARCHES DURING H. M. S. BEAGLE'S VOYAGE
ROUND THE WORLD.'

LONDON:
JOHN MURRAY, ALBEMARLE STREET.
1859.

The right of Translation is reserved.

Charles Darwin's monumental work was published in November 1859. (Library of Congress)

ationism as there is for evolution. In many states, biology teachers often place little or no emphasis on evolution (Weld and McNew 1999). Finally, a 1999 Gallup poll found that 47 percent of Americans believe that "God created man pretty much in his present form at one time within the last 10,000 years." Only 9 percent believe that "man has developed over millions of years from less advanced forms of life. God had no part in this process" (Gallup and Newport 1991). By comparison, a majority of scientists take the naturalist view shared by only 9 percent of Americans. It is hard to imagine any other issue for which there is such a difference between laypeople and experts (see discussion in Shermer 1997).

Darwin in the Courtroom

Charles Darwin's monumental *On the Origin of Species by Means of Natural Selection* refuted teleology and purpose as explanations of life's diversity and suggested that humans are not exempt from processes that affect other organisms. Despite *Origin*'s message and implications, there was considerable acceptance of Darwin's ideas by American Protestants. That acceptance resulted largely from the advocacy of Darwin's ideas by Harvard's Asa Gray, an evangelical Christian who was the leading botanist in the United States in the mid-nineteenth century and president of the American Association for the Advancement of Science (AAAS). Gray, who espoused a progressive, God-driven evolution, arranged for the initial publication of Darwin's *Origin* in the United States (see Moore 1997 and references therein).[1] When Gray proclaimed that he had reconciled God and evolution, many American Protestants were relieved and accepted the idea (Scott 1994). However, that acceptance didn't last long, for by the end of World War I, religious attitudes had shifted; a collective nostalgia for the relative simplicity of prewar life, combined with a perceived decline in morality, led many people to rely increasingly on their religious faith for stability and comfort. Religious fundamentalism, based on a literal interpretation of the Bible, became very popular.[2]

Creationism is not a single concept; rather, there are several distinguishable varieties of creationism (e.g., young-Earth, day-age, progressive, theistic; see Pennock 1999). The different sects of creationism are distinguished largely by what part(s) of science each is willing to accept. For example, intelligent-design creationists avoid topics such as the age of Earth, the Great Flood, and Noah's ark, and—as far as possible—interpretations of the Book of Genesis. Although creationists disagree on some of the details (e.g., see Scott 1997), the essence of their beliefs is summarized in the following six tenets, each of which arises from a fundamentalist Christian interpretation of the creation story in Genesis (Shermer 1997; Taylor 1992; and references therein):

- Evolution cannot adequately account for the development of life and its various forms.
- The universe, energy, and life were created suddenly from nothing by a Creator.
- Humans and apes do not share a common ancestry.
- Changes occur only within fixed limits or within originally created forms of life.
- Geological history is best explained by catastrophism, including a Noachian flood.[3] Many claims of creationists are not falsifiable.[4]
- The Earth is young (less than 10,000 years old).

The Controversy Begins: Fundamentalists and Darwin

Following World War I and the successful campaign to outlaw liquor, fundamentalists turned their attention to Darwin. Led by religious leaders such as William Bell Riley, John Roach Straton, J. Frank Norris, Aimee Semple McPherson, and—most prominently—William Jennings Bryan, fundamentalists denounced Darwin's ideas as being responsible for the decline of the nation's morals and feared that evolution was "the most present threat to the truth they were sure they alone possessed" (Smith 1965). Fundamentalist preachers such as William A. "Billy" Sunday (a former Chicago Cubs outfielder) used theatrical services to link evolution with eugenics, prostitution, and crime; McPherson presided at ritual hangings of "monkey teachers"; Straton told his followers that it was "better to wipe out all the schools than . . . permit the teaching of evolution"; Norris called evolution "that hell-born, Bible-destroying, German rationalism" as he campaigned to have "evolutionists" fired from their teaching positions. Other preachers cited Darwin as a primary supporter of the four p's: prostitution, perversion, pornography, and permissiveness (Gould 1983; Larson 1997; de Camp 1969). To these and other people, antievolution laws represented a return to prewar normalcy, just as creationism in the public schools represented a public validation of a populist lifestyle (Larson 1997; Taylor and Condit 1988).

In the early 1920s, religious fundamentalists—especially those in the South—sensed that something was wrong with the country. Nostalgically longing for simpler times, religious fundamentalists tried to save the nation's soul by eliminating discussions of evolution from society, beginning with the public schools. In Kentucky, where "Fundamentalists were probably more firmly entrenched among the Baptists . . . than in any other state," administrators at Campbellsville College told faculty to condemn evolution (Bailey 1964). Soon thereafter, the Kentucky Baptist Board of Missions demanded that the state eradicate the teaching of the "false and degrading" theory of evolution at the University of Kentucky. William Jennings Bryan, the rich, populist Democrat and three-time candidate for president of the United States, joined the Baptists' crusade by sending a letter to Kentucky Baptists saying that "the movement [to ban the teaching of evolution] will sweep the country and will drive Darwinism from our schools." He then told a joint session of the Kentucky General Assembly to pass a law that would ban the teaching of "atheism, agnosticism or the theory of evolution" in the state's public schools. Legislation for such a law was opposed by the University of Kentucky's president, Frank McVey, and a few other leaders in the state. On 9 March 1922, within weeks after a Kentucky teacher was fired for teaching that the Earth was round, the state legislature debated the legislation for five hours, after which it defeated the legislation by a vote of 42–41. This was the first legislative vote to ban the teaching of evolution, but it would not be the last ("One Legislator's Vote" 1999).

Southern Baptists were usually the leaders of the fundamentalists. At their national convention in 1922, the Southern Baptists reiterated their belief that the Bible and evolution are irreconcilable. At their convention the following year, the Southern Baptists instructed scientists to concede the authority of the Bible, including the Virgin Birth and the physical Resurrection. Meanwhile, in Arkansas, the Baptist State Convention passed a resolution stating that the state's Baptist institutions could not employ anyone—not even someone to pick up trash—who believed in Darwinism.

Late in 1922, the Oklahoma Baptist Convention demanded that the state's legislators pass a law banning the teaching of evolution in the state's public schools. Two months later, the Baptists' plea was answered when lawmakers, recognizing the public's support for such a ban, added a rider to a free-textbook bill that banned the use of any textbook that promoted "a materialistic conception of history, that is, the Darwin theory of evolution versus the Bible theory of creation." That rider, which was suggested by William Jennings Bryan, passed overwhelmingly in the Oklahoma House of Representatives, but it survived by a margin of only four votes in the state Senate.

On 24 March 1923, with little fanfare, Governor John C. Walton (a progressive Democrat) of Oklahoma signed the legislation, thereby creating the first antievolution law in the United States.[5] As the state Baptist Sunday School Convention congratulated the legislature and governor for their work (Bailey 1964), the California Board of Education instructed teachers to present evolution "as a theory only," and the North Carolina Board of Education—with the governor's support—barred public high schools from using biology textbooks that presented an origin for humans that differed from that described in the Bible (Larson 1989). Tennessee and Arkansas, with the backing of groups including the Ku Klux Klan, made it a crime to teach nonbiblical ideas such as evolution in public schools (Larson 1997; Shermer 1997).

Forty-three years after Darwin's death, the clash between science and fundamentalism went on trial in the infamous Scopes "Monkey Trial" in Dayton, Tennessee, a small town nestled among the Cumberland hills, 40 miles north of Chattanooga. Despite the fact that it has often been misreported and misinterpreted (Cornelius 1990), the Scopes trial has profoundly influenced virtually all legislation, court decisions, and local actions involving the evolution/creationism controversy since 1925 (Larson 1997; Cornelius 1991). The Scopes trial has become the standard to which all subsequent "evolution trials" have been compared (Cornelius 1991). Although Scopes's misdemeanor carried the same penalties as the minor drinking violations that were heard in batches in Dayton's court every day, it became the basis for one of the most influential and celebrated trials of all time, as well as an important event that shaped the twentieth century (Larson 1997; Puente 1999).

Notes

1. Gray's *First Lessons in Botany and Vegetable Physiology* (1857; later renamed *The Elements of Botany*) was the leading botany text of the late nineteenth century and the first high school text after the publication of *Origin* to include Darwin's ideas about evolution. Gray was the only American taken into Charles Darwin's confidence prior to the publication of *Origin* (Larson 1989).

2. Fundamentalists got their name from a series of twelve small pamphlets (containing ninety articles) titled *The Fundamentals* that were written between 1910 and 1915. These pamphlets, which were to be sent free of charge to "every pastor, evangelist, missionary, theological student, Sunday school superintendent, Y.M.C.A. and Y.W.C.A. secretary in the English speaking world, so far as the addresses of these can be obtained," proclaimed biblical literalism as the antidote to "modernism." The volumes stated that it is "evident to every intelligent layman that [Darwin's ideas] can have no possible points of contact with Christianity." Millions of the pamphlets were given away (Larson 1989). This project was financed by Lyman and Milton Stewart, who founded the Union Oil Company (Clouse 1995). Before the fifth volume was printed, 275,000 people had received copies; eventually, 3 million copies were distributed.

3. A popular book promoting the flood—*The Genesis Flood: The Biblical Record and Its Scientific Implications* (Whitcomb and Morris 1961)—became the flash point for the subsequent demand by creationists for "equal time" in the classroom (see Moore 1998b, 1998c).

4. John Whitcomb and Henry Morris (1961) demonstrate the unfalsifiability of creationists' claims by stating that the "geological record . . . can give no information as to the process . . . employed by God during the Creation, since God has plainly said that those processes no longer operate."

5. Oklahoma's antievolution law was repealed soon after Walton was impeached in 1925.

"WITH FLAMING BANNERS AND BEATING DRUMS": STATE OF TENNESSEE V. JOHN THOMAS SCOPES

[The Tennessee antievolution law] is as brazen and as bold an attempt to destroy learning as was ever made in the Middle Ages. The only difference is we have not provided that they [the violators of the law] will be burned at the stake. But there is time for that, Your Honor. We have to approach these things gradually.
—Clarence Darrow

It is utterly foolish for a man to talk about teaching biology and not teaching evolution.
—Andrew Lee Pickens, 1926, after Southern Baptists forced him to resign from Furman University for declaring his support for the theory of evolution

Keep your Bible in the world of theology where it belongs and do not try to . . . put [it] into a course of science.
—Dudley Field Malone, shouting at prosecutors during the Scopes trial, July 1925

May the son of Charles Darwin send you one word of warm encouragement. To state that which is true cannot be irreligious.
—Leonard Darwin, in a letter to John Scopes

The evolution/creationism controversy exploded in front of a worldwide audience in July 1925, when twenty-four-year-old coach and substitute science teacher John Thomas Scopes volunteered to be tried in Dayton, Tennessee, for violating Tennessee's newly passed statute that made it a crime to teach human evolution in public schools.[1] That law, like Scopes's trial, was influenced by William Jennings Bryan. In 1924, Bryan was a fading influence in the Democratic Party, but he realized that his political aspirations could be reinvigorated by a "great cause" like the antievolution campaign. Bryan told his son that he was going to shift "from the politics of ballot boxes to the politics of saving souls." As part of his plan to save souls, Bryan remade himself into "a sort of Fundamentalist Pope" and lectured in 1924 in Nashville on "Is the Bible True?" as the legislature was discussing the evolution question (Cornelius 1991). Bryan's lectures catapulted the evolution/creationism issue to public attention. Copies of Bryan's talk were printed as a pamphlet and sent twice to the state's legislators, one of whom was John Washington Butler.

Butler, an amiable part-time teacher and clerk of the Round Lick Association of Primitive Baptists, was a prosperous farmer and legislator who had taken up the antievolution cause in 1922 after hearing a preacher tell of a woman whose faith had been shaken after she went to a university and was told about evolution (Scopes Trial Museum). Butler worried that his five children would be similarly corrupted by the public schools and knew that his desire to ban the teaching of evolution was popular, claiming that "ninety-nine people out of a hundred in my district [think] just as I do. . . . I know there isn't a one in the whole district who thinks evolution of man can be the way scientists tell it."

In 1924, convinced that evolution "undermines the foundation of our government," Butler spent his forty-ninth birthday (17 December 1924) at home writing House Bill 185, "An Act Prohibiting the Teaching of the Evolution Theory in all the Universities, Normals, and all other public schools of Tennessee, which are supported in whole or in part by the public school funds of the State, and to provide penalties for the violations thereof," which became known as the "Butler Law." That bill, which Butler had promised in an election campaign several years earlier, made it "unlawful for any teacher in any of the Universities, Normals and all other public schools of the state . . . to teach any theory that denies the story of the Divine Creation of man as taught in the Bible, and to teach instead that man is descended from a lower order of animals" (Cornelius 1991). However, Butler was beaten to the punch when, on 20 January 1925, Senator John A. Shelton introduced a bill banning the teaching of evolution in Tennessee's public schools. Shelton's bill was rejected by the Senate Judiciary Committee by one vote; the committee did not want to pass laws dealing with religious beliefs.

Although Shelton's bill languished, Butler introduced his bill in the House of Representatives. There was virtually no opposition to Butler's legislation. Faculty and administrators at the University of Tennessee remained silent, fearing that the legislature would cut the university's budget if they opposed the law. Officials at the State Department of Education also were silent, as were leaders of the Tennessee Academy of Science. Major newspapers in Tennessee either endorsed the legislation or ignored it (Ginger 1958). Among the many public figures who praised the legislation was famed evangelist Billy Sunday, whose eighteen-day revival in Memphis in February 1925 attracted more than 10 percent of Tennessee's residents ("First Verse" 1925). Throughout the revival, Sunday denounced evolution as "the old bastard theory of evolution," Darwin as an "infidel," and education as being "chained to the devil's throne."

Butler's statute appeared in the same form that Butler "wrote it out after breakfast at home" and was passed without debate on 28 January 1925 by the Tennessee House in a vote of 71–5. The next month in the Senate, however, Butler's bill met the same fate as Shelton's had in the Judiciary Committee. After both bills were referred back to the committee, the legislature recessed for four weeks. When the Senate reconvened, the Senate Judiciary Committee reversed itself and passed Butler's bill on 10 March by a vote of 7–4. Three days later in the full Senate, there were cries to "Save our children for God" as Butler's legislation passed by a vote of 24–6. It was then signed into law—under pressure by fellow Baptists—by Governor Austin Peay on 21 March 1925, thereby becoming Chapter 27 of the Public Acts of Tennessee for 1925. Peay feared that "there is a deep and widespread belief that something is shaking the fundamentals of the country . . . an abandonment of the old-fashioned faith and belief in the Bible is our trouble." And he believed he knew the remedy for the problem: "The people have the right, and must have the right, to regulate what is taught in their schools."

Although the Butler Law took effect immediately, Peay tried to disarm critics by claiming that "it will not put our teachers in any jeopardy. . . . Nobody believes that it is going to be an active statute" (de Camp 1969; Larson 1997). Neither Peay nor the legislature intended to enforce the law. Within just a few weeks, however, the governor would be proven wrong.

Scopes's trial—a world-class event in its day—resulted from an ad the American Civil Liberties Union (ACLU) placed in the 4 May 1925 issue of the *Chattanooga Daily Times*. The ACLU announced: "We are looking for a Tennessee teacher who is willing to accept our services in testing this law in the courts. Our lawyers think a friendly test case can be arranged without costing a teacher his or her job. Distinguished counsel have volunteered their services. All we need now is a willing client."

Dr. George Rappleyea, a thirty-one-year-old chemical engineer and the manager of Dayton's ailing Cumberland Coal and Iron Company, saw the ACLU's ad and was intrigued. With the newspaper in hand, Rappleyea headed for Robinson's Drugstore, a popular gathering spot where he, Fred E. "The Hustling Druggist" Robinson (president of the school board and owner of the drugstore), and other local residents decided to concoct a trial to test the law and, in the process, boost Dayton's struggling economy (see, e.g., Allem 1959).[2] Rappleyea summoned Scopes from a tennis match to Robinson's Drugstore—"if it's convenient"—and asked if he'd be willing to be arrested for violating the new law. When Scopes agreed to be the law-breaking villain, the *Chattanooga News* was given the story (Cornelius 1990). Rappleyea found a piece of brown wrapping paper and wrote the text of a telegram to the ACLU office in New York:

Professor J. T. Scopes, teacher of science at Rhea County high school, Dayton, Tenn., will be arrested and charged with teaching evolution. Consent of superintendent of education for test case to be defended by you. Wire me collect if you wish to co-operate and arrest will follow.

The ACLU agreed to finance the case, and Rappleyea swore out a warrant for Scopes's arrest, after which a deputy found and "arrested" Scopes where Rappleyea said he'd be, in Robinson's Drugstore, drinking a Coke.[3] After a preliminary hearing on 10 May, Scopes was arraigned and bound over to the grand jury under a $1,000 bond. No one anticipated that the case would become one of the most famous trials in U.S. history (Scopes 1961). But before it was over, Scopes's trial would test the First Amendment's protection of freedom of speech and the establishment of religion, as well as the Fourteenth Amendment's provision for personal liberty. The trial would also pit science against religion, the academic freedom of teachers against the academic freedom of students, and governmental authority against parental rights. Scopes, who described the trial as "just a drugstore discussion that got past control," quickly became irrelevant as the trial became a battle of evangelical faith and majoritarianism against scientific secularism and individual liberty (Cornelius 1990).

When the public learned that Scopes would test the Butler Law, local ministers began raising funds to prosecute him (Ginger 1958). Residents began choosing sides. On the same day that Scopes agreed to be tried, the World's Christian Fundamentals Association denounced "the teaching of the unscientific, anti-Christian, atheistic, anarchistic, pagan rationalistic evolutionary theory" (Irons 1988). On 28 May, the American Medical Association struck for the other side when it unanimously condemned the prosecution of Scopes and restrictions on the teaching of evolution (Ginger 1958). The American Federation of Teachers also came out on Scopes's side when it passed a resolution stating that "it is neither science nor religion that is on trial, but the public school." However, the larger National Education Association rejected a similar resolution as "inadvisable." The Tennessee Academy of Science, which included most of Tennessee's leading scientists, said nothing against the Butler Law until several months after it became law (Larson 1997).

Scopes's trial (*State of Tennessee v. John Thomas Scopes*, Nos. 5231, 5232 [1925]) opened on 10 July 1925 and ended on 21 July 1925. It was a spectacular media event. Dayton was overrun by vendors, street salvationists, interested spectators, and money-based promotions—a gathering described by Scopes as consisting of "screwballs, con men, and devotees" (Ipsen 1973). Dayton's residents were entertained and outraged by the arrival of two apes and Jo Viens, a 3-feet-tall man claiming to be "The Missing Link" ("Dayton Keyed Up" 1925); the town's wrath was placated only

Three principals of the Scopes trial strolling through Dayton, Tennessee, in July 1925. Left to right: John Scopes (defendant), John R. Neal (defense attorney), and George Rappleyea (trial instigator). (Bryan College)

after it was said that "they may be used to disprove evolution." William Jennings Bryan and the jury visited the "monkey house" and posed for photos at Robinson's Drugstore as headlines told readers that CRANKS AND FREAKS FLOCK TO DAYTON, EUROPE IS AMAZED BY THE SCOPES CASE (one article in a European newspaper began by stating that "the assumptions of fundamentalism are so preposterous . . ."), and STRANGE CREEDS AND THEORIES ARE PREACHED AND SUNG WITHIN SHADOWS OF THE COURT HOUSE. Princeton University's president, John Hibben, denounced the Butler Law as "outrageous" and the upcoming trial as "absurd," and Yale's president, James Angell, reminded people that "the educated man must recognize and knit into his view of life the undeniable physical basis of the world" (Larson 1997). Albert Einstein warned that "any restriction of academic freedom heaps coals of shame upon the community"; Luther Burbank (a famed horticulturist well known to many Tennessee farmers) called the trial "a great joke"; and George Bernard Shaw condemned the "monstrous nonsense of Fundamentalism," adding that "it is not often that a single state can make a whole Continent ridiculous, or a single man set Europe asking whether America has ever really been civilized, but Tennessee and Mr. Bryan have brought off the double event" (Church 1925; Kuh 1925; "Shaw and Coleman on Scopes Trial" 1925; Burbank to Holmes 1925; Ginger 1958; Larson 1997).

Dayton's visitors included circus performers, Lewis Levi Johnson Marshall ("Absolute Ruler of the Entire World, without Military, Naval or other Physical Force"), Elmer Chubb (who claimed that he could "withstand the

John Scopes being arraigned for the crime of teaching human evolution, July 1925. Over Scopes's left shoulder is prosecutor William Jennings Bryan. Scopes's trial was the first to be broadcast on the radio (note the WGN microphone in the left foreground). (Bryan College)

bite of any venomous serpent"), flat-Earth advocate Wilber Glenn Voliva, "some of the world's champion freaks," monkeys (Mindy the Monkey arrived in Dayton with golf clubs and presented several piano concerts) and monkey-based advertisements by local merchants, religious fanatics (including a hairy prophet who billed himself as "John the Baptist the Third"), and unabashed religiosity. Signs outside the courthouse urged SWEETHEARTS, COME TO JESUS; a 10-foot-long banner on the courthouse proclaimed READ YOUR BIBLE; and hand-lettered signs posted by Deck Carter (the self-proclaimed "Bible Champion of the World") warned that the kingdom of God was at hand. *Monkey* became the most popular word in Dayton; documents were delivered by a courier service renamed "The Monkey Express"; a constable's motorcycle was dubbed "Monkeyville Police"; and Robinson's Drugstore sold "simian" sodas (Larson 1997). Even William Jennings Bryan, who argued in 1924 that God had created each species "separate and distinct," exploited the monkey theme: "How can teachers tell students that they came from monkeys and not expect them to act like monkeys?"[4]

Dayton, described as being "literally drunk on religious excitement" ("Famous Trials in American History"), welcomed about 500 visitors and almost 200 newspeople during the trial. The courthouse seated about 400, but 200 more crammed in to watch Dayton's most historic event ("Famous Trials in American History"). Robinson's Drugstore hung a banner that bragged WHERE IT STARTED, as Western Union strung extra telegraph wires, the telephone company hired extra staff, Southern Railway added extra service, and the Chattanooga-Dayton Bus Line added extra buses (and ran ads urging, LET'S ALL GO TO THE SCOPES TRIAL). The Dayton Progressive Club, which budgeted $5,000 for diversions and announced accommodations for 30,000 attendees, sold souvenir coins stamped with an image of a monkey wearing a straw hat (Larson 1997). There seemed to be something for everyone.

More than 2,300 daily newspapers tracked the trial; "no periodical of any sort, agricultural or trade as well . . . ignored the subject" (Lienesch 1993). The *Chattanooga Daily Times* published full transcripts of the daily proceedings, and in China alone, twenty-seven newspapers bought and published full telegraphic transcripts of events in Dayton (Metzger 1978; "Trial Transcript" 1925). Newspapers such as the *New York Journal* gave the Scopes trial front-page coverage in war-type headlines almost 5 centimeters high. Reporters, who came from as far as Hong Kong, sometimes invented stories about the trial (Allem 1959; de Camp 1968). Among them was the cynical and caustic H. L. Mencken of the *Baltimore Sun*. Mencken, whose coverage of the trial is ranked as one of the top ten works of journalism of the twentieth century ("The Top 100 Works" 2001), arrived in Dayton with four bottles of Scotch and a typewriter, and he found plenty to write about. After referring to the popular Bryan as an "unmitigated ass" and to the people of Dayton as "yokels," "morons," "anthropoid rabble," "gaping primates," and "hillbillies," Mencken had to be rescued from an angry mob by the Dayton sheriff (de Camp 1969; "Famous Trials in American History"). During the trial, Mencken reported that he was "converted" at a local meeting of the Holy Rollers, then "saved" several times by the secretary of the Anti-Evolution League (Ipsen 1973), adding, "Oh, well, I have always said I would be converted to any religion for a cigar and baptized in it for a box of them" (de Camp 1968). Scopes's trial was the first in history that included daily broadcasts of trial updates on the radio (see Scopes 1961; Cornelius 1991).[5]

Scopes was tried for teaching evolution as presented in a textbook that he used titled *A Civic Biology: Presented in Problems*, by George William Hunter (Hunter 1914; also see Gillis 1994).[6] *Civic Biology* had been used in Tennessee's schools since 1909 and was officially adopted by the state textbook commission in 1919 (Ginger 1958). Hunter's book was a bestseller and included sections titled "The Doctrine of Evolution," "Evolution of Man," and "Charles Darwin and Natural Selection." Hunter credited Darwin with "the proofs of the theory on which we today base the progress of the world." Other biology textbooks popular before Scopes's trial (e.g., Truman J. Moon's *Biology for Beginners* [1921]) were also decidedly proevolution; the word *evolution* appeared extensively throughout the books, and several chapters were devoted to the topic. Moon's book even identified evolution as a fundamental and unifying concept of biology, noting that "both man and the apes are descended from a common ancestor from which both lines have developed." Books that treated evolution cautiously (e.g., *Biology and Human Welfare* by James E. Peabody and Arthur E. Hunt [1924]) excused their timidity by citing a report by the College Entrance Examination Board claiming that a discussion of evolution might be too hard for high school students to understand (Grabiner and Miller 1974).

The Primary Players: Scopes, Raulston, Bryan, and Darrow

State of Tennessee v. John Thomas Scopes was an all-but-manufactured test case that involved four primary players, all of whom became national bywords.

John Scopes became involved in the case when W. F. Ferguson, the school's regular biology teacher, refused to participate in the case. Scopes never testified at his own trial, but he encouraged his students to testify.[7] Unlike Ferguson, who had a family and administrative responsibilities, Scopes was single, easygoing, and had no long-term plans to stay in Dayton. Scopes opposed the Butler Law; like most biologists, Scopes didn't understand how anyone could teach biology without considering Darwin's theory. Scopes was largely irrelevant to the trial, but he took the issues seriously; he had been a student at the University of Kentucky a few years earlier when its president fought against antievolution legislation (Larson 1997).

Judge John Tate Raulston was a devout Baptist who felt called by God to preside at the trial. Raulston began each day's proceedings with a prayer to the Christian God. During these prayers, prosecutors bowed their heads and defendants stared out the window (Larson 1997).

William Jennings Bryan, known throughout the country as "the Great Commoner," helped prosecutor A. Thomas Stewart, attorney general of Tennessee.[8] Bryan, a former secretary of state to Woodrow Wilson (1913–1915), championed the creationists' fundamentalist cause.[9] In 1909, Bryan had no fear of evolution, saying that "I am not yet convinced that man is a lineal descendant of the lower animals. I do not mean to find fault with you if you want to accept the theory." Even in 1922, Bryan had written an article for the *New York Times* in which he noted the position adopted by "theistic evolutionists"—namely, "Did God Use Evolution in His Plan?" Bryan stated: "If it could be shown that man, instead of being made in the image of God, is a development of beasts, we would have to accept it, regardless of its effect, for truth is truth and will prevail" (Ginger 1958).

Although Bryan described the Scopes trial as a "contest between evolution and Christianity . . . a duel to the death" (Smith 1965) and scientists as "dishonest scoundrels . . . stealing away the faith of your children," he did not reject all of evolutionary biology; he merely objected to humans having evolved from other animals (Larson 1997).[10] Bryan—a great orator who worked on the Scopes case without salary—insisted on the divine creation of humans and objected to an evolutionary tree because it included humans "in a little ring with lions and tigers and everything that smells in the jungle" (Ginger 1958; Gillis 1994). Bryan believed that evolution was responsible for World War I, the decline of morals and Christianity, and the evils of society. As he said in 1923, "I am trying to protect the students from atheistic professors. . . . Ramming poison down the throats of our children is nothing compared with damning their souls with the teaching of evolution" (Ginger 1958; Cowen 1986). By 1924, Bryan—the most widely known creationist of his generation—claimed that "all the ills from which America suffers can be traced back to the teaching of evolution. It would be better to destroy every other book ever written, and just save the first three verses of Genesis" (Irons 1988).[11]

Bryan had been instrumental in the passage of the Sixteenth Amendment (income tax) and the Eighteenth Amendment (prohibition); he had even drafted a law that would have made it a crime, punishable by loss of citizenship, for U.S. citizens to drink alcoholic beverages while abroad or on the high seas (Ginger 1958). Bryan hoped to add an antievolution amendment to the U.S. Constitution. Fiery evangelist T. T. Martin's *God or Gorilla* and *Hell and the High Schools*, which laid out Bryan's case against evolution, were best-sellers on the streets of Dayton during the Scopes trial. When Bryan, a member of the American Association for the Advancement of Science, agreed to participate in the trial on 13 May 1925, the trial assumed major-league status (Cornelius 1991). Bryan went to Dayton not as a lawyer goes to court, but as a preacher goes to a revival meeting.

Clarence Darrow—the labor advocate whom Bryan labeled as "the greatest atheist or agnostic in the United States"—was the leading criminal defense attorney in the country at the time and one of several lawyers for the ACLU-sponsored defense.[12] Unlike Bryan, Darrow put his faith in doubt and inquiry and his trust in reason instead of revelation. Darrow, who had once campaigned for Bryan's presidency, now "wanted to put Bryan in his place as a bigot" (Smith 1965). Although the ACLU wanted to remove Darrow from the case, Scopes resolved the controversy by calmly saying, "I want Darrow" (Ipsen 1973). And although residents of Dayton were nice to Darrow, H. L. Mencken reported that "there is ample space around him when he negotiates the streets. . . . A newspaper woman was warned by her landlady to keep out of the courtroom when Darrow was on his legs. All the local sorcerers predict that a bolt from heaven will fetch him in the end." Interestingly, Scopes's case was the only case for which Darrow ever volunteered his services (Tompkins 1965). In Darrow's words, "For the first, the

Clarence Darrow, the most famous defense attorney of his day, was the most prominent member of Scopes's defense team. (Bryan College)

last, the only time in my life, I volunteered my services in a case. I really wanted to take part in it."

Before the trial, Bryan wrote articles and gave speeches describing the scientific and moral failings of evolution. At a rally in Nashville, Bryan proclaimed that scientists "have not found a single link" and—remembering that the Butler Law pertained only to the teaching of human evolution—stressed the missing links between humans and their simian relatives (Larson 1997). Darrow also used the media to make his points: "Nero tried to kill Christianity with persecution and law. Bryan would block enlightenment with law. Had we Mr. Bryan's ideas of what a man may do towards free thinking, we would still be hanging and burning witches and punishing persons who thought the earth was round. . . . America is founded on liberty and not on narrow, mean, intolerable, and brainless prejudice of soulless religio-maniacs" ("Darrow Likens Bryan to Nero" 1925; "Darrow Loud in His Protest" 1925).

Darrow tried to replace Scopes's teaching of evolution with Bryan's threat to individual liberty; that strategy persisted until Darrow hounded Bryan into the witness chair on the seventh day of the trial (Larson 1997). Bryan's response to Darrow was simple: "Darrow is an atheist, I'm an upholder of Christianity. That's the difference between us. . . . If evolution wins, Christianity loses" (Larson 1997; Scopes 1989).

The ACLU staged photo opportunities for Scopes at the Statue of Liberty and in front of the original copy of the U.S. Constitution in the Library of Congress, during which Scopes professed his "deep" religious feelings ("Scopes Rests Hope in U.S. Constitution" 1925; Larson 1997). Most people idolized Bryan but were fiercely against Scopes and Darrow.[13] Scopes's father attended the trial, as did Butler, who cheered for Bryan against the "infidel outsiders."[14] Ben McKenzie, assistant attorney general of Tennessee and dean of the local bar, invoked regionalism and southern pride in his overstated attacks on the defense:[15]

> We don't need anybody from New York to come down here to tell us what [the Butler Law] means. . . . As for the Northern lawyers, who

have come down to teach the "ignorant yokels" what to believe, they had better go back to their homes, the seat of thugs, thieves, and Haymarket rioters, and educate their criminals rather than to try and proselyte here in the South, where people believe in the Christian religion, and know that Genesis tells the full and complete story of creation. . . . [It is] better to kill all children under two years of age than to have teachers who will wreck the lives of children with atheist theories which will put them on the toboggan slide which leads to hell.[16] ("Famous Trials of American History"; Larson 1997)

Throughout the country, there were exhibits of the public's strong feelings against evolution. For example, the Board of Regents at the University of Texas said it would hire no atheists, and in Dayton, Scopes's boss—Superintendent Walter White—proclaimed that he would "recommend no one as a teacher in the Rhea County schools who is not a Fundamentalist" (de Camp 1968).

Realizing the publicity and economic benefits that the trial could bring, leaders in nearby Chattanooga tried to capitalize on a delay in Dayton's legal proceedings in mid-May to move the trial from Dayton to their Memorial Auditorium. When this ploy failed, Chattanooga's leaders tried to stage their own case involving a local teacher (Cornelius 1990, 1995). Entrepreneurs in Dayton responded by threatening a boycott of Chattanooga merchants, by recalling Scopes from his vacation in Paducah, Kentucky, by arranging a special meeting of the grand jury (instead of waiting until the regular session in August), and by staging two fistfights to keep the media interested in the case (Cornelius 1991, 1995).

In early July 1925 in New York, the defense team decided to use the Scopes trial as a test case to pit science against fundamentalism and to sacrifice Scopes's acquittal for the chance to appeal the verdict to a higher court (Allem 1959; Scopes and Presley 1967). As a Baptist preacher called evolution "a lie of hell" and Scopes "an ambassador of the devil" (Ginger 1958), people began gathering in Dayton for the trial. When Darrow arrived in Dayton on the evening of 9 July, everything was set for "the trial of the century."

The Trial of the Century

State of Tennessee v. John Thomas Scopes opened on Friday, 10 July 1925, two days after the twenty-ninth anniversary of Bryan's famous "Cross of Gold" speech.[17] The trial included many memorable and dramatic moments.[18] For example, Judge Raulston opened the trial with a fundamentalist prayer described by Scopes as "interminable." Raulston then read the thirty-one verses of Genesis 1, after which he seated a grand jury that reindicted Scopes. (Mindful of the publicity and economic stimulus the trial could produce, Raulston had allowed Scopes to be indicted on 25 May by a grand jury whose term had expired so that another town did not "steal the show" [Larson 1997; Cornelius 1991; Scopes 1965].) The court then chose twelve jurors, three of whom said that they had never read any book except the Bible and one of whom admitted that he couldn't read. When questioned as a potential juror by the defense, a local preacher was applauded by spectators when he proudly stated that he preached against evolution; he wasn't chosen for the jury (see Scopes 1961). Scopes, sitting between his father and George Rappleyea, stated the obvious: "This is incredible."

As Monday's (13 July) newspapers promoted the upcoming confrontation between Darrow and Bryan, the defense claimed that the Butler Law should be overturned so that "a teacher may tell the truth without being sent to jail" (Scopes 1961). Clarence Darrow then argued that the Butler Law was unconstitutional because it established a particular religion in public schools, noting that "[Scopes] is here because ignorance and bigotry are rampant, and [that] is a mighty combination" (Scopes 1961).

In response, chief prosecutor Tom Stewart—described by Mencken as "a man of apparent education and sense"—said, "The state, through the legislature, has the right to control its schools by controlling the content of their curriculum. . . . The laws of the land recognize the Bible. We are not living in a heathen country." This argument was the basis for the prosecution's subsequent motion to ban expert testimony that supported evolution. Later, as testimony strayed from the Butler Law, the prosecution asked Judge Raulston about the purpose of Darrow's questions. Darrow again made his point: "We have the purpose of preventing bigots and ignoramuses from controlling the education of the United States. . . . The fundamentalists will make the ages roll back. . . . Ignorance and fanaticism are ever busy and need feeding."

The *Chattanooga Daily Times* described the trial as a "crusade against intelligence" and wondered why the state hadn't avoided "the humiliation that has come upon [us]" (Ginger 1958). When the electricity went out in Dayton on Monday night, believers proclaimed that Dayton was being punished for allowing evolutionists to speak against the Bible (Ipsen 1973).

Tuesday (14 July) began with Darrow objecting to the opening prayer. After Raulston overruled Darrow's objection, Stewart called Darrow "the agnostic counsel for the defense."

On Wednesday (15 July), Darrow expressed pride in being an agnostic: "I do not pretend to know where many ignorant men are sure; that is all *agnosticism* means." After Scopes entered a plea of not guilty, the well-dressed Dudley Field Malone (defense attorney who was an undersecretary of state during Bryan's service as secretary of state for Woodrow Wilson) told the court that "science and religion embrace two separate and distinct fields of thought and learning. . . . There is no conflict between evolution and Christianity." The court then heard testimonies from Superintendent of Schools Walter White, School Board Chairman Fred E. Robinson, and two of Scopes's students (Scopes had used the backseat of "Stumpy" Reed's taxi to coach the prospective student witnesses on evolution so that they could truthfully say that they learned the subject from Scopes [Allem 1959; Cornelius 1990]). These were the only witnesses whose testimony was part of the official court record.[19] After the trial, Scopes admitted that he wasn't sure if he had taught evolution (Scopes and Presley 1967; Cornelius 1999). But he was never called to the witness stand because, as Darrow told Judge Raulston, "Your Honor, every single word that was said against this defendant, everything was true."

On Thursday (16 July), William Jennings Bryan broke his virtual silence by pointing out the dangers associated with evolution being taught and the Bible being excluded from schools. After his speech, Bryan received loud applause and shouts of "Amen." Malone then did what Scopes described as "the most effective act anyone could have thought of to get the audience's undivided attention" (Ipsen 1973): he slowly stood up, deliberately removed and folded his coat, and responded for the defense. Invoking Bryan's claim that they were in a "duel to the death," Malone chided Bryan:

> After all, whether Mr. Bryan knows it or not, he is a mammal, he is an animal and he is a man. . . . I have never seen harm in learning and understanding, in humility and open-mindedness. . . . This is not a conflict of personages; it is a conflict of ideas. . . . There is never a duel with truth; the truth always wins, and we are not afraid of it. The truth is no coward. The truth does not need the law. The truth does not need the forces of government. The truth does not need Mr. Bryan. The truth is imperishable, eternal and immortal and needs no human agency to support it. We are ready to tell the truth as we understand it and we do not fear all the truth that they can present as facts. . . . We feel we stand with progress. We feel we stand with science. We feel we stand with intelligence. We feel we stand with fundamental freedom in America. We are not afraid.

To many, this was the highlight of the trial. Mencken proclaimed that Malone's speech, which lasted about twenty-five minutes, "roared out of the open windows like the sound of artillery." Butler described Malone's speech as "the finest speech of the century," and forty years later, Scopes described it as "the most dramatic event I attended in my life" (Tracy 1925; Butler

Judge Raulston
forgives Clarence
Darrow for his
contempt of court
on 20 July 1925.
Left to right in the
foreground: Dudley
Field Malone,
Thomas Stewart,
William Jennings
Bryan, John
Raulston, and
Clarence Darrow.
(Bryan College)

1925; Scopes and Presley 1967). One reporter described Bryan as an "old gladiator" who had been "tumbled in the dust by the shining spear of Dudley Field Malone's logic," and another reporter from the *Des Moines Register* acknowledged that Malone had "stirred even [the] loyal partisans of the idol Bryan to applause" (Clapper 1925). Even Bryan conceded that Malone's speech was "the greatest speech I've ever heard." Afterward, Malone said, "I am sorry it was I who had to make it." After Malone's speech, people applauded and yelled wildly. The press broke its customary silence of neutrality and gave Malone a standing ovation. When order was restored, Stewart refocused attention on the issues at hand, proclaiming that he didn't come "from the same cell with the monkey and the ass."

On Friday (17 July), after less than an hour of testimony, the state rested its case.

Over the weekend of 18–19 July, most reporters and some of the attorneys left town; as Scopes would later note, "many of the army of newspapermen had evidently deserted" (de Camp 1968; Scopes 1967). However, others suspected that there could be excitement ahead when Sunday's *Nashville Banner* reported that the defense was "preparing to spring a *coup d'etat*" (see Larson 1997 and references therein). They were right.

Monday (20 July) was the climax of the trial. Court opened with Judge Raulston citing Darrow for contempt of court (the first such citation of his career) and setting his bail bond at $5,000. Darrow apologized, and Raulston—quoting Scripture—forgave Darrow. Meanwhile, Dayton continued to be gripped by a sweltering heatwave. One newspaper reported that "only the judge, Malone, and one juror have the fortitude to wear their coats"

in the hot courtroom. Because of the intense heat and a fear that the court-house floor might collapse under the weight of the throng attending the trial, Raulston reconvened the court on a dais under shade trees on the courthouse lawn. Only about six reporters attended the afternoon session; others spent the afternoon away from the trial looking for relief from the heat.[20]

Clarence Darrow (right) questioning William Jennings Bryan about the Bible, 20 July 1925. (Bryan College)

After ACLU attorney Arthur Garfield Hays finished reading the statements of expert witnesses, Darrow objected to the READ YOUR BIBLE banner on the courthouse and had it removed. Then, as Malone told Scopes that, "Hell is going to pop now" (Scopes and Presley 1967), almost 2,000 spectators watched the trial reach its peak of excitement. After having baited Bryan earlier by saying that "Bryan has not dared test his views in open court under oath," Hays announced to the court, "The defense desires to call Mr. Bryan as a witness." Prosecutors jumped to their feet to object. Bryan did not have to testify, and Raulston left the decision to Bryan. Bryan, falling for Darrow's trap, took the witness chair "to protect the word of God against the greatest atheist or agnostic in the United States." When Judge Raulston asked Darrow if he wanted Bryan sworn, Darrow replied, "No . . . I take it you will tell the truth, Mr. Bryan."

Before agreeing to testify, however, Bryan had insisted that he later be allowed to question Darrow, Malone, and Hays (Cornelius 1991; de Camp 1969). After sparring at a distance for more than a week, Darrow and Bryan were set to go head-to-head in a clash of faith versus science as the way of best understanding nature.

During his ninety-minute examination, Darrow covered about fifty topics. He referred to Bryan's "fool religion" and questioned Bryan about his "fool ideas" (e.g., Jonah being swallowed by a whale, Joshua commanding the sun to stand still to lengthen the day, the worldwide flood). Darrow eventually forced Bryan to admit that he didn't believe in a literal interpretation of the Bible. When Darrow asked Bryan how the serpent had walked before God told it to crawl on its belly, the audience laughed and Bryan became flustered. After Darrow told Bryan, "I am examining you on your fool ideas that no intelligent Christian on earth believes," there was a near riot and court was adjourned.

On Tuesday (21 July), the last day of the trial, rain moved the proceedings back indoors. Following an opening prayer, Raulston expunged Bryan's testimony from the record (de Camp 1969; Cornelius 1991) because it was irrelevant to the case. Darrow then told Judge Raulston "to bring in the jury and instruct [them] to find the defendant guilty."[21] Stewart then stated that the jury should set Scopes's fine. Although Stewart was correct, he was overruled. Darrow then promised that the defense would "not take an exception, either way you want it, because we want the case passed on by the higher court." Darrow had just sanctioned the error that would ultimately prevent the case from reaching the U.S. Supreme Court.

The Verdict

The jury, which was in court for little more than three hours during the entire trial, deliberated for nine minutes on the courthouse lawn. It then delivered its verdict: Scopes, who was labeled by a Baptist minister as "an ambassador of the devil" for supporting "a lie of hell," was guilty of the crime of teaching evolution.

Raulston fined Scopes $100 (plus legal costs), the minimum allowed. Mencken, acting on behalf of the *Baltimore Sun*, promised to pay Scopes's fine. After a prompt by defense attorney John Neal, Raulston asked Scopes if he had anything to say. In his only statement to the court, Scopes said: "Your Honor, I feel that I have been convicted of violating an unjust statute. I will continue in the future, as I have in the past, to oppose this law in any way I can. Any other action would be in violation of my idea of academic freedom. . . . I believe the fine is unjust."[22]

Bryan then noted that the trial was about one of the causes that "stir the world," and Darrow said, "I think this case will be remembered because it is the first case of this sort since we stopped trying people in America for witchcraft—because here we have done our best to turn back the tide that has sought to force itself upon this . . . modern world, of testing every fact in science by a religious dictum."

After yet another Christian prayer, the "trial of the century" was over.

The Appeal

For six months after the verdict, the fate of Scopes's conviction was plagued by confusion, missed deadlines, and conflict. Tennessee's newly elected attorney general, Frank M. Thompson, was responsible for defending the Butler Law before the Tennessee Supreme Court. Despite a serious illness that would soon kill him, Governor Peay, who claimed that the "reckless teaching of evolution" had been converting students to agnosticism "in shocking numbers" (Ginger 1958), also wanted to be involved in the appeal.

In early January, Scopes's defense team filed their brief with the Tennessee Supreme Court in Nashville. The appeal dragged on for eighteen months. John Neal wasted time by filing two petitions in federal court in Chattanooga seeking to halt enforcement of the Butler Law based on two violations of the Fourteenth Amendment: denial of property without due process and denial of equal protection of the law (despite the fact that Scopes had already left Tennessee). Neal and Darrow also requested a federal restraining order on behalf of a Rhea County farmer, who claimed that the Butler Law robbed his children of a proper education (de Camp 1968; Ginger 1958). Meanwhile, opposition intensified to Darrow's involvement in the appeal. Forrest Bailey, an associate director of the ACLU, pleaded with Scopes that someone besides Darrow should handle the appeal, noting that "there is no need for attorneys outside Tennessee" (Scopes 1989). Despite these protests, Scopes stood by Darrow, and Darrow remained on the defense team (Ginger 1958; de Camp 1968).

In November, the Tennessee Academy of Science—finally entering the fray—denounced the Butler Law, soon after which it filed a brief with the Tennessee Supreme Court on Scopes's behalf.[23] The scientists who had been called as expert witnesses in Scopes's trial had endorsed Darrow, but Rappleyea and others feared that if Darrow remained on the case, "It will not be our cause on trial, but it will be a case of the State of Tennessee vs. Clarence Darrow, the man who spiritually and literally crucified Bryan on the cross examination" (ACLU Executive Committee 1925).

Amid charges that someone had tampered with the court record, Neal missed the deadline for filing the bill of exceptions with the Tennessee Supreme Court, thereby precluding the defense from challenging any of Raulston's rulings during the original trial (e.g., his rulings about expert testimony, opening court with prayer, etc.). The only option remaining for the defense was to challenge the validity of the Butler Law (Larson 1997). All occurrences of Arthur Garfield Hays standing to say "Exception!" during the Scopes trial now meant nothing.

The appeal hearing of Scopes's conviction began on 31 May 1926. Scopes, who was spending the summer working for the Illinois Geological Survey, did not return to Tennessee for the hearing (Ginger 1958). The con-

tinuing defense team of Clarence Darrow, Dudley Field Malone, Arthur
Garfield Hays, and F. B. McElwee was joined by Frank Spurlock of Chattanooga, Robert Keebler of Memphis, and Walter Pollack and Samuel
Rosensohn of the ACLU (Cornelius 1991; Ginger 1958). The state was represented by E. T. Seay, K. T. McConnico, and William Jennings Bryan Jr.

With John Butler and George Rappleyea sitting in the front row, the
hearing commenced with the state stressing Darrow's agnosticism, the
ACLU's radicalism, and Darrow's treatment of Bryan during the trial.
(Bryan had died five days after the trial; see below.) The state argued that
the legislature had tried to preserve the Bible for all faiths, not just fundamentalists. The defense responded with the only argument it had—namely,
that the Butler Law was unconstitutional because it unreasonably restricted the liberty of teachers and students by establishing a preference in
public schools for a particular religion (de Camp 1968; Larson 1997).
Darrow chided the fundamentalists: "With flaming banners and beating
drums we are marching backward to the glorious ages of the sixteenth century." The defense pleaded for "freedom of education" and noted that the
teaching of evolution would not cause students to lose faith in God. The
Tennessee Academy of Science added that the Butler Law would damage
science education ("Supreme Court Hears Scopes Case" 1926).

The state's rebuttal gave the law a secular purpose; Darrow's earlier de-
fenses of murderers and Communists were used to link the acceptance of
evolution with the acceptance of murder and communism.[24] The state then
equated the ACLU's interest in the case with a pro-Communist agenda, after which the defense argued that the Butler Law promoted fundamentalism and that there is no conflict between the acceptance of evolution and
man's divine origin (see discussion in Larson 1997). The gallery cheered
when the state's attorney—invoking the majoritarian legacy of William Jennings Bryan—reminded the Supreme Court justices that the idea of life after death was very popular among Tennesseeans and that evolution undermined their faith. He then closed by asking, "Would not the state of
Tennessee be committing a tragedy . . . if it did not intervene to prevent the
teaching in her public schools of a dogma conceded to destroy the minds of
the people, whether it is right or wrong?"

In response, Darrow linked science with progress and stressed that religion should be a personal issue. He also reminded the court that "the
schools of this state were not established to teach religion. They were established to teach science" (Larson 1997; Hutchinson 1926). Darrow concluded his hour-long presentation to great applause as he said, "We are once
more fighting the old question, which after all is nothing but a question of
intellectual freedom of man."

All in all, the hearing was rather boring; the *Chattanooga Daily Times* described it as "a flop of a news story compared with the trial." The hearing ended with the court taking arguments under advisement.

During the seven months that followed the hearing, both sides were optimistic of victory. The ACLU continued to pursue the case, during which time it became resolute about eliminating Darrow, Malone, and Hays from the defense team. Darrow refused to step aside, and Scopes later said that he would have stuck with Darrow. But it was a moot point.

On 15 January 1927, Chief Justice Grafton Green of the Tennessee Supreme Court announced the court's split decision. Three judges—a bare majority—upheld the Butler Law as constitutional because (1) it did not infringe on Scopes's individual liberties and (2) it did not require the teaching of any doctrine and therefore did not give preference to any religion (*John Thomas Scopes v. The State of Tennessee*, 154 Tenn. [1 Smith] 105, 289 S.W. 363 [1927]). However, the court reversed Scopes's conviction on a technicality; as per Article VI, Section 6, of the Tennessee Constitution, fines greater than $50 were to be set by the jury, not the judge. The question of who should impose the fine had been discussed at the original trial, but both sides had agreed not to raise the issue on appeal (Raulston had given the jury the chance to set a higher fine, but he established the $100 fine that Scopes received [Ginger 1958]). The Supreme Court justices ruled that Scopes's case was subject to a retrial but added that since Scopes was no longer employed by the state, "We see nothing to be gained by prolonging the life of this bizarre case. . . . On the contrary, we think the peace and dignity of the state . . . would be better conserved by the entry of a nolle prosequi herein. Such a course is suggested to the Attorney General" ("Trial Transcript" 1925; Cornelius 1991). Tennessee's new attorney general—without comment—complied, thereby leaving the ACLU with no conviction to appeal and closing Darrow's hoped-for route to the U.S. Supreme Court (de Camp 1968). None of the original principals in the Scopes trial was present for the announcement of the decision.

Three days after the Tennessee Supreme Court decision, Darrow sent an optimistic letter to Scopes, saying that "I am pretty well satisfied that the law is dead but we want to make sure, if possible" (Scopes 1989). Darrow's hopes were soon dashed; all motions for a new hearing were rejected, and the Butler Law would remain on the books for more than forty years thereafter. The most famous misdemeanor case in U.S. history was over.

John Scopes was the only teacher ever prosecuted for breaking the Butler Law. There would be no more serious attempts to enforce the Butler Law during the remaining four decades of its existence.

In the Wake of the Scopes Trial

Bryan Responds to Darrow

As mentioned earlier, before agreeing to be questioned by Darrow at Scopes's trial, Bryan—described by Theodore Roosevelt as "an amiable, windy creature who knows almost nothing" (de Camp 1968)—insisted that he be given a chance to question Darrow, Malone, and Hays in kind. However, Darrow's request that Scopes be convicted (to provide the basis for an appeal to a higher court) caused Judge Raulston to expunge Bryan's testimony from the trial's record and cancel plans for Bryan to question Darrow. The abrupt end of the trial also deprived Bryan of making his much-anticipated closing statement to the court. Journalists and others at the trial were so interested in Bryan's remarks that Bryan promised to prepare them for publication.

Two days after the Scopes verdict, Bryan suggested that his supporters establish a college for young men on one of the hills surrounding Dayton. Bryan pledged $50,000 for this project and committed himself to raise the rest of the money necessary to establish the college. For most of that Thursday, Bryan evaluated sites for the proposed college.[25] Two days later, Bryan fulfilled a promise to Attorney General Stewart (who later became a U.S. senator) by speaking at the county fair in Winchester, Tennessee. When he returned to Chattanooga, Bryan was warned by a physician about his diabetes and a heart condition, and he was told to rest for a few days. In Chattanooga, Bryan also corrected proofs of his 15,000-word speech, which he hoped would ensure support for an antievolution amendment to the U.S. Constitution[26] and maybe even lead to the formation of a new political party that would revive his faded hopes for the presidency. That speech, which suggested that evolution would cause students to commit murder, included several indictments that stressed familiar themes:

> The majority . . . is trying to protect itself from . . . an insolent minority [trying] to force irreligion upon the children under the guise of teaching science. . . . Christians . . . oppose the teaching of [evolution] that encourages godlessness among the students. . . . Evolution is not truth. . . . There is no more reason to believe that man descended from some inferior animal than there is to believe that a stately mansion has descended from a small cottage. . . . The law is a very conservative statement of the people's opposition to an anti-Biblical hypothesis. . . . What shall we say of . . . those who . . . put a man with an immortal soul in the same circle with the wolf, the hyena and the skunk? . . . Evolution . . . is also creating doubt as to a heaven at the end of life. . . . Evolution . . . disputes the truth of the Bible's account of man's creation and shakes faith in the Bible as the Word of God.

Bryan Dies, Leaving the Antievolution Movement without a Leader

On Sunday morning, 26 July 1925, Bryan drove to Dayton, where he led a prayer at the First Southern Methodist Church. That afternoon, the sixty-five-year-old Bryan did the most effective thing possible to rally his fundamentalist supporters: he died in his sleep, just a few blocks from the Rhea County Courthouse.

Many people praised Bryan and blamed Scopes for Bryan's death. According to one man from North Carolina, "The public holds you [Scopes] personally responsible for ending the life of William Jennings Bryan. Mark my word, you are next. God will not permit [you] to live" (Scopes 1989). Not surprisingly, antievolutionists made Bryan a martyr. Fundamentalists compared Bryan to Christ and Scopes's defense team to King Herod, Pontius Pilate, and other biblical villains (see discussion in de Camp 1968). Governor Peay proclaimed that Bryan had died "a martyr to the faith of our fathers" and announced a state holiday to commemorate the funeral (Scopes and Presley 1967; Peay 1929). However, others were apparently glad that Bryan was gone. Eugene Debs wrote that "the cause of human progress sustains no loss in the death of Mr. Bryan," and H. L. Mencken continued his attack on Bryan by writing that Bryan's "last secular act on this globe of sin was to catch flies."

Bryan's funeral was a national event; thousands filed by his open coffin in Dayton. Elsewhere, shops closed and flags flew at half-mast before his burial in Arlington National Cemetery under the small inscription HE KEPT THE FAITH. America's political elite attended the burial, where even Bryan's foes praised his passion and integrity (Larson 1997). Many people wrote "Scopes songs" (e.g., Charles Oaks's "The Death of William Jennings Bryan," Arthur Fields's "Bryan Believed in Heaven"; see Cornelius 1998) that lionized Bryan, and the *New York Herald Tribune* wrote that "he tried to do the right thing as he saw it. His passing will be a profound shock to millions who, however often he misled them, looked upon him as their prophet and counselor."

On 28 July, while Bryan's body still lay in state in Dayton, Bryan's Last Message was given to the press (see Bryan 1925). Those remarks, which were superimposed over an image of Bryan's face, were originally titled "Fighting to Death for the Bible"; many hoped that they would be another "Cross of Gold" speech. In his essay, Bryan again emphasized familiar themes—namely, that Christians have a right to control the public schools, that the Bible is true, and that science breeds atheism. Bryan repeated his claim that evolution is a "bloody, brutal doctrine," adding that "evolution is not the truth; it is merely a hypothesis . . . it is millions of guesses strung together" (de Camp 1968).

Meanwhile, the Controversy Continues

Although Scopes knew that his defense had "all of the facts, logic and justice," he also knew that "these weapons are often ineffective in a battle against bigotry and prejudice" (Scopes 1965). He was right. Religious groups—especially the Baptists—denounced Scopes and evolution as "Christless," proclaimed that "every . . . evolutionist . . . is an agnostic, infidel, or atheist," labeled the ACLU as "a diminutive aggregation of atheistic asses," and emphasized "the choice between Christ and Darwin" ("The Scopes Trial" 1925). A resolution adopted unanimously by the 1926 Southern Baptist Convention in Houston repudiated "as unscriptural and scientifically false every claim of evolution that declares or implies that man evolved to his present state from some lower order of life. . . . This convention . . . rejects every theory, evolutionary or other, which teaches that man originated or came by way of lower animal ancestry" (Ginger 1958).

Shortly thereafter, the Education Board of the Southern Baptist Convention adopted the same resolution. J. Frank Norris's *Searchlight* ran headlines proclaiming that SOUTHERN BAPTIST CONVENTION HEROICALLY AND TRIUMPHANTLY DELIVERS KNOCKOUT BLOW AGAINST EVOLUTION AND EVOLUTIONISTS, and the *American Baptist* rejoiced that the "evolution question has been satisfactorily disposed of" (Bailey 1964). The *Moody Bible Institute Monthly* declared evolution to be "propaganda of the Devil" and urged readers to "boycott every school" that taught evolution (Nelson 1925). Repeated references to the Scopes trial spurred sales of the stenographic record of the trial—aptly titled *The World's Most Famous Court Trial* (published one month after the verdict)—to almost 20,000 copies (at $2.00 each) in less than a year (Cornelius 1990).[27]

Darrow, who accepted only two more cases after the Scopes trial,[28] predicted that young people would soon repeal Tennessee's Butler Law, but he was wrong. As noted earlier, the constitutionality of the Butler Law was upheld by the Tennessee Supreme Court after the Scopes trial. The ACLU looked for another volunteer to challenge the Butler Law, but "nobody was willing to make the sacrifice" (Larson 1989).[29] Once in place, no southern antievolution law was repealed for more than forty years (Larson 1997).[30] No other lawsuits to repeal antievolution were filed until Susan Epperson of Arkansas challenged the ban on evolution in 1965.

Early in 1925, Mississippi lawmakers had rejected antievolution legislation. However, soon after Scopes's trial, the fundamentalist governor of Mississippi predicted that his state would "follow the lead of Tennessee and bar the teaching of evolution in the schools" (Larson 1989, 1997). Supporters of antievolution legislation in Mississippi warned that evolution would destroy the state and claimed that 90 percent of Mississippians supported the legislation; one prominent supporter even claimed that it was better to have the leadership of one Christian mother than of all the scientists in the world (Larson 1989).[31]

In January 1926, as a group of Baptists pleaded with the Mississippi legislature to prevent evolution "from injecting its poison into the minds and hearts of school-children of this State," legislator and preacher L. Walter Evans introduced a Butler-like bill, but the bill was rejected by the House Education Committee in a 10–4 vote. The committee's minority members then filed a separate report, thereby ensuring that the bill would come before the entire House. In February, T. T. Martin—now heading the newly formed Bible Crusaders of America—came to Mississippi to lobby and address a joint session of the legislature. Soon afterward, the House approved Evans's bill by a vote of 76–32. Although the Senate Education Committee recommended that the bill be rejected, it passed the full Senate by a vote of 29–16 and was sent to Governor Henry L. Whitfield for his signature. Chancellor Alfred Hume of the University of Mississippi wanted the governor to reject the bill, but he assured the governor that his university was a Christian institution "shot through and through with the teaching of Our Lord" (Halliburton 1973). Mississippi's scientists and educators were largely indifferent about the legislation, and Whitfield signed the law on 12 March. The ACLU repeatedly offered to support a teacher willing to challenge Mississippi's antievolution statute, but there were no volunteers.[32] Prominent businesspeople and lawyers endorsed the antievolution campaign.

There were victories for the antievolutionists. For example, Baylor University announced that it would not employ any teacher who "doubts God as the creator of the world or discounts the Bible as God's revelation to man," and Baptist groups forced proevolution biology professors to resign in Georgia, South Carolina, and elsewhere (Numbers 1992).

Yet antievolution activists also suffered some defeats, such as the instance of the Education Association of Southern Methodists opposing "all legislation that would interfere with the proper teaching of science in American schools and colleges"; and one antievolution bill was met by a companion bill requiring all water in the state to run uphill (Ginger 1958). In Missouri, a facetious legislator suggested that the penalty for violating a proposed antievolution statute be imprisonment "for not less than thirty days nor more than forty nights in the St. Louis Zoo," and another proposed that the bill apply only to areas whose citizens believed "that the earth is flat, that the sun travels around the earth, and that the storms of the sea are caused by the fury of the monsters of the deep." Despite this sarcasm, these antievolution efforts were narrowly defeated (Ginger 1958). Throughout the United States, many teachers were "afraid to express acceptance of the theory of evolution," and biology teachers who mentioned evolution were often reprimanded.

Although the front page of the 27 July 1925 edition of the *Knoxville News* had lamented William Jennings Bryan's death with a headline claiming that there was NO ONE LEFT TO CHAMPION BRYAN'S CAUSES, several groups (e.g., the Bryan Bible League, the Defenders of the Christian Faith, and the Ku Klux Klan) picked up the fundamentalists' creationist mantle. For example:

The short-lived Supreme Kingdom was formed in January 1926 in Atlanta, Georgia, by Edward Young Clarke, a shady fundamentalist with a lurid past and an impressive arrest record. Clarke, who had been a successful membership director in the Ku Klux Klan, hired Billy Sunday's business manager to promote his antievolution cause. John Raulston, the presiding judge at the Scopes trial, lectured for the Supreme Kingdom (de Camp 1968). After importing John Roach Straton[33] from New York to give sixty lectures about evolution (for the selfless fee of $30,000), the Kingdom disintegrated amid a financial scandal. Clarke had been pocketing two-thirds of every $12.50 initiation fee (Ginger 1958).

The Ku Klux Klan, which had supported many leaders of the antievolution crusade (e.g., the Klan publicized William Jennings Bryan's speeches that led to the passage of Tennessee's Butler Law; see "William Jennings Bryan Here Saturday" 1924), held a variety of ceremonies to pay homage to Bryan and his creationist beliefs (Moore 2001a). Within weeks of Bryan's death, the Klan became the first national organization to demand that creationism and evolution be given "equal time" in public schools. Decades later, this demand would be renewed by creationists.

The Bible Crusaders of America was formed in Florida in November 1925 by George F. Washburn, who declared that God had appointed him to succeed Bryan. Washburn enlisted virtually all of the leading antievolutionists of the day (including Straton and William Bell Riley) and made apocalyptic speeches in which he claimed that "the great battle of the age is now on between Christianity and evolution" (de Camp 1968). The Crusaders' campaign director was wild-eyed evangelist T. T. Martin, a world-class religious huckster.[34]

The Anti-Evolution League of Minnesota was founded in 1923 by a group of preachers that included William Bell Riley, founder of the World's Christian Fundamentals Association in 1919. By the time of the Scopes trial, the league had expanded and was known as the Anti-Evolution League of America. The league started a nationwide "Bible-Christ-and-Constitution Campaign against Evolution in Tax-Supported Schools" (Ginger 1958). When Riley became ill, leadership of the league was transferred to T. T. Martin of Mississippi. Martin's fundamentalist magazine, *Conflict*, became the league's official publication. Martin, with the help of famed fundamentalist preacher George McCready Price and others, denounced several schools for hiring "unsafe" teachers. One chapter of the Anti-Evolution League of America was presided over by William Jennings Bryan Jr.

These groups were associated with many organizations trying "to wipe out all the new knowledge in the schools and to clear all modern books out of the libraries." Antievolution groups often exaggerated the nationalistic arguments made at the Scopes trial, deplored "alien ideas and Yankee infidelity," and warned the public that evolution would lead to communism and other social ills. As evangelist Mordechai Ham told his followers in Louisville, Kentucky, "The day is not distant when you will be in the grip of the Red Terror and your children will be taught free love by the damnable theory of evolution" (de Camp 1968). In addition to claiming that the teaching of evolution would destroy southern womanhood, the antievolution groups stressed that evolution made blacks as good as whites (Cash 1941). For fundamentalist groups such as the Southern Baptists, the Bible-based hierarchies—especially white over black and man over woman—could not be weakened (Rosenberg 1989).

By 1927, the fanaticism for antievolution laws began to fade. Antievolution groups such as the misnamed Research Science Bureau and the American Science Foundation declined in number. Oklahoma, which had repealed its antievolution law in 1925, defeated another antievolution bill in 1927. Similar legislation in Florida, Delaware, Maine, and elsewhere failed in 1927 as fundamentalists redirected their attacks to Jews, Catholics, and the evils of booze (Ginger 1958).[35] Meanwhile, in Tennessee, interest in religion diminished after the Scopes trial. In May 1926, for example, Chattanooga's school board discontinued its Bible classes in public schools and stopped awarding credit for religious study. During the decade following the Scopes trial, church membership dropped more than 10 percent. This drop was especially pronounced among Baptists (who lost 40,000 members) and Methodists (who lost 60,000 members; see Ginger 1958).

During the next few decades, creationists changed; whereas creationists at the Scopes trial were "ballyhoo artists . . . preachers . . . revivalists of all shapes and sects and . . . holy rollers" (Nelkin 1982), more contemporary creationists began using more sophisticated arguments to claim that there is credible scientific evidence to prove the biblical story of creation. By the 1950s, fundamentalists had become more politically active about the perceived loss of traditional values and growing secularism in the United States. In the 1960s and 1970s, creationists organized groups such as the Creation Research Society to promote their beliefs and legislation.[36] This movement emphasized a literal interpretation of the Bible and the Book of Genesis as the only source of knowledge about origins.

Evolution Disappears from Biology Textbooks

The Scopes trial made textbook publishers and school boards throughout the country reluctant to deal with evolution. The amount of evolution taught in public schools decreased dramatically (Larson 1989); virtually all publishers removed Darwin's ideas about evolution as the unifying theme of life from their biology books (Grabiner and Miller 1974). Within a few months after the Scopes trial, Governor Miriam Ferguson of Texas—the first female governor in the South—ordered her state's textbook commission to delete the theory of evolution from its high school biology books; for years, this ban forced publishers to produce special, sanitized books for use in Texas.[37] The following year, Louisiana's superintendent of education took a similar step. Tennessee abandoned George Hunter's popular textbook (i.e., the textbook that Scopes used in Dayton) soon after Scopes was indicted. The publisher of Hunter's textbook gave it a new title (*New Civic Biology*, presumably to distinguish it from the previous edition that was linked with the Scopes verdict); when producing the new book, the publisher deleted the section on evolution, eliminated charts showing the evolution of species, and added vague qualifiers such as "suggested" and "believed" when describing evolution. The word *evolution* disappeared from Hunter's book, as it did from most other biology textbooks. After the Scopes trial, one publisher even asked Bryan to endorse its book (Grabiner and Miller 1974; Larson 1997; Moore 2001b). The antievolutionists had won, for by 1942, most high school science teachers in the United States taught their students nothing about evolution (Futuyma 1983). Even George McCready Price acknowledged that "virtually all textbooks on the market have been revised to meet the needs of Fundamentalists" (Price 1929).

In the decades that followed, evolution slowly began to reappear in biology textbooks. Yet religious quotations also appeared in many biology textbooks (Grabiner and Miller 1974).[38] As one publisher noted, "Creation has no place in biology books, but after all we are in the business of selling textbooks" (Gorman 1980). However, the best-selling textbooks downplayed or ignored evolution. Proevolution texts such as Alfred Kinsey's *Introduction to Biology* did not sell well, and the best-selling biology textbook at the time (A. O. Baker and L. N. Mills's *Dynamic Biology*) did not use the word *evolution* at all. Indeed, *Dynamic Biology* even included an attack on evolution, likening Darwin's ideas to Lamarck's and noting that Darwin's theory was "no longer generally accepted" (Grabiner and Miller 1974). That attack on Darwin was followed by a tribute to God.

By the late 1950s, many legislators worried that the scientific and technological prowess of the United States had fallen behind that of the Soviet Union.[39] In 1958, President Dwight D. Eisenhower requested (and Congress passed) the National Defense Education Act, which encouraged the National Science Foundation (NSF) to fund and develop state-of-the-art science textbooks. The most important collaboration to result from this legislation involved the American Institute of Biological Sciences, which formed the Biological Sciences Curriculum Study (BSCS) at the University of Colorado in 1959 with $143,000 from the NSF. The three books the BSCS produced, which were identified by the green, blue, or yellow color that dominated their covers, unapologetically stressed evolution as the unifying theme of biology and "put evolution back in the biology classroom." The BSCS's books were based on the best professional science available rather than the consensus-oriented, nondescript nonevolutionism typical of most textbooks (e.g., a popular textbook in 1957, by Moon, Mann, and Otto, treated evolution only at the end of the book as "racial development" instead of "evolution"). The biologists who wrote the BSCS books were shocked when they reviewed the competition; as noted by Nobel laureate Hermann Muller, "One hundred years without Darwin are enough." In fact, the implied century was really just the thirty-five years that had elapsed since the Scopes trial (Grabiner and Miller 1974).

Not surprisingly, the BSCS books were criticized. The harshest attacks occurred in Texas, where the books were denounced in newspapers, in church sermons, and at hearings of the Texas Textbook Commission (Grabiner and Miller 1974). The attacks were often led by Melvin and Norma Gabler, self-appointed censors who condemned evolution as well as statements about religions other than Christianity, statements emphasizing contributions by minorities, and statements critical of slave owners. When the BSCS refused to concede to creationists' demands, their books disappeared from the Texas list. One critic even linked evolution with the assassination of John F. Kennedy.

Thanks to the endorsement of the federal government, increased interest in public education, and legal precedents limiting religious influences in public schools (i.e., the same forces that helped overturn Tennessee's Butler Law in 1967; see Grabiner and Miller 1974), the BSCS books were popular nationwide and completely transformed the profile of high school biology textbooks. The books were adopted throughout the country (by nearly half of the high schools in the United States by 1970), including the three southern states having antievolution laws (Grobman 1969; Skoog 1979). Commercial publishers, trying to keep up, began reinstating evolution in their books (Moore 2001b).

John Scopes Seeks and Finds Anonymity
Soon after the trial, the Rhea County School Board offered Scopes a new contract (at a salary of $150 per month) if he would adhere "to the spirit of

the evolution law" (Ginger 1958). Scopes rejected the offer and left town.[40] He accepted a scholarship (offered by scientists and reporters who attended the trial) to attend graduate school at the University of Chicago in September 1925 and spent the rest of his life as a geologist who only occasionally spoke in public about his trial (e.g., the reluctant Scopes was convinced by his wife, Mildred, to promote and attend the 1960 world premiere of *Inherit the Wind* in Dayton, where he was given a parade and a key to the city; see Cornelius 1991).[41]

Scopes never discussed his famous case with his children except when they asked questions about it. Wanting to be "just another man instead of the Monkey Trial defendant," he was content to let his hour of fame pass by. In doing so, Scopes passed up many lucrative offers to cash in on his fame (e.g., a New York agent offered him $2,000 per week to appear in the *Tarzan* movies, and another offered him $50,000 to lecture about evolution from a vaudeville stage; see Scopes 1989). As Scopes said thirty-nine years after the trial, "Least of all did I want to make a quick dollar out of my experience; I had too much respect for the issues involved in the trial. . . . I knew that none of these offers . . . could give me two things I wanted above all else: peace and emotional stability. . . . I could not live happily in a spotlight" (Tompkins 1965; Scopes and Presley 1967). Within a year after the trial, Scopes was returned to the world of anonymity; he would never again be significantly involved in the issues that stormed around him during the summer of 1925 (Tompkins 1965). After having defended his ideas, Scopes went contentedly to a quieter life.

After the Scopes trial, there were no prosecutions under the various antievolution laws. Although the introduction of the BSCS's evolution-based books prompted many teachers to question the decades-old laws, no teacher dared risk the defeat and public humiliation that Scopes had endured. Finally, however, a teacher summoned the courage to challenge the law. That teacher was a churchgoing, twenty-four-year-old born-again Christian in Arkansas named Susan Epperson (see Chapter 3).

Who Won?
Before the Scopes trial began, William Jennings Bryan told reporters, "It is not the decision but the discussion which will follow that I consider important. It will bring the issue before the attention of the world" (Cross 1925). Everyone knew that the issue would be controversial. For example, as John Scopes helped visitors leave Dayton, legislator-turned-correspondent John Butler reported that "the Dayton trial is the beginning of a great battle between infidelity and Christianity. . . . This is the controversy of the age" (de Camp 1968).

Inherent in the controversy was deciding who had "won." Some of the responses were predictable. For instance, Bryan proclaimed victory and branded Darrow as "all that is cruel, heartless, and destructive in evolution." Ben McKenzie, the oldest of the prosecution lawyers, used a harsh antievolutionary sermon to continue Bryan's attack on evolution: "The modern-day evolutionist is an atheist, and if he is not an atheist he is an agnostic." An Oklahoma newspaper gave the victory to Bryan: "Mr. Bryan came out more than victorious. He made a monkey out of the defense counsel and left them gasping" (Ginger 1958).

Dudley Field Malone—while speaking at the request of Will Rogers from the stage of New York's *Ziegfeld Follies* two days after the trial—called Scopes's conviction a "victorious defeat" that would ensure that "future generations will know the truth" (Scopes 1961; Ginger 1958). Many agreed with Malone. For example, the *New York Times* described Bryan's performance as "absurdly pathetic," and others declared that "Darrow's manhandling of Bryan had a shattering impact" (Ginger 1958). H. L. Mencken described the trial like this: "On the one side was bigotry, ignorance, hatred, superstition, every sort of blackness that the human mind is capable of. On the other side was sense. And sense achieved a great victory" (Mencken 1925). And the *Arkansas Gazette*, which would later report on an important trial that overturned the Butler Law, reported that "for the state of Tennessee, the Scopes trial has been a moral disaster. It will plague the citizen of Tennessee wherever he may go."

Amid suggestions that northern universities deny credits from colleges in states having "monkey laws," both sides claimed victory. Editors of newspapers such as the *New York Times*, the *New York Evening Post*, and the *Chicago Tribune* predicted that the evolution/creationism controversy would continue unabated ("Ended at Last" 1925; "As Expected, Bryan Wins" 1925; "Dayton's 'Amazing' Trial" 1925). They were all right.

Notes

1. Scopes had planned to leave Dayton for the summer to be with his family and to sell Fords for a 5 percent commission; he was available for the trial in July only because he had a date with "a beautiful blonde" at a forthcoming church social (Ginger 1958; Larson 1997). In 1925, Dayton had 1,500 residents and nine churches. Ironically, Rhea County was named for John Rhea, a Revolutionary soldier and an early leader in higher education in Tennessee (de Camp 1968).

2. Rappleyea's dislike for fundamentalism increased when he heard a fundamentalist preacher tell weeping parents that their dead child was "awrithin' in the flames of hell" because the parents hadn't had the child baptized. According to Rappleyea, "A few days later I heard that this same bunch, the Fundamentalists, had passed that Anti-Evolution Law, and I made up my mind I'd show them up to the world."

3. The original table from Robinson's Drugstore at which the decision was made to test the Butler Law is now in the Scopes Trial Museum in the basement of the

Rhea County Courthouse in Dayton, Tennessee. In 1977, the ninety-year-old courthouse was designated as a national historic landmark by the U.S. National Park Service. In 1979, a $1 million restoration of the courthouse was completed; the courthouse remains in use today.

4. Bryan invoked nationalism when he later proclaimed that humans didn't evolve from monkeys, "not even from American monkeys." Bryan, who hadn't practiced law in the thirty years before the Scopes trial, believed that (1) there is no scientific proof for human evolution, (2) the teaching of human evolution undermines students' faith and social values, and (3) the "Bible believing" majority should control public schools. Bryan's typical speech in Dayton attacked Clarence Darrow and was similar to the many stump speeches he had used to attack academic freedom ("Trial Transcript" 1925).

5. The *New York Times* received an average of 10,000 words per day from its writers in Dayton. Telegraphers there sent out 165,000 words per day about the trial; these telegraphers sent more words to Europe and Australia than had ever been cabled about any other event in U.S. history. The trial was broadcast by the *Chicago Tribune*'s WGN radio from the Rhea County Courthouse (at a cost of $1,000 per day for the telephone line; Cornelius 1991). Judge John Tate Raulston was thrilled that this was the first trial ever broadcast, noting that "my gavel will be heard around the world!" (Ginger 1958).

6. Scopes didn't teach evolution; he was not even in school on the day mentioned in the indictment (he had assigned the evolution chapter on 23 April, but he was sick the next day so the class recitation never took place). The textbook by Hunter, a former biology teacher, was sold at Robinson's Drugstore and was the state-approved text in Tennessee high schools (Dayton schools had used the book since 1919). Hunter's book—oriented toward public health rather than theoretical biology—was blatantly racist; in its discussion of five races of humans, Hunter concluded that "the Caucasians represented by the civilized white inhabitants of Europe and America" were "the highest type of all."

7. Two of Scopes's students testified at the trial. One of those students, fourteen-year-old Howard Morgan, was the son of a banker who offered the use of his home to the Darrow family while they were in town for the trial.

8. The prosecutorial team included Bryan, Bryan's son William Jennings Bryan Jr., Ben McKenzie (former assistant attorney general and a practicing lawyer in Dayton for more than thirty years), J. Gordon McKenzie (Ben McKenzie's son and former county judge), A. Thomas Stewart (the chief prosecutor in the trial and attorney general for the Eighteenth Judicial Circuit, which included Rhea County), Wallace Haggard (Fred E. Robinson's brother-in-law), and brothers Sue and Herbert Hicks (Dayton attorneys). Ben McKenzie's practice of calling other attorneys by military titles (e.g., "Captain Malone," "Colonel Darrow") was adopted by other participants in the trial, including, on occasion, Judge Raulston. Sue Hicks, a close friend of Scopes, was the original "Boy Named Sue" of the Johnny Cash hit song (Cornelius 1991); he was named for his mother, who died when he was born.

9. Bryan had achieved national prominence in 1896 (at the age of thirty-six) with his "Cross of Gold" speech at the Democratic National Convention in Chicago, where he was nominated for president. Clarence Darrow was a delegate at that convention. Although Bryan swept the South in each of his three tries for president, he never carried Rhea County, the location of Dayton, Tennessee (Larson 1997).

10. Bryan's syndicated column was published in over 100 newspapers with an estimated readership of 15 million. Bryan's weekly Bible class in Miami had 5,000 members and had to meet in a park (Cornelius 1997).

11. Scopes met Bryan years before the trial when Bryan spoke at Scopes's high school graduation in the spring of 1919 in Salem, Illinois. Scopes remembered Bryan as "one of the most prefect speakers I have heard" (Ipsen 1973).

12. The defense included Darrow, the eccentric John R. Neal (Rhea County native and former dean of the University of Tennessee Law School at Knoxville), Arthur Garfield Hays (the defense team's chief strategist and New York counsel to the ACLU), Dudley Field Malone (New York divorce attorney and "backslidden" Catholic; see discussion in Cornelius 1991), W. O. Thompson (Darrow's law partner and replacement for Bainbridge Colby, who resigned the day before the trial started), and F. B. McElwee (one of Neal's former students and replacement for John L. Godsey, who resigned on the first day of the trial). By some accounts, Bryan was outdebated by Malone, a former subordinate of Bryan's in the State Department. (When his law practice later declined, Malone gave up law and became a bit-part actor for the next decade.) The defense was assisted by librarian and biblical authority Charles F. Potter, a Unitarian preacher (Scopes and Presley 1967; de Camp 1968). The short and stocky Hays, who was named after three presidents, had played a key role in the Sacco-Vanzetti case. At the end of the Scopes trial, Hays offered to give Judge Raulston a copy of *On the Origin of Species*, which the judge laughingly accepted.

13. Scopes and Darrow received thousands of letters such as the one from a woman in Kentucky that contained this excerpt: "If you convert everybody to your way of thinking, what will you accomplish? The churches will be torn down, men will have to go armed to protect themselves from murder and lust, and sin will be rampant in the world, for men will not fear God and therefore will do as they please. . . . The only thing you will accomplish will be the making of infidels and the sending of innumerable souls to hell." As another example, a man in North Carolina wrote: "God will not permit [you] to live. You are the enemy of everything that is Christian and decent" (Scopes 1989). Scopes burned most of his mail in large bonfires.

14. Although the public liked Bryan, some reporters were biased against him; he was referred to as an "old buzzard" who gave "a grotesque performance . . . touching in its imbecility" (Cornelius 1990). Mencken said that if Bryan was sincere, "then so was P. T. Barnum" and that "the thing to do is make a fool out of Bryan" (Fletcher 1978). Butler attended the trial after a newspaper offered to pay him for his commentary (Larson 1997).

15. Two weeks after the trial, the lighthearted McKenzie—who was often referred to as the "official jester" of the trial—wrote letters praising Darrow's work at Dayton. When McKenzie was arrested near Dayton for illegally transporting whiskey, Darrow asked if he needed counsel. McKenzie declined Darrow's offer.

16. References to nationalism and southern pride occurred throughout the trial. For example, on the fifth day of the trial, Herbert Hicks proclaimed that "the most ignorant man in Tennessee is a highly educated, polished gentleman [when compared] to the most ignorant man in some of our northern states" ("Trial Transcript" 1925).

17. This portion of that speech became famous: "We will answer their demand for a gold standard by saying to them: you shall not press down upon the brow of labor this crown of thorns, you shall not crucify mankind upon a cross of gold."

18. Unless specified otherwise, all quotations from the courtroom are from the stenographer's court transcript ("Trial Transcript" 1925).

19. The fourth day of the trial ended with zoologist Maynard Metcalf on the witness stand saying that "I doubt very much if any two [scientists] agree as to the exact method by which evolution has been brought about, but . . . there is not a single one among them who has the least doubt of the fact of evolution." When Darrow asked his last question of this witness—"And you say that evolution as you speak of it means including man?"—Metcalf answered: "Surely." However, Metcalf's testimony, as well as that of other expert witnesses for the defense, was not allowed to be considered as evidence in the trial.

20. Scopes was recruited to write news stories for the delinquent reporters (Scopes 1967).

21. This move paved the way for the case toward an appeal, spared Darrow from having to be questioned by Bryan, and avoided the closing argument that Bryan had been preparing (Scopes 1967). When Darrow waived the closing argument for the defense, the prosecution was denied its opportunity for a closing argument as well.

22. The ACLU—which had entered the trial to help publicize the facts of the controversy—spent $8,993.01 on Scopes's case, most of which went to expert witnesses. Scopes's bill for court costs totaled $343.87, all of which was paid by the ACLU (Scopes and Presley 1967). Darrow and other attorneys worked without pay and covered all of their own expenses. (Darrow, who spent about $2,000 of his own money for the trial, told the ACLU, "I don't want you to think about my expenses. I could afford it and I never got more for my money" [de Camp 1968].) Malone raised $1,350 for the trial (Ginger 1958), but the ACLU didn't pay off its Scopes-related debts until 1926, thanks to a plea mailed to members of the AAAS; that mailing turned the deficit into a surplus of more than $2,000 (de Camp 1968). If churchgoers and lawyers were upset by Darrow's tactics, many scientists were not (Ginger 1958).

23. The brief filed by the Tennessee Academy of Science included a list of "leading ministers" in Tennessee who condemned the Butler Law (the only other group to file a brief was the Unitarian Laymen's League). At the hearing, the Tennessee Academy of Science also contributed to the presentation made by the defense.

24. Darrow had gained fame by defending socialist Eugene V. Debs and more than 100 accused murderers, including Nathan Leopold and Richard Loeb in 1924 (Cornelius 1990).

25. Most of the initial meeting to plan the college was devoted to denouncing Darrow. After gathering pledges totaling almost $1 million (over half of which was erased by the Great Depression) and a donation of 81 acres by the citizens of Dayton, ground for William Jennings Bryan University (later abbreviated to Bryan College) was broken on 5 November 1926 by Governor Peay before a crowd of more than 10,000 onlookers (Traylor 1990). The college opened in 1930 in the old high school building where John Scopes had supposedly taught evolution. Tobacco and liquor were banned, and applicants for admission had to take a loyalty oath to biblical literalism (Ginger 1958). Today, Bryan College is a 100-acre, nonsectarian, independent, coeducational liberal arts college that enrolls about 700 students committed to biblical Christianity and "Christ Above All." A variety of roads, schools, and other public facilities throughout the United States are named after Bryan (Cor-

nelius 1997). Although the Liberal Church of Denver conferred the rank of bishop on Scopes and Rappleyea, Rappleyea's plans to create a liberal college to offset the plans for William Jennings Bryan University never materialized (de Camp 1968).

26. Before the Scopes trial, two congressmen (William Taylor of Tennessee and W. D. Upshaw of Georgia) talked about introducing a national antievolution bill. However, both later decided that such restrictions were best handled at the local level (de Camp 1968).

27. *The World's Most Famous Court Trial* was originally produced at God's Bible School in Cincinnati, Ohio. Today, copies of the trial's transcripts are published by Bryan College.

28. After the Scopes trial, Darrow defended twelve African Americans in Detroit who had allegedly committed murder while defending their home against a white mob (Ginger 1958).

29. Despite repeated attempts to overturn the Butler Law, the statute remained on the books (and unenforced) until it was repealed in 1967, following a debate in which a monkey was brought to the Tennessee House of Representatives ("Tennessee House Votes to Repeal Antievolution Law" 1967). As the monkey watched from the well of the House, only two representatives defended the law (Larson 1989), and the repeal bill passed by a vote of 59–30. In the Tennessee Senate, Senator Ernest Crouch (who opposed repeal) read a letter from a soldier in Vietnam whose life, he claimed, had been saved by a Bible he carried in a pocket struck by a bullet (de Camp 1968). The vote initially tied at 16–16, meaning that the bill failed. The Senate then amended the existing law to forbid the teaching of evolution "as a fact" (the House voted to table this motion). On a second try, the repeal bill passed the Tennessee Senate by a vote of 20–13. On 18 May 1967, Governor Buford Ellington signed the repeal bill into law, thereby ending the Butler era (de Camp 1968).

30. For a discussion of the heritage of the Scopes trial and its players, see Ginger (1958), Marsden (1980), Cornelius (1991), and Larson (1997).

31. Representatives of student groups in Arkansas denounced the bill, claiming that they "did not want to be laughed at, as are the graduates of the University of Tennessee, and practically boycotted by larger university and medical schools when we seek to pursue our education further" (Ginger 1958).

32. During a heated debate in the Mississippi Senate, an opponent of the antievolution law proposed an amendment to make the penalty "death by burning at the stake, it being the spirit of this bill to restore the Spanish Inquisition" (de Camp 1968). The amendment failed, but the law passed the Senate by a vote of 29–16. The Mississippi statute, which later became the last surviving antievolution law, was not declared unconstitutional until 21 December 1970.

33. Straton, who announced his candidacy for Bryan's role, challenged Darrow and Malone to debates but was rudely rebuffed (de Camp 1968).

34. During Scopes's trial, Martin had set up a booth near the courthouse to sell his book *Hell and the High Schools: Christ or Evolution—Which?* However, realizing that money could also be made with the evolutionists, Martin later invented a pen name and wrote "Why Evolution Should Be Taught in Our Schools Instead of the Book of Genesis" (his concealed identity was later revealed). In early 1926, Martin spoke to the Mississippi legislature in support of its antievolution statute, telling the legislators to "go back to the fathers and mothers of Mississippi and tell them because you could not face the scorn and abuse of Bolsheviks and Anarchists and

Atheists and agnostics and their co-workers, you turned over their children to a teaching that God's Word is a tissue of lies" (Ginger 1958). Local papers credited the passage of the bill to Martin (Ginger 1958).

35. A relic of the antievolution crusade was the passage of laws in many states requiring Bible reading in public schools. Those laws remained in effect for decades until the U.S. Supreme Court ruled them all unconstitutional.

36. The Creation Research Society (http://www.iclnet.org/pub/resources/text/crs/crs-home.html) produces and distributes booklets such as *Science and Creation* (introduced in twenty-eight states in 1973–1974), Robert Kofahl's *Handy Dandy Evolution Refuter* (1977), and Kelly Segraves and Robert Kohfal's *The Creation Explanation: A Scientific Alternative to Evolution* (1975). These creationists want "to reach the 63 million children of the United States with the scientific knowledge of Biblical creationism" (Overton 1985). Creationists have influenced legislation in many states. For example, in 1963, Tennessee passed by a vote of 69–16 a bill requiring that all textbooks include a disclaimer that any idea about "the origin and creation of man and his world . . . is not represented to be scientific fact" (see Bennetta 1986). Not surprisingly, the Bible—listed as a reference book instead of a textbook—was made exempt from the disclaimer (Shermer 1997). The bill was later appealed by the National Association of Biology Teachers (NABT) at about the same time that Susan Epperson filed her lawsuit in Arkansas.

37. Ferguson was actually a stand-in for her husband, who had been impeached in 1917 over a road contract scandal (de Camp 1968). As head of the state textbook commission, Ferguson approved Truman J. Moon's *Biology for Beginners*, but only after three chapters that mentioned evolution were deleted. Contracts permitting the removal of offensive pages were arranged with such publishers as Henry Holt, Macmillan, and Allyn and Bacon (Ginger 1958). About evolution, Ferguson proclaimed that "I'm a Christian mother who believes Jesus Christ died to save humanity, and I am not going to let that kind of rot go into Texas textbooks" (de Camp 1968). The commission threatened to fire any teacher using books that had not been approved.

38. Organizations such as the California Board of Education argued that the inclusion of religious quotations made a book worthy of adoption because they showed that the book presented evolution as a "theory and not as an established fact" (see Grabiner and Miller 1974).

39. These worries were heightened by the Soviet Union's launch on 4 October 1957 of *Sputnik I*, the first orbiting artificial satellite. This launch announced to Americans that nature's secrets—unlike political secrets—cannot be concealed and that no nation holds a monopoly on the laws of nature (Shermer 1997).

40. Not surprisingly, Scopes's successor (Raleigh Reece, a reporter from Nashville) was a strict fundamentalist (de Camp 1968; Ginger 1958). George Rappleyea, who kept in touch with Scopes after the trial, noted with great amusement that when Reece missed the first week of classes in the fall of 1925, his substitute was Darius Darwin (Scopes 1989).

41. Scopes's application for a fellowship was rejected because of his "godlessness" (de Camp 1968). When he returned to Dayton for the premiere of *Inherit the Wind*, "Scopes" sodas and "simian" sodas were again priced at 15 cents, just as they were during the trial (Scopes 1989). During Scopes's visit to Dayton, a local preacher denounced him as "the devil," and Scopes noted that teachers were still re-

quired to sign a pledge that they would not teach evolution (Scopes and Presley 1967). In 1972, Dayton hosted the world-premiere of *The Darwin Adventure*, a British-made film about Charles Darwin's voyage aboard the HMS *Beagle*. Francis W. Darwin (Charles Darwin's great-grandson) was a special guest at that premiere (Mercer 1978; Cornelius 1991).

3

"THIS IS THE BIBLE, BUDDY":
EPPERSON V. ARKANSAS

Arkansas' anti-evolution law has disturbed me more than a little. . . . This law, prohibiting any teacher from discussing in any way the Darwinian theory of evolution, compels me either to neglect my responsibility as a teacher or to violate my responsibility as a citizen.
—Susan Epperson

It will probably take another case to clear up the matter.
—Clarence Darrow, upon hearing that the Tennessee Supreme Court upheld Tennessee's Butler Law banning the teaching of evolution, 1927

You don't protect any of your individual liberties by lying down and going to sleep.
—John Scopes

The main conclusion arrived at in my work, namely, that man is descended from some lowly organized form, will, I regret to think, be highly distasteful to many. But there can hardly be a doubt that we are descended from barbarians.
—Charles Darwin

After John Scopes's conviction in 1925 for teaching human evolution, the American Civil Liberties Union could find no one willing to challenge the Butler Law ("Scopes Goes Free" 1927; "Will Ask Court to Rehear Case" 1927). In the ensuing decades, biology teachers avoided the subject of evolution, and the word *evolution* disappeared from biology textbooks. The award-winning movie *Inherit the Wind* popularized the Scopes trial's legend as it warned the nation of the perils of zealotry. No antievolution law would be tested until the 1960s. That test would occur in Arkansas.

Arkansas' Antievolution Law

Efforts to pass an antievolution law in Arkansas began soon after the Scopes trial. Although the fundamentalists' antievolution crusade was beginning to lose steam elsewhere, it was not in Arkansas. The crusade in Arkansas was led by Baptist preacher Ben M. Bogard, who toured the state proclaiming the evils of evolution. Encouraged by Bogard's lobbying and the growing legend of the Scopes trial, state Representative T. P. Atkins of Prairie County introduced the first antievolution legislation in Arkansas on 12 January

1927. On the following day, Representative Astor L. Rotenberry of Pulaski County submitted another antievolution bill (House Bill 34). Rotenberry's bill made no references to Genesis but did ban the teaching of human evolution; it also punished violators with up to a $1,000 fine and the possible loss of their teaching license. When Bogard said that he favored Rotenberry's bill, Atkins withdrew his legislation (Kazan 1966c; "Antievolution in Arkansas" 1966). Not wanting to go on record as blocking a bill that would keep the Bible in the state's classrooms, Rotenberry's supporters called for a roll-call vote, after which the bill was referred to the House Education Committee.[1]

At the committee's first hearing about the bill on 28 January 1927, Bogard pleaded with legislators: "I ask in the name of God, don't teach my boy or my girl anything contrary to the Christian religion and make me pay for it. . . . I warn you politicians that your folks back home are going to hold you accountable for your vote on this thing" (Kazan 1966c; "Antievolution in Arkansas" 1966). The Evolution Committee of the Baptist State Convention joined the fray, warning representatives that "every county in the state will be organized to defeat those who fail to support the [antievolution] bill."[2]

On 2 February 1927, only four of the thirteen members of the House Education Committee attended a subsequent hearing about Rotenberry's bill. At that meeting, Rotenberry read "poisonous stuff" from a popular biology textbook used in many Arkansas high schools (Moon's *Biology for Beginners* [1921]).[3] The next day, the committee voted 5–2 to recommend that the House not pass the bill. When the bill was brought before the entire House on 9 February as a special order of business, Bogard again warned legislators, "We will defeat every monk or monkey who favors evolution. If that is a threat, make the most of it. . . . This all has been brought about by the John D. Rockefeller Foundation, which has been controlled by skeptics and infidels and atheists." After a three-hour debate, the House voted 49–48 against the bill. Two dissenting members then changed their votes, and the bill passed 50–47. The bill was then sent to the Senate, but it was tabled after a discussion lasting fifteen minutes. Five days later, the Senate tabled an attempt to reconsider the Rotenberry bill. The fate of Rotenberry's bill was uncertain.

Bogard then made good on his earlier threat by forming and making himself president of the American Anti-Evolution Association, an organization that was open to everyone except "Negros [*sic*], and persons of African decent, Atheists, Infidels, Agnostics, such persons as hold to the theory of Evolution, habitual drunkards, gamblers, profane swearers, despoilers of the domestic life of others, desecrators of the Lord's Day, and those who would depreciate feminine virtue by vulgarly discussing relationships" (de Camp 1969; "Antievolution in Arkansas" 1966; McLester 1966).[4] When the *Chicago Tribune* claimed that Arkansas was "being more primitive than the Tennesseans," the *Arkansas Gazette* published a front-page article the next day describing nine violent deaths in Chicago (Kazan 1966c).

Bogard, with the help of the Southern Baptists, began a petition drive to get an initiated act on the ballot of the 1928 general election (Larson 1989). To become an "initiated bill" on the general ballot, Arkansas law required that the petition be signed by only 8 percent of the voters in the 1926 gubernatorial election. The following advertisement was typical of the public appeals used to convince voters to endorse the Arkansas law:

> THE BIBLE OR ATHEISM, WHICH? ALL ATHEISTS FAVOR EVOLUTION. IF YOU AGREE WITH ATHEISM VOTE AGAINST ACT NO. 1. IF YOU AGREE WITH THE BIBLE VOTE FOR ACT NO. 1. . . . SHALL CONSCIENTIOUS CHURCH MEMBERS BE FORCED TO PAY TAXES TO SUPPORT TEACHERS TO TEACH EVOLUTION WHICH WILL UNDERMINE THE FAITH OF THEIR CHILDREN? THE *GAZETTE* SAID RUSSIAN BOLSHEVIKS LAUGHED AT TENNESSEE. TRUE, AND THAT SORT WILL LAUGH AT ARKANSAS. WHO CARES? VOTE FOR ACT NO. 1.[5] (Irons 1988; also see *Arkansas Gazette* [Little Rock ed.], 4 November 1928, p. 12)

On 6 June 1928, Bogard filed more than 19,000 signatures with the Arkansas secretary of state, and the act—now referred to as "Initiated Act No. 1" (Arkansas Statutes 80–1267, 1268)—was placed on the ballot. Educators such as Virgil Jones of the University of Arkansas described the bill as "a long step backward," and Presbyterian preacher Hay Watson Smith likened the bill to "going back to the Middle Ages." Nevertheless, the modified legislation was passed by 63 percent (108,991 to 63,406) of the voters of Arkansas just three years after the Scopes trial. Only five counties failed to approve the measure. Initiated Act No. 1—the only antievolution law ever approved by a popular vote—read as follows:

1. It shall be unlawful for any teacher or other instructor in any University, College, Normal, Public School, or other institution of the State, which is supported in whole or part from public funds derived by State and local taxation to teach the theory or doctrine that mankind ascended or descended from a lower order of animals and also it shall be unlawful for any teacher, textbook commission, or other authority exercising the power to select textbooks for above mentioned education institutions to adopt or use at any such institution a textbook that teaches the doctrine or theory that mankind descended or ascended from a lower order of animals.

2. Any teacher or other instructor or textbook or commissioner who is found guilty of violation of this act by teaching the theory or doctrine mentioned in Section 1 hereof, or by using or adopting any such textbooks in any such educational institution shall be guilty of a misdemeanor and upon conviction shall vacate the position thus held in any educational institutions of the character above mentioned or any commission of which he may be a member.

Thus, in 1928, it became a crime to teach about human evolution in Arkansas.

Trying to Repeal the Arkansas Antievolution Law

The first attempt to repeal the antievolution law failed in 1937, when a proposal died in committee without coming to a vote (Sweeney 1966; Keienburg 1978). In 1959, another attempt to repeal the law emerged when Little Rock was gripped by racial strife. When the public schools were closed, a group including high school student Griffin Smith Jr.[6] asked Pulaski County Representative Willie Oates to "have restrictions imposed on teaching in this state lifted" (Keienburg 1978). Soon thereafter, Oates introduced House Bill 418, an "equal-time" bill to repeal the state's antievolution law and allow students "to study both sides of an issue and decide for themselves what is true in an atmosphere of complete academic freedom" (Keienburg 1978). Oates was labeled an atheist and, facing overwhelming opposition, withdrew the bill, stating that "we must compromise with each other in an effort to reach conclusions that are mutually beneficial. . . . The majority of the people in my county do not wish to grant the academic freedom these young people requested. Therefore, Mr. Speaker, I wish to permanently withdraw my H.B. 418—The Evolution Bill" (Keienburg 1978). When Oates lost her next election, she noted that "the Evolution Bill was a contributing factor to my not being re-elected."[7]

By 1965, the teaching of human evolution in Arkansas had been a crime for almost forty years. In that year, Garland County Representative Nathan Schoenfeld introduced another bill calling for the repeal of the antievolution law. The *Arkansas Gazette* praised Schoenfeld for trying to bring Arkansas into the modern era, but his bill failed to pass through committee and was never called for a vote (Susan Epperson, personal papers; Keienburg 1978).

Soon after, however, the Arkansas Education Association (AEA, a 17,000-member affiliate of the National Education Association), the Arkansas School Board Association, and the Arkansas Parent Teacher Association spoke out against the antievolution law, as did the American Association of University Women (AAUW). Supporters of the law also spoke out. For example, the Central Baptist Association supported the law, and a prominent Baptist preacher declared evolution "impossible" ("Baptist Cleric Says Evolution Is 'Impossible'" 1965). The State Association of Missionary Baptist Churches, meeting at the Antioch Baptist Church, where Ben Bogard had been a preacher, urged authorities to enforce the law ("Baptists Seek 'Monkey Law' Enforcement" 1965). Governor and famed segregationist Orval Faubus insisted that the 1928 antievolution law was still "the will of the people" and proclaimed that the Genesis account of creation was "good enough for me" (Tompkins 1966). Faubus (a Baptist who had used armed troops in 1957 to keep black students out of

Arkansas Governor Orval Faubus strongly opposed Susan Epperson's challenge to Arkansas' law banning the teaching of human evolution. (AP Photos/stf)

Little Rock Central High School) supported the antievolution law "as a safeguard to keep way-out teachers in line" (Irons 1988). Amid this renewal of interest in the antievolution law, the AEA began to consider challenging the statute.

Susan Epperson Agrees to Test the Law

The AEA enlisted Virginia Minor, a kindergarten teacher at Little Rock Central High School, to help find a plaintiff to challenge the antievolution law. At about the same time, Susan Epperson, then in her second year as a biology teacher at Central High,[8] read an article in the *Arkansas Gazette* about the AAUW's stand against the law. In 1965, administrators at Central High School—in response to a recommendation from the school's biology teachers—adopted *Modern Biology* (Otto and Towle 1965); whereas evolution had disappeared from earlier editions of *Modern Biology* after Scopes's conviction, the new edition adopted at the high school stated that evidence of "changes in plants and animals" over time showed that humans and apes "may have had a common, generalized ancestor in the remote past" (see Irons 1988).[9] Although these statements were cautious and qualified, they nevertheless violated Initiated Act No. 1.[10] Thus, in 1965, Epperson faced a dilemma: she was required to use the prescribed textbook, but doing so would be a crime and subject her to being fired. Most teachers avoided this dilemma by skipping the chapters on evolution; some schools even omitted biology altogether (de Camp 1969). Epperson, however, decided to challenge the law.

Epperson was an ideal plaintiff for the AEA. She was a public school teacher who had been born, raised, and educated in Arkansas; she had graduated from a church-affiliated college in the state; and her husband, Jon, was in the Strategic Air Command at the Little Rock Air Force Base, thereby neutralizing charges of "outside agitation" that had surfaced during the racial confrontations in Little Rock (as well as during the Scopes trial).[11] Epperson was also a devout Christian. It is hard to imagine a better plaintiff.

Epperson's challenge of the antievolution law began in mid-September 1965, when Forrest Rozzell, the executive director of the AEA, called a press conference to issue a "personal position" statement outlining the importance of understanding nature and recommending the repeal of the state's 1928 law. Rozzell's statement was endorsed by State Commissioner of Education Arch Ford, who argued that the law "was a dead issue and there was no reason for keeping it on the statute books." Two months later, Rozzell met with Epperson, Minor, and Eugene R. Warren (attorney for the AEA) in Minor's kindergarten classroom to discuss the 1928 antievolution law.[12] The group sat in tiny chairs around a tiny table. Epperson was shown a complaint drafted by the AEA. She later recalled, "I was aware of the possible negative results of the case. But when a law is wrong you should try to do something about it. The brief was written for me—it was all there expressing in legal terms everything that I felt. It was really nothing but cowardice that would have kept me from signing the complaint for the suit."

Epperson agreed to test the law "because of my concept of my responsibilities both as a teacher of biology and as an American citizen." With Epperson now serving as the nominal plaintiff, the AEA asked the court to declare that the antievolution law was unconstitutional because it violated two clauses of the First Amendment. Epperson also charged that the law impeded the "free communication of thoughts and opinions" protected by the Arkansas Constitution (Irons 1988) and sought to enjoin the administrators of the school from firing her for breaking the law.

On 4 December 1965, after teachers had used the offending textbook but before they had reached the illegal chapter, the AEA Board of Directors agreed to use "the judicial process for determining the constitutionality of the [antievolution] law" (Larson 1989). Two days later, Warren filed the complaint, asked for a declaratory judgment[13] of the antievolution law, and requested that the school board not be allowed to fire Epperson. Hubert H. Blanchard Jr., associate executive secretary of the AEA and a parent who wanted his two sons to "be informed of all scientific theories and hypotheses," supported Epperson's action as an intervenor; he believed that his children were being denied a good education. For the first time since the Scopes trial in 1925, there would be a lawsuit to challenge an antievolution law.

People Choose Sides

When Epperson's lawsuit was made public, people began taking sides. The *Arkansas Gazette* praised Epperson, and in April 1966, the Little Rock branch of the AAUW commended Epperson "for her courage and intellectual integrity." Little Rock Central High School's *Tiger* newspaper noted that "Mrs. Epperson has shown admirable courage in filing her law suit" ("Maintaining One's Ideas" 1965). In response, the Baptist Bible Fellowship announced that "we firmly believe and accept the Genesis account of creation; that man was created in the image of God by the direct and immediate act of God without the process of evolution" (de Camp 1968).

Concerned citizens sent Epperson an assortment of religious texts, including one written by Willard Henning of Bryan College (Dayton, TN) titled "How Valid Is the Theory of Evolution?" A letter from the Creation Research Society informed Epperson that "evolution is on its way out" and asked, "Can't you delay your action against [the law] while you study the facts?"

Others attacked Epperson; she was labeled an atheist and depicted as a monkey. A letter addressed to "The Monkey Teacher" told Epperson that "there is a striking resemblance between you and a monkey. I would advise you to go ahead and teach it. You are living proof of it." One Charlotte Blair told Epperson:

> I am sure you are not aware of the Havoc you are causing among the young with your Darwin theory, teaching. As United States is mostly Christian, this is an affront to Christians, and in favor of the atheists, it is about time that Christians rise up and demand recognition for their beliefs. The Bible reading was removed as an affront to atheists, well this Darwin theory is an affront to the Christian, and we are footing the bills for the nation. Even the Jew would object to being descended from a monkey, as it sure would not fit into their religious views. Not knowing you, it could be true, in your case, but why brag about it, you are proving it.

Concerned Christians also had comments for Epperson: "If I had a daughter like you, I would of asked God to of let you died while young" and "Go on, teach evolution and may God have mercy on your soul. We will live to see the day when . . . others will [go] to hell and you will go there also."

Although Warren had warned against making Epperson's trial a "Bar-

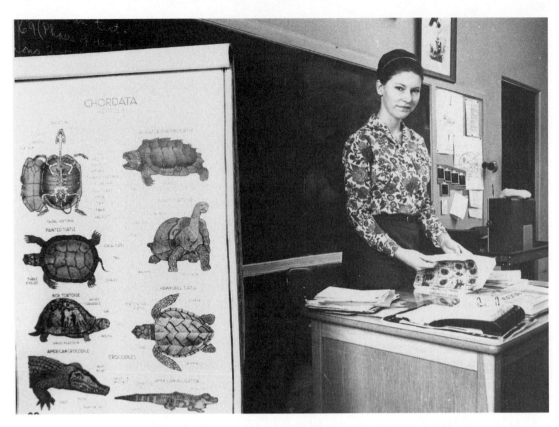

Late in 1965, Susan Epperson, a second-year biology teacher at Central High School in Little Rock, challenged the Arkansas law banning the teaching of evolution. Her lawsuit was the first challenge of an antievolution law since the trial of John Scopes in 1925. (AP Photos)

num and Bailey circus" and had said that he wanted to avoid "the carnival atmosphere that went on in Tennessee" ("Arkansas 'Monkey' Battle" 1966; Bentley 1966), many people tried to sensationalize the trial. For example, on the Sunday before the trial opened, a popular Baptist preacher told his congregation that "the acceptance of organic evolution means the death of Christianity" (Kazan 1966a) and that "the U.S. Supreme Court is now in the process of reversing all previous decisions that recognized our Nation as a Christian Nation" ("Trial of 1966" 1966). Governor Faubus told his Sunday school class that the law was good and declared that he "was not ready to repeal the Bible" ("Antievolution Law Is Good" 1966). Bruce Bennett, the attorney general of Arkansas, complained to Murray O. Reed, the judge for the trial, that Epperson "was the only person since the law was approved to 'clamor' in favor of teaching that man evolved from monkeys, apes, sharks, porpoises, seaweed, or any other form of animal or vegetable" and that the teaching of evolution would make it possible for "crackpots" to teach the "God is Dead" theory, the theory that "man came from a gorilla," and the "Ham and Eggs Theory of California" (Bennett did not explain this "Ham and Eggs Theory" [Kazan 1966b]). Bennett also proclaimed that evolution was an atheistic doctrine, that Epperson wanted to convert her students to atheism, and that he wanted to have preachers and other witnesses testify about the inadequacies of the theory of evolution (Keienburg

1978). On the day before the trial, Bennett continued his tirade, claiming that Epperson "wants . . . to advance an atheistic doctrine" ("Arkansas 'Monkey' Battle" 1966). He then reassured citizens by reminding them that, "This is the Bible, buddy; I intend to defend it."

Epperson, meanwhile, released her own statement:

I am a teacher by profession. I chose to become a teacher because I believe that teaching is the most important profession to which a person can dedicate his talents and energies. I pursued an education course in college to become a science teacher as competent as my capabilities will permit. I received a bachelor's degree from the College of the Ozarks and a Master of Science degree from the University of Illinois.

My mother is a public school librarian and my father has been a professor of biology for almost half a century. They are both dedicated Christians who see no conflict between their belief in God and the scientific search for truth. I share this belief.

As a new teacher (this is my second year), and, as a native Arkansan, Arkansas' anti-evolution law has disturbed me more than a little.

I do not try to teach my students what to think. I try to teach them how to think, how to make sound judgments about the various relevant alternatives. In doing this, it is my responsibility to expose my students to and encourage them to seek after as much of the accumulated scientific knowledge and theories as possible. Rational knowledge, as accurate and balanced as humanly possible at any given time, is essential to the making of sound value judgments.

When [I was asked] to become the plaintiff in this test suit I agreed to do so because of my concept of my responsibilities both as a teacher of biology and as an American citizen. This law, prohibiting any teacher from discussing in any way the Darwinian theory of evolution, compels me either to neglect my responsibility as a teacher or to violate my responsibility as a citizen. As a responsible biology teacher, it is my duty to discuss with my students and to explain to them various scientific theories and hypotheses in order that they may be as educated and enlightened as possible about matters pertaining to science, including the theories of Darwin as set forth in *On the Origin of Species* and in *The Descent of Man.* However, when I do this, I become an irresponsible citizen—a law violator—a criminal subject to fine and dismissal from my job. On the other hand, if I obey the law, I neglect the obligations of a responsible teacher of biology. This is the sure path to the perpetuation of ignorance, prejudice and bigotry.

The only recourse available to me which is consistent with my concept of my responsibilities as a teacher and citizen is this test suit. It is my fervent hope that this suit will resolve this dilemma not only for me but also for all other Arkansas teachers.

The "New Scopes Trial" Begins

There were two judges in Little Rock who presided over cases in chancery court. Eugene Warren wanted Epperson's case to be heard by Chancellor Murray O. Reed. To accomplish this, Warren used two different lawsuits—the Epperson suit and another unimportant "placeholder" suit—to ensure that Epperson's case would be assigned to Reed for a hearing and decision without a jury. The trial occurred on 1 April 1966[14] before a packed courtroom. Reed had tripled the usual number of bailiffs present, banned all media coverage, limited the case to constitutional issues, refused to allow questions about the personal beliefs of witnesses, and would not hear arguments about the validity of evolution or its relative merits when compared to creationism. Warren hardly questioned the state's four witnesses and questioned Epperson for only about ten minutes, during which she focused on the central issue: "I brought this lawsuit because I have a textbook which includes the theory about the origin or the descent or the ascent of man from a lower form of animals. This seemed to be a widely accepted theory and I feel it is my responsibility to acquaint my students with it."

Bennett took personal charge of Epperson's trial, as he had in the 1957 trial of Daisy Bates for refusing to give Bennett the National Association for the Advancement of Colored People's membership list (see Larson 1989). Bennett questioned Epperson for almost an hour, after which he argued that Arkansas, like most employers, has "certain things about which they command their employees to keep silent during their hours of employment." Bennett then invoked the majoritarian legacy of William Jennings Bryan by reminding the court that

> the people have spoken on this subject and have shown by an overwhelming vote that they do not want their children taught the theory of evolution in the public schools. Are the rights and wishes of the majority to be ignored in order that Mrs. Epperson's desire to teach evolution may be gratified? . . . Have the people no right or power, by majority vote, to forbid the teaching of a theory in which they do not believe, to which they violently object, which has no basis in fact, and which is detrimental to the spiritual and mental

well-being of their children? If not, then this is no longer a government of the people, by the people, and for the people.

Bennett also reminded the court of Scopes's case and its legacy, as well as the fact that two of Arkansas' neighboring states had similar statutes: Tennessee (*Tenn. Code Ann.* 49-1922, enacted 1925) and Mississippi (*Miss. Code Ann.* 6798, 6799, enacted 1926).[15] He then added, "These two states evidently regard the statutes as being reasonable. The only challenge to either of these was the Scopes case, and there the Tennessee statute was held to be valid. The Scopes decision was in 1927; since then the evolution statutes have gone unchallenged."

Bennett proceeded to attack Epperson—"Mrs. Epperson seeks to foist the beliefs of Darwin which she advocates upon a captive audience . . . she insists that it is her right under the freedom of speech provision of the Constitution to indoctrinate our children with this unproven theory"—and then described the case as a choice of "whether we succumb to the atheistic, materialistic concept which is attempting to conquer the world or whether we provide a climate in which our children will be encouraged to retain the spiritual, moral, and human values which our forefathers, in drafting our Constitution, tried so steadfastly to protect" ("Memorandum Brief" 1966).

The trial—billed by the *New York Times* as the "New 'Scopes Trial'" ("New 'Scopes Trial' Opens in Arkansas" 1966)—was attended by ministers, seminary students, civil rights workers, and interested spectators. Although there was seating for only 60, more than 100 people were in the courtroom, and onlookers stood 10-deep in doorways to hear testimony. Twice during the proceedings Chancellor Reed threatened to clear the court when spectators laughed and became unruly. Like Bryan before him, Bennett played to the courtroom with swagger and claimed that Epperson's teaching would "becloud" the minds of her students, which would be "warped by anti-religious propaganda." Reed barred Bennett's witnesses who were to testify on behalf of the law (and, simultaneously, question and denounce evolution), stating that the issue at hand was a constitutional, not a religious or scientific, one.

Bennett, searching for an opening to bring in his parade of witnesses, asked a variety of unusual questions. For example:

BENNETT: The protozoa is an infinite little cell, isn't it?
EPPERSON: I believe it is finite.
BENNETT: Do you know of a theory that man evolved from algae?
EPPERSON: No sir.
BENNETT: From seaweed?
EPPERSON: Seaweed? No, not as a strict theory.

Despite his bravado and self-confidence, Bennett was poorly prepared, ignorant of science, and outperformed by Warren. (One account described Bennett as a "silver-haired, but scarcely silver-tongued counterpart of William Jennings Bryan.") Reed sustained all of Warren's sixty-three objections. Whereas Scopes's trial more than forty years earlier had dragged on for two weeks, Epperson's trial involved only six witnesses and ended after only two hours (Irons 1988). Bennett rested the state's case just thirty minutes into the afternoon session. Warren then rested his case, and Reed—asking for additional briefs—took the case under advisement.

Although Chancellor Reed did not reject "creation" in his nine-page per curiam opinion (which was issued two months later), he did reject the law forbidding the teaching of evolution: "This Court is of the opinion that a chapter in a biology book, adopted by the school administrative authorities, stating that a specific theory has been advanced by an individual that man ascended or descended from a lower form of animal life, does not constitute such a hazard to the safety, health and morals of the community that the constitutional freedoms may justifiably be suppressed by the state." Reed, citing the legacy of the Scopes trial and acknowledging that "this Court is not unmindful of the public interest in this case," ruled that the Arkansas statute violated the Fourteenth Amendment because it was arbitrary and vague, thereby making interpretation difficult. Reed went on to add that "Act No. 1 . . . tends to hinder the quest for knowledge, restrict the freedom to learn, and restrain the freedom to teach" ("Memorandum Opinion" 1966).

Reed's handling of the case was praised by the press and individuals alike ("A Dignified Trial" 1966). But many people—especially those hoping for another Scopes fiasco—were disappointed in the trial. Headlines on 2 April 1966 made it clear that Epperson's trial lacked the drama of the Scopes trial:

> *Washington Daily News:* COURT DRAMA LACKING: 2D EVOLUTION
> TRIAL IS A DRAG
> *Oakland Tribune:* EVOLUTION TRIAL FAILS TO IMPRESS
> *Washington Post:* '66 EVOLUTION CASE IS ONLY A SHADOW OF FA-
> MOUS SCOPES MONKEY TRIAL
> *Shreveport Times:* "MONKEY TRIAL" FIZZLES ON LACK OF SENSATION
> *Los Angeles Times:* "MONKEY TRIAL" RERUN STRIPPED OF DRAMA
> *New York Herald Tribune:* ARKANSAS EVOLUTION TRIAL LACKS
> 1925 SCOPES DRAMA

Although Epperson had won, Warren knew that to get a definitive decision, Epperson's case would have to get to the U.S. Supreme Court. That meant that the state would need to appeal Reed's decision to the Arkansas Supreme Court and that Epperson must lose that appeal.

Soon after Reed's decision, Tennessee—a state that had become known as the "Monkey State" ("The *Press-Scimitar* Blitzes" 1967; "Monkey Law Bill" 1967)—repealed its antievolution law.[16] John Scopes, who had just published his memoirs (Scopes and Presley 1967), noted that "it's been a long fight for the people of Tennessee. I think the people there realized that it was a bad law and would have to be repealed sooner or later. I suppose the time had come" ("House Act Fails to Stir Scopes" 1967). But the appeal of Reed's decision would change everything.

The Appeal

As Bennett had promised, Arkansas' Attorney General's Office appealed Reed's ruling to the Arkansas Supreme Court less than one month after the decision. The appeal included no oral arguments. On 5 June 1967, the Arkansas Supreme Court issued a bizarre, unsigned, two-sentence per curiam ruling. Unlike most decisions by the court, this decision was not written by any one justice and did not include the usual published opinion (five of the seven judges had written opinions, but "some were unhappy with the way some of [the opinions] read" [Keienburg 1978]). The first sentence of the decision ruled that the state law "is a valid exercise of the state's power to specify the curriculum in its public schools." The second sentence puzzled everyone: "The court expresses no opinion on the question whether the Act prohibits any explanation of the theory of evolution or merely prohibits teaching that the theory is true."[17]

Although the 6–1 decision did not address whether Epperson could assign "the evolution chapter" (titled "The History of Man") of *Modern Biology* to her students, the appeal did reverse the chancery court's ruling, thereby sustaining the statute as an exercise of the state's power to specify the curriculum in public schools. On 26 July 1967, the Arkansas Supreme Court refused to reconsider its ruling.[18] After being legal for just over a year, the teaching of evolution was again a crime in Arkansas. However, four decades after the Scopes fiasco, there was a case—not in Tennessee, but in Arkansas—to appeal to the U.S. Supreme Court.

The Evolution/Creationism Controversy Goes to the U.S. Supreme Court

On 4 March 1968, the U.S. Supreme Court agreed to hear *Epperson v. Arkansas*, despite the fact that there was no record of any prosecutions under the statute and the statute was more of a curiosity than a fact of life in Arkansas. Epperson's case, like all cases involving evolution since Scopes's trial, was viewed in light of Scopes's trial. For example, a front-page article in the *New York Times* described Epperson's case as "the nation's second 'monkey trial'" (Graham 1968).

On 16 October 1968, Eugene Warren addressed the Court for only ten minutes of the half hour allotted to him. Warren's presentation ignored the free speech and establishment of religion issues that had been addressed in his brief and instead focused on the vagueness of the Arkansas law.[19] Warren claimed that teachers were so confused and frightened that "biology is not even taught" in many Arkansas schools (Irons 1988).

The state's argument was made by Don Langston, a young assistant to Arkansas' new attorney general, Joe Purcell (Bennett had been sent back to private practice by Arkansas' voters in 1966). Langston complained that he had inherited the case and that the Arkansas Supreme Court had not provided any basis for its decision. After apologetically claiming that the law was a "neutrality act" that equally proscribed Darwin's ideas and "opposing theories" of human origins, Langston admitted that the law did not prohibit "the literal reading of Genesis" in biology classes (Irons 1988). Langston argued that the antievolution law was a valid use of the state's power to govern the curriculum and instruction in public schools, adding that "if Mrs. Epperson would tell her students that 'Here is Darwin's Theory, that man ascended or descended from a lower form of being' then I think she would be under this statute liable for prosecution."

Although Langston would not concede that the law was invalid (to which U.S. Supreme Court Justice Abe Fortas replied, "It might not be too late, you know"), he smiled when Justice Thurgood Marshall asked whether, since the Arkansas Supreme Court disposed of the case in two sentences, he would "object to us disposing of [the case] in one sentence" (Irons 1988). At another point, Langston complained that Arkansas "didn't file a written opinion with reasoning." When a justice responded that "maybe they couldn't," Langston replied, "I have heard rumors to that effect." Clearly, Langston knew that he would lose the case.

One month later (on 12 November 1968), the Supreme Court proved Langston right. Strongly influenced by the legacy of the Scopes trial,[20] the Court ruled unanimously in *Epperson v. Arkansas* (393 U.S. 97 [1968]) that banning the teaching of evolution violated the Due Process Clause of the Fourteenth Amendment and the Establishment Clause of the First Amendment to the Constitution (Levy 1986).[21] The Court ruled that the Arkansas law was too vague to enforce, attempted to establish a religious position in a public school, reflected religious dogma, and tried to bar the teaching of evolution because evolution contradicted the religious beliefs of people who favored a literal biblical explanation for the origin of humans:[22]

> Arkansas has sought to prevent its teachers from discussing the theory of evolution because it is contrary to the belief of some that the Book of Genesis must be the exclusive source of doctrine as to the

origin of man. It is clear that fundamentalist sectarian conviction was and is the law's reason for existence. . . . Arkansas did not seek to excise from the curricula of its schools and universities all discussion of the origin of man. The law's effort was confined to an attempt to blot out a particular theory because of its supposed conflict with the Biblical account. . . . The overriding fact is that Arkansas' law selects from the body of knowledge a particular segment which it proscribes for the sole reason that it is deemed to conflict with a particular religious doctrine; that is, with a particular interpretation of the Book of Genesis by a particular religious group. . . . [Government] may not be hostile to any religion or to the advocacy of no religion; and it may not aid, foster, or promote one religion or religious theory against another or even against the militant opposite. The First Amendment mandates governmental neutrality between religion and religion, and between religion and nonreligion.

Finally, more than three years after it started, Epperson's case was over.

Many applauded the Supreme Court's decision; for example, the *Arkansas Gazette* told its readers that the U.S. Supreme Court had provided "an overdue rescue from a law of ignorance" ("An Overdue Rescue" 1968).[23] As people in Dayton, Tennessee, reiterated their claim that they would "convict Scopes still" ("Dayton Says It'd Convict Scopes Still" 1968),[24] John Scopes—by this time sixty-eight years old—emerged from his retirement in Louisiana to speak out in support of Epperson: "This is what I've been working for all along. . . . I'm very happy about the decision. I thought all along—ever since 1925—that the law was unconstitutional" ("A Darwinism Ban" 1968).

Meanwhile, Back in Tennessee . . .

As Epperson's lawsuit made its way to the U.S. Supreme Court, events began in Tennessee that eventually led to the repeal of the state's Butler Law. On 13 January 1967, Knoxville attorney Martin Southern filed suit on behalf of his fourteen-year-old son, Thomas, in the Knox County Chancery Court to test the validity of the Butler Law, claiming that the law limited his son's education. On 1 March 1967, before there was any action on Southern's lawsuit, a coalition of legislators from Memphis and Nashville introduced House Bill 48 to repeal the Butler Law. On the following day, the bill was referred to the House Judiciary Committee, the chairperson of which (Charles Galbreath) had cosponsored the legislation. On 5 April, the committee recommended passage of the bill, and a week later, the House—in a session "marked by emotion and comedy"—began debating the bill. The House, amid proclamations of people's dedication to God, passed House Bill

To Jan and Susan Epperson
December 6, 1969
John T. Scopes
Jerry R. Tompkins

In January 1969, John Scopes (left) and Susan Epperson met and discussed their famous lawsuits. Scopes told Epperson that he continued to receive about seven letters per week regarding his trial. At that meeting, Scopes autographed Epperson's copy of Jerry Tomkins's book, D-Days at Dayton: Reflections on the Scopes Trial. *(Photo by Jerry Tomkins)*

48 by a vote of 59–30. However, even the supporters expressed reservations; as Representative Curtis Person Jr. noted, "I pray that teachers will use discrimination and care in teaching Darwin's theory so as not to mislead young minds in their formative stages" (Webb 1994).

On 20 April 1967, the Tennessee Senate began considering the legislation. Soon thereafter, the Senate voted 16–16 on the legislation, thereby killing the repeal. In its place, the Senate passed by a vote of 23–10 Senate Bill 536, which amended the Butler Law. The House refused to accept the amendment, and the repeal was dead.

Meanwhile, Gary L. Scott, a twenty-four-year-old science teacher in rural Jacksboro, Tennessee, was fired for allegedly teaching evolution. Scott's dismissal was instigated by a complaint by Archie Cotton, a member of the Campbell County Board of Education. At a closed meeting on 13 April, the board agreed with Cotton's claim that Scott had neglected his job and violated the Butler Law, and members voted unanimously to fire Scott. By the end of April, Scott had enlisted the help of the ACLU, but he had virtually no local support. The National Education Association agreed to pay Scott's living-expenses while he was unemployed and hired famed civil rights attorney William Kunstler to represent Scott. Scott immediately sued the Campbell County School System for breach of contract and damages; he also challenged the Butler Law but agreed that he would withdraw his challenge if the law was repealed before his trial.

Facing unwanted publicity and the costs of an expensive legal battle, the Campbell County Board of Education reversed itself on 11 May 1967 and voted 7–1 to reinstate Scott. Even Cotton supported Scott's reinstatement. Four days later, however, Scott filed a class action lawsuit in federal district court in Nashville on behalf of himself, two of his students, the National Science Teachers Association, and fifty-nine faculty members at Tennessee colleges and universities. Scott's lawsuit claimed that the Butler Law violated teachers' constitutional rights and sought a permanent injunction to restrain local and state officials from enforcing the law. On 16 May, the state Senate reconsidered House Bill 48 and, after less than three minutes of debate, passed the repeal by a vote of 20–13. Two days later, the legislation was signed by Governor Buford Ellington. The Butler Law had been repealed. Scott and Southern withdrew their lawsuits, and it was again legal to teach evolution in Tennessee's public schools. But the legal challenges in Tennessee and elsewhere were not over.

Notes

1. Rotenberry's bill made it a misdemeanor to teach that "man ascended or descended from any lower order of animals." Like Tennessee's Butler Law, Rotenberry's bill did not prohibit the teaching of evolution; rather, it banned only the teaching of human evolution.

2. The House passed a resolution condemning this action by the Baptist State Convention, but only by a 43–34 vote (Kazan 1966c).

3. *Biology for Beginners* (Moon 1921) was the last of the evolution books in the 1920s. (As explained in Chapter 2, following the Scopes verdict in 1925, evolution had been deleted from other biology textbooks.) Moon's book included several thorough chapters about evolution, and its frontispiece was a picture of Darwin. In the preface, Moon stated that evolution was the fundamental unifying theme of biology. In the 1926 edition, the picture of Darwin had been replaced by a cartoon of the digestive system, and the statement that biology was based on the "fundamental idea of evolution" was replaced by the claim that biology was based on the "fundamental idea of development." A variety of religious quotations were added to the chapters about evolution (see Grabiner and Miller 1974).

4. When a prominent atheist (Charles Smith, president of the American Association for the Advancement of Atheism) came to Little Rock to protest the antievolution legislation, he was jailed for twenty-six days for distributing literature "calculated to disturb the peace." The mayor proclaimed that "no atheist will be permitted to maintain headquarters in Little Rock, Arkansas, if I can prevent it" (Kazan 1966c).

5. For other examples of the public's reaction to the statute, see footnote 16 of *Epperson v. Arkansas*. That ruling can be found at: http://cns.bu.edu/pub/dorman/epperson_v_arkansas.html.

6. Smith's teacher had told him that Arkansas banned her from teaching Darwin's theory. Smith learned more about the law from his grandfather (a former chief justice of the Arkansas Supreme Court) and his father, who was an attorney (Keienburg 1978).

Gary Scott, a high school science teacher in Jacksboro, Tennessee, was fired in 1967 for teaching evolution. Scott's subsequent lawsuit helped convince the Tennessee legislature to repeal its law banning the teaching of human evolution. (AP Photos)

7. Years later, Oates wrote to Susan Epperson, recounting her attempt to repeal the law and offering support.

8. Little Rock Central High School was the infamous site where federal troops were used to enforce desegregation according to the U.S. Supreme Court's *Brown v. Board of Education* decision. Although racism did not play a role in Epperson's case, she received many letters that linked racism with the teaching of evolution (Susan Epperson, personal letters). The community's division over race affected attitudes about Darwin's theory being taught in the public schools. As Wilbur J. Cash noted, "The anti-evolution organizers were explicitly engaged in attempting to wipe out all new knowledge in the schools. They warned constantly that evolution was certain to breed Communism, it was breaking down Southern morals, destroying the ideal of Southern Womanhood. One of the most stressed notions that went around was that evolution made a Negro as good as a white man, that it threatened White Supremacy" (1941).

9. *Modern Biology* was the best-selling biology textbook for more than fifteen years; at one point, more than half of all biology teachers used it (Grabiner and Miller 1974).

10. In fact, Act No. 1 had already been violated, for the Central High School library was "well-stocked with books of and by Charles Darwin," including *Origin of Species* ("Teacher's Challenge" 1965).

11. The ACLU, which had financed John Scopes's test of the antievolution law in Tennessee, offered legal assistance to Epperson, but her attorney declined because of the negative connotations that the entrance of the ACLU would produce.

12. Like Epperson, Rozzell was a graduate of the College of the Ozarks and had studied biology under Epperson's father.

13. A declaratory judgment would put the law, not Epperson, on trial.

14. The April Fools' date was not an accident. Chancellor Reed, who had made no secret of his contempt for the antievolution law, scheduled the trial for one day instead of the usual two weeks allotted for most other cases (Larson 1989).

15. Tennessee's Butler Law would be repealed in 1967. On 21 December 1970, the Mississippi Supreme Court blamed *Epperson v. Arkansas* for unanimously declaring the Mississippi antievolution statute—the last antievolution law in the United States—to be "void and of no effect" (Larson 1989; also see *Pine v. Mississippi State Textbook Purchasing Board*, 322 F.S. 1131 [1971]).

16. The Butler Law was repealed after a controversy that erupted when Gary L. Scott, a science teacher in the rural Campbell County School System, was fired for teaching evolution and for allegedly telling students that the Bible is "a bunch of fairy tales." Scott challenged the Butler Law in federal court on 15 May 1967. Soon thereafter, the Butler Law was voted down by a two-to-one majority in the Tennessee House, but a 16–16 stalemate in the state Senate—punctuated by many professions of faith—preserved the status quo. When Scott's attorneys offered to dismiss the lawsuit if the Senate repealed the Butler Law, senators voted to strike the law. Scott then dismissed his lawsuit and was reinstated ("Teacher in Tennessee Is Fired" 1967).

17. This sentence (and its nonfinal "decision") was meant to deny the U.S. Supreme Court the jurisdiction of the case (i.e., only a final decision could be appealed [Keienburg 1978]).

18. Governor Faubus attended one of the Supreme Court sessions and intimidated the members of the court. Even Justice George Smith (whose father, Hay Wat-

son Smith, had opposed passage of the original legislation in 1928) went along with the majority, saying only, "You will have to be satisfied with the decision in the record" (Keienburg 1978).

19. The written brief alleged that appellants were denied freedom of speech and freedom to learn, equal protection of the law, due process of law, and religious freedom (see Keienburg 1978).

20. Justice Fortas, who had followed the Scopes trial as a fifteen-year-old student in Memphis, Tennessee, volunteered to write the Court's majority opinion. In that opinion, Fortas repeatedly cited "the celebrated Scopes case" and scornfully linked both the Tennessee and Arkansas antievolution laws to "the upsurge of 'fundamentalist' fervor of the twenties" (Irons 1988). Interestingly, Fortas's opinion in *Epperson v. Arkansas* would later be used by creationists to argue for "equal time" in the classroom for their ideas.

21. By 1922, the U.S. Supreme Court had used the Due Process Clause to protect academic freedom by striking down a Nebraska law making it a crime to teach any subject in any language other than English to students who had not passed the eighth grade. The First Amendment mandates governmental neutrality between religion and religion and between religion and nonreligion. The Establishment Clause of the First Amendment states that "Congress shall make no law respecting an establishment of religion." For a discussion of the First Amendment and religion, see Levy 1986.

22. Justice Hugo Black, who issued a separate opinion, questioned the truth of evolution and did not believe that the antievolution laws had a religious purpose. Black's opinion was influenced by his background (e.g., he was raised by devout Baptists and had been supported in earlier elections by the Ku Klux Klan; see Larson 1989).

23. *Epperson v. Arkansas* has been applied in a variety of court decisions, including those involving "release time" from public schooling for religious training (*Smith v. Smith*, 391 F.S. 443 [1975]), censorship of textbooks (*Daniel v. Waters*, 515 F. 2d 485, 6th Cir. [1975]), Bible readings in public schools (*Meltzer v. Board of Public Instruction of Orange County, Florida*, 548 F. 2d 559 [1977]), sex education (*Cornwell v. State Board of Education*, 341 F.S. 340 [1969]), exhaustion of administrative remedies (*Lopez v. Williams*, 373 F.S. 1279 [1973]), the Establishment Clause of the First Amendment (*Meek v. Pittenger*, 421 U.S. 349 [1975]), First Amendment rights for students (*Tinker v. Des Moines*, 89 Sup. Ct. 733, 736 [1969]), and the academic freedom of teachers (*Parducci v. Rutland*, 316 F.S. 352 [1970]).

24. In 1968, Mrs. J. D. Goodrich, widow of a juror in the Scopes trial, repeated the belief from more than forty years before: "William Jennings Bryan was a wonderful Christian, but Clarence Darrow was an agent of the devil and an infidel" ("Dayton Says It'd Convict Scopes Still" 1968).

4
IN EPPERSON'S WAKE

The scientific facts, rightly interpreted, will give the same testimony as that of Scripture. There is not the slightest possibility that the facts of science can contradict the Bible.
—Henry Morris, 1974

However much the creationist leaders might hammer away at their "scientific" and "philosophical" points, they would be helpless and a laughing-stock if that were all they had. It is religion that recruits their squadrons. Tens of millions of Americans, who neither know nor understand the actual arguments for—or even against—evolution, march in the army of the night with their Bibles held high. And they are a strong and frightening force, impervious to, and immunized against, the feeble lance of mere reason.
—Isaac Asimov, 1981

The final and conclusive evidence against evolution is the fact that the Bible denies it.
—Henry Morris

Epperson v. Arkansas outraged conservative Christians and galvanized them into action (Eve and Harrold 1991). For example, between 1967 and 1985, the Watchtower Bible and Tract Society distributed 18 million copies of *Did Man Get Here by Evolution or by Creation?* and other creationist groups produced hundreds of books and millions of pamphlets. Millions of copies of books from the Institute for Creation Research (ICR) were in circulation, and several of those books were translated into several languages and endorsed by such fundamentalists as Tim LaHaye and Jerry Falwell. In one decade, the ICR published more than fifty books, despite its meager record of research.

In the 1970s, creationists banned the Biological Sciences Curriculum Study textbooks from science classes in Texas, and by 1974, all textbooks in Texas were required to prominently display a disclaimer stating that evolution is a theory and one of the several explanations of origins.[1] At about the same time, protests erupted throughout the United States about a federally funded, proevolution curriculum titled MACOS (Man: A Course of Study). MACOS had started in 1963 with a grant from the National Science Foundation and was finally published in 1970 by the Education Development Center as an introduction to evolution and the social and behavioral sciences for elementary school students. Earlier, MACOS had won national awards and had been praised by teachers, students, and parents as a major innovation in science teaching. By 1974, 1,700 school districts in forty-seven states had adopted MACOS. The curriculum urged that students should learn what is needed to become "citizen scientists" so that they could help solve science-based problems. MACOS sometimes used language that enraged opponents: "It will not do to dream nostalgically of simpler times when children presumably grew up believing in the love of God, the virtue of hard work, the sanctity of the family, and the nobility of the Western historical tradition. . . . We must understand . . . what causes . . . these things." As a result, parents in some areas "stormed the schools" and argued that equal time be given to traditional views (Nelkin 1982). By 1976, MACOS sales had plummeted 70 percent. In 1980, Ronald Reagan used MACOS as an example of how the federal government subsidized subversive values and asked why the NSF had not instead developed curricula that supported Christian values. Many of the opponents of the MACOS program had also opposed the introduction of the BSCS books.

As creationists became increasingly active and politically successful, the National Academy of Sciences, the National Science Teachers Association, and the National Association of Biology Teachers began organizing campaigns to try to slow the growing popularity of "scientific creationism." The NABT received $12,000 in donations for its "Fund for Freedom in Science Teaching," but it was quickly met with a vigorous backlash from its many members who were creationists. To placate these members, the NABT sponsored a creationism panel at its 1973 national meeting, and 1,500 biologists attended. William Mayer of the BSCS, in a letter published in the *American Biology Teacher* (April 1974, p. 246), condemned the NABT's actions, labeling the creationists as "religious missionaries . . . smuggling religious dogma into classrooms in a Trojan horse." Mayer branded the NABT as "schizoid" because it fought the inclusion of creationists' ideas via legal means while simultaneously providing them with a forum at meetings.[2]

Feeling vulnerable, threatened by the BSCS-driven return of evolution to textbooks and the curriculum, and convinced that their beliefs and rights were not being protected, creationists turned to the courts for relief, as had leaders of earlier social movements. There, creationists became involved in a variety of legal battles.

Segraves v. State of California
Controversy about California's *The Scientific Framework for California Public Schools, Kindergarten–Grades One through Twelve* began in 1969, when the California Board of Education starting reviewing a draft of the document that had been prepared over a span of four years by a committee of scientists and teachers. *The Scientific Framework* contained two paragraphs

about evolution that were innocuous to scientists (e.g., "From the origin of the first living particles, the evolution of living organisms was probably directed by environmental conditions and changes occurring in them").

However, Vernon Grose, a Pentecostal untrained in biology who claimed that his "citizenship is in heaven," was outraged by the paragraphs. Grose felt that evolution would "destroy . . . moral values," "deny any racial differences," eradicate "the distinction between male and female," and "mix all ethnic groups in cookbook proportions." Claiming that he "felt something like Jesus did when he overthrew the tables and the money changers in the temple," Grose announced that the evolutionary bias of the *Framework* threatened "our national heritage." He sent a thirteen-page memo to the Board of Education arguing that (1) creationism should be included in the state's science classes and textbooks and (2) at least two theories about origins should be presented to science students (Nelkin 1982).

In October, seven members of the board appointed by Ronald Reagan demanded that the evolution paragraphs be taken out of the *Framework*; other members, such as physician John Ford, wanted creationism included. In November, creationists—citing materials provided by the Creation Research Society—presented petitions and testimony to the board claiming that evolution is scientifically invalid and that the guidelines promoted atheism at the detriment of Christianity. Soon thereafter, the state education superintendent, Max Rafferty, announced that the guidelines would be rewritten to include creationism.

In December, the scientists who advised the board resigned, stating that the changes would damage science education and were "offensive to the very essence of science." Various groups (including one consisting of nineteen Nobel laureates) condemned the creationists' ignorance of science. Nevertheless, publishers quickly changed their books to include creationism; one proposed replacing the descriptions of archeological discoveries with a reproduction of Michelangelo's Sistine Chapel painting of the Creation and a drawing of Moses. Another publisher produced a book claiming that science says nothing about who made the world and why; one chapter even included an investigation of the biblical account of creation. The California Textbook Committee screened many books, changing *evolved* to *appeared*, deleting words such as *ancestors* and *descendants*, and adding qualifiers such as "according to one point of view" and "it is believed, in the theory of evolution" (see discussion in Nelkin 1982). Many scientists were relieved that the changes were not more drastic.[3]

In 1972, California changed its way of selecting instructional materials when it replaced its Curriculum Commission with a Curriculum Development and Supplemental Materials Commission. Although the new commission was loaded with creationists (including Vernon Grose), in September

Kelly Segraves and his children (from left) Jason, Kasey, and Kevin. In 1981, the boys challenged the way evolution was taught in California. (AP Photos)

1972, it recommended no creationist texts to the board. By November of that year, however, Grose wanted creationist texts on adoption lists. Scientists throughout the country protested, as did the National Academy of Sciences. As *Science* editor William Bevan wrote, "If the state can dictate the content of a science, it makes little difference that its motivation is religious rather than political." Nell Segraves, an ardent creationist, countered by claiming that "Christian children are losing their faith because an increasingly unrelenting flood of anti-Biblical teaching in the public schools disguises historical fact and scientific truth."

In May 1974, as public opinion polls indicated that in some parts of California more than 80 percent of the residents wanted both evolution and creationism taught in public schools, the board reversed its earlier decision. Frustrated and bitter, the creationists repeated William Jennings Bryan's majoritarian arguments. As noted by Kelly Segraves, the son of Nell Segraves and a Baptist preacher who headed the *Bible Science* radio program, "The public schools are not controlled by the public nor does the public have any say in the educational process. It seems that the public through taxes simply pays for that which they do not want."

In 1979, Kelly Segraves petitioned a California court to block the distribution of the California Board of Education's *The Scientific Framework for California Public Schools* because the document was too dogmatic. When Segraves's petition was denied, he sued in state court, claiming that the state was violating his children's rights because evolution was taught dogmatically as fact and because classroom discussions of "evolutionary dogma" prohibited his and his children's free exercise of religion. The plaintiffs had school-children plead that they should not be taught that their religious beliefs are wrong. Segraves also objected to several features of a textbook titled *Principles of Science*, including a chart listing successive geologic periods over the last 4.5 billion years (and placing the development of different life-forms in different periods), because those features were "clearly in opposition to [their] Christian faith." Segraves asked the court to mandate equal time for creationism in science classrooms of the state's public schools. When the trial opened on 2 March 1981, however, the creationists abandoned their request for equal treatment of the biblical account of creation. Soon thereafter, they reduced their complaint to details regarding the wording of the *Framework*.

In *Segraves v. State of California* (No. 278978, Sacramento Superior Court [1981]), in what Kelly Segraves called "the trial of the century" and a "rerun of the Scopes trial," Judge Irving Perluss ruled on 6 March that (1) the California Board of Education must circulate a statement stressing the need to eliminate dogmatism and include qualifying statements about spec-ulations on the origins of life and (2) the *Framework*, as written and as qualified by its antidogmatism policy (e.g., that scientific explanations fo-cus on "how," not "ultimate cause"), gave "sufficient accommodation for the views of [Segraves]" and his children.[4] An appeals court acknowledged the balance between religious beliefs and the right to disseminate knowledge through schools and other institutions, but it precluded a courtroom trial for religious challenges to the teaching of evolution.

Segraves hailed Perluss's decision as a victory for creationists, an-nouncing that it would "protect the rights of the Christian child." In 1989, the antidogmatism policy was expanded to include all areas of science, not just those about origins. Pleased with the promise this held for the future, Henry Morris—the most influential creationist of the late twentieth cen-tury—proclaimed, "Creationism is on the way back."

Smith v. State

Epperson v. Arkansas was a death knell for other antievolution laws. The de-mise of the last of those laws, the ban on teaching evolution in Mississippi, began in late 1969 in Jackson, when Mrs. Arthur G. Smith filed suit in state court on behalf of her daughter Frances. Mississippi had no declaratory judg-ment law, so Smith could not ask that the law be declared unconstitutional. However, she did claim that the Mississippi law deprived Frances of a qual-ity education and therefore put her at a disadvantage relative to students from states in which evolution was taught, and she also asked for an injunc-tion prohibiting the enforcement of the law, on the basis that it violated the Establishment Clause of the U.S. Constitution (as had been noted in *Epper-son v. Arkansas* for the Arkansas law banning the teaching of evolution).

On 21 January 1970, while *Smith v. State* was being considered in state court, legislators began debating the merits of repealing their law banning the teaching of evolution in the state's public schools. During the debate, legislators made it clear that they were not impressed with the U.S. Supreme Court's ruling in *Epperson v. Arkansas.* Legislators repeatedly urged that the repeal be rejected because, for example, they should "hold the line as a Christian state" and because if "it is against the law to teach religion, it should be against the law to teach atheism." The repeal failed by a vote of 70–42, meaning that the state's courts would have to decide the issue.

Soon after the vote, *Smith v. State* was dismissed because the state had not tried to enforce the law, and the law was therefore not considered legitimate. The dismissal included a statement upholding the constitutionality of the law, despite the clear ruling to the contrary in *Epperson v. Arkansas.* Smith appealed the decision to the Mississippi Supreme Court, which announced its decision on 21 December 1970. Citing *Epperson v. Arkansas,* the court unanimously overturned the lower court's decision, noting that "there is little doubt, if any, that [the U.S. Supreme Court] would make the same finding relative to our statute." The nation's last antievolution law had been declared "void and of no effect."

Wright v. Houston Independent School District

The year 1970 witnessed the first lawsuit initiated by creationists. In November, Leona Wilson sued the Houston (Texas) Independent School District in federal court on behalf of her daughter Rita Wright, claiming that the schools had violated her daughter's constitutional rights by teaching evolution "without critical analysis and without reference to other theories which purport to explain the origin of the human species." Wright's lawsuit was delayed until June 1972, at which time the plaintiffs claimed that the schools' teaching of evolution endorsed a "religion of secularism" that implied that beliefs in creationism are wrong, thereby inhibiting students' free exercise of religion. The plaintiffs further argued that there was little difference between the Arkansas ban on the teaching of evolution and the Houston school district's attempt to avoid teaching creationism; according to Wright, neither policy was religiously neutral, as demanded by *Epperson v. Arkansas.* Wright's lawsuit tried to mandate such neutrality.

Wright's suit (366 F. Supp. 1208, 1208–09, S.D. Tex. [1972]) was dismissed before reaching trial, when Judge Woodrow B. Seals ruled that Wright had "wholly failed to establish the analogy"—unlike the censorship imposed by Arkansas before *Epperson v. Arkansas,* there was no evidence that the school district discouraged free discussion. Seals also ruled that (1) the Houston school district had not followed any policy to promote secularism as a religion, (2) the free exercise of religion was not accompanied by a right to be shielded from scientific findings incompatible with one's beliefs, and (3) Wright's proposed solution of "equal time" for creationism was "an unwarranted intrusion into the authority of public school systems to control the academic curriculum." As Seals wrote,

> All that can be said is that certain textbooks selected by school officials present what Plaintiffs deem a biased view in support of the theory [of evolution]. This court has been cited to no case in which so nebulous an intrusion upon the principle of religious neutrality has been condemned by the Supreme Court. . . . Teachers of science in the public schools should not be expected to avoid the discussion of every scientific issue on which some religions claim expertise. . . . [The case of the plaintiffs] must ultimately fail, then, because the proposed solutions are more onerous than the problem they purport to alleviate.

The *Wright* decision made it clear that scientific findings can be taught, even if those findings are offensive. One year later, the Fifth Circuit Court of Appeals issued an unsigned opinion that supported Seals's decision to dismiss the *Wright* case. When the U.S. Supreme Court refused to hear Wright's appeal in June 1974, the case was over. Subsequent cases to restrict the teaching of evolution were dismissed by repeated reaffirmations of the *Wright* decision.

Willoughby v. Stever

Late in the summer of 1972, William Willoughby (an evangelist and the religion editor of the conservative *Washington Evening Star*) sued H. Guyton Stever (director of the National Science Foundation) and the Board of Regents of the University of Colorado for funding the BSCS textbooks. Willoughby, who claimed to be acting "in the interest of forty million evangelistic Christians in the United States," argued that creationists should receive the same amount of money "for the promulgation of the creationist theory of the origin of man." Willoughby believed that the government was establishing "secular humanism" as "the official religion of the United States," decried the "intellectual snobbery" of scientists, and opposed using tax revenues to support educational programs that are "one-sided, biased, and damaging" to religious views.

Willoughby received much public support, but his lawsuit (Civil Action No. 1574–72, D.D.C. [25 Aug. 1972]) was dismissed in May 1973 by the U.S. District Court in Washington, D.C., because (1) books supported by taxes allocated to the National Science Foundation disseminate scientific findings, not religion, and (2) the First Amendment does not allow the state

Judge Barrington Parker, the presiding judge in Crowley v. Smithsonian Institution. *(AP Photos)*

to demand that teaching be tailored to particular religious beliefs. Willoughby's case ended in February 1975, when the U.S. Supreme Court refused to hear his appeal.

Crowley v. Smithsonian Institution

In the mid-1970s, Congress provided almost $500,000 for an exhibit titled "The Emergence of Man: Dynamics of Evolution" at the Museum of Natural History, a division of the Smithsonian Institution. When Dale Crowley Jr.—a retired missionary and the executive director of the National Foundation for Fairness in Education—learned of the plans for the exhibit early in 1978, he believed that the Smithsonian Institution was using tax money to establish the religion of secular humanism. In Crowley's opinion, the exhibit forced fundamentalists to choose between violating their religious views by entering the museum or abandoning the right to access public property. Crowley sued the Smithsonian Foundation in U.S. District Court, demanding that either the proevolution exhibit be closed or the Smithsonian give equal money and space for an exhibit promoting the biblical story of creation.

In December 1978, citing *Epperson v. Arkansas* and *Daniel v. Waters* (see below), District Judge Barrington D. Parker ruled that the Smithsonian's exhibit was "wholly secular" and that the Smithsonian had treated evolution as science, not religion. Parker rejected Crowley's claim that the Museum of Natural History had restricted the exercise of religion, noting that "the plaintiffs can carry their beliefs into the Museum with them, though they risk seeing science exhibits that are contrary to that faith."

Crowley v. Smithsonian Institution (462 F. Supp. 725, 725, D.D.C. [1978]) was dismissed on the same grounds as *Willoughby v. Stever.* Like the *Willoughby* decision, the *Crowley* decision was supported in appeals courts. When the U.S. Supreme Court refused to hear Crowley's appeal in 1980, the case was over. In the fall of 1981, Republican Representative William Dannemeyer used Crowley's arguments to urge Congress to review the exhibit and limit its funding, but his pleas attracted little support.

Hendren v. Campbell

The Creation Science Research Center was formed in 1970 by Nell Segraves, Kelly Segraves, and Henry Morris, soon after which Morris's Creation Research Society produced a high school biology textbook titled *Biology: A*

Search for Order in Complexity (Moore 1974), a book whose contributors included a high school biology teacher and three biology professors. That book, which blatantly promoted the biblical story of creation and declared that "there is no way to support the doctrine of evolution," was offered to teachers interested in a "balanced treatment" of studies of origins. The book's "two-model approach"—that is, the "evolution model" and the "creation model"—became popular at several public schools and many private schools. Henry Morris himself used the model in his influential *Scientific Creationism* (Morris 1974), a handbook for biology teachers that repackaged creationism as science.

In the early 1970s, the Indiana Textbook Commission approved *Biology: A Search for Order in Complexity* for use in biology classes of its public schools. In the spring of 1976, the West Clark Community Schools adopted this text, after which their action was challenged by the Indiana Civil Liberties Union (ICLU). After trying to reach a compromise for nine months, the ICLU filed suit on behalf of parent Jon Hendren in February 1977, claiming that the use of the textbook in public schools was unconstitutional. The court sent the ICLU's complaint to the textbook commission for an administrative hearing, at which time scientists recommended that the book not be used. Nevertheless, the commission upheld its original ruling, thereby returning the lawsuit to court.

In April 1977, Superior Court Judge Michael T. Dugan agreed with the ICLU. In *Hendren v. Campbell* (Superior Court No. 5, Marion County, Indiana, 14 April 1977), Dugan rejected the use of *Biology: A Search for Order in Complexity* in public schools because it advanced a specific religious point of view (i.e., "the fundamentalist doctrine") and it violated the separation of church and state. As Dugan noted, the use of *Biology* would ensure "the prospect of biology teachers and students alike forced to answer and respond to continued demand for correct fundamentalist Christian doctrine in public schools." The West Clark schools kept *Biology* on their list of supplemental materials, but Indiana's textbook commission (and those elsewhere, such as in Dallas) dropped the book from its approved list. Dugan's decision was not appealed.

Daniel v. Waters: **The Genesis Act**
Throughout the 1960s, Russell Artist had been active in the creation science movement. He had been an expert witness in various parts of the country and, as a biology professor at David Lipscomb College in Nashville, used his biology class to promote biblical creationism and the alleged errors in evolution. In 1970, Artist convinced Tennessee education officials to approve the procreationism textbook *Biology: A Search for Order in Complexity* as a supplemental text for the state's public schools. When no school bought the

book, Artist decided to try to enact a law in Tennessee to ensure the teaching of creationism in the state's public schools.

Early in 1973, Artist convinced Senator Milton Hamilton (a Democrat from rural Union City) that the state's public schools should include biblical creationism in their curricula. On 26 March 1973, Hamilton and four of his colleagues—all of whom had witnessed the repeal of the Butler Law but none of whom had voted for the repeal—introduced Senate Bill 394, a bill mandating "balanced treatment" for creationism and evolution. The legislation, which became known as the "Genesis Act," required biology textbooks (1) to identify evolution as a theory rather than a "scientific fact" and (2) to give "equal emphasis" (i.e., equal number of words, space, and emphasis) to "the Genesis account in the Bible."[5] The legislation neither banned evolution nor promoted scientific creationism, yet it defended creationists by qualifying the teaching of evolution. When a group of Tennessee professors formed the Committee to Prevent Anti-Evolution Law in Tennessee and claimed that the bill was "utterly repugnant to the American idea of democracy," Hamilton responded, "This is not a Ph.D. bill. It is a people's bill."

Amid overwhelming public support and claims by legislators "that the Biblical account of creation is fact, not theory," the bill was approved—in front of television cameras on the state Senate floor—by a vote of 29–1. In the Tennessee House of Representatives, a coalition of seven representatives introduced a similar "equal-time" bill on 3 April, despite the fact that the state's attorney general had declared that the bill was probably unconstitutional. There was strong public support for the legislation; House Speaker Ned Ray McWherter received more than 500 letters supporting the bill but only a single letter opposing it. The legislation was amended to (1) include a literal reading of Genesis in the state's biology classrooms, (2) exclude "the teaching of all occult or satanical beliefs of human origin," and (3) endorse the Holy Bible as a reference work rather than a textbook, thus making the Bible immune to any disclaimers that might be put in biology books. The legislation passed the House by a vote of 69–15 and became law one week later when Governor Winfield Dunn refused to either sign or veto the bill.

The newly passed Genesis Act was promptly challenged by the NABT and three coplaintiffs (two professors from the University of Tennessee and a public school teacher).[6] The plaintiffs contended that the bill interfered with free speech, freedom of religion, and freedom of the press, as guaranteed by the First and Fourteenth Amendments (see Nelkin 1982). The plaintiffs also argued that the law included no secular purpose.

On 10 April 1975, the Sixth Circuit Court of Appeals in Cincinnati struck down Tennessee's Genesis Act by a vote of 2–1 because it (1) violated the Establishment Clause of the U.S. Constitution by mandating the instruction of a religious doctrine in public schools and (2) was little more than a revision of the Butler Law that had led to the Scopes trial almost fifty years earlier (the law's purpose was "establishing the Biblical version of the creation of man"). The court emphasized that "no state court interpretation of [this law] can save it." Tennessee did not appeal the court's decision, but support for creationism in Tennessee remained strong. For example, in 1972, 75 percent of the students at Rhea County High School—the school at which John Scopes taught—still believed in creationism and claimed that "Darwinian evolution breeds corruption, lust, immorality, greed, and such acts of criminal depravity as drug addiction, war, and atrocious acts of genocide."

The overturning of the Genesis Act (*Daniel v. Waters*, 515 F. 2d 485, 6th Cir. [1975]) caused many "equal time for religion" bills to die quiet deaths in several state legislatures (Larson 1989). For instance, Georgia had passed an equal-time bill in 1973, but it had tabled the legislation while the Divine Creation Committee of the Georgia House of Representatives held hearings. The committee reported that the public wanted all theories of creation to be available in public schools, but it recommended that the issue be dealt with via textbook selection rather than legislation. Soon afterward, the "Science and Creation Series" of books was approved for state adoption.

Inventing "Creation Science"

Following the defeats outlined above, creationists concluded that their best hope was to mount a credible *scientific* challenge to evolution. Realizing that the teaching of religious beliefs (*creationism* and similar terms) would violate the Establishment Clause of the Constitution, creationists repackaged the Bible as "creation science"[7] and demanded "equal time" and "balanced treatment" for creationism in the public schools. The creation science movement was triggered a few years earlier with the publication of *The Genesis Flood*, a book by John Whitcomb and Henry Morris that developed the dormant ideas of flood geologist George McCready Price and triggered the revival of creationism in the United States. Suddenly, thanks to the efforts of Morris in particular, creationists stopped fighting science and enlisted it as an ally. Science, according to creation scientists, was their proof of the literal truth of Genesis and the basis for including creationism in public schools.

Although Tennessee's Genesis Act had mandated that biology textbooks give equal emphasis to alternative theories of origins (especially the Genesis account), the most popular balanced-treatment strategy took shape in 1978, when Yale law student and avowed creationist Wendell Bird presented an award-winning legal justification for teaching evolution and creation science in public schools (Bird 1978).[8] Bird built his equal-time argument on Supreme Court decisions that recognized the rights of religious

minorities, such as Jehovah's Witnesses and the Amish, to practice their beliefs without state interference (Irons 1988).

According to creation scientists, the Bible is a science book, and scientific observations must conform to what we read in the Bible. If human observations do not conform, either they are illusions or they are interpreted incorrectly. And if they are interpreted incorrectly, it may be because of Satan, who wants to use evolution to damn humankind forever. In this sense, creation science became a modern-day version of the ageless battle between Good and Evil.

Bird's strategy was remarkably effective, for it changed the discussion from the realm of science to the realm of popular idiom (Taylor and Condit 1988). In doing so, Bird held the teaching of evolution not to the scientific standard of testable evidence, but rather to the political concept of equal time.

After graduating from law school, Bird joined the Institute for Creation Research[9] as a legal adviser. There, he used

Attorney Wendell Bird's resolution for "equal time" for creationism in public schools received much support. Bird represented Louisiana before the U.S. Supreme Court in Edwards v. Aguillard. *(AP Photos)*

his award-winning article as a basis for revising and providing a constitutional justification for the ICR's equal-time resolution, which Henry Morris had drafted early in 1975 (Larson 1989). Bird's revision was a Baconian effort to equate creationism with science and was based on several key arguments (Bird 1979):

Creationism is as scientific as evolution, and evolution is as religious as creationism.

Because scientific creationism is science rather than religion, it is not subject to Establishment Clause challenges.

Although teaching only creationism may violate religious freedoms, the presentation of "both the theory of evolution and the theory of creationism would not [violate religious freedoms] because it would involve presenting the scientific evidence for each theory rather than any religious doctrine."

Presentations of both theories "must be limited to scientific evidence and must not include religious doctrine."

There must be a "balanced treatment" of both theories in classroom lectures, library materials, and other educational programs. Neutralizing the public schools' instruction with a balanced treatment of origins would not advance religion.

Not teaching scientific creationism violates the First Amendment because it gives "preference to religious Liberalism, Humanism, and other religious faiths." It does this by implying an official disapproval of some religious beliefs while simultaneously putting the prestige of science and the state behind other religions.

Teaching scientific creationism would ensure the state's neutrality, for both major theories would be taught.[10] This, in turn, would ensure academic freedom, a well-rounded scientific education, and the protection of everyone's First Amendment rights.

Like many creationists before him, Bird invoked the legacy of William Jennings Bryan by reminding people of the popularity of the balanced-treatment proposition: "Most citizens, whether they personally believe in evolution or creation, favor balanced treatment in public schools."

The ICR distributed thousands of copies of Bird's resolution in mid-1979, each with a disclaimer that the language was a suggested resolution for boards of education, not legislation to be enacted as law (Larson 1989). Bird's efforts prompted several fundamentalist organizations (e.g., Henry Morris's ICR, the Bible Science Association; see Scott 1994) to produce propaganda for convincing school boards, administrators, and teachers that creationism should be taught in public schools "to protect academic freedom," to protect freedom of religion, and to bar discrimination. The religious agenda of these publications was always obvious. For example, the ICR began publishing two versions of its science textbooks, one for Christian schools and one for public schools. The versions were identical except for avoiding specific references to God, the Bible, and Noah in the public school editions. The "creative work of God" became "Creation," and "God" became the "Master Designer" (see discussion in Nelkin 1982). Other publications by the ICR blamed the teaching of evolution for societal problems such as the spread of venereal disease.

Creationists' demands for equal time and balanced treatment in public schools received strong public support. Language supporting such treatments of evolution and creationism appeared in textbook adoption guidelines in several states. For instance, the Texas Education Agency told publishers that books submitted for adoption should discuss "scientific evidence of evolution and reliable scientific theories to the contrary." By the late 1970s, many state legislatures were considering equal-time laws. Arkansas and Louisiana were among the states that passed balanced-treatment statutes, which required creation science to be taught in schools in which evolution was taught and forbade the teaching of evolution unless it was accompanied by instruction in creation science.

By 1980, creationism instruction was officially available in several states (e.g., Wisconsin, Missouri, South Dakota), and in other states, a de facto equal-time formula was used in many school districts. Textbook publishers, acknowledging that they "are in the business of selling textbooks," quickly inserted creationism back into biology textbooks.

The first challenge to an "equal-time" law would occur in Susan Epperson's home state of Arkansas.

Notes

1. In 1975, 80 percent of the biology textbooks adopted for approval by the Texas Board of Education did not mention evolution (Webb 1994).

2. By 1973, biologists had become increasingly reluctant to acknowledge creationism; the NABT's 1973 annual meeting did not mention the controversy (Nelkin 1982).

3. Soon thereafter, the BSCS was also condemned by scientists for having "sold out" by producing an audio slide-show program titled "An Inquiry into the Origin of Man: Science and Religion" (see discussion in Nelkin 1982).

4. In 1963, Nell Segraves (Kelly's mother, a Baptist and a member of the Bible Science Association and the Creation Research Society) had petitioned the California Board of Education to require that evolution be presented as a theory in all state-approved textbooks; this was done to "seek justice for the Christian child." The petition was based on the 1963 U.S. Supreme Court *Abington School District v. Schempp* decision that declared it unconstitutional to force nonbelieving children to read prayers in school. Segraves used this decision to claim that if it is unconstitutional "to teach God in the school," then it must also be unconstitutional "to teach the absence of God." Her effort failed. Later, Nell and Kelly became directors of the Creation Science Research Center (CSRC), which "had a distinctive Baptist flavor" and fought evolution, sex education, women's rights, and gay rights. The CSRC studied issues such as the relation of teaching evolution to the incidence of venereal diseases; in 1977, it reported that "the results of evolutionary interpretations of scientific data result in a widespread breakdown in law and order" that "leads to divorce, abortion, and rampant venereal disease" (see discussion in Numbers 1992).

5. Unlike Tennessee's earlier antievolution law that was challenged by John Scopes, the Genesis Act was restricted to textbooks; teachers were not mentioned in the legislation.

6. One month later, and unbeknownst to the NABT, America United for the Separation of Church and State, Inc., filed a similar suit in the state chancery court in Nashville. This suit delayed action in the NABT's suit, which prompted the NABT to appeal the case to the U.S. Supreme Court. The Supreme Court refused to hear the case, soon after which a court of appeals in Tennessee overturned the Genesis Act.

7. In the 1970s and 1980s, creation science became increasingly popular. On occasion, the antievolution sentiment that accompanies creation science influenced federal funding for science. For example, in 1976, Arizona Congressman John Conlan—partially in response to complaints about MACOS—sponsored an amendment to the National Defense Education Act that would "prohibit federal funding of any curriculum project with evolutionary content or implications." The amendment passed by a vote of 222–174 (Taylor 1992). Although the U.S. Senate narrowly rejected the amendment, funding for some projects (including many at the National Science Foundation) was delayed, pending a review of their "evolutionary content." Today, the NSF remains afraid of the evolution/creationism controversy; talks about the controversy are seldom publicized, administrators often refuse to discuss the controversy, and the word *evolution* is often expunged from lists of funded projects that are submitted to Congress (e.g., see McDonald 1986; Zimmerman 1989; Eve and Harrold 1991).

8. At Yale, Bird studied under later Supreme Court nominee Robert Bork (Eve and Harrold 1991).

9. The ICR (http://www.icr.org) originated as an affiliate of Christian Heritage College, which was established as an unaccredited Baptist college linked with the Moral Majority in San Diego, California (see Gilkey 1985). Christian Heritage College is presided over by Reverend Tim LaHaye, a longtime associate of Moral Majority leader Jerry Falwell and author of such books as *The Battle for the Schools*. The ICR has been supported by various Baptist churches and was established to address the "urgent need for our nation to return to belief in a personal, omnipotent Creator, who has a purpose for His creation and to whom all people must eventually give account." A goal of the ICR is "a revival of belief in special creation as the true explanation of the origin of the world." The institute publishes a variety of antievolution books (e.g., Bird 1989) and offers graduate degrees from a "somewhat unique perspective." The ICR often helps with local efforts to mandate the teaching of creationism (Berman 1997). The president of the ICR is John Morris (Henry Morris's son), who searches for Noah's ark and promotes the alleged coexistence of dinosaur tracks and human footprints in the Paluxy riverbed in Texas. His *The Young Earth* (Morris 1994) includes seventy pages of overhead projector masters designed to "be shared with your church or Bible study groups."

10. The emphasis on neutrality in this and other cases involving religion came from the 1963 U.S. Supreme Court ruling that mandatory Bible readings and prayers in public schools were unconstitutional. This decision, prompted by efforts of atheist Madeline Murray, endorsed a policy of governmental neutrality (see Numbers 1992). U.S. Supreme Court Justice Abe Fortas's opinion in *Epperson v. Arkansas* overturned the ban on the teaching of evolution because the antievolution law's primary effect was not neutral. What, argued the creationists, would be more neutral than "balanced treatment" of and "equal time" for creationism and evolution?

5

"THIS IS A TERRIBLE BILL": *MCLEAN V. ARKANSAS BOARD OF EDUCATION*

I want you to have all the academic freedom you want, as long as you wind up saying the Bible account [of creation] is true and all others are not.
—Jerry Falwell, 1979

I have a great many questions about [evolution]. I think that recent discoveries down through the years have pointed up great flaws in it. . . . If [evolution] is going to be taught in the schools, then I think that the biblical theory of creation should also be taught.
—Presidential candidate Ronald Reagan, 1980

The god who is reputed to have created fleas to keep dogs from moping over their situation must also have created fundamentalists to keep rationalists from getting flabby. Let us be duly thankful for our blessings.
—Garrett Hardin

It has often and confidently been asserted, that man's origin can never be known; but ignorance more frequently begets confidence than does knowledge; it is those who know little, and not those who know much, who so positively assert that this or that problem will never be solved by science.
—Charles Darwin

McLean v. Arkansas Board of Education was a pivotal test of creationists' efforts, for it was the first test of legislation designed to avoid the constitutional problems that had doomed previous attempts by creationists to force their beliefs into public schools (La Follette 1983; Nelkin 1982; Prelli 1989). In addressing the reasonableness of giving "balanced treatment" to creationism in the science curriculum, *McLean v. Arkansas Board of Education* is unique and instructive, not just for understanding the evolution/creationism debate, but also because it provides a legal analysis of what science is and what science isn't, as well as how science is defined by a nonscientific legal system.

McLean began in late 1980, when Paul Ellwanger (founder in 1978 of the South Carolina–based Citizens for Fairness in Education) used Wendell Bird's "equal-time" resolution as a basis for a sample bill to introduce "creation science" into the classrooms of public schools (Taylor and Condit 1988).[1] The intent of Ellwanger's bill was summarized in its opening sen-

tence: "Public schools within this State shall give balanced treatment to creation-science and to evolution-science." Ellwanger wanted Arkansas to require its science teachers to give equal time and attention to "competing
theories" of human origins. Ellwanger and other creationists portrayed this
requirement as a way of protecting academic freedom, ensuring freedom of
religious exercise, guaranteeing freedom of belief and speech, preventing
"the establishment of theologically liberal, humanistic, nontheist, or atheist
religion," and prohibiting discrimination on the basis of either belief ("Balanced Treatment" 1981). Ellwanger's bill made its way to Reverend W. A.
Blount, a biblical literalist and chairman of the Greater Little Rock Evangelical Fellowship. Blount thought that the bill was interesting, but he put
it aside, where it would remain for more than a year.

Meanwhile, Larry Fisher, a creationist and math teacher at a school in
Little Rock, became interested in forcing creationism into the science curriculum in Little Rock's public schools. In 1980, schools in Fisher's district
were considering adopting new textbooks. Fisher, who "knew from [his]
reading of creation science literature that there were a lot of problems with
the idea of evolution," saw Wendell Bird's "balanced-presentation" resolution in May 1979 in the Institute for Creation Research's "Impact" series of
publications. Fisher copied the resolution and on 12 December 1980 included it in a letter to Tom Hardin, the superintendent of the Pulaski
County Special School District. Invoking the majoritarian claims of William
Jennings Bryan, Fisher argued that "school districts across the country are
beginning to pass similar resolutions. Our district would be promoting good
public relations by adopting this resolution since surveys across the country
indicate that about 80% of the patrons support it. By adopting this resolution, I feel our district would be providing a leadership role by promoting
academic integrity and responsibility on this issue."

Fisher sent copies of the resolution to members of the school board, who
had recently been lobbied by various Christian fundamentalists and the
Moral Majority, both of whom were concerned about "liberal" textbooks
and issues such as sex education. When the school board met in January,
Fisher told the board that, given the convincing scientific evidence for creationism, it was only fair to give students all of the evidence for origins
rather than censoring some of it because some scientists didn't like it. The
board agreed and created a subcommittee to develop a curriculum based on
scientific creationism. Local residents, sensing victory, wrote letters to Little Rock's newspapers claiming that evolution was finally going to be vanquished from their schools.

Fisher lobbied the subcommittee, but he met with resistance. As Little
Rock science teacher Bill Wood noted, "I could find no science at all in the
material that I had been given. The things I read were full of religious ref-

erences." On 10 March 1981, Wood presented the subcommittee's report to the school board and a large group of Fisher's supporters. According to the official record of the meeting, "The committee did not support implementing instruction in creationism in the district's classrooms, nor would the committee endorse the materials submitted by Fisher." Nevertheless, Gene Jones, the director of secondary education, assured the board that "the committee would continue to work on a sample curriculum which would offer several alternative theories to evolution." At the meeting, Wood was jeered and booed; Fisher was cheered.

When news of the school board's actions hit the local papers, Blount remembered Ellwanger's bill and knew that it represented "an idea whose time had come" (Luxenberg 1981; Taylor and Condit 1988; Larson 1989). Blount and other preachers presented seminars on creation science and, with the blessing of the school board, gave copies of *The Genesis Flood* to science teachers and libraries in every junior and senior high school in the county.

At Blount's request, the Greater Little Rock Evangelical Fellowship voted unanimously to try to introduce Ellwanger's bill in the Arkansas legislature. In 1981, Ellwanger's bill was given to a member of Blount's congregation, a self-described "born-again fundamentalist" named James Holsted. Holsted, a state senator from North Little Rock, agreed to sponsor the bill in the state legislature despite the fact that he had not written a single word of the bill and did not know who had (Taylor and Condit 1988). Although Holsted's bill listed seven "legislative findings of fact" about what was being taught in public schools, there was no meaningful fact-finding by the General Assembly. Moreover, Holsted did not discuss his bill with scientists, science educators, anyone from the Arkansas Attorney General's Office, or the state Board of Education. The Greater Little Rock Evangelical Fellowship joined a group called FLAG (Family Life, America, and God) to lobby for the bill (Eve and Harrold 1991). Holsted admitted that the bill favored religious fundamentalists and acknowledged that he "didn't know anything about that [creation science] stuff." Nevertheless, he sponsored the bill because of his own religious convictions and because the legislation was "of course" related to religion: "I think you should teach the scientific theory of a Creator. . . . I believe in a Creator and I believe that God created this universe. I can't separate the bill from that belief. All of we legislators have prejudices and beliefs that affect what legislation we introduce. . . . Probably the ones who are going to be the strongest supporters of the legislation are fundamentalists" (Brummett 1981a).

When that bill was introduced on 24 February, it was quickly approved by the Judiciary Committee, which was chaired by born-again Christian Max Howell and included Holsted as a member. On Friday, 13 March 1981—in the waning days of the legislative session—the bill (now referred to as "Act

Arkansas Governor Frank White signed Arkansas' Balanced Treatment for Creation-Science and Evolution-Science Act into law even though he had not read the legislation. (AP Photos)

590: Balanced Treatment for Creation Science and Evolution Science ") was debated for fifteen minutes, after which it passed the Senate by a vote of 22–2; following a vote to suspend parliamentary rules, cheering members of the House passed the law on 17 March 1981 by a vote of 69–18. As legislators rushed to finish last-minute business, all attempts to amend or debate the bill on the House floor were ruled out of order. Two days later, Republican Governor Frank White signed the bill into law, despite the fact, as he would later admit, that he didn't read it (e.g., "Law on Creation" 1981; Taylor and Condit 1988; Brummett 1981b). His justification for supporting the bill was simple: "If we're going to teach evolution in the public school system, why not teach scientific creationism? Both of them are theories" (Larson 1989). White was also pragmatic, adding that, "This is a terrible bill, but it's worded so cleverly that none of us can vote against it if we want to come back up here." The entire legislative process for Act 590—from its initial consideration in the Senate to its approval by the governor—took less than a week.

Arkansas' new antievolution law was immediately challenged by a variety of people and groups. Susan Epperson, whose earlier challenge had reversed the ban on teaching evolution in public schools, emerged to denounce Act 590 as an effort to teach religion in schools, adding that creation science is religion and that "I am a strong Christian, but I feel that Christianity, or religion whatever it might be, is not proper in the science classroom. . . . [Creationists] seem to think that their religion will be wiped out if the concept of evolution is taught" ("Creation Science Act Improper" 1981).

Yet the fact remained: thanks to the legal theories of Wendell Bird and the scientific claims of Henry Morris of the Institute for Creation Research, "equal time" was the law in Arkansas.

Challenging Act 590

On 27 May 1981, the Little Rock chapter of the American Civil Liberties Union filed suit on behalf of twenty-three Arkansas citizens and organizations (including the National Association of Biology Teachers and various groups of Catholics, Jews, Methodists, and Presbyterians) in U.S. District Court, charging that Act 590 was an attempt to establish religion in the public schools and therefore violated the First Amendment (Griffee 1981b).[2] Holsted, like others before him, was confident that his legislation was constitutional: "I welcome a court challenge, so we can settle it once and for all" (Brummett 1981a).

The plaintiffs—represented by Little Rock ACLU attorneys Phillip Kaplan and Robert Cearley—asked the court to void Act 590 and issue a permanent injunction against the law's enforcement because it violated constitutional guarantees of academic freedom and was unacceptably vague (Griffee 1981b; Taylor and Condit 1988). Cearley's opening statement summarized the case:

> We . . . challenge this law as unconstitutional, as contrary to the First Amendment since it represents in fact the teaching of a religious doctrine in the guise of science. We will seek to prove that creation science, far from being science, is actually a religious apologetic. . . . Thus the Act represents the establishment of a particular religious point of view, the preference of one religion over another in the public schools, and the inevitable involvement as a consequence of the State in the affairs of religion. . . . Scientists will show that creation science . . . is not science, that its theory does not, and could not . . . exist in the world of science, and does not use the scientific method. . . . Liberty of religion has been given to us all; this Act violates these fundamental principles of our common life. (Gilkey 1985)

The antievolution defendants of Act 590 were the Arkansas Board of Education and its members, the director of the Arkansas Department of Education, and the State Textbooks and Instructional Materials Selecting Committee. Despite his "personal qualms" about the law, Arkansas Attorney General Steve Clark headed the state's defense (Taylor and Condit 1988), for which the Creation Science Research Center offered its help ("No Help Needed" 1981). Clark denounced press descriptions of the case as the "creationism trial" and claimed instead that the trial was about two political concepts: fairness and tolerance (Taylor and Condit 1988). Clark also argued that the legislation broadened the search for truth:

> The fact that some of the implications of the Act are parallel with, or consistent with, so called "religious doctrines" in Genesis or in fundamentalist documents, is quite irrelevant. . . . The purpose of

the Act is definitely not religious. On the contrary, it has a secular purpose, namely to broaden the discussion of origins to more than one exclusive model. Thus, far from restricting teaching, the law broadens the search for truth and furthers academic freedom. The issue is not whether creation science is science or not; neither model qualifies strictly as science, as we will show. We will also show that creation science is at least as scientific as is evolutionary science, and so at least as nonreligious as the latter. . . . The act is neutral and immensely educational. (Gilkey 1985)

Although Clark angered many creationists when he rejected Wendell Bird's offer to participate in the trial (Eve and Harrold 1991), he based his defense on Bird's outline (Irons 1988).[3] Clark argued that (1) there was enough scientific evidence to make creationism a legitimate alternative theory of human origins, (2) creationism deserved balanced treatment in the classroom to compete with the theory of evolution, (3) creationism could be taught without reference to religion, and (4) the exclusion of creationism from the classrooms of public schools was an infringement on academic freedom (Stuart 1981; Taylor and Condit 1988).

Understanding the precedent established by *Epperson v. Arkansas*, creationists did not ostensibly try to ban or criminalize the teaching of evolution from public schools. Rather, they wanted a guarantee that creation science would be given equal time if a teacher taught evolution. With this strategy, the creationists used Act 590 to try to move the discussion from the evidentiary realm of science to "fairness" of the popular idiom; that is, they equated the teaching of creationism with fairness and equity. This use of a powerful sociocultural motive (i.e., the demand of similar treatment regardless of merit, as is given for voting rights, freedom of belief and expression, and other aspects of the "American way") guaranteed a hearing by the national media (Taylor and Condit 1988). The state argued that "the question is not what the majority opinion [of scientists] is, but whether a majority should be allowed to squelch a minority [scientific] view" (Stuart 1981). Some newspapers sided with creationists by stating that "calls for fairness are at the heart" of the creation science movement (Horowitz 1981). William Jennings Bryan would have been proud.

The creationists' strategy was successful: a 1981 poll by *NBC News* found that 76 percent of Americans favored equal presentations of evolution and creationism in public schools. Incredibly, 18 percent favored the presentation of only creationism, while only 6 percent favored a central focus on evolution (see Nelkin 1982; Eckberg and Nesterenko 1985; Miller 1987).

To help their cause, creationists tried to "get their message out" before the trial. Their pamphlets defined *creation science* according to traditional fundamentalist tenets (e.g., a young Earth, explanation of the Earth's geology by catastrophism) and presented evolution and creationism as intellectually equal ideas, both of which are ultimately grounded in nothing more than personal conviction (Taylor and Condit 1988). As creationist Robert Kofahl suggested, "Neither evolution nor creationism are testable theories—that is theories that can be proved false in the laboratory. These are faith views. . . . We have two groups of thinkers who interpret in a way to support their own philosophy" (Sehlstedt 1981). If this view was accepted by the court, fairness would dictate balanced treatment—that is, creationism would be taught in public schools.

Creationists also claimed that scientists were censoring academic inquiry; one creationist referred to science as "thought control," and Irving Seager, an Arkansas biology teacher who had included creationism in his course since 1968, told the *Arkansas Gazette* that "most science teachers don't know anything but evolution and won't even consider accepting anything else. . . . [T]hey are just as intolerant as they accuse the creationists of being" (Griffee 1981a; also see discussion in Taylor and Condit 1988). In the midst of these charges and countercharges, the trial began.

Yet Another "Monkey Trial" Begins

McLean v. Arkansas Board of Education (529 F. Supp. 1255, 50 *U.S. Law Week* 2412 [1982]) took place in federal district court in Little Rock, Arkansas, and was presided over by Judge William R. Overton. Overton, who was appointed to the Arkansas federal bench by President Jimmy Carter, allowed both sides to present a parade of expert witnesses on religion and theology (Irons 1988). Overton was a judicial traditionalist who relied heavily on precedent and shied away from making new laws (Trimble 1981; Taylor and Condit 1988). The ICR's Wendell Bird petitioned to intervene on behalf of the creationists, but his petition was rejected.[4] The trial consisted almost exclusively of legal arguments rather than performance. There was no Darrow to confront Bryan.

Clark argued that creationist instruction would serve the constitutionally valid purpose of neutralizing evolutionary teaching, after which he presented evidence of the overwhelming public support for the equal-time statute ("Defendants' Trial Brief" 1981). Newspapers labeled the trial as a "monkey trial," and Bruce Ennis (of the ACLU) and Kelly Segraves (director of the CSRC) debated the issues on television shows such as *Donahue* ("Monkey Trial Seen in Suit over Act 590" 1981).[5] Despite the huge amount of public attention paid to the trial (e.g., more than seventy-five news organizations asked for press credentials required to get into the Little Rock Federal Courthouse; see "Seventy-five News Organizations" 1981) and occasional courtroom antics by religious people attending the trial,[6]

Judge William R. Overton presided in McLean v. Arkansas Board of Education. *His opinion, which included an analysis of what science is and what it is not, destroyed the legal credibility of "creation science." (AP Photo)*

Overton (an appointed judge not concerned with reelection) made it clear that his decision would not be affected by public opinion. As he said, "I don't read letters that are sent to me about the case and I don't accept collect calls either" (Wells 1981). And as he later wrote in his decision: "The application and content of First Amendment principles are not determined by public opinion polls or by a majority vote. Whether the proponents of Act 590 constitute the majority or the minority is quite irrelevant under a constitutional form of government. No group, no matter how large or small, may use the organs of government, of which the public schools are the most conspicuous and influential."

The trial began on 7 December 1981 and ended on 17 December 1981, "not with a bang but a whimper" (Gilkey 1985). On 5 January 1982, the same day that Mississippi enacted into law its "Balanced Treatment for Creation Science and Evolution Science Act," Overton issued a thirty-eight-page "sharp and unambiguous" decision (Nelkin 1982).[7] The first part of his decision addressed a fundamental question: Did Act 590 violate the First Amendment of the U.S. Constitution?

Act 590 and the First Amendment

To determine whether Act 590 violated the Establishment Clause of the U.S. Constitution, Overton relied on the so-called Lemon Test. This test, which was derived from the 1970 U.S. Supreme Court decision in *Lemon v. Kurtzman* (403 U.S. 602, 612–613), required school boards and legislators to ensure that statutes (1) have a secular purpose, (2) neither advance nor inhibit religion, and (3) do not result in excessive entanglement of government with religion.[8] If an action by a board or legislature violates any one of these requirements, it is unconstitutional. The plaintiffs tried to show that Act 590 violated *all* of the tenets of the Lemon Test (see Prelli 1989).

Did Act 590 Have a Secular Legislative Purpose?

The plaintiffs argued that Act 590 did not have a secular purpose by exposing the sectarian motives behind the legislative efforts to enact the bill. Overton agreed with the plaintiffs (see Pope 1982; Taylor and Condit 1988): "The only inference which can be drawn from these circumstances is that the Act was passed with the specific purpose by the General Assembly of advancing religion. The Act therefore fails the first prong of the three-pronged test, that of secular legislative purpose. . . . The evidence is overwhelming that both the purpose and effect of the creationism act is the advancement of religion in public schools."

The *Epperson v. Arkansas* decision had not addressed this part of the Lemon Test, probably because the justices didn't believe that the antievolution laws had any effect in modern America. But the equal-time requirement *could* have an effect. Overton concluded that the effect would be religious.

Did Act 590 Advance Religion?

The plaintiffs emphasized the "inescapable religiosity" of Act 590 by using theologians to establish that claims of "creation from nothing," a worldwide flood, and the relatively recent inception of Earth, along with use of the term *creator*, identified themes peculiar to Western religion and held no scientific meaning (Taylor and Condit 1988; Prelli 1989). Overton concluded that Ellwanger, Blount, Holsted, and the Greater Little Rock Evangelical Fellowship were motivated by their religious beliefs, that Act 590 "was simply and purely an effort to introduce the Biblical version of creationism into the public school curricula," and that "the only real effect of Act 590 is the advancement of religion." The plaintiffs portrayed creationism as an extensive, encompassing framework of fundamentalist Christian thought and argued that creationists' claims are derived from the belief that God has made supernatural interventions. Overton responded: "If the unifying ideas of supernatural creation by God are removed from [the Act], the remaining parts of the section explain nothing and are meaningless assertions."

Would Act 590 Produce an Excessive Entanglement of
Government with Religion?

Overton concluded that Act 590 would create "an excessive and prohibited entanglement [of government] with religion" because compliance would involve federal and state authorities in "delicate religious judgments" when asked to screen course materials and classroom discussions for religious references (see Taylor and Condit 1988).

Early in the trial, the state tried to exclude all evidence about the religious roots of creationism, arguing that because Act 590 prohibited religious references, evidence of religious links was irrelevant (Taylor and Condit 1988). Overton disagreed; he ruled that such testimony was relevant because "an ACLU contention is that creation-science is religion in disguise" ("Attempts Thwarted" 1981). As Overton said, "They can't wear two hats. The writers can't call it religion for one purpose and science for another" (Kenyon 1981; Taylor and Condit 1988). Later, Overton was more explicit: "The problem was that all these 'creation-science' writers have permeated their materials with a religiosity that they can't shed" (Wells 1984).

Overton also noted that Ellwanger—the founder of Citizens for Fairness in Education and the author of Act 590—had no legal or scientific credentials for advocating Act 590. Like fundamentalists before him, Ellwanger—a respiratory therapist trained in neither law nor science—believed that evolution is responsible for social ills such as Nazism and abortion. Overton concluded that Ellwanger had religious intentions for sponsoring Act 590, citing Ellwanger's letter to Louisiana Senator William Keith saying that "I view this whole battle as between God and anti-God forces, though I know there are a large number of evolutionists who believe in God. . . . It behooves Satan to do all he can to thwart our efforts and confuse the issue at every turn."

Although Overton considered the defendants' intentions when making his ruling, he concluded that if only the language of the act were considered, it would still be evident "that both the purpose and effect of Act 590 is the advancement of religion in the public schools." Overton's decision indicated that Act 590 failed all three tests for constitutionality. However, Overton's ruling didn't stop there; he also addressed whether creation science is, in fact, science.

Is "Creation Science" Really Science?

To answer this question, Overton decided that science is what is "accepted by the scientific community" and "what scientists do." Overton also declared political standards of reasonableness irrelevant to deciding what is scientific: "In a free society, knowledge does not require the imprimatur of legislation in order to become science." This decision to defend the scientific community as the appropriate agency for deciding what does and does not count as science (i.e., that "science is as science does")[9] was critical. ACLU counsel Mark Herlihy invoked the claim of Clarence Darrow when he suggested that "the greatest success of the *McLean* opinion was its . . . implicit reliance on the efficacy and integrity of specialized communities—such as the scientific and educational communities—to be the proper arbiters of claims of legitimacy made within their proper spheres" (La Follette 1983; also see Taylor and Condit 1988).

Overton's decision had two important consequences, both of which were setbacks for creationists (Taylor and Condit 1988). First, it denied creationists the moral, political, and religious standards that are their strongest sources of persuasive arguments with nonexpert audiences. Second, it validated professional scientific societies and excluded providers of "similar" services who falsely claim to be within the profession (Gieryn, Bevins, and Zehr 1985; Prelli 1989). This enabled the plaintiffs to define creationists as scientific outsiders and creationism as beyond the pale of scientific reasonableness.

Despite these setbacks, creationists tried to convince Overton that they were legitimate scientists and that creation science is, in fact, science. The plaintiffs argued the opposite—namely, that creationists are not scientists, "that creation-science is less than a weak or bad science; it is not science at all" (Taylor and Condit 1988), and that "creationism . . . is thinly disguised religion." Overton had to answer several important questions: Do creationists' claims constitute reasonable scientific claims? Do creationists have the traits of professional scientists? Do creationists do what scientists do—specifically, publish articles frequently in authorized scientific journals and submit their claims about creationism for peer review? Are creationists employed by leading scientific research institutions? And do creationists support their claims with scientific evidence?

Do Creationists' Claims Constitute Reasonable Scientific Claim-Making?
The plaintiffs argued that creationists' claims do not constitute reasonable scientific claim-making by showing that (1) creationists lack the hallmarks of science—that is, the virtues of skepticism, universality, and disinterestedness; (2) creationists are not credible scientific witnesses because they do not think or act like scientists; (3) creationists are dogmatic rather than skeptical; (4) creationists will not acknowledge the validity of universal and obvious scientific facts; and (5) creationists' conclusions are biased by their greater interest in advancing religion than in discovering truth.

The plaintiffs used these arguments to try to convince Overton that creationists are not scientists at all, but instead are dogmatically proclaiming the inerrancy of Scripture. The plaintiffs supported their arguments by noting that most creation scientists were members of the Creation Research Society and, as such, were required to take oaths to attest to their belief in a literal interpretation of the Genesis story of creation and the literal truth of Scripture, as well as to their fidelity to belief in God (Taylor and Condit 1988; *Amicus Curiae* 1986). The fact that members were required to sign such oaths showed that they didn't have the skeptical outlook proper for scientists.[10]

Do Creationists Display the Qualities of Professional Scientists?

The plaintiffs argued that creationists do not have good standing in the scientific community because they refuse to share in scientific debates about noncontroversial issues and do not participate actively in a scientific intellectual life (Gieryn, Bevins, and Zehr 1985).[11] For example, a creationist geologist admitted under cross-examination that "he had [published] only two articles in standard scientific journals since getting his Ph.D. in 1955"— hardly a publication record for a geologist actively engaged in the intellectual life of his professional community (Gieryn, Bevins, and Zehr 1985; also see below). Such admissions weakened the credibility of "expert" witnesses produced by the procreationism defense and helped convince Overton that creationists do not display the qualities of professional scientists.

Do Creationists Do What Scientists Do?

The plaintiffs argued that creationists do not display the scientific virtue of community because they neither produce nor disseminate credible scientific knowledge, practices that characterize scientific communities. Creationists display a lack of scientific community by failing to submit their technical claims about creationism to peer review.[12] The creationists argued that they could not publish in standard journals because of editorial bias, claiming that editors and evolutionary biologists were guilty of "censorship," of "country-club exclusion," and of trying to keep theories that "were incompatible with their personal or philosophical views out of the marketplace of ideas" (see Taylor and Condit 1988). However, no proponent of creationism offered a rejected submission to a scientific journal, prompting Overton to dismiss creationists' claims that they had been unfairly ignored by the scientific community.[13] Overton concluded that the absence of reputably published articles supporting creation science was evidence that creationists were either unwilling to submit or unable to meet the standards recognized by scientific journals.

Are Creationists Employed by Leading Scientific Research Institutions?

The state rested its case on the claim that competent scientists accept creationism as good science. However, creationists had problems finding recognized scientists who could testify on behalf of creationism without being discredited for their religious presuppositions. Morris and his colleagues at the ICR were not considered because they had already admitted their religious uses of creationism, and those purposes conflicted with the law.[14] Norman Geisler, who was used as an expert witness for the state to show the "enlightened and scientific attitude of today's creationists," embarrassed some creationists when he claimed that demonic possession, exorcism, occultism, and UFOs are "a satanic manifestation in the world for the purpose of deception" (cited in Nelkin 1982). Geisler went on to say that UFOs "represent the Devil's major, in fact, final, attack on the earth" and that he knew that UFOs exist because he had "read it in *The Reader's Digest.*" Another expert witness for the state claimed that interstellar space is littered with genes that can be carried by comets and seed life on Earth and that insects may be more intelligent than humans, but "they're not letting on." Even that witness admitted that no rational scientist could believe that Earth was less than a million years old and that belief in a separate ancestry for apes and man was "clap trap" (Nelkin 1982).[15]

Overton concluded that creationists are not employed by leading scientific research institutions. Harold Morowitz, a biophysicist at Yale University, said he could not name a creationist who held a position at an Ivy League university and emphasized Overton's conclusion by adding, "I can't give you the name of an Ivy League school, graduate school, or journal which houses a flat-earth theorist either" (Gieryn, Bevins, and Zehr 1985).

Do Creationists Have Scientific Evidence to Support Their Claims?
McLean v. Arkansas Board of Education did not focus on the comparative technical merits of creationism and evolution. Such a strategy would have labeled creationism a science (albeit a weak one) and therefore a reasonable source (again, albeit a weak one) for meaningful explanation of origins and other scientific claims. The plaintiffs knew that it was imperative that creationism be denied the status of being even a weak science; otherwise, proposals such as Act 590 could not be judged unconstitutional.

The plaintiffs built their case by arguing that there is no valid evidence for creationists' claims, that there are no scientifically meaningful ideas within the framework of creationism, and that creationists' claims are not scientifically legitimate. The plaintiffs also questioned creationists' ability to make scientifically meaningful interpretive statements about evolutionary theory. Overton agreed with the plaintiffs; he was not convinced by creationists' arguments against the empirical adequacy of evolutionary theory, and he dismissed the claims of creationists by noting the lack of scientific evidence for their claims: "The arguments asserted by creationists are not based upon new scientific evidence or laboratory data which has been ignored by the scientific community. . . . [The claims of creationists about the existence of present life-forms are] simply a hodgepodge of limited assertions, many of which are factually inaccurate."

Overton also noted that experimental/observational work is virtually absent from creationist literature and that creationism "proceeds by showing evolution (specifically Darwinism) wrong, rather than by showing Creationism right." He concluded that creationists' methodology is indicative that their work is not science. Later, Overton added, "I didn't have to define what creationism was—it was all down in black and white [in the law]. . . . Creation science . . . is simply not science" (Wells 1984).

In a word, then, Overton flunked "creation science" on all counts.[16]

Overton and the Demise of Creation Science

Before *McLean v. Arkansas Board of Education*, judges who heard cases associated with the evolution/creationism controversy were hesitant to define science or evaluate scientific evidence because they recognized the limits of their competence. For example, in *Wright v. Houston Independent School District*, Judge Seals noted that the "Court is hardly qualified to select from among the available theories those which merit attention in a public school biology class." Overton, however, met the issue head-on.

Overton's decision, which cited the *Epperson*, *Willoughby*, and *Wright* decisions, included several key features:[17]

> The Arkansas "balanced-treatment" statute is unconstitutional because it violates the First Amendment.
>
> Creationism is not science; rather, it is religion masquerading as science.
>
> Creationism has no scientific significance.
>
> Creationism subverts, rather than contributes to, natural order.
>
> Creationists cannot display a scientific ethos because, unlike scientists, creationists are not involved in a disinterested search for scientific knowledge.
>
> Creationism fails as science because creationists are not scientists and do not function like scientists.

McLean v. Arkansas Board of Education doomed future legislative initiatives involving creation science because it destroyed creationists' arguments about the credibility of creation science (Taylor 1992). An ACLU attorney proclaimed that "the case will deal creation science a fatal blow" (Cearley, quoted in "Federal Judge Denies" 1982). Indeed, creation science legislation declined after the *McLean* case (Heard 1982).

Overton, who had read sixty to sixty-five creationist texts during his decision-making process, later warned against the teaching of creationism in public schools: "The general public has very little understanding of what 'creation science' is. [Most] people would really be amazed if they knew what 'creation-science' is really about. [Much of the material] is more like propaganda than educational material" (Wells 1984). Overton was also discouraged by the "lack of understanding of the Constitution and a lack of understanding of what this country is all about and what we're about. . . . Any time the state adopts a religious view, it degrades all citizens who do not subscribe to that particular religion"; he then quoted one writer who summed it up by saying that "public schools ought to teach religion— my kind" (Wells 1984).

Not surprisingly, creationists attacked Overton's decision; Duane T. Gish of the ICR labeled Overton as biased, and Wendell Bird—an architect of the ICR's equal-time policy on which the Arkansas statute was based—claimed that Overton's decision was "constitutionally erroneous and factually inaccurate." Henry Morris also attacked Overton as biased and claimed that Steve Clark did a poor job of defending the law.

On 4 February 1982 (one month after Overton's decision), Attorney General Clark recognized the strength of Overton's ruling and decided to cut his losses. Harshly criticized for his handling of the suit but convinced that the law was unconstitutional, Clark decided not to appeal Overton's decision (Heard 1982; Novik 1983).[18]

Arkansas Attorney General Steve Clark announces that he will not appeal Judge William Overton's decision in McLean v. Arkansas Board of Education. *(AP Photo)*

After Overton's ruling, the ACLU asked Overton to award $1.4 million in attorneys' fees. Overton reduced the award to $357,768. Clark appealed the award, but the award was upheld (along with 8.75 percent interest) by the U.S. Eighth Circuit Court of Appeals. The *Arkansas Gazette* estimated that the legal fees surrounding Act 590 cost taxpayers almost $1 million. It also offered some advice: "Arkansas has been given an expensive lesson in its dalliance with 'creation science,' and legislatures and governors in the future would be well-advised to shun those creationists who would lead the state astray" ("Putting 'Creation-Science' to Rest" 1984).

Although the case concerning Act 590 in Arkansas was permanently closed, not everyone took the advice of the *Arkansas Gazette*. Despite Overton's ruling, the balanced-treatment issue remained alive. The new stage was Louisiana, and the new actor was a young biology teacher named Don Aguillard.

Notes

1. Ellwanger had failed to introduce a similar resolution in South Carolina, but comparable bills were introduced in the legislatures of eight states in 1980 and in fourteen such assemblies in 1981 (Heard 1982).

2. Among the plaintiffs was the late Reverend Bill McLean, a Methodist minister for whom the trial would be remembered (i.e., *McLean v. Arkansas Board of Education*). The NABT was the only scientific organization listed on the suit. No religious groups appeared on the list of defendants.

3. Bird was upset by his exclusion from the case and told many of the witnesses for the state that the defense was poorly prepared to defend the law. As a result, several of the state's witnesses failed to appear (Nelkin 1982). Clark could find no credible scientists who accepted creationist arguments or creationists with scientific credentials. Clark ended up with witnesses who testified that they believed life on Earth began from "cometary seeding" and biblical literalists who denied that contrary evidence could shake their beliefs (Irons 1988; also see the discussion later is this chapter about the question regarding creationists' employers). Bird and other creationists (including television preachers Pat Robertson and Jerry Falwell) responded by denouncing Clark as an ACLU stooge who did not want to win the case (Eve and Harrold 1991; Irons 1988). In response, there was a defamation action against Robertson (Nelkin 1982).

4. Soon after being excluded from the Arkansas trial, Bird went to Louisiana and became involved in another lawsuit by creationists. That lawsuit eventually made it to the U.S. Supreme Court (see Chapter 6).

5. Bill Aldridge (then the executive director of the National Science Teachers Association) and Wayne Moyer (then the executive director of the NABT) spoke out against Act 590, claiming that the teaching of creation science in biology classes was like propounding the flat-Earth theory in physics classes. Both Aldridge and Moyer declared that Act 590 was a disguise for teaching religion in public schools. As Moyer said, "The law is going to be laughed at. Good teachers will realize they have an obligation to the subject matter. . . . [Act 590] places the state in the position of defining by law what is truth in science" ("Educators Criticize Creationism Bill" 1981).

6. When Professor Dorothy Nelkin said during the trial that she did not believe in a personal God, three spectators rose from their seats, stepped into the aisle, sank to their knees, and began "very audible prayers" for the skeptical professor (Gilkey 1985).

7. Overton's *McLean v. Arkansas Board of Education* ruling, which has been referred to as "an amazing intellectual document" (Gilkey 1985), is available on the Internet (http://cns-web.bu.edu/pub/dorman/McLean_vs_Arkansas.html) and in "Creationism in Schools" (1982).

8. The "secular purpose" prong of the Lemon Test resulted largely from the *Epperson v. Arkansas* decision that legalized the teaching of evolution. Note that the test doesn't say that a law may not also have a religious purpose or that the secular purpose has to be the primary purpose of the law. Similarly, the test doesn't mean that a law can't have *any* effect on advancing religion or that a law needn't have *any* entanglement with religion.

9. In the trial, scientists defined science by its hallmarks: critical thinking, rational examination of evidence, and intellectual honesty enforced by skeptical

scrutiny. In light of these criteria, creationist doctrines were easily identified as non-scientific. The Committee on Science and Creationism of the National Academy of Sciences concluded that "creationism, with its accounts of the origin of life by supernatural means, is not science" (National Academy of Sciences 1984).

10. Similarly, the editorial policy of the *Creation Research Society Quarterly* includes a "Statement of Belief" that proclaims that "the Bible is the written word of God . . . all its assertions are historically and scientifically true in all of the original autographs. To a student of nature, this means that the account of origins in Genesis is a factual presentation of simple historical truths" (see Taylor 1992; Eve and Harrold 1991). Members of the Creation Research Society, "an organization of Christian men of science, who accept Jesus Christ as [their] Lord and Savior," must also subscribe to additional claims: "All . . . living things, including man, were made by direct creative acts of God . . . as described in Genesis. . . . The special creation of Adam and Eve as one man and one woman, and their subsequent Fall into sin, is the basis for your belief in the necessity of a Savior for all mankind. . . . Salvation can come only thru [*sic*] accepting Jesus Christ as your Savior" (see note 3 of *Edwards v. Aguillard*).

11. Many prominent creationists have advanced degrees from prestigious institutions. For example, Duane T. Gish (associate director of the ICR) has a Ph.D. in biochemistry from the University of California at Berkeley, Henry M. Morris (director of the ICR) has a Ph.D. in hydraulics from the University of Minnesota (Taylor 1992), and Kurt Wise (a science professor at Bryan College) was trained at Harvard University by Stephen J. Gould. Morris blames evolutionary theory for "communism, fascism, Freudianism, social Darwinism, behaviorism, Kinseyism, materialism, and atheism," to name just a few. Morris also claims that people who believe in evolution are "lost to salvation" and "face eternal damnation" (see discussion in Scott 1994).

12. Most of the creationist literature at the time was published by Creation-Life Publishers, which Overton concluded was a religiously motivated publishing company, not a legitimate forum for communicating or testing scientific ideas (Prelli 1989).

13. Creationists continue to blame editorial bias for the huge quantitative disparity between scientific articles supporting evolution and their own work. However, studies show that only a few creationists have submitted articles to scientific journals and that those that were submitted were uniformly rejected for not adhering to the most rudimentary standards of scientific research (Cole and Scott 1982; Taylor 1992).

14. For example, Steven Austin (chair of the ICR's Department of Geology) has produced a college-level textbook titled *Grand Canyon: Monument to Catastrophe* (Austin 1994) that states that "the real battle in regard to understanding the Grand Canyon is founded not just upon Creation and Noah's Flood versus evolution, but upon Christianity versus humanism." Similarly, the ICR's *Science, Scripture, and the Young Earth* (Morris and Morris 1989) claims that "the data of geology . . . should be interpreted in light of the Scriptures, rather than distorting Scripture to accommodate current geological philosophy." Henry Morris believes that the scientific study of nature is subordinate to theology and to his God and that his God's word has priority over that of people: "If the Bible teaches it, that settles it, whatever scientists might say, because it's the word of God" (quoted in Donaldson 1988).

Morris believes that creationism is an excellent "ministry" for leading students to Christ (Larson 1989).

15. Virtually all of the geologists recruited to creationism have deserted the belief after being exposed to scientific evidence (Wise 1998; Numbers 1992).

16. Overton was criticized for his emphasis on the nonfalsifiability of some creationists' claims to deny their scientific merits. Indeed, Overton's decision neglected the strongest argument against creationism—namely, that many of the claims of creationists *have* been falsified (Lauden 1983; Numbers 1992). Similarly, Overton's argument that scientific conclusions are always "tentative" does not mean that all scientific conclusions are equally tentative; some are supported weakly, whereas others, such as evolution, are firmly established.

17. One month after issuing his decision, Overton announced that he'd decided "fairly early on" in the trial how he would rule: "I would say we weren't far into that trial before the attorney general [Steve Clark] was rearranging the chairs on the deck of the *Titanic*. . . . It was clear cut. . . . The ACLU lawyers ran through the State like the British took the Argentines" (Wells 1984).

18. When Overton heard lawyers say that it was possible to draft a creationist law that would meet constitutional standards, he said, "All I can say . . . is that it would take a better lawyer than me to do that" (Wells 1984).

6
BAD SCIENCE: EDWARDS V. AGUILLARD

Evolution is a laughing matter for anybody that's got a rational mind.
—Merle Haggard, 1990

The scientific case for special creation . . . is much stronger than the case for evolution. The more I study and the more I learn, the more I become convinced that evolution is a false theory and that special creation offers a much more satisfactory interpretive framework for correlating and explaining the scientific evidence related to origins.
—Duane T. Gish, Institute for Creation Research, 1985

There is no significant scientific doubt about the close evolutionary relationships among all primates or between apes and humans. The "missing links" that troubled Darwin and his followers are no longer missing. Today, not one but many such connecting links, intermediate between various branches of the primate evolutionary family tree, have been found as fossils. The linking fossils are intermediate in form and occur in geological deposits of intermediate age. They thus document the time and rate at which primate and human evolution occurred.
—National Academy of Sciences, 1984

After suffering a stunning defeat in *McLean v. Arkansas Board of Education*, creationists turned their attention to Louisiana, which also had a "balanced-treatment" law. The constitutionality of the Louisiana law wasn't covered by the *McLean* decision because the Louisiana law did not include the traditional biblical features that were prominent in the Arkansas law. Whereas the Arkansas balanced-treatment statute had linked "creation science" to the study of a biblically inspired list of creation events (e.g., a worldwide flood), the Louisiana statute lacked religious references. Moreover, the Louisiana law defined creation science as "scientific evidence for creation and inferences from those scientific evidences" (see Larson 1989 and references therein), but it did not list those inferences (as Act 590 had), nor did it define the term *creation* or mention God.

Wendell Bird demanded a trial on the *scientific* merits of creation science, arguing that such a trial was justified because Louisiana's balanced-treatment legislation (1) was a substantially different statute than the Arkansas law, (2) was based on a different definition of creation science than was the Arkansas law, and (3) had a different legislative purpose than did the Arkansas law.

The Origin of Louisiana's Balanced-Treatment Law

Louisiana's balanced-treatment legislation was introduced by Senator Bill Keith on the opening day of the 1981 legislative session.[1] Keith, who rejected evolution because it was contrary to his religious beliefs, wanted to use "academic freedom" to (1) require the development of curriculum guides and resource services for creation science, (2) appoint only creation scientists to the "research services panels," (3) prohibit school boards from discriminating against anyone who "chooses to be a creation-scientist" (Keith's bill did not offer similar protections for those who chose to teach evolution or who refused to teach creation science), and (4) ban the teaching of evolution in public elementary and secondary schools unless it was accompanied by instruction of creation science.

Keith produced an "expert" on creation science (Edward Boudreaux), who admitted in legislative hearings that creation science included believing in the existence of a supernatural creator. Boudreaux claimed that there were "something like a thousand [creation scientists] who hold doctorate and master's degrees in all areas of science who are affiliated with either or both the Institute for Creation Research and the Creation Research Society." Several vocal legislators who supported Keith's bill proudly revealed their religious intentions; one legislator argued that the existence of God is "a scientific fact."

During hearings, Keith's bill was amended so that teachers could refer to the Bible and other religious texts to support the creation science theory. Keith urged his colleagues to support the legislation by telling them that "evolution is no more than a fairy tale about a frog that turns into a prince. We force our children to go to school, and when they get there we teach them man came from monkeys" (Larson 1989). Although Keith's bill did not require the teaching of either subject unless the other was taught, each—when taught—had to "be taught as a theory, rather than as proven scientific fact."

The Louisiana House of Representatives passed Keith's balanced-treatment bill by a vote of 71–19, and on 6 July, Keith distributed pamphlets claiming that creationism is "pure science" that "has no missing links." The state Senate passed Keith's legislation by a vote of 26–12. Although Republican Governor David Treen had reservations about the legislation, he signed the bill two weeks later. In Louisiana, balanced treatment was the law.

Wendell Bird, recently excluded from *McLean v. Arkansas Board of Education*, wanted the balanced-treatment law to be enacted immediately. To accomplish this, Bird went to Louisiana, where on 2 December 1981, in federal court in Baton Rouge, he filed a lawsuit (*Keith v. Louisiana*) to force Louisiana educational agencies to comply with the newly signed law: "It seems only clear and reasonable that if one science, evolution, is taught, another—that of creation science—should be also" ("One Case" 1987).

In 1981, biology teacher Don Aguillard filed a lawsuit challenging the constitutionality of Louisiana's "balanced treatment" law. Six years later, the U.S. Supreme Court decided Aguillard's case. (AP Photo)

The next day, the American Civil Liberties Union—on behalf of twenty-six organizational and individual plaintiffs (including the National Association of Biology Teachers, the National Science Teachers Association, and the American Association for the Advancement of Science)—challenged the constitutionality of the balanced-treatment law (*Aguillard v. Treen*). Serving as the nominal plaintiff was Don Aguillard, a biology teacher at Acadiana High School in Lafayette, Louisiana. The ACLU claimed that the law "does not have any secular legislative purpose in that creation-science is inherently religious, it is religious apologetics calculated to advance a particular religious belief, it is not science and it has no educational merit."

Aguillard realized the damage the law would inflict on students and science education; as he later said, "I knew that creationism didn't belong in science classrooms. I couldn't stand by and do nothing . . . . We just don't have the money to be spending on bad science." Many biology teachers were prepared to not teach evolution rather than give equal time to creationism (Aguillard 1989). Like John Scopes, Susan Epperson, and others before him, Aguillard was harshly criticized; supporters of creation science viewed his position as a threat to their religious beliefs (Aguillard 1989).

Bird was deputized a special attorney general for both *Keith v. Louisiana* and *Aguillard v. Treen*. The ACLU's defense followed the strategy that it had used successfully in *McLean v. Arkansas Board of Education*, claiming that the Louisiana law advanced religion. When *Keith v. Louisiana* was dismissed in June 1982 because it did not raise a federal question, all attention shifted to *Aguillard v. Treen*.

In *Aguillard v. Treen* (634 F. Supp. 426 [ED La. 1985]), the constitutionality of Keith's balanced-treatment statute was challenged by Louisiana parents, teachers, and religious leaders in U.S. District Court in New Orleans. Judge Adrian Duplantier, acting without a trial, ignored the scientific aspects of the case, focusing instead on the argument that the teaching of creation science requires teaching the existence of a divine creator. On 10 January 1985, Duplantier ruled that the legislature wrongly dictated "to the public schools not only that a subject must be taught, but also how it must get taught" and that the statute violated the Establishment Clause of the First Amendment of the U.S. Constitution. Duplantier's ruling, which prohibited the state of Louisiana from implementing the law, sided with the

The U.S. Supreme Court upheld Judge Adrian Duplantier's ruling that Louisiana's "balanced treatment" law was unconstitutional. (AP Photo)

appellees, noting that (1) there can be no valid secular reason for prohibiting the teaching of evolution, (2) "creation science" is "tailored to the principles" of a particular religious sect, (3) the statute's avowed purpose of protecting academic freedom was inconsistent with the statute's legislative history and its requirement for teaching creation science whenever evolution is taught, and (4) creationism is a religious belief.[2] Duplantier's decision noted that no conceivable trial testimony could save the balanced-treatment law.

As Keith claimed that Duplantier was biased, Bird convinced the state to file its intention to appeal the decision. At this point, the case became *Edwards v. Aguillard*, since the state and governor (Edwin Edwards) were now the plaintiffs. The appeal in the Fifth Circuit Court of Appeals did not involve a trial. On 8 July 1985, the appellate panel of the court, which consisted of three judges, unanimously affirmed Duplantier's ruling:

> The Act violates the Establishment Clause of the First Amendment because the purpose of the statute is to promote a religious belief. . . . We must recognize that the theory of creation is a religious belief. Nor can we ignore the fact that through the years religious fundamentalists have publicly scorned the theory of evolution and worked to discredit it. . . . [The state intended] to discredit evolu-

tion by counterbalancing its teaching at every turn with the teaching of creationism, a religious belief.

When Louisiana Attorney General William Guste petitioned for a rehearing by the entire fifteen-member court, the full U.S. Court of Appeals for the Fifth Circuit—noting the ongoing influence of the Scopes legacy in the case[3]—affirmed Duplantier's ruling by a vote of 8–7. The ACLU again proclaimed that the controversy was over, as it had after the *Scopes*, *Epperson*, and *McLean* decisions. As claimed by Martha Kegel, Louisiana's ACLU executive director, "This is the death knell for the entire creation science movement across the country."

Although the dissenting opinion by Judge Thomas Gee ("there *are* two bona fide views" of origins) was the first published judicial support for creationist claims since the Scopes trial (Larson 1989), the case wasn't over, for when a federal court rules that a state law is unconstitutional, by "mandatory jurisdiction," the U.S. Supreme Court must consider hearing the case (Shermer 1997). On 5 May 1986, the U.S. Supreme Court said that it would hear the case. The evolution/creationism controversy was again headed to the highest court in the land.

The Fate of "Balanced Treatment"

The validity of the balanced-treatment strategy was decided in 1987 by the U.S. Supreme Court in *Edwards, Governor of Louisiana, et al. v. Aguillard et al.* (No. 85–1513, 482 U.S. 578; 107 Sup. Ct. 2573; 1987 U.S. Lexis 2729; 96 L. Ed. 2d 510; 55 *U.S. Law Week* 4860).[4] In that trial, which occurred on 10 December 1987, the state's case for balanced treatment was presented by Wendell Bird; Aguillard was defended by Jay Topkis, a volunteer for the ACLU who was frequently challenged by Justice Antonin Scalia at the hearing.

When Supreme Court Justice John Paul Stevens asked, "What . . . [is] the factual issue that [has] to be resolved?" Bird told the Court, "Your Honor, the definition of 'creation science' is one very important factual issue, what the statute's about." Although Bird admitted that "some legislators had a desire to teach religious doctrine in the classroom," he added that this group was a "small minority." He then argued that the law had a primary secular purpose based on "fairness" and the "academic freedom" of students.

Topkis responded by stating that what the legislators said at the time they enacted the statute "is nothing but religion. . . . We can go through this entire record without finding anybody talking about a secular purpose."

Bird countered: "Teaching creation science does not entail, necessarily, the teachings of [a personal God]. . . . In other words, with creation science consisting of scientific evidence, such as the abrupt appearance of complex life in the fossil record, the systematic gaps between fossil categories, the mathematical improbability of evolution . . . in none of that is there any concept of a creator, and certainly no concept of Genesis. That is scientific data."

Bird was repeatedly interrupted by questions from the justices. Topkis scoffed at Bird's argument by comparing him to Tweedledum in *Alice in Wonderland:* "[Bird] wants words to mean what he says they mean, and that didn't fool Alice—and I doubt very much that it will fool this court. . . . This statute calls for the very antithesis of academic freedom" ("One Case" 1987).

On 19 June 1987, the U.S. Supreme Court ruled in a 7–2 decision that Don Aguillard did not have to teach creation science in his classes. The Court, noting that evolution has been "historically opposed by some religious denominations," affirmed that (1) it is unconstitutional to mandate or advocate creationism in public schools, for creationism is inherently a religious idea; (2) Louisiana's balanced-treatment and equal-time law was unconstitutional because it impermissibly endorsed religion by advancing the religious belief that a supernatural being created humankind (i.e., it violated the Establishment Clause); (3) banning the teaching of evolution when creation science is not also taught undermines a comprehensive science education; (4) the contention that teaching creation science is required as "a basic concept of fairness" is "without merit"; and (5) the act discriminated for the teaching of creation science and against the teaching of evolution by requiring that curriculum guides be developed and resource services be supplied for teaching creationism but not for teaching evolution.

The Court did not mince words, noting that the statute was "facially invalid as violative of the Establishment Clause of the First Amendment, because it lacks a clear secular purpose."[5] The Court also noted that it was not happenstance that the legislature required the teaching of a theory that coincided with a particular religious view, noting that creationists

have identified no clear purpose for the Louisiana Act. . . . The preeminent purpose of the Louisiana legislature was clearly to advance the religious viewpoint that a supernatural being created humankind. . . . [The] purpose of the Creationism Act was to restructure the science curriculum to conform with a particular religious viewpoint. . . . The goal of providing a more comprehensive science curriculum is not furthered either by outlawing the teaching of evolution or by requiring the teaching of creation science. . . . Requiring schools to teach creation science with evolution does not advance academic freedom.

The Supreme Court ruled that the law's requirement that creationism be taught "advances a religious doctrine" and "seeks to employ the symbolic and financial support of government to achieve a religious purpose." Again invoking the Scopes legacy, *Time* magazine described the *Edwards v. Aguillard* decision as "a major setback for fundamentalist Christians" (Sanders 1987).

After *Edwards v. Aguillard*, attempts to pass equal-time laws dwindled (Scott 1994). Ironically, however, many creationists were encouraged by a part of Justice William Brennan's majority opinion: "Teaching a variety of scientific theories about the origins of humankind to school children might be validly done with the clear secular interest of enhancing the effectiveness of science instruction." They were also encouraged by Justice Scalia's dissenting opinion (which Justice William H. Rehnquist joined)[6] that accepted creationists' claims when concluding that "the people of Louisiana, including those who are Christian fundamentalists, are quite entitled, as a secular matter, to have whatever scientific evidence there may be against evolution presented in their schools, just as Mr. Scopes was entitled to present whatever scientific evidence there was for it." Scalia also pointed out:

> The body of scientific evidence supporting creation science is as strong as that supporting evolution. In fact, it may be stronger. Evolution is merely a scientific theory or "guess." Creation science is educationally valuable. Students exposed to it better understand the current state of scientific evidence about the origin of life. . . . Although creation science is educationally valuable and strictly scientific, it is now being censored from or misrepresented in the public schools. . . . Teachers have been brainwashed by an entrenched scientific establishment composed almost exclusively of scientists to whom evolution is like a "religion." These scientists discriminate against creation scientists so as to prevent evolution's weaknesses from being exposed.

Although both Rehnquist and Scalia ignored the fact that there are no reputable alternatives to evolution as a scientific explanation, they did suggest that alternative theories could be taught in public schools.

Notes

1. Keith had introduced a scientific creationism bill in 1980, but it had died in committee. Keith's 1981 attempt was based on a version of Paul Ellwanger's proposal that was adopted in Arkansas. Keith subsequently founded the Creation Science Legal Defense Fund (later the Academic Freedom Legal Defense Fund; see Eve and Harrold 1991).

2. Among those urging affirmation were the American Federation of Teachers, Americans United for Separation of Church and State, and the National Academy of Sciences. Louisiana officials, charged with implementing the act, defended the statute on the grounds that it had a secular interest—namely, academic freedom.

3. The appeals court noted that "the Act continues that battle that William Jennings Bryan carried to his grave" and that "the case comes to us against a historical background that cannot be denied or ignored" (Numbers 1992).

4. The *Edwards v. Aguillard* ruling by the U.S. Supreme Court can be accessed at http://cns-web.bu.edu/pub/dorman/edwards_v_aguillard.html or in Irons and Guitton (1993). The ruling cites a variety of related issues and court opinions, including those involving "meditation periods" in public schools, posting of the Ten Commandments, opening a legislative session with a prayer by a chaplain paid by the state, and so forth. The appellants agreed not to implement the creationism act pending the outcome of this litigation.

5. This decision came to be known as "the Edwards restriction." Today, this restriction is the controlling legal position on attempts to require the teaching of creationism in public schools. Such attempts are unconstitutional.

6. Scalia and Rehnquist were appointees of President Ronald Reagan, who supported balanced treatment. Indeed, Reagan supported school prayer, questioned the theory of evolution, supported biblical creationism, repeatedly complained that "I don't believe we should ever have expelled God from the classroom," and promised to appoint federal judges willing to include religion in public education (Larson 1989). Bill Keith, the sponsor of Louisiana's balanced-treatment legislation, claimed that God had delayed the lawsuit so that President Reagan could appoint more judges to the bench (Reagan had appointed six of the fifteen judges in the Fifth Circuit Court).

7

THE ONGOING BATTLE

*Causes stir the world, and this cause has stirred the world. . . . The world
is interested because it raises an issue, and that issue will someday be settled.
The people will determine this issue.*
—William Jennings Bryan, at the Scopes trial, July 1925

*Scientific creationism may be poor science, but it is powerful politics.
And politically, it may succeed.*
—Laurie Godfrey, 1981

If the Bible and the microscope do not agree, the microscope is wrong.
—William Jennings Bryan, 1925

Webster v. New Lenox School District 122

After *Edwards v. Aguillard*, the evolution/creationism controversy raged.
The next court proceeding in the controversy began in 1990, when Ray
Webster, a social science teacher in a junior high in New Lenox, Illinois, was
told by his superintendent to stop teaching creation science in his classes.
Webster sued the school district (917 F. 2d 1004 [7th Cir. 1990]), claiming
that the district was violating his right to free speech.

In November 1990, the Seventh Circuit Court of Appeals relied heavily
on the earlier *Edwards* decision to rule that a teacher does not have a First
Amendment right to teach creation science in a public school and that a
school district may ban a teacher from teaching creationism (i.e., the teaching of creation science violates the First Amendment).

John E. Peloza v. Capistrano Unified School District

In 1991, John Peloza was teaching creationism and promoting conservative
Christianity in his biology classes at Capistrano High School in Orange
County, California. Parents and teachers complained, after which Peloza
was reprimanded and instructed by administrators to stop teaching creationism and follow California's educational guidelines for teaching evolution. Peloza sued the school district (37 F. 3d 517 [9th Cir. 1994]), claiming that the district was violating his right to free speech and forcing him to
teach the religion of evolution.

In January 1992, Judge David W. Williams dismissed Peloza's lawsuit
because the school district acted appropriately in demanding that Peloza
not teach creationism. In his ruling, Williams emphasized that teachers can-

not teach their own curriculum if it violates the state's educational guidelines. When Peloza appealed Williams's decision, the Ninth Circuit Court of Appeals declared that because evolution is not a religion, requiring an instructor to teach evolution does not violate the Establishment Clause of the U.S. Constitution. That is, a teacher's First Amendment right to religious freedom is not violated by a school district's requirement that evolution be taught in biology classes.

Freiler v. Tangipahoa Parish Board of Education

Freiler v. Tangipahoa Parish Board of Education (No. 94–3577 [E.D. La. Aug. 8, 1997]) began on 19 April 1994 when the Tangipahoa (Louisiana) Parish Board of Education passed (by a vote of 5–4) the following resolution:

> Whenever, in classes of elementary or high school, the scientific theory of evolution is to be presented, whether from textbook, workbook, pamphlet, other written material, or oral presentation, the following statement shall be quoted immediately before the unit of study begins as a disclaimer from endorsement of such theory:
>
> "It is hereby recognized by the Tangipahoa Board of Education, that the lesson to be presented, regarding the origin of life and matter, is know as the Scientific Theory of Evolution and should be presented to inform students of the scientific concept and not intended to influence or dissuade the Biblical version of Creation or any other concept."
>
> "It is further recognized by the Board of Education that it is the basic right and privilege of each student to form his/her own opinion and maintain beliefs taught by parents on this very important matter of the origin of life and matter. Students are urged to exercise critical thinking and gather all information possible and closely examine each alternative toward forming an opinion."

Seven months later, several parents of children in the Tangipahoa Parish Public Schools sued in U.S. District Court, on the basis that the disclaimer was unconstitutional because it endorsed religion. In August 1997, U.S. District Court Judge Marcel Livaudais Jr. ruled in *Freiler v. Tangipahoa Parish Board of Education* that (1) it is unlawful to require teachers to read aloud disclaimers saying that the biblical version of creation is the only concept "from which students [are] not to be dissuaded" and (2) proposals for teaching "intelligent design" are equivalent to proposals for teaching "creation science." The court awarded $49,444.50 to Herb Freiler's attorneys.

On 13 August 1999, the Fifth Circuit Court of Appeals affirmed the *Freiler* decision, stating that a school board cannot require that a disclaimer be read immediately before the teaching of evolution in elementary and secondary classes. The following month, the Tangipahoa Parish board proposed an alternative disclaimer. When the plaintiffs rejected this disclaimer, the board asked for a hearing by all fifteen members of the Fifth Circuit Court. On 24 January 2000, the court denied the board's petition by a vote of 8–7. The following month, the board voted 5–4 against further appeals. Two members of the board then changed their votes, prompting the issue to be placed on the agenda for the board's next meeting. On 22 February, the board voted 7–2 to ask the U.S. Supreme Court to consider hearing an appeal of the lower court's rulings opposing the controversial disclaimer. On 19 June 2000, the U.S. Supreme Court voted 6–3 to let the lower court's decision stand in *Freiler v. Tangipahoa Parish Board of Education.* Creationists on the board responded by proclaiming, "The war isn't over."

Rodney LeVake v. Independent School District #656, et al.

In 1997, middle school science teacher Rodney LeVake applied for a job as a biology teacher at the Faribault, Minnesota, high school. Soon after LeVake got the job, his fellow teachers became uneasy with his approach to the teaching of evolution, noting that he "was openly professing his Christianity" and "would argue things from a fundamentalist point of view." Biologist Ken Hubert, the chair of the science division at the high school, met with LeVake. After that meeting, Hubert decided that LeVake needed to discuss how he was teaching evolution with the principal and the district science coordinator. At that meeting, LeVake claimed that he was willing to teach evolution but had not gotten around to it during his first year of teaching at the high school. LeVake also demanded to teach the alleged "evidence against evolution." When school officials asked LeVake to describe more precisely what he wanted to teach, he made a variety of creationist claims, such as that (1) "evolution itself is not only impossible from a biochemical, anatomical, and physiological standpoint, but the theory of evolution has no evidence to show that it actually occurred," (2) "neither evolution or creation can be considered a science because neither are [*sic*] observable at the present," (3) "proponents of either interpretation must accept it as a matter of faith," (4) "the theory of evolution is in clear violation of" the second law of thermodynamics, and (5) there is an "amazing lack of transitional forms in the fossil record." LeVake cited Michael Denton's *Evolution: A Theory in Crisis* (1986), Phillip Johnson's *Darwin on Trial* (1993), and Michael Behe's *Darwin's Black Box* (1996), even though he had "not personally read" the latter two books.

The school district had a prescribed curriculum for biology that included instruction about evolution. Since LeVake had not taught evolution and continued to demand that he be allowed to teach the "evidence against evolution," he was reassigned to teach freshman general science, a course in which evolution was not a part. In response, LeVake sued the school in May 1999 in Minnesota state court, claiming that the district had discriminated against him because of his "adherence or non-adherence to certain religious or philosophical beliefs" and that his right to free speech entitled him to teach whatever he wanted to teach. LeVake asked the court for two things: to find "the district's policy, of excluding from biology teaching positions persons whose religious beliefs conflict with acceptance of evolution as an unquestionable fact, to be unconstitutional and illegal under the U.S. and Minnesota Constitutions" and to award him $50,000 plus court costs.

LeVake was represented by the American Center for Law and Justice, a branch of television preacher Pat Robertson's Christian Coalition. LeVake's lawyers called his reassignment an example of "educational McCarthyism." In June 2000, District Court Judge Bernard E. Borene issued a summary judgment dismissing *Rodney LeVake v. Independent School District #656* (Order Granting Defendants' Motion for Summary Judgment and Memorandum, Court File Nr. CX–99–793, District Court for the Third Judicial District of the State of Minnesota [2000]) because LeVake's right to free speech did not override the right of the school to set its curriculum. One month later, LeVake appealed Borene's decision. In May of 2001, the Minnesota Appeals Court rejected LeVake's appeal.

Other Skirmishes

Creationists have consistently lost court cases involving the insertion of creationism into (and the banning of evolution from) public schools. Many scientists and others have praised these court decisions as protections against the establishment of religion in public schools. Nevertheless, evolutionary biology continues to face the opposition that it has been experiencing since before the Scopes trial (Bull and Wichman 1998). One of the newest strategies of creationists involves demanding equal time to teach the alleged evidence *against* evolution and, correspondingly, that evolution did not occur. This strategy, which resembles pre-*Edwards* creationism, typically entails claims that radiometric dating is unreliable, that it is impossible that life could have originated at random, that there are no transitional life-forms, and that evolution is disproved by the second law of thermodynamics. To garner scholarly support for these and similar ideas, creationists have developed reference materials filled with scientific terminology (e.g., "critical thinking") without significant theoretical or intellectual underpinning.[1] These strategies, combined with euphemisms such as "intelligent design" and "abrupt appearance theory," have created significant inroads for fundamentalists in public schools.

Aided by organizations such as the Creation Research Society, the Creation Science Research Center, Answers in Genesis, and the Institute for Creation Research, creationists continue to try to force their ideas into science classes of public schools. Here are a few of the most recent examples of their activities:

In 1995, Alabama required that evolution be taught as a "theory rather than fact" (Scott 1995), and in 1997, the Washington State Senate took up yet another measure "not to teach evolution as fact" (Pigliucci 1998). North Carolina House Bill 511, proposed in March 1997, attempted to "ensure that evolution is not taught as fact in North Carolina public schools" (Lewis 1997). Creationists continue to argue that the exclusion of creationism from classrooms of public schools is unfair and unscientific, that evolutionists need governmental authorities to shield students from the "scientific truth" of creationism, and that national leaders have an "evolutionary bias" that must be overcome (e.g., see Gabler and Gabler 1985a, 1985b).

A school district in Kentucky that had an equal-time rule in place before the *Edwards* case revised its science curriculum to "avoid mention of creationism in its curriculum guide, calling it 'alternative theories to evolution' and adding it to the science classes" (Kennedy 1992).

The religious right often exploits the evolution/creationism controversy to promote its goal of instituting Christianity in public education (Berman 1997). In 1992, the religious right won control of the school board in Vista, California. The board quickly began promoting the teaching of creationism; it also reduced support programs for poor children, tried to limit sex education and multicultural classes, and reintroduced school prayer, in direct violation of Supreme Court rulings (see Berman 1997). Many fundamentalists view the evolution/creationism controversy as a "holy war" (e.g., see Paterson and Rossow 1999).

Some politicians, such as Alabama's former governor Fob James, openly ridicule science (and especially evolution) and vow to disregard court decisions that favor it (e.g., see Poovey 1998). Recently, House Republican Whip Tom DeLay has linked the teaching of evolution with school shootings, birth control, and abortion ("Mr. DeLay's Power Play" 1999).

In rural Draffenville, Kentucky, at the start of the 1996–1997 school year, the Marshall County superintendent learned that the science textbooks being used by fifth- and sixth-graders contained a two-page discussion of the "big bang" theory for the origin of the universe but no parallel account of the biblical version from Genesis. Invoking the balanced-treatment argument by claiming that "we're not going to teach one theory and not teach another theory," the superintendent recalled the textbooks to his office, where staff were told to glue the two offending pages together (e.g., see Berman 1997).

Every year, legislatures in several states consider antievolution bills, some of which contradict Supreme Court decisions (e.g., *Edwards v. Aguillard*; see discussion in Paterson and Rossow 1999).

Some political platforms now include antievolution planks (Patterson and Rossow 1999). For example, in 1996, the Iowa Republican Party included this statement in its platform: "We believe the theory of Creation Science should be taught in public schools along with other theories . . . [and] support the stocking of Creationist produced resources in all tax-funded public schools and school libraries." That same year, creationists in Tennessee proposed in a Senate bill that "no teacher or administrator in a local education agency shall teach the theory of evolution except as a scientific theory." Although biology teachers found this statement to be rather puzzling (after all, evolution *is* a scientific theory), they were not amused by the provision that anyone teaching evolution as fact would be suspended or fired. After a five-hour debate, the measure was defeated by a vote of 20–13.

In several states, curriculum guides no longer include the word *evolution.*

In Tennessee, where the Scopes legacy remains strong, legislation to restrict the teaching of evolution in public schools appeared in the state Senate in 1994. Reporters flocked to Tennessee, the BBC sent crews, and *Inherit the Wind* had yet another revival of popularity.[2] The Senate Education Committee approved the two-sentence proposal by a vote of 8–1, after which the full Senate debated the proposal for three days. Following many professions of faith, the bill failed by a vote of 20–13.

In 2001, legislatures throughout the country considered various antievolution bills. For example, in March, the Michigan House of Representatives began considering House Bill 4382, which would require science standards to refer to evolution as an unproven theory and to give equal time to "the theory that life is the result of the purposeful, intelligent design of the creator."

Court decisions such as *McLean v. Arkansas Board of Education* and *Edwards v. Aguillard* have given relief and time to use education to change public opinion. However, as noted by American Civil Liberties Union attorney Jack Novik after the *McLean* decision: "The problem of creationism will persist because it is a legal problem only in part. The law can provide only temporary relief. . . . [The solution requires] meaningful science education"(Novik 1983). Court decisions and constitutional practices often have only a limited (and delayed) effect on what happens in schools. For instance, many public schools continue to endorse public prayer and give equal time to creationism. Although the Establishment Clause of the Constitution protects the rights of minorities, even the smallest minority must include at least one person who will seek his or her rights. In many areas, no one opposes creationism in the science classroom. As a result, many students are taught that creationism is legitimate science.

Notes

1. Among the most popular of these materials is *Of Pandas and People* (Davis and Kenyon 1989), which was produced by a Texas-based creationist group called the Foundation for Thought and Ethics. This book, which has been used in many schools as a supplement to biology books, claims to present a balanced treatment of evolution and "intelligent design theory" (see discussion in Scott 1994).

2. A sign in a Broadway theater lobby quoted 1996 presidential candidate Pat Buchanan's comments in support of the Tennessee bill.

8

KEY PEOPLE IN THE EVOLUTION/ CREATIONISM CONTROVERSY

Agassiz, Louis (1807–1873)

Famed protégé of Georges Cuvier, son of a Protestant preacher, and Harvard paleontologist who vigorously opposed Darwin's claims about evolution and natural selection because he could not reconcile himself to any theory that did not involve design. Agassiz argued that "we are children of God, and not of monkeys." Agassiz's claim that different races are the products of several different creations has often been used by creationists to justify racism. Unlike Darwin, who argued that organisms and their interrelationships are "complex facts, to be analyzed and interpreted scientifically," Agassiz believed that such phenomena are "ultimate facts" to be interpreted theologically. Agassiz's design-based arguments against evolution have also been repeated by modern-day creationists such as Michael Behe (author of *Darwin's Black Box*). Agassiz believed that embryology, ecology, biogeography, and paleontology must contribute to any classification scheme that claims to show true relationships of organisms, even if those relationships (according to Agassiz) exist only in God's mind. Agassiz, who is remembered primarily for proposing the existence of the Ice Ages, was one of the founding fathers of modern American science and considered himself to be an intellectual heir to Cuvier; for his entire life, Agassiz defended Cuvier's catastrophism. Agassiz believed that new species could arise only through the intervention of God. Despite his rejection of evolution, Agassiz was America's leading scientist in his day. He was also one of the last reputable scientists to reject evolution outright for any period of time after the publication of Darwin's *On the Origin of Species.* Many of the phrases used by "creation scientists" can be found in the works of Agassiz.

Famed Harvard University paleontologist Louis Agassiz was among the last reputable scientists to adamantly reject evolution. (Library of Congress)

Aguillard, Don

High school biology teacher and nominal plaintiff who challenged Louisiana's "balanced-treatment" law in 1981. In 1987, the U.S. Supreme Court declared in *Edwards v. Aguillard* that the Louisiana law was unconstitutional.

Aquinas, St. Thomas (1225–1274)

Italian philosopher and theologian who founded the system declared by Pope Leo XIII to be the official Catholic philosophy. Aquinas is the greatest figure of scholasticism and was one of the first philosophers to merge science and theology in the thirteenth century, which ultimately led to the "Great Chain of Being." In this scheme, life led inexorably from simple organisms through increasingly complex animals to humans, and then to angels and God. The Great Chain was fixed; there was no movement from one link to another.

Aristotle (384–322 B.C.)

The first major theorist of science and foremost natural philosopher in the ancient world. Aristotle believed that to understand nature, one must explain the purpose of the event or structure that one is studying. Aristotle believed that the natural world is static, with each form of life having its own set position on a ladder of nature that reflected its degree of "perfection." Aristotle's ideas were unchallenged for centuries. By the time of the Renaissance more than 1,800 years later, Aristotle's scale of nature was absorbed into the "Great Chain of Being," an infinite graduation of species that stretched from the simplest forms of life to humans.

Bateson, William (1861–1926)

British biologist who realized that chromosomes must carry a variety of "factors" (i.e., genes) that control several characteristics. Bateson endorsed evolution but questioned its linkages with chromosome theory. In a famous address to the American Association for the Advancement of Science in Toronto in late 1921, Bateson described the origin and nature of species as "utterly mysterious." Bateson's comments were published in *Science* magazine, with Bateson's warning that they would by used by the "enemies of science." Bateson was right; reporters filed stories that told of the "collapse of Darwinism" and implied that Bateson supported religious and political leaders opposed to the teaching of evolution.

Behe, Michael

Biochemist and modern-day William Paley who in 1996 wrote *Darwin's Black Box*, a best-seller based on the type of arguments presented by Darwin's arch-foe, Louis Agassiz. Behe believes that Darwinian evolution cannot account for "molecular machines" and biochemical pathways that he calls "irreducibly complex." *Darwin's Black Box*, like Phillip Johnson's *Darwin on Trial*, argues for "intelligent design" yet admits that Darwin's model for evolution (i.e., natural selection operating on variability) can explain "many things." In 1997, *Christianity Today* declared *Darwin's Black Box* its "Book of the Year."

Bennett, Bruce

Arkansas attorney general and ardent segregationist who defended Arkansas' antievolution law when it was challenged by Susan Epperson in 1965. Bennett claimed that Epperson believed that humans "evolved from monkeys, apes, sharks, porpoises, seaweed, or any other form of animal or vegetable." He sensationalized the trial and attacked Epperson as someone who wanted to promote atheism, despite the fact that she was a devout Christian.

Bird, Wendell (1954–)

Leading architect of creationists' demands for "equal time" and "balanced treatment" in public schools. Bird devised his strategy in 1978 and subsequently worked at the Institute for Creation Research as a legal adviser. In the 1980s, Bird represented Louisiana in *Edwards v. Aguillard* as the state tried to protect its antievolution law. Bird's two-volume *The Origin of Species Revisited*, which in 1989 introduced euphemisms such as "theories of abrupt appearance," was an outgrowth of his experiences in the *Edwards* case.

Blanchard, Hubert H., Jr.

Associate executive secretary of the Arkansas Education Association who joined Susan Epperson's challenge to Arkansas' 1928 antievolution law. Blanchard claimed that the law diminished the quality of the education received by his two sons.

Bogard, Ben M.

Baptist preacher who believed that evolution had "been brought about by the John D. Rockefeller Foundation, which has been controlled by skeptics and infidels and atheists." Bogard, whose approach to the controversy resembled that of J. Frank Norris, gathered more than 19,000 signatures supporting antievolution legislation in Arkansas. In 1928, the legislation was supported by almost two-thirds of Arkansas voters and became law. Bogard created the American Anti-Evolution Association, which threatened to "blacklist" legislators who did not want to ban the teaching of evolution.

Brown, Arthur I. (1875–1947)

Preacher, surgeon, and public lecturer who, along with Harry Rimmer, was one of the most prolific creationist writers of the 1930s and 1940s. Brown's popularity as a creationist led him to abandon his lucrative medical practice to devote all his time to writing and lecturing about science and the Bible. Brown's popular books included *God's Masterpiece—Man's Body* (1946), *Footprints of God* (1943), and *Miracles of Science* (1945). Although often considered a biblical literalist, he believed that Earth is very old and that the Noachian flood was a regional event. Brown was a gap creationist (believing that after the first creation, life on Earth became extinct; after a long period, another supernatural creation of life occurred) but did not discuss gap creationism in his books.

Bruno, Giordano (1548–1600)

Dominican friar who was burned at the stake after a seven-year trial for, among other things, embracing the claims of Copernicus's heliocentric model of the solar system.

Bryan, William Jennings (1860–1925)

Three-time Democratic candidate for president, religious fundamentalist, newspaper editor (of the *Omaha World Herald*), editor (of the *Commoner*, a weekly paper with a circulation of 140,000), former secretary of state, and part of the team of lawyers who prosecuted John Scopes in 1925 in Dayton, Tennessee. Bryan was the only person to run as a major-party candidate for president three times without winning. As a politician, he stressed a variety of progressive ideas, including women's suffrage, direct election of senators, and minimum wage. Bryan was a relatively late convert to the antievolution cause, but he pursued the cause with typical zeal. Bryan often chided scientists with statements such as, "There is no more reason to believe that man descended from some inferior animal than there is to believe that a stately mansion has descended from a small cottage." Bryan's lectures in Nashville about biblical literalism and the moral failings of evolution in 1924 helped ensure the passage of the Butler Law, an antievolution law under which Scopes was prosecuted. Bryan's entry into the Scopes trial gave the controversy tornado-like dimensions; he proclaimed that he was in Dayton to defend revealed religion. Bryan, who rejected human evolution, argued that the "Bible-believing" majority should control public schools. Bryan disappointed fundamentalists when, called by Darrow as a witness on the seventh day of the Scopes trial, he admitted that he did not believe in a literal interpretation of the Bible. Bryan died five days after the Scopes trial and was buried in Arlington National Cemetery under the tiny inscription HE KEPT THE FAITH.

Bryan, William Jennings, Jr.

Son of William Jennings Bryan and part of the team of lawyers that prosecuted John Scopes in Dayton, Tennessee, in 1925. The young Bryan, a former assistant U.S. attorney in Arizona, also assisted the state when Scopes appealed his conviction in 1926–1927. Bryan later led a chapter of the Anti-Evolution League of America.

Buffon, Georges-Louis Leclerc de (1707–1788)

French scientist and aristocratic eccentric whose forty-four-volume illustrated *Histoire naturelle* speculated (in volume 4) that similar species might have come from the same original ancestor—that is, that life had evolved.[1] Unlike Carolus Linnaeus, Buffon rejected the idea that

Georges-Louis Leclerc de Buffon was one of the first people to suggest that the Earth is much older than 6,000 years. (Wellcome Institute Library, London)

life reflects a divine plan of creation. Although Buffon's claim came 100 years before Darwin, he could not provide a coherent mechanism for change; moreover, he often argued against evolution. In his *Les Epoques de la nature* in 1788, Buffon suggested that Earth is much older than 6,000 years. Buffon was the first person to formulate the modern concept of species as units that are reproductively isolated. Many of Buffon's ideas are similar to Charles Lyell's uniformitarianism, which was proposed forty years later. The Catholic church demanded that Buffon recant his ideas, but Buffon never got around to doing so.

Butler, John Washington

Tennessee farmer, preacher, and legislator who, fearing that his children would be corrupted by the public schools, drafted the antievolution legislation that became known as the "Butler Law" ("An Act Prohibiting the Teaching of the Evolution Theory . . ."). Butler justified his bill by arguing that "the evolutionist who denies the Bible story of creation, as well as other biblical accounts, cannot be a Christian. . . . I regard evolution to be the greatest menace to civilization in the world today." Butler's legislation was used to prosecute John Scopes in Dayton, Tennessee, in 1925. During Scopes's trial, Butler worked as a reporter and often dispatched poems.

Chambers, Robert (1802–1871)

Scottish writer, publisher, and amateur geologist who (anonymously) published the 400-page *Vestiges of the Natural History of Creation* in 1844, a popular and eccentric book that presented biological evolution (controlled by unknown laws) as steady upward progress. Chambers was acknowledged as the author of *Vestiges* in 1884, long after his death. Although *Vestiges* was attacked by scientists and theologians alike, it went through ten editions in ten years. Chambers's ideas about hereditary change may have been influenced by the fact that he and his brother were born with six digits on both hands and feet (the extra digits were removed when Chambers was a child, but the operation left him lame). *Vestiges* showed Darwin some obstacles he would have to overcome to gain acceptance of his own theory of evolution.

Chetverikov, Sergei S.

Russian geneticist who used sophisticated mathematical techniques to confirm his claim that variability would be most apparent in small populations. Chetverikov's conclusions, which became an important part of the "modern synthesis" in biology in the 1940s and were reached independently by Ronald A. Fisher, J. B. S. Haldane, and Sewall Wright, introduced the idea of gene pools as reservoirs of genetic variability based on the interactions of genes and the laws of probability.

Chick, Jack T.

Wrote and published *Big Daddy* in 1972, a comic-book tract in which a college student stands up to an obnoxious biology professor. The student hero reduces the professor to a babbling idiot. The nasty-toned tract is probably the most popular and widely distributed piece of creationist literature ever.

Clark, Steve

Arkansas attorney general who headed the state's defense of efforts to include "creation science" in public schools. In 1982, the state lost the case (*McLean v. Arkansas Board of Education*). Clark's handling of the case was denounced by Pat Robertson, Jerry Falwell, and others.

Clarke, Edward Young

Founder in 1926 of the Supreme Kingdom, a prominent antievolution organization linked with the Ku Klux Klan.

Copernicus, Nicolaus (1473–1543)

Polish prelate who in 1543 described a heliocentric solar system in his posthumous book *On the Revolutions of the Heavenly Spheres*. Copernicus's idea would be confirmed in Galileo's *The Starry Messenger* (1610) and *Di-*

alogue concerning the Two Chief World Systems (1632). Copernicus provided us with our modern view of the universe. Seventy-two years after its publication, *On the Revolutions of the Heavenly Spheres* was banned as heretical.

Cotton, Archie

Local coal mine operator and member of Tennessee's Campbell County Board of Education who in April 1967 charged science teacher Gary Scott with unprofessional conduct, neglect of duty, and violation of Tennessee's Butler Law. Cotton convinced the Board of Education to vote unanimously to fire Scott, which ultimately led to the repeal of the law.

Crowley, Dale Jr.

Sued the Smithsonian Foundation in 1978 to eliminate federal support for an evolution-based exhibit. His lawsuit (*Crowley v. Smithsonian Institution*) was dismissed in late 1978 by Judge Barrington Parker. Crowley's subsequent appeals to the U.S. District Court for the District of Columbia and the U.S. Supreme Court failed. Crowley believed that evolution is a "lie," "evil fraud," and "satanic plot" against God.

Georges Cuvier established the science of vertebrate paleontology but rejected evolution. (Archive Photos)

Cuvier, Baron Georges (1769–1832)

French Lutheran, scientist, and antievolutionist who established vertebrate paleontology as a scientific discipline and the fact of extinctions of past forms of life. Cuvier, who identified the first pterodactyl in the early 1800s as a flying reptile, knew Earth was immensely old. He rejected organic evolution; he believed that any similarities between organisms were due to common functions, not to common ancestry. In his twelve-volume *Researches on Fossil Bones*, Cuvier argued that a series of regional (not worldwide) "revolutions" (i.e., *catastrophes*, a word that Cuvier avoided because of its supernatural overtones) had wiped out species. Cuvier's "catastrophism" was later supplanted by James Hutton's and Charles Lyell's "uniformitarianism." Cuvier considered evolution to be "contrary to moral law, to the Bible, and to the progress of natural science itself." In his day, Cuvier was the most famous naturalist in Europe.

Darrow, Clarence S. (1857–1938)

Famous labor advocate who was the leading defender of John Scopes in Dayton, Tennessee, in July 1925. Darrow, an agnostic, was America's foremost criminal defense attorney of his day and was sixty-eight years old when John Scopes's trial began. At the time of the Scopes trial, Darrow was in high demand, despite the fact that he charged as much as $200,000 per case. He volunteered his services directly to Scopes and therefore could not be replaced by his critics at the American Civil Liberties Union. Scopes ignored the advice of many people in choosing Darrow, stating that "I know of no two lawyers in the country who are more capable of de-

Charles Darwin's On the Origin of Species remains one of the greatest books ever written. Although the book was not published until late 1859, Darwin was convinced of evolution much earlier; as he wrote in 1838, "Man in his arrogance thinks himself a great work worthy the interposition of a deity. More humble and I think truer to consider him created from animals." (Library of Congress)

fending a great cause than Mr. Darrow and Mr. Malone." When Darrow returned to Dayton several years after the Scopes trial and saw a church being built across the street from Robinson's Drugstore, he commented that "I guess I didn't do much good after all." Scopes's case was the only case for which Darrow ever volunteered his services. At the trial, Darrow promoted secularism more than individual freedom. His entry into the Scopes trial determined the direction of the defense; his questioning of William Jennings Bryan provided an incomparable opportunity to dramatize the issues associated with the trial.

Darwin, Charles (1809–1882)

Author of *On the Origin of Species by Means of Natural Selection; Or, The Preservation of Favoured Races in the Struggle for Life*, the most influential book in the history of biology. Darwin's ideas were shaped by decades of scientific investigations (e.g., his voyage as the de facto naturalist aboard the 90-foot-long HMS *Beagle* from 1831 to 1836), as well as by how he could transfer the laissez-faire economic principles of Adam Smith to nature. Darwin developed the idea of natural selection (chapter 4 of *Origin*) as a mechanism for evolutionary change in 1838, but—like his grandfather Erasmus—did not publish his ideas for more than twenty years. *Origin*, published in 1859, refuted teleology and purpose as explanations of life's diversity and suggested that humans are not exempt from processes that affect other organisms. *Origin* did not contain the word *evolution*; instead, Darwin used the word *transmutation* (the more common phrase during his time) or his own preferred phrase, *descent with modification*. Before his death in 1882, Darwin produced six editions of *Origin* (each including some changes to clarify his ideas and some to answer critics)[2] and published eight more books, including *The Descent of Man and Selection in Relation to Sex* (1871), *The Expression of the Emotions in Man and Animals* (1872), and *The Variation of Animals and Plants under Domestication* (1868). Darwin, who believed that evolution by natural selection is proven "beyond reasonable doubt," died forty-three years before the Scopes trial.

Darwin, Erasmus (1731–1802)

Charles Darwin's freethinking grandfather who, while not stating that adaptation occurs via natural selection, suggested that animals may evolve via active adaptation to the environment, including the inheritance of acquired characteristics. As his grandson Charles would do decades later, Erasmus waited almost twenty years before publishing his book *Zoonomia*, which contained a poetic dissertation about evolution. Although Erasmus was probably the first confirmed evolutionist, grandson Charles was not impressed by Erasmus's work.

Darwin, George (1845–1912)

Charles Darwin's son and one of several scientists who used Antoine-Henri Becquerel's (1852–1908) discoveries about radiation to show that Earth is approximately 4.6 billion years old, which is much older than Lord Kelvin (1824–1907) claimed.

Dawkins, Richard (1941–)

Oxford biologist whose popular book titled *The Blind Watchmaker* in 1986 refuted "intelligent design." Dawkins became the arch-enemy of creationists by making statements such as "I am against religion because it teaches us to be satisfied with not understanding the world," and "Religions do make claims about the universe—the same kinds of claims that science makes, except they're usually wrong."

Dobzhansky, Theodosius Gregorievitch (1900–1975)

Russian émigré whose work with Thomas Hunt Morgan, Alfred Sturtevant, and Sewall Wright culminated in *Genetics and the Origin of Species* (1937). This book combined experimental genetics, mathematical analyses, and naturalists' evolutionary views and, in the process, stimulated a flurry of work that ultimately established the "modern synthesis." Dobzhansky later argued that "nothing in biology makes sense except in the light of evolution," and that biology without evolution is "a pile of sundry facts—some of them interesting or curious but making no meaningful picture as a whole."

Television evangelist and creationist Jerry Falwell helped trigger the revival of creationism in the late 1900s. (Institute for Creation Research)

Duplantier, Adrian

Presiding judge in U.S. District Court who in 1985 ruled that Louisiana's "balanced-treatment" law was unconstitutional. Duplantier's decision would be upheld in 1987 by the U.S. Supreme Court in *Edwards v. Aguillard.*

Eldredge, Niles

American paleontologist who, with Stephen Jay Gould, announced in 1972 the theory of punctuated equilibrium, which holds that evolution proceeds through relatively short bursts of rapid change followed by long periods of stasis.

Ellington, Buford (1907–1972)

Tennessee governor who in April 1967 signed the legislation that repealed the Butler Law, thereby making it legal to teach human evolution in Tennessee.

Ellwanger, Paul

Used Wendell Bird's proposal for "equal time" and "balanced treatment" as a means of trying to introduce "creation science" into public schools. Ellwanger founded Citizens for Fairness in Education, "a citizen group, national in scope, who favor academic freedom and are opposed to suppression of information about evolution and creation." Ellwanger's efforts convinced numerous state legislatures to debate granting equal time to creationism. The creation science movement culminated in 1981 with *McLean v. Arkansas Board of Education,* which declared, among other things, that creation science is not science.

Epperson, Susan (1941–)

Biology teacher at Little Rock Central High School who in 1965 challenged the antievolution law in Arkansas. Epperson's case (*Epperson v. Arkansas*) would eventually reach the U.S. Supreme Court, which in 1968 ruled unanimously that laws banning the teaching of evolution in public schools are unconstitutional.

Falwell, Jerry (1933–)

Fundamentalist preacher and founder of Liberty University in Lynchburg, Virginia. The university's Center for Creation Studies has a creationism-based biology education program that is accredited by the Virginia Board of Education to train teachers. Falwell merged the religious and political worlds in 1979 when he formed Moral Majority (in 1989 he disbanded the organization). Falwell and his followers view the teaching of evolution in public schools as one of the major problems in society.

Faubus, Orval (1910–1994)

Arkansas governor and ardent segregationist who campaigned against Susan Epperson's challenge of the state's antievolution law. In 1957, Faubus gained national attention when he used the Arkansas National Guard to block the integration of Central High School in Little Rock.

Ferguson, Miriam A. "Ma" (1875–1961)

Texas governor who in 1925 ordered the state's textbook commission to delete the theory of evolution from its high school biology books. For years, this ban forced publishers to produce special, sanitized books for Texas.

Ferguson, W. F.

Full-time biology teacher at Rhea County High School who in 1925 refused to participate in a test of Tennessee's antievolution law. Local businesspeople then convinced substitute teacher John Scopes to test the law.

Fisher, Larry

Creationist and math teacher who sent the "balanced-presentation" resolution of the Institute for Creation Research to Tom Hardin, the superintendent of the Pulaski (AR) County Special School District. Fisher's lobbying ultimately led to passage of "Act 590: Balanced Treatment for Creation Science and Evolution Science" in Arkansas, which was overturned in 1982 by *McLean v. Arkansas Board of Education*.

Fisher, Ronald A. (1890–1962)

British biologist who used mathematical models to predict the effects of natural selection. Although many biologists believed that Darwin's gradualism was not consistent with Mendelian genetics, Fisher statistically reconciled Mendelian inheritance with natural selection by showing that natural selection could produce the range of variation present in life. Fisher's seminal work was *The Genetical Theory of Natural Selection* in 1930.

FitzRoy, Robert (1805–1865)

Captain of the HMS *Beagle* who recruited Charles Darwin as an educated companion for the *Beagle*'s five-year voyage. FitzRoy later criticized Darwin for his ideas about natural selection.

Fortas, Abe (1910–1982)

U.S. Supreme Court justice who in 1968 wrote the majority opinion in *Epperson v. Arkansas*. Fortas had followed the Scopes trial as a high school

student. In 1969, Fortas became the first justice to resign from the Supreme Court after it was revealed that he had accepted $20,000 from a private foundation.

Freiler, Herb

Lead plaintiff in *Freiler v. Tangipahoa Board of Education*, in which the U.S. District Court for the Eastern District of Louisiana ruled in 1997 that (1) proposals for teaching "intelligent design" are equivalent to teaching "creation science" and (2) it is unlawful to force teachers to read aloud disclaimers saying that the biblical version of creation is the only concept "from which students are not to be dissuaded." This ruling was affirmed by the U.S. Court of Appeals on 19 August 1999 and by the U.S. Supreme Court on 19 June 2000.

Duane Gish, a creationist who became famous by effectively debating scientists. Gish's last debate was in 2001. (Institute for Creation Research)

Gabler, Mel and Norma

Self-appointed textbook censors who founded the influential Educational Research Analysts in Longview, Texas. The Gablers began monitoring textbooks in 1963, and their strong antievolution beliefs convinced many publishers to weaken the coverage of evolution in their textbooks. In 1985, the Gablers claimed that Soviet writers worked on the BSCS biology textbooks.

Galilei, Galileo (1564–1642)

First scientist to raise a telescope to the sky and, in the process, start the scientific revolution that transformed ancient natural philosophy into modern science. Galileo endorsed Copernicus's theory of a Sun-centered solar system in 1610 in his book titled *The Starry Messenger.* When he again deposed Earth from a central position in his 1632 book *Dialogue concerning the Two Chief World Systems*, he was called before the commissary general of the Vatican's Holy Office (known unofficially as "the Inquisition"). Hoping to avoid Giordano Bruno's fate, Galileo recanted his theory and spent the last six years of his life under house arrest. Galileo's *Dialogue* was not removed from the Catholic Church's list of banned books until 1757.

Gish, Duane T. (1921–)

One-time science professor and now senior vice president of the Institute for Creation Research, who became a prominent creationist in the late 1900s. In 1972, Gish wrote *Evolution? The Fossils Say No!*, a creationist sourcebook that includes many quotes by scientists critical of evolution.

Gosse, Philip H. (1810–1888)

English religious naturalist who developed the omphalos theory, which denied that there had been a gradual modification of Earth: "When the catastrophic act of creation took place, the world presented instantly the structural appearance of a planet in which life had long existed."

Gould, Stephen Jay (1941–)

American paleontologist who, in 1972, announced the theory of punctuated equilibrium, which holds that evolution proceeds through relatively short bursts of rapid change followed by long periods of stasis. Gould became one of the most effective and articulate advocates for evolution education.

Gray, Asa (1810–1888)

Prominent botanist, Harvard professor, and evangelical Christian who was Charles Darwin's chief supporter in the United States. Gray met Darwin in London in 1839 and again in 1850, but they did not correspond with each other until 1856. A letter from Darwin to Gray in 1857 was part of the 1858 Darwin/Wallace paper. Gray, who espoused a progressive, God-driven evolution, arranged for the initial publication of Darwin's *Origin* in the United States. Gray believed that nature is filled with "unmistakable and irresistable indications of design" and that "God himself is the very last, irreducible causal factor and, hence, the source of all evolutionary change." Gray's textbook *First Lessons in Botany and Vegetable Physiology* was the first high school textbook to include Darwin's ideas about evolution. After the publication of *Origin*, Gray devoted himself to spreading Darwin's ideas in America and to overcoming the creationist ideas of Louis Agassiz, his colleague at Harvard.

Asa Gray, despite his endorsement of "intelligent design," was Darwin's strongest supporter in the United States following the publication of On the Origin of Species. *(Library of Congress)*

Grose, Vernon (1928–)

In 1969, Grose asked that California's curriculum guidelines be changed to include creationism. Grose's complaints resulted in evolution being diminished or eliminated from the state's textbooks and triggered years of debate and legal wrangling about evolution and creationism in California.

Guyot, Arnold (1807–1884)

New Jersey geologist who believed that the Earth was ancient, but that Genesis I provided a broad outline of the Earth's history. Each "day" of the Genesis story represented a long period of geological time. Like Asa Gray, Guyot rejected human evolution. Guyot's ideas became known as day-age creationism. Guyot had introduced the discipline of scientific geography to America and was one of the last prominent scientists who did not fully accept evolution in the 1880s.

Haeckel, Ernst H. (1834–1919)

Zoologist who became a prolific and vocal supporter of evolution. After reading Darwin's *Origin*, Haeckel quit his medical practice and attacked entrenched religious dogma. Haeckel is best known for his famous statement "Ontogeny recapitulates phylogeny," but he also coined such terms as *phylum* and *ecology*. Haeckel, who believed that evolution inevitably leads to increased complexity, popularized "evolutionary trees" as ways of showing how species might have split and evolved into groups that we recognize today. Nazis used Haeckel's ideas and statements (e.g., "Politics is applied biology") to justify racism, nationalism, and social Darwinism.

Haggard, Wallace

Part of the team of lawyers that prosecuted John Scopes in Dayton, Tennessee, in 1925. After losing virtually everything in the Great Depression, Haggard committed suicide.

Haldane, John B. S. (1892–1964)

British geneticist who formulated a mathematical approach to the study of evolution that led to biologists being able to estimate the rates of genetic changes in populations. Haldane, a Marxist and popularizer of science, was one of the most influential scientists of the twentieth century. He predicted human cloning and hailed its potential uses.

Ham, Kenneth A. (1951–)

Executive director of Answers in Genesis, an influential and well-funded creationist organization based near Cincinnati, Ohio. In 2002, Answers in Genesis will open a $14 million, 95,000–square foot Creation Museum and Family Discovery Center at a 47-acre complex in Kentucky.

Hays, Arthur Garfield (1881–1954)

American Civil Liberties Union attorney and part of the team of lawyers that defended John Scopes in Dayton, Tennessee, in 1925. A law partner of Dudley Field Malone, Hays, who had challenged censorship laws and later defended Jews in Nazi Germany charged with burning the Reichstag, was in charge of the defense team's strategy. During the trial, Hays objected to the introduction of the Bible into evidence, arguing that the King James Version that had been introduced represented only one of several different versions of Scripture. This surprised many in the audience (including John Butler) who did not know that there were different versions of the Bible.

Hendren, Jon

Sued the West Clark (Indiana) school board in 1977, claiming that the use of the creationist textbook *Biology: A Search for Order in Complexity* was unconstitutional. In *Hendren v. Campbell*, the court agreed with Hendren. The decision was not appealed.

Henslow, Reverend John Stevens (1796–1861)

Botany professor at Cambridge who befriended Charles Darwin and was responsible for his appointment to the *Beagle*. Henslow, an obstinate creationist who maintained a lifelong correspondence with Darwin, chaired the 1860 British Association for the Advancement of Science meeting at which Thomas Huxley argued for Darwin's ideas.

Hicks, Herbert and Sue

Part of the team of lawyers that prosecuted John Scopes in Dayton, Tennessee, in 1925. Sue Hicks, named after his mother who died at his birth, later became a judge and was immortalized as the original "Boy Named Sue" of the Johnny Cash hit song.

Holsted, James

A self-described "born-again fundamentalist" who in 1981 introduced legislation promoting the teaching of "creation science" in public schools. The efforts culminated in 1982 in *McLean v. Arkansas Board of Education*, which declared, among other things, that creation science is not science.

Hooker, Sir Joseph Dalton (1817–1911)

Botanist and close friend of Charles Darwin who founded the science of plant geography.[3] Hooker was the first person to whom Darwin showed the outline of his theory of natural selection in 1844 and an essay describing it in 1847. Although he initially had misgivings about Darwin's ideas, Hooker became one of Darwin's most prominent advocates. Hooker, with Charles Lyell, arranged for the publication of the Darwin/Wallace paper in 1858.

Houghton, William H. (1887–1947)

President of the Moody Bible Institute who in 1940 blamed universities for causing people to replace traditional faith with Darwinism and Marxism. Houghton believed that Nazism was produced by evolution and materialism.

Hume, David (1711–1776)

Scottish philosopher, diplomat, and skeptic whose *Dialogues Concerning Natural Religion* (1779) refuted the "intelligent-design" argument later made popular by many creationists. Hume also argued that we cannot establish that relations of cause and effect exist in the external world.

Hunter, George W.

Author of the best-selling *A Civic Biology: Presented in Problems*, the state-adopted and racist textbook used by John Scopes when he was a substitute biology teacher in Dayton, Tennessee, in 1925. Hunter was a teacher at New York's De-Witt Clinton High School.

Hutton, James (1726–1797)

Scottish farmer and geologist who argued in his densely verbose *Theory of the Earth* (1795) that Earth is constantly yet imperceptibly changing. Hutton, one of the first people to convincingly challenge that Earth is only 6,000 years old, became known for his famous statement that rocks of the Earth provide "no vestige of a beginning, no prospect of an end." Hutton's ideas, which were largely overlooked by his immediate contemporaries, became known as "uniformitarianism," the doctrine that the distant past is best explained by common forces that operate today. Hutton's uniformitarianism directly opposed Georges Cuvier's catastrophism and was an inspiration to Darwin's thinking that led to *Origin*.

Thomas Henry Huxley was Charles Darwin's most vocal supporter in England. (Haeckel-Haus, Jena)

Huxley, Thomas H. (1825–1895)

Zoologist and teacher whose ideas about evolution were molded, like Darwin's, aboard a voyage of a Royal Navy surveying ship (HMS *Rattlesnake*, 1846–1850). After qualifying as a physician, Huxley was a professor at the Royal School of Mines in London and later at the Royal College of Surgeons. When Darwin's *Origin* was published, Huxley became an immediate convert, noting, "How extremely stupid [of me] not to have thought of that." Huxley became an advocate for Darwin in England (and was thus nicknamed "Darwin's Bulldog"), most notably at the 1860 meeting of the British Association for the Advancement of Science in Oxford, when he debated the bishop of Oxford and had several battles with Richard Owen.

Huxley wrote numerous books (e.g., *Evolution and Ethics*, 1893) and held numerous public offices.

Johannsen, Wilhelm (1857–1927)
Danish botanist who coined the term *gene* in 1909.

Johnson, Phillip E.
Author of *Darwin on Trial*, an argument for "intelligent design" and one of the most influential creationism books in the late 1900s. Johnson is a chaired professor at the University of California's Boalt Hall Law School and was a former clerk to Chief Justice Earl Warren.

Keith, William
Louisiana state legislator and old-earth creationist who in 1981 introduced what would become the state's "balanced-treatment" law requiring that "creation science" be taught side by side with evolution. That law was declared unconstitutional in 1987 by the U.S. Supreme Court in *Edwards v. Aguillard*. Keith claimed that Darwinian evolution is the "greatest hoax of the twentieth century" and is a fairy tale like the Easter Bunny and Tooth Fairy.

Kellogg, Vernon L. (1867–1937)
Author of *Headquarters Nights*, a book that convinced William Jennings Bryan that German militarists had used evolutionary theory to justify their actions and lead people away from Christianity. Kellogg, a zoologist, studied insects and was well-known for his interpretations of science for laypeople.

Kidd, Benjamin
Author of *The Science of Power*, a book that convinced William Jennings Bryan that German militarists had used evolutionary theory to justify their actions and lead people away from Christianity.

Kramer, Stanley (1913–2001)
Director of the 1960 movie version of *Inherit the Wind*.

Kunstler, William M.
Famed attorney who represented Tennessee science teacher Gary Scott when Scott was fired for allegedly teaching evolution in 1967. Scott's lawsuit ultimately prompted the Tennessee legislature to repeal the state's anti-evolution law.

LaHaye, Tim F. (1926–)
Founder of Christian Heritage College, sponsored by the Scott Memorial Baptist Church complex and including the Creation Science Research Cen-

ter. The Center publishes materials such as Robert Kofahl's *Handy Dandy Evolution Refuter.* LaHaye, the leader of Californians for a Biblical Majority, wrote several best-selling "end time" books in the late 1990s.

Lamarck, Jean-Baptiste-Pierre-Antoine de Monet de (Chevalier de Lamarck) (1744–1829)

French naturalist and protégé of Georges-Louis Buffon who was the first to publish a reasoned theory of evolution (or *transformation*, as it was called then) in 1809 in his major work *Philosophie zoologique*, which supported his theory of evolution with some of the same evidence that Darwin would later use in *Origin*. Lamarck believed unequivocally in evolution; as he stated, "Species have only a limited or temporary constancy in their characters, and . . . there is no species which is absolutely constant."

Jean Baptiste de Lamarck was among the first to claim that changes in species could result from natural laws rather than miracles. (Wellcome Institute Library, London)

Lamarck believed that evolution is a process of "gradually complicating and perfecting not only the organism as a whole, but each system or organ in particular." *Lamarckism* is now often used derogatorily to refer to the idea that acquired traits can be inherited, as suggested earlier by Erasmus Darwin; as Lamarck wrote, "We know that [a giraffe], the tallest of mammals, dwells in the interior of Africa, in places where the soil, almost always arid and with herbage, obliges it to browse on trees and to strain itself continuously to reach them. This habit sustained for long, has had the result in all members of its race that the forelegs have grown longer than the hind legs and that its neck has become so stretched, that the giraffe, without standing on its hind legs, lifts its head to the height of six meters." Lamarck, who introduced the terms *biology* and *Invertebrata*, was among the first to propose that changes in species could be the result of natural laws rather than miraculous interposition. Although Charles Darwin, Charles Lyell, and others admired Lamarck, his ideas were attacked and vilified (especially by Baron Cuvier) during his lifetime. Lamarck, who named the invertebrates and did not believe in extinction (he believed that species that disappeared did so because they evolved into different species), died in poverty and obscurity.

Lang, Walter (1913–)
Missouri Synod Lutheran preacher who in 1963 founded the Bible Science Association to support scientific creationism. Despite its name, the association has always been a society of nonscientists. The Bible Science Association, along with the Creation Research Society, convinced people that they did not have to accept evolution in order to be scientific and modern.

Langston, Don
Arkansas assistant attorney general who in 1968 argued unenthusiastically and unsuccessfully in *Epperson v. Arkansas* for the validity of Arkansas' antievolution law before the U.S. Supreme Court.

Lawrence, Jerome
Coauthor of *Inherit the Wind*, a fictional account of the Scopes trial.

LeConte, Joseph (1823–1901)
Famed geologist and student of Louis Agassiz who claimed that species are the products of divine intelligence. According to LeConte, the "transmutation of species was as impossible as the transmutation of metals." LeConte's *Evolution and Its Relation to Religious Thought* in 1888 merged neo-Lamarckism and design and rejected explanations based on natural selection.

Lee, Robert E.
Coauthor of *Inherit the Wind*, a fictional account of the Scopes trial.

Leonardo da Vinci (1452–1519)
Italian painter, sculptor, architect, engineer, and scientist who, when noting that fossil shells in the Alps were often found in pairs and rows, concluded that "if the shells had been carried by the muddy deluge they would have been mixed up, and not in the regular steps and layers, as we see them now in our time." In 1508, Leonardo rejected claims involving a universal flood.

Leuba, James H. (1868–1946)
Bryn Mawr College psychologist who reported in *The Belief in God and Immorality* that many students had lost their religious faith during college after being exposed to modern ideas. Leuba's work helped convince William Jennings Bryan to become involved in the antievolution campaign.

Lightfoot, John (1602–1675)
Contemporary of James Ussher who, as vice-chancellor of Cambridge University, claimed in his wonderfully titled pamphlet *A Few, and New Observations, Upon the Book of Genesis; The Most of Them Certain, the Rest of*

them Probable, All Harmless, Strange, and Rarely Heard of Before that the final act of creation was the genesis of the human race at 9:00 A.M. on Sunday, 23 October 4004 B.C. Lightfoot based his conclusion on genealogies of Genesis 5 and 11 and the assumption that creation would have occurred on the autumnal equinox.

Linnaeus, Carolus (Carl von Linné) (1707–1778)

Swedish naturalist and energetic traveler who laid the foundation of systematic biology with his binomial system of naming and classifying plants and animals. Linnaeus was not an evolutionist; on the contrary, his ever-expanding *Systema Naturae* (which started as a slim pamphlet and later expanded to several volumes) was an attempt to reflect the divine plan of creation. In *Systema Naturae*, Linnaeus writes that, "It is remarkable that the stupidest ape differs so little from the wisest man, that the surveyor of nature has yet to be found who can draw the line between them." However, Linnaeus's system of classification is readily adapted to evolutionary interpretations. Modern botanical nomenclature dates from Linnaeus's *Species Plantarum* (1753) and zoological nomenclature from *Systema Naturae* (10th ed., 1758). Linnaeus was also known as Carl Linné (of which Carolus Linnaeus is a Latinized version); when he was ennobled in 1761 he formally adopted the name Carl von Linné.

Lyell, Charles (1797–1875)

Geologist and sometime lawyer whose three-volume *The Principles of Geology, Being an Attempt to Explain the Earth's Surface by Reference to Causes Now in Operation* (1830) described for the first time the story of a very old Earth having species that are constantly becoming extinct as others emerge. As the title of his book suggests, Lyell believed that Earth's features could be explained by forces now in operation. As Thomas Huxley noted, "I cannot but believe that Lyell was for others, as for me, the chief agent in smoothing the road for Darwin." Lyell's ideas, considered by many to be the foundation of modern geology, solidified James Hutton's uniformitarianism as a theory without which Charles Darwin's theory of natural selection would have been impossible. Lyell's ideas greatly influenced Darwin's formulation of his theory of evolution by natural selection. Darwin appealed to Lyell for advice when he received Alfred Wallace's manuscript in 1858. There was no other person whom Charles Darwin admired as greatly as Lyell.

Lysenko, Trofim D. (1898–1976)

Prominent Russian scientist and charlatan who promised quick, easy, and fallacious ways of obtaining desired genetic results. Lysenko, the leader of the Soviet school of genetics, rejected Gregor Mendel and Charles Darwin as capitalistic, thereby blocking the advancement of science in a world power.

Malone, Dudley Field (1882–1950)

Law partner of Arthur Garfield Hays and part of the team that defended John Scopes in Dayton, Tennessee, in 1925. Malone's stirring speech defending academic freedom and free speech on the fifth day of the Scopes trial was described by William Jennings Bryan as "the greatest speech I've ever heard." The *New York Times* reprinted the speeches by Malone and Bryan, calling them the "greatest debate on science and religion in recent years." After the Scopes trial, Malone spent a decade as a Hollywood actor.

Malthus, Thomas R. (1766–1834)

Author of *Essay on the Principle of Population*, a classic in British political economy that warned in 1798 that populations of all organisms increase geometrically, whereas the ability of humans to increase their food supply increases only arithmetically. Malthus wrote that "Population, when unchecked, increases in a geometrical ratio. Subsistence increases only in an arithmetical ratio. A slight acquaintance with numbers will show the immensity of the first power in comparison of the second, "and that, "As many more individuals of each species are born than can possibly survive . . . it follows that any being, if it vary ever so slightly in a manner profitable to itself . . . will have a better chance of survival, and thus be naturally selected." Malthus's *Essay*, which Charles Darwin read in 1838 "for pleasure," told how suffering and misery are part of nature and that famines and plagues are nature's way of controlling the sizes of populations. Over time, Malthus's essay was associated with repressive measures against the poor, but Malthus advocated more humane solutions (e.g., education to reduce family size). In September 1838, Darwin read the sixth edition of Malthus's pamphlet, which had been published in 1826. Malthus's conclusions were a key part of Darwin's hypothesis that evolution occurs by natural selection.

Martin, Thomas T. (1862–1939)

Itinerant Southern Baptist preacher, professor, and author of *Hell and the High Schools: Christ or Evolution—Which?*, a book that described many aspects of William Jennings Bryan's opposition to the teaching of human evolution. In 1926, Martin helped secure passage of an antievolution law in Mississippi, and later he was active in the Anti-Evolution League of America and the Bible Crusaders of America.

Mayr, Ernst (1904–)

Ornithologist and systematist whose 1942 masterwork *Systematics and the Origin of Species* argues that geographic isolation and small selective advantages can be evolutionarily significant. Mayr's work, heavily influenced by that of Theodosius Dobzhansky, formed part of the "modern synthesis" of biology which linked the theories of Charles Darwin and Gregor Mendel.

McElwee, F. B.
Part of the team of lawyers that defended John Scopes in Dayton, Tennessee, in 1925.

McKenzie, Ben
Part of the team of lawyers that prosecuted John Scopes in Dayton, Tennessee, in 1925. McKenzie later became friends with Clarence Darrow and hosted Darrow's return to Dayton in 1938.

McKenzie, J. Gordon
Son of Ben McKenzie and part of the team of lawyers that prosecuted John Scopes in Dayton, Tennessee, in 1925.

McLean, Bill
Methodist minister who opposed the introduction of "creation science" into Arkansas' public schools in the early 1980s. McLean was the nominal plaintiff in *McLean v. Arkansas Board of Education.*

McPherson, Aimee Semple (1890–1944)
Prominent fundamentalist preacher who, like many others, attacked evolution as the source of societal ills in the early 1900s. McPherson died as a result of an overdose of sleeping pills.

McVey, Frank
President of the University of Kentucky who argued forcefully against the passage of an antievolution bill in 1922. McVey's advocacy impressed John Scopes, who in 1925 agreed to be arrested to test the validity of an antievolution law in Tennessee.

Mencken, H. L. (1880–1956)
Caustic journalist and critic who covered the Scopes trial for the *Baltimore Sun.* At the time of Scopes's trial, Mencken was America's best-known journalist; his columns often attacked censorship, prohibition, and other attempts to purify the United States. Mencken was bombastic; he referred to William Jennings Bryan as "a charlatan, a mountebank, a zany without shame or dignity" and likened the trial to a "religious orgy." Mencken coined the enduring description of the Scopes trial as "the Monkey Trial." He also described the South as "the Bible Belt," another phrase that remains common today. In the 1960s, Scopes said, "In a way, [my trial] was Mencken's

show." Mencken's thirteen essays about the trial are considered by many to be masterpieces of journalism.

Mendel, Gregor J. (1822–1884)
Austrian monk whose studies of inheritance in the garden pea (*Pisum sativum*) laid the foundation of modern genetics. Mendel published his work in 1866, but it was not recognized widely until it was "rediscovered" in 1900.

Minor, Virginia
A kindergarten teacher in Little Rock, Arkansas, who in 1965 helped convince Susan Epperson to challenge Arkansas's antievolution law.

Moore, John N. (1920–)
Prominent creationist and coeditor of *Biology: A Search for Order in Complexity* (1970). This procreationism and antievolution biology textbook, developed by the Creation Research Society, was adopted by a variety of schools, but its use in public schools was later declared unconstitutional. Moore later claimed that evolution leads to communism and that evolution is "mathematically impossible and really quite irrational."

Morgan, Howard
Student of John Scopes who testified at Scopes's trial in Dayton, Tennessee, in 1925. Morgan was the son of a Dayton banker who let Clarence Darrow and his wife use his family's home during the trial.

Morgan, Thomas Hunt (1866–1945)
Drosophila geneticist at Columbia University whose work (along with that of Alfred Sturtevant, Calvin Bridges, and Nobel laureate Hermann Muller) helped produce a new theory of heredity. Morgan's work, disseminated widely in *The Mechanism of Mendelian Heredity* (1915), helped revitalize Darwinism, explained many of the old problems with heredity, and later became a major part of the "modern synthesis." Morgan received the 1933 Nobel Prize in Physiology or Medicine.

Morris, Henry (1918–)
Virginia Tech engineering professor and creationist who in 1961 coauthored (with theologian John Whitcomb of Grace Theological Seminary) *The Genesis Flood: The Biblical Record and Its Scientific Implications*, a biblically orthodox book that revived George McCready Price's flood geology, ignited the creationist movement in the late twentieth century, and became a foundation for creationists' demands for "equal time" in classrooms. While

studying hydraulic engineering at Rice University in the 1930s, Morris was a theistic evolutionist. Later, however, he became a biblical literalist. In 1970, Morris cofounded the Creation Science Research Center and the Creation Research Society, which produced procreationism and antievolution textbooks. In 1975, Morris drafted an "equal-time" resolution that would later be used by Wendell Bird to promote the creationists' cause. In *The Troubled Waters of Evolution* (1982), Morris claimed that "Satan himself is the originator of the concept of evolution." Morris, a prolific writer, admits that the purpose of his many books is to help people find Jesus. In the late 1900s, no one did more to popularize "scientific creationism" and "creation science" than Morris and his colleagues at the Institute for Creation Research.

Henry Morris transformed George McCready Price's "flood geology" into "creation science" and became the most famous and influential creationist of the second half of the twentieth century. (Institute for Creation Research)

Neal, John R. (1876–1959)
Part of the team of lawyers that defended John Scopes in Dayton, Tennessee, in 1925. Neal was also the chief counsel of record when Scopes appealed his conviction in 1926–1927. Neal's mishandling of the appeal limited Scopes's options during the appeal.

Norris, J. Frank (John Franklin) (1877–1952)
Fiery Fort Worth, Texas, preacher and champion of the antievolution movement. In 1922, Norris began making sensational attacks on gambling, drinking, dancing, and the Rockefellers. A product of Baylor University, Norris exposed the teaching of evolution at Baylor University and elsewhere, and in 1923, he convinced the Texas state legislature to consider a bill censoring textbooks that discuss evolution. In 1925, Norris—who feared Catholics and hated Jews—turned the attention of the Southern Baptist Convention to evolution. He succeeded in driving proevolution professors from Baylor and Southern Methodist University. In that same year, Norris's church became the world's largest Baptist church (its congregation exceeded 8,000), but he was tried for (and acquitted of) murdering D. E Chipps in 1926. Although Norris tried to use the trial to increase his popularity, his influence soon faded.

Oparin, Aleksandr Ivanovich

Russian biochemist who argued in *The Origin of Life* that life originated through chemical evolution of pre-living organisms. Oparin, a key figure in Russian science, was a strong supporter of Trofim Lysenko.

Overton, William R. (1939–1987)

Presiding judge at *McLean v. Arkansas Board of Education.* Overton's devastating critique of creationism and "creation science" in 1982 doomed future legal efforts by creationists involving creation science. Although Overton's decision was denounced by creationists, it was not appealed.

Owen, Richard (1804–1892)

British anatomist and student of Georges Cuvier who campaigned against Charles Darwin. Owen did not dismiss evolution, but he could not accept natural selection over divine guidance. Owen, who coined the term *dinosaur,* introduced the concepts of homology and analogy of animal structure. Owen predicted that Darwin's work would be forgotten within a decade.

Richard Owen, a vocal critic of Charles Darwin, believed that Darwin's work would have no significant impact. (Way We Were)

Paley, William (1743–1805)

English Anglican clergyman and articulate defender of Christian faith whose popular 1802 treatise *Natural Theology: Or, Evidences of the Existence and Attributes of the Deity, Collected from the Appearances of Nature* was an influential argument for natural design, a popular claim of creationists. Paley's book was written to counter arguments like those made by David Hume in *Dialogues Concerning Natural Religion.* Paley believed that changes in organisms are unnecessary and unthinkable. Reverend Archdeacon Paley argued that living organisms are so complex and well fitted to their tasks that they could have been fashioned only by infallible design; the complexity of nature is thus evidence of God and God's involvement in shaping living things. Paley's treatise, which included the famous analogy about a watch and watchmaker, stated: "Were there no example except that of the eye, it would be alone sufficient to support the conclusion which we draw from it, as to the necessity of an intelligent Creator. . . . The marks of design are too strong to be gotten over. Design must have a designer. That designer must have been a person. That person is God." In 1794, Paley published *View of the Evidences of Christianity,* in which he argued that the New Testament's miracles prove the existence of God.

Parker, Barrington D.

District judge who in *Crowley v. Smithsonian Institution* rejected the claim that the Smithsonian Institution had to provide equal time to the biblical story of creation in its exhibits. Parker noted that the Smithsonian's exhibits about evolution did not restrict anyone's exercise of religion.

Peay, Austin (1876–1927)

Tennessee Democrat governor who signed Tennessee's antievolution law (also known as the "Butler Law") on 21 March 1925. Although Tennessee newspaper editors called the legislation "a jackass measure," Peay signed the bill—the most famous of all the antievolution bills—because it was popular and represented his "deep and widespread belief that something is shaking the fundamentals of the country, both in religion and morals. . . . An abandonment of the old-fashioned faith and belief in the Bible is our trouble in large degree. . . . The people have the right and must have the right to regulate what is taught in their schools." The Butler Law made it a crime to teach human evolution in Tennessee and led to the prosecution of John Scopes in Dayton, Tennessee, four months later. There was no opposition to the Butler Law before it became law. John Scopes was the only teacher ever charged with violating the Butler Law. The law was not repealed until 1967.

Peloza, John E.

High school biology teacher who sued the Capistrano Unified School District and various individuals associated with the district, alleging that the district forced him to teach "evolutionism" and that evolution is a religious belief. In 1994, the Ninth Circuit Court of Appeals upheld a district court's ruling that a teacher's First Amendment rights to freedom of speech are not violated by a district's requirement that evolution be taught in biology classes (*John E. Peloza v. Capistrano Unified School District*).

Potter, Charles F.

Unitarian preacher, librarian, and biblical authority who assisted the defense of John Scopes in Dayton, Tennessee, in 1925.

Price, George McCready (1870–1963)

Self-described geologist and conservative creationist who has been called the "greatest of the antievolutionists." Price was influenced by Seventh-Day Adventist founder Ellen White, who claimed that God had carried her back to the Creation and revealed that the Creation had lasted six days. In 1938, Price formed the Deluge Geology Society, an organization that (1) promoted biblical literalism, (2) claimed that a flood had disrupted geological strata so much that they were now incomprehensible, and (3) believed that a flood caused all major geological changes after creation. Price reserved his harshest criticism for uniformitarianist geology, since he believed that "the modern theory of evolution is about 95% due to the geology of Lyell and only about 5% to the biology of Darwin." Price claimed that Charles Darwin had a "slow lumbering type" of mind and did not understand the "facts of science." Like many creationists after him, Price declared that anyone who pretended to have knowledge contrary to the revealed word of God was "anti-Christian." Starting in 1909, Price published twenty-five major antievolution books. He was the only person cited as a creation scientist by William Jennings Bryan at the Scopes trial. (Darrow and the scientific community derided this citation.) Price's views were rejected by scientists and initially attracted little support among the faithful, but they later became the foundation for Henry Morris and John Whitcomb's *The Genesis Flood*, a book that triggered the creationist revival in the late 1900s. Price was the most important creationist of the early twentieth century.

Rappleyea, George (1894–1967)

Engineer and businessman in Dayton, Tennessee, who in 1925 instigated the trial of John Scopes for allegedly violating the state's antievolution law. Rappleyea and other businessmen in Dayton hoped the trial would boost their town's faltering economy. During Scopes's trial, Rappleyea sat with defense attorneys and was Scopes's most visible and vocal local supporter.

Raulston, John T.

Presiding judge at the Scopes trial in Dayton, Tennessee, in 1925. Raulston, a devout Baptist, felt led by God to preside at the trial. Raulston's bias against Scopes was evident when he started each day's proceedings with a prayer, thereby prompting defense attorney Clarence Darrow to try to make his point with scientific experts and a public questioning of prosecuting attorney William Jennings Bryan.

Ray, John (1627–1705)

Famed British naturalist who claimed in *The Wisdom of God Manifested in the Works of the Creation* (1701) that living organisms have no history— they have always been the same, lived in the same places, and done the same things as when they were first created by God. Ray, the first to name and make the distinction between monocots and dicots, was also the first to define and explain the term *species* in the modern sense of the word.

Reece, Raleigh

Fundamentalist teacher who replaced John Scopes at Rhea County High School in 1925.

Reed, Murray

Presiding Arkansas chancery court judge who in 1966 sided with Susan Epperson when ruling that it was unconstitutional to ban the teaching of evolution from classrooms of public schools. Reed's decision would be overturned in 1967 by the Arkansas Supreme Court but supported the following year by the U.S. Supreme Court (*Epperson v. Arkansas*).

Rice, Edward L.

Ohio Wesleyan zoologist (and American Association for the Advancement of Science vice-president) who published a widely read essay in *Science* in March 1925 claiming that William Jennings Bryan's opposition to the teaching of evolution "is due to Mr. Bryan's simple ignorance of the facts." Rice was one of the expert witnesses for John Scopes at his trial. In a subsequent essay published in 1926 in *Current History*, Rice noted the parallels between the Scopes trial and the treatment of Galileo in the seventeenth century, declaring that the "spirit of intolerance and persecution" was identical in both cases.

Riddle, Oscar

Biologist at the Carnegie Institution of Washington who reported in 1936 to the American Association for the Advancement of Science that the antievolution movement remained alive because of poor textbooks, the failure of biologists to educate the public about evolution, and poor teaching.

Riley, William Bell (1861–1947)

Dynamic evangelist and "Grand Old Man of Fundamentalism" who in 1923 founded the Anti-Evolution League of Minnesota. The league soon became the Anti-Evolution League of America as Riley campaigned against the teaching of evolution. In 1919, Riley—one of the most diligent fundamentalists in history—founded and became the first president of the World's Christian Fundamentals Association, which was instrumental in sending William Jennings Bryan to Dayton, Tennessee, in 1925 to help with the criminal prosecution of John Scopes. Riley led his campaigns from his First Baptist Church of Minneapolis. The sermons Riley gave while traveling, in which evolution was denounced as speculation rather than science, were often attended by thousands of people who were told that without "a sense of sin, man would revert to the brute morality of his monkey ancestors."

Rimmer, Harry (1890–1952)

Flamboyant Presbyterian preacher and outspoken proponent of gap-theory creationism who held the first public debates with evolutionists. Rimmer, who tried to use science to prove the literal truth of the Bible, pledged $1,000 (which he never paid) to anyone who could prove evolution to his satisfaction. Pastor of the First Presbyterian Church of Duluth, Minnesota, Rimmer founded the Research Science Bureau in 1921 and was field secretary for the World Christian Fundamentals Association in the late 1920s. With George McCready Price, Rimmer served as a leading scientific authority for those who embraced fundamentalism. Although Rimmer was often considered to be a biblical literalist, he believed that Earth is very old and that the Noachian flood was a regional event. Rimmer influenced Henry Morris, who became the most influential creationist of the twentieth century. Rimmer's popular books included *Modern Science and the Genesis Record* (1940), *The Theory of Evolution and the Facts of Science* (1941), and *Lot's Wife and the Science of Physics* (1947).

Robertson, Pat (1930–)

Yale Law School graduate and popular television preacher who told his followers that evolution is the cause of many societal ills. Robertson failed in his attempt to secure the 1988 Republican presidential nomination, but he remains active in politics.

Robinson, Fred E.

Owner of Robinson's Drugstore in Dayton, Tennessee, where local businesspeople in 1925 concocted a plan to prosecute John Scopes for allegedly violating the state's recently passed antievolution law. The business community in Dayton hoped that Scopes's trial would stimulate the area's slumping economy. After the trial, Robinson became a founder, incorporator, and chairman of the Board of Trustees at Bryan College.

Rotenberry, Astor L.

Arkansas legislator who in 1927 introduced legislation that eventually became the basis for that state's antievolution law.

Rozzell, Forrest

Executive director of the Arkansas Education Association who in 1965 helped convince Susan Epperson to challenge Arkansas' antievolution law.

Scofield, Cyrus I. (1843–1921)

Lawyer, preacher, and conservative biblical scholar who produced the overwhelmingly popular *The Scofield Reference Bible* in 1909. Scofield suggested in annotations that "heaven and the earth" of Genesis 1:1 "refers to the dateless past, and gives scope for all geologic ages." Later Scofield noted that if we "relegate fossils to the primitive creation . . . no conflict of science with the Genesis cosmology remains." Scofield's comments supported and helped popularize the gap theory of creation. The revised edition in 1967 omits the comments supporting the gap theory. More than 10 million copies of *The Scofield Reference Bible* were sold.

Scopes, John Thomas (1900–1970)

Coach and substitute science teacher who was tried and convicted of teaching human evolution in Dayton, Tennessee, in July 1925. Scopes opposed the state's antievolution law but was largely irrelevant in his trial. Scopes's conviction was later overturned on a technicality. Scopes's trial was one of the most influential events in the twentieth century; it influenced the evolution/creationism debate for decades. After the trial, Scopes rejected an offer to return to Rhea County High School. Instead, he went to graduate school and became a geologist. In subsequent years, Scopes rarely spoke publicly about his trial. He was buried in 1970 in Paducah, Kentucky, under the inscription A MAN OF COURAGE.

Scott, Gary L.

Science teacher at Tennessee's Jacksboro High School who was fired on 14 April 1967 for allegedly teaching evolution. Scott was helped by the American Civil Liberties Union and the National Education Association, who arranged for Scott to be represented by William Kunstler. Scott's lawsuit ultimately convinced the Tennessee legislature to repeal the state's Butler Law banning the teaching of evolution.

Seals, Woodrow

Judge who dismissed *Wright v. Houston Independent School District* on the grounds that the free exercise of religion is not accompanied by a right to be shielded from scientific findings incompatible with one's beliefs.

Sedgwick, Adam (1785–1873)

Cambridge geology professor, evangelical Christian, and catastrophist who condemned Robert Chambers's *Vestiges of the Natural History of Creation* as being bad science as well as irreverent. The attacks by Sedgwick and others on *Vestiges* showed Darwin some obstacles he would have to overcome to gain acceptance of his own theory of evolution. Sedgwick detested Darwin's theory because "it utterly repudiates final causes and thereby indicates a demoralized understanding on the part of its advocates." Sedgwick claimed that if evolution were true, then "religion is a lie, human law is a mass of folly . . . , morality is moonshine. . . ."

Segraves, Nell (1922–) and Kelly (1942–)

Cofounders (with Henry Morris) of the Creation Science Research Center in 1970. In 1963, Nell petitioned the California Board of Education to require that evolution be taught as a theory, not fact. In 1975, Kelly (a Southern Baptist preacher who headed the *Bible-Science* radio program) cowrote a procreationism (and antievolution) book titled *The Creation Explanation: A Scientific Alternative to Evolution.* Kelly was later involved in several evolution-related disputes, including *Segraves v. State of California* in 1981, which challenged how evolution was taught in California. Nell briefed President Ronald Reagan about evolution for many years.

Shelton, Harry
A student of John Scopes who testified at Scopes' trial. Years later, Shelton said that, "Evolution should be taught as a theory. Teaching it as a fact, however, is a different matter."

Shipley, Maynard
Founder in the 1920s of the Science League of America, an organization that opposes the antievolution movement.

Simpson, George Gaylord (1902–1984)
Prominent paleontologist whose 1944 book *Tempo and Mode in Evolution* bridged his field with genetics in the "modern synthesis" of biology. In the late 1950s, Simpson—the most influential paleontologist of the twentieth century—contributed to the Biological Sciences Curriculum Study textbooks that "put evolution back in biology."

Slusher, Harold S. (1934–)
Coeditor (with John N. Moore) of *Biology: A Search for Order in Complexity*, an antievolution biology textbook. *Biology*, developed by the Creation Research Society, was adopted by a variety of schools, but its use in public schools was later declared unconstitutional.

Smith, Mrs. Arthur G.
Resident of Jackson, Mississippi, who, acting on behalf of her daughter Frances, sued in state court in late 1969 for an injunction against the enforcement of the state's antievolution law. Smith argued that her daughter was being denied a proper education and, citing *Epperson v. Arkansas*, that the antievolution law was unconstitutional. Smith's lawsuit was later dismissed.

Smith, Charles
Proevolution crusader who, while campaigning against Arkansas' antievolution law, was jailed for twenty-six days for his views.

Herbert Spencer coined the terms "evolution" and "survival of the fittest" to refer to Darwin's theories. (Library of Congress)

Smith, Ella T.

Biology author whose *Exploring Biology* in 1938 was one of the few bright spots for evolutionists in the 1930s. Smith's book was vigorously proevolution, noting that "evolution is a fact." Virtually all other textbooks at the time, however, ignored evolution.

Smith, William (1769–1839)

English surveyor, civil engineer, and mill builder who, with Germany's Abraham Werner, claimed that rocks are deposited as strata that follow a set sequence in time. Smith's *Strata Identified by Organized Fossils*, published in 1816, showed that fossils are not distributed randomly, as they would be following a flood, but instead are arranged in a definite order. Smith's linking of fossils with past geological eras changed fossils from random relics to pages in the history of life.

Spencer, Herbert (1820–1903)

British social theorist and maverick philosopher who first used the word *evolution* to refer to Darwin's theory. When Spencer later coined the phrase *survival of the fittest* in his *Principles of Biology* in 1864 to refer to Darwin's ideas, Darwin replied that Spencer's phrase was "more accurate, and is sometimes equally convenient." Spencer claimed that society advances through "the stern discipline of Nature" and that governmental policies protecting the poor contradict natural law. Many of Spencer's ideas about society were rejected even before his death. Nevertheless, Spencer's writings helped establish sociology as a discipline.

Steno, Nicolaus (1638–1686)

Danish geologist and Roman Catholic prelate who first claimed that fossils have an organic origin. Steno's devotion to missionary work caused him to virtually abandon science later in his life.

Stewart, A. Thomas (1892–1972)

No-nonsense attorney general for the Eighteenth Judicial Circuit of Tennessee in 1925. Stewart, who had regularly argued cases before Judge John

Raulston throughout the district, was the lead prosecutor of John Scopes in Dayton, Tennessee, in 1925. After serving one term as a U.S. senator, Stewart operated a law office in Nashville.

Stewart, Lyman and Milton
Cofounders of the Union Oil Company who financed the publication and distribution of *The Fundamentals* in the early 1900s. These booklets, funded with $300,000 from the Milton Stewart Evangelistic Fund, promoted biblical literalism as the antidote to "modernism." Nearly 3 million copies of *The Fundamentals* were distributed throughout the United States and elsewhere.

Straton, John Roach (1875–1929)
The "Fundamentalist Pope" who led various campaigns against the teaching of evolution. In 1922, Straton founded the Baptist Fundamentalist League of Greater New York, but the organization had little impact.

Sunday, William A. "Billy" (1862–1935)
Famed fundamentalist preacher who used flamboyant, theatrical services to link evolution with prostitution, eugenics, and crime in the early 1900s. Sunday, who had been a professional baseball player, raised much of the popular support for prohibition.

Thompson, Frank M.
Tennessee attorney general who defended the state's Butler Law when John Scopes appealed his conviction in 1926–1927.

Thompson, W. O.
Clarence Darrow's law partner and part of the team of lawyers that defended John Scopes in Dayton, Tennessee, in 1925.

Thomson, William (Lord Kelvin) (1824–1907)
Scientist who used cooling rates of Earth's crust to estimate that the planet is 20–100 million years old (with 98 million the most likely figure). This calculation troubled Darwin, for it was not enough time for natural selection to have accounted for life's biodiversity. In response, Darwin was forced to accept the idea of inheritance of acquired characteristics to speed up the evolutionary process.

Topkis, Jay
American Civil Liberties Union attorney who argued against Louisiana's balanced-treatment law before the U.S. Supreme Court in *Edwards v. Aguil-*

Alfred Russel Wallace co-discovered (with Charles Darwin) the theory of natural selection. (Corbis)

lard. In June 1987, the Court upheld lower courts' decisions when it declared the law to be unconstitutional.

Ussher, James (1581–1656)

Irish archbishop who wrote *Annales Veteris et Nove Testamenti,* in which he concluded that the universe was created in 4004 B.C. Ussher's genealogy of the Creation was printed in some versions of the King James Bible from 1701 until the last half of the twentieth century.

de Vries, Hugo Marie (1848–1935)

Dutch botanist who "rediscovered" Gregor Mendel's studies of inheritance.

Wallace, Alfred Russel (1823–1913)

English surveyor, botanist, and collector who codiscovered (with Charles Darwin) the theory of natural selection. Like Darwin, Wallace was strongly influenced by the writings of Thomas Malthus and Charles Lyell. In 1858, while suffering from malaria on an island near New Guinea, Wallace wrote and sent a manuscript to Charles Darwin that showed that he had independently arrived at exactly the same theory as Darwin. As Wallace later recalled, "[Evolution] presented itself to me, and something led me to think of the positive checks described by Malthus in his *Essay on Population,* a work I had read several years before, and which made a deep and permanent impression on my mind. These checks—war, disease, famine, and the like—must, it occurred to me, act on animals as well as man. Then I thought of the enormously rapid multiplication of animals, causing these checks to be much more effective in them than in the case of man; and while pondering vaguely on this fact, there suddenly flashed upon me the idea of the survival of the fittest— that the individuals removed by these checks must be on the whole inferior to those that survived. I sketched the draft of my paper . . . and sent it by the next post to Mr. Darwin." As Darwin noted about Wallace, "We have thought much alike." Wallace traveled and collected on the Amazon and in the Indo-Australian regions of the Malay Archipelago. In his later years, Wallace published a major work on the distribution of animals, as well as books on travel, natural selection, and evolution. Wallace, a kind and gentle man who never accepted that evolution could explain the human brain, was an ardent spiritualist, socialist, and opponent of vaccination. The imaginary boundary that separates species of Australasia from those of Southeast Asia is known as "Wallace's line."

Walton, John C. (1881–1949)
Democrat governor of Oklahoma who in 1923 signed the first antievolution law in the United States. That law offered free textbooks to public schools whose teachers would not discuss evolution. Walton was impeached in 1925, soon after which the state's antievolution law was repealed.

Warren, Eugene R.
Attorney for the Arkansas Education Association who helped convince Susan Epperson to challenge the Arkansas antievolution law. Warren represented Epperson throughout her legal battle, which concluded successfully in 1968 as *Epperson v. Arkansas* before the U.S. Supreme Court.

Washburn, George F.
Founder in 1925 of the Bible Crusaders of America, a prominent antievolution organization. Like many others, Washburn claimed that God had appointed him to succeed William Jennings Bryan.

Werner, Abraham G. (1750–1817)
German geologist who, with William Smith, claimed that rocks and fossils are deposited as strata that follow a set sequence in time. Werner remained a disciple of catastrophism (e.g., the biblical flood) and successive creations, each with its own set of species.

Whitcomb, John C., Jr. (1924–)
Conservative Christian theologian at Grace Theological Seminary who, with Henry Morris, wrote *The Genesis Flood*, a popular book that claimed that mainstream geology and evolution are badly flawed. *The Genesis Flood*, published in 1961, was hardly noticed in the secular world, but it galvanized evangelicals and began the modern "creation science" movement in the United States.

White, Ellen G. (1827–1915)
Seventh-Day Adventist cofounder who averred that science could not possibly contradict the Bible. White, whose claims strongly influenced other creationists such as George McCready Price, said that God had carried her back to the Creation and revealed that it had lasted six days. In *Testimony for the Church*, White warns believers that, "Again and again we shall be called to meet the influence of men who are studying sciences of satanic ori-

gin, through which Satan is working to make a nonentity of God and of Christ . . . . The Bible is not to be tested by men's ideas or science, but science is to be brought to the test of this unerring standard." To White and other creationists, science must bow to scriptures.

White, Frank

Arkansas governor and born-again Christian who in 1981 signed the Arkansas equal-time law, despite the fact that he never read the bill. The law was eventually overturned by *McLean v. Arkansas Board of Education.*

White, Walter

Superintendent of Rhea County schools and first witness for the state in the Scopes trial.

Wilberforce, Samuel "Soapy Sam" (1805–1873)

Bishop of Oxford who was the leading clerical critic of Charles Darwin's *On the Origin of Species.* In a historic encounter during the summer of 1880 at the meeting of the British Association for the Advancement of Science in Oxford (a meeting that Wilberforce hoped to use to "smash Darwin"), Wilberforce delivered a thirty-minute speech in which he ridiculed Darwin's ideas and asked Thomas Huxley if it was through his grandfather's or his grandmother's side of the family that Huxley claimed descent from a monkey. Huxley, a defender of Darwin, responded: "If, then, the question is put to me, would I rather have a miserable ape for a grandfather, or a man highly endowed by nature and possessing great means and influence, and yet who employs those faculties and that influence for the mere purpose of ridicule into a grave scientific discussion—I unhesitatingly affirm my preference for the ape." Samuel was the son of William Wilberforce, who achieved fame in England as an opponent of slavery.

Willis, Tom

President of the Creation Science Association for Mid-America, an antievolution group that advised some members of the Kansas Board of Education to delete evolution and cosmology from its science standards in 1999. Willis claims that "Christians or anybody who teaches evolution as science is likely to be causing harm. Some of [the teachers] are evil." Willis believes that exhibits at the University of Kansas' Natural History Museum are blasphemous; he leads yearly "creation safaris" to the building to mock the exhibits for their lack of biblical accuracy.

Willoughby, William

Evangelist who in 1972 sued the director of the National Science Foundation and others for funding the proevolution textbooks produced by the Biological Sciences Curriculum Study. His lawsuit (*Willoughby v. Stever*) was dismissed the next year. Soon thereafter, Willoughby became editor of *The Crusader: The Voice of Religious Freedom*, the official publication of the Religious Freedom Crusade.

Wilson, Leona

Resident of Houston who sued the Houston Independent School District on behalf of her daughter Rita Wright and other students in 1970 because the school district had violated the students' constitutional rights by teaching evolution as fact and without referring to other theories. Wright's lawsuit (*Wright v. Houston Independent School District*), the first lawsuit initiated by creationists, was dismissed before reaching trial.

Winchell, Alexander (1824–1891)

Science professor who was fired in 1878 from Vanderbilt University "for holding questionable views on Genesis." Winchell, who argued that humans existed before Adam, helped popularize geology in America. Among his best-known books were *Sketches of Creation: A Popular View of Some of the Grand Conclusions of the Sciences in Reference to the History of Matter and Life* (1870) and *Preadamites, or a Demonstration of the Existence of Man Before Adam (1890)*.

Wright, G. Frederick (1838–1921)

Theologian and coauthor (with Asa Gray) of *Darwiniana* in 1876. Like Gray, Wright reconciled religion and evolution; he believed that God's purposes are understandable and interrelated. Wright's *Studies in Science and Religion* in 1882 was a more sophisticated description of induction and its use in understanding nature. He argued that scientists accept evolution because it agrees with observed facts, as does Christianity. The work of Wright and Gray helped calm the fears of most people about evolution.

Wright, Rita

Student in the Houston Independent School District in 1970 whose mother (Leona Wilson) sued the district because it had violated Rita's constitutional rights by teaching evolution without referring to other theories. Wright's lawsuit (*Wright v. Houston Independent School District*), the first lawsuit initiated by creationists, was dismissed before reaching trial.

Wright, Sewall (1889–1988)

Agricultural geneticist whose biological and mathematical analyses of small populations (especially bloodlines of cattle) ultimately led to the concept of genetic drift. Wright's "shifting balance theory" was based on "adaptive landscape," his famous pictorial metaphor. Wright's work, made accessible to many people by Theodosius Dobzhansky's 1937 book *Genetics and the Origin of Species*, became a foundation of the "modern synthesis" in biology.

Notes

1. The first three volumes were published in 1749, and the last nine appeared after his death in 1788.

2. The first edition of *Origin* is distinguished by the fact that in that edition, chapter 4 (i.e., the chapter in which Darwin introduces natural selection) does not contain Herbert Spencer's phrase *survival of the fittest*. Later editions of *Origin* contain Spencer's phrase.

3. Hooker was director of the Royal Botanic Gardens at Kew, which had been established by his father.

9

HISTORY OF THE EVOLUTION/CREATIONISM CONTROVERSY

circa 415 B.C.   Greek philosopher Empedocles claims that the universe and everything in it is gradually changing (e.g., "Many races of living creatures must have been unable to continue their breed").

circa 310 B.C.   Aristotle proposes that each form of life has its own static position that reflects its degree of "perfection" on a ladder of nature, a view that is accepted for centuries.

circa A.D. 350   St. Augustine declares that "nothing is to be accepted save on the authority of Scripture, since that authority is greater than all the powers of the human mind."

1543   Polish prelate Nicolaus Copernicus describes a heliocentric model of the solar system in his book *De Revolutionibus Orbium Coelestium* (*On the Revolutions of Heavenly Spheres*).

1550   Mapmakers help travelers identify the geographic origins of plants, animals, and human cultures.

1600   Dominican friar Giordano Bruno is tried by the Vatican's Holy Office (during what is informally known as "the Inquisition") for criticizing Aristotelian logic and embracing Copernicus's heliocentric model of the solar system. After a seven-year trial conducted by the Catholic Church, Bruno is convicted of heresy. In the Square of the Flowers before the Theatre of Pompey, the Master Inquisitor stands before Bruno with a lit torch in one hand and a picture of Jesus in the other, demanding repentance. When Bruno turns his head, he is burned at the stake.

1610   Galileo publishes *The Starry Messenger*, in which he affirms Copernicus's heliocentric solar system.

1616   *5 March*   The Catholic Church decrees Copernicus's theory that Earth moves around the Sun "false and erroneous."

1632	Galileo publishes *Dialogue concerning the Two Chief World Systems*, in which he again affirms the Copernican model of the solar system.
1636	Galileo is called before the Vatican's Holy Office and branded a heretic for his belief in a heliocentric solar system. Galileo avoids Bruno's fate by recanting his ideas but spends the last six years of his life under house arrest.
1642	Biblical scholar John Lightfoot publishes a 20-page pamphlet entitled *A Few, and New Observations, Upon the Book of Genesis, The Most of Them Certain, the Rest of Them Probable, All Harmless, Strange, and Rarely Heard of Before* in which he claims that "man was created by the Trinity on the twenty-third of October, 4004 B.C., at nine o'clock in the morning."
1650–1654	Irish archbishop James Ussher writes his *Annales Veteris et Nove Testamenti,* in which he uses biblical genealogy to argue that creation occurred in 4004 B.C. Ussher's 4004 B.C. date will be included in the margins of some printings of the King James Version of the Bible until the last half of the twentieth century.
1660	Italian physician Francesco Redi strikes a blow against spontaneous generation by showing that maggots form when meat is exposed to open air but do not form when meat is isolated from flies.
1660–1667	Antoni van Leeuwenhoek improves lens-making methods and observes bacteria and other microbes. This discovery makes possible Matthias Schleiden and Theodor Schwann's development of the cell theory in 1838–1839.
1665	In *Micrographia*, Robert Hooke uses the word *cell* to describe the plant structures that he sees with a microscope.
1691	Fossils are identified as the remains of animals and plants from earlier eras.
1701	British naturalist John Ray writes in his *Wisdom of God Manifested in the Works of the Creation* that all living and

nonliving things were "created by God at first, and by Him conserved to this Day in the same State and Condition in which they were first made." Ray believed that organisms have no history—they have always been the same, lived in the same places, and done the same things as when they were first created.

1735   Carolus Linnaeus publishes the first volume of *Systema Naturae*, which establishes the foundation of systematic biology. Linnaeus is not an evolutionist; on the contrary, his system places every plant and animal into its own unique and static place in the divinely created order of nature. Nevertheless, Linnaeus's system is later adapted to evolutionary interpretations.

1749   In the first volume *Histoire naturelle*, Georges-Louis Leclerc argues that Earth might have been created more than 70,000 years ago. Other volumes of *Histoire naturelle* reject Linnaeus's claim that life reflects a divine plan of creation and contain some of the first modern speculations about evolution.

1757   The Catholic Church removes Galileo's *Dialogue Concerning the Two Chief World Systems* from its list of banned books.

1779   The posthumous publication of Scottish philosopher David Hume's *Dialogues Concerning Natural Religion* presents devastating criticisms of the argument from design.

1794–1796   Erasmus Darwin, the grandfather of Charles Darwin, publishes *Zoonomia*.

1795   Scottish farmer and geologist James Hutton publishes his *Theory of the Earth*, which plants the seeds of modern geology. Hutton argues that "in examining things present we have data from which to reason with regard to what has been." Hutton concludes that "rest exists not anywhere" and that the prominent features of Earth have been produced by ordinary forces (e.g., wind, water) acting slowly and uniformly over long periods of time. Hutton's ideas are later developed by Charles Lyell and become the basis of uniformitarianism.

1798	Clergyman, philosopher, and economist Thomas Malthus publishes his *Essay on the Principle of Population*, pointing out that the sizes of populations increase geometrically and therefore outstrip the availability of food. Malthus's basic idea—namely, that there is a competition and struggle for existence—becomes a key part of Charles Darwin's hypothesis that evolution occurs by natural selection.
1802	English archdeacon William Paley publishes his best-seller, *Natural Theology: Or, Evidences of the Existence and Attributes of the Deity, Collected from the Appearances of Nature*, which begins with an analogy of a watch and a watchmaker (i.e., if a person finds a watch in a field, he or she would assume the watch had a designer and maker). Paley claims that God created organisms perfectly adapted to their environment; his argument for "intelligent design" will become a favorite of creationists.
	In a famous letter to the Baptist Association of Danbury, Connecticut, Thomas Jefferson praises the Establishment Clause of the U.S. Constitution for "building a wall of separation between church and state."
1809	Jean-Baptiste Lamarck publishes *Philosophie zoologique*, which contains the first theory of evolution to explain how and why change occurs. Until Darwin publishes his theory of evolution by natural selection decades later, Lamarck's ideas—ideas about acquired characters and the fact that evolution is driven by the needs of organisms as they strive to fulfill their way of life—remain the only detailed arguments for how change might occur across generations.
	12 February Charles Robert Darwin is born in Shrewsbury, Shropshire, England.
1811	Twelve-year-old Mary Anning discovers the first ichthyosaurus, prompting many to reject the claims that dinosaurs are rare, undiscovered, living organisms. When Anning's discovery is declared an extinct reptile by famed French anatomist Georges Cuvier, many people concede extinction.

1813   Biologist Georges Cuvier publishes his *Essay on the Theory of the Earth* in which he argues that fossils prove that extinctions occurred. Cuvier's "correlation of parts" convince him that animals could not evolve. Cuvier considered evolution to be "contrary to moral law."

1816   English surveyor William Smith's *Strata Identified by Organized Fossils* argues that fossils are not distributed randomly, as by a flood, but instead are arranged in a definite order. Smith's linking of fossils with past geological eras changes fossils from random relics to pages in the history of life.

1822   English physician Gideon Mantell (1790–1852) links fossilized teeth with a 40-foot-long lizardlike dinosaur called *iguanodon* ("iguana tooth").

1826   Thomas Malthus publishes the sixth edition of his *Essay on the Principle of Population;* he argues that competition for limited resources must produce a struggle for existence. In 1838, Darwin will read and be greatly influenced by Malthus's ideas.

1827   Charles Darwin enters Christ's College in Cambridge to begin three years of study of divinity, classics, and mathematics. While there, Darwin attends botany lectures by John Henslow, who later helps Darwin secure a position on the HMS *Beagle*.

1830–1833   Charles Lyell publishes his three-volume *The Principles of Geology, Being an Attempt to Explain the Earth's Surface by Reference to Causes Now in Operation*, which outlines for the first time the story of a very old Earth whose plants and animals have been in flux. Lyell argues that species are constantly becoming extinct as others emerge. Rejecting catastrophism, Lyell instead suggests that Earth's features have been formed by ordinary forces still in operation. This was the world that Darwin wanted to explain.

1831   *30 August*   Charles Darwin is invited to sail aboard the HMS *Beagle*.

27 December   Darwin sets sail from Plymouth, England, aboard the HMS *Beagle* on what will be a five-year trip to chart the coastal waters of Chile, Peru, and Patagonia. This voyage, which shows Darwin that each part of the world has its own species, will be instrumental in helping him formulate his theory of evolution by natural selection.

1832   *26 October*   Charles Darwin receives the second volume of Charles Lyell's *Principles of Geology* in which Lyell indignantly criticizes Lamarck's theory of the transmutation of species.

1835   *September*   The *Beagle* spends a month at the rocky Galápagos Islands. Darwin's observations at the islands will be important for developing his theory of evolution by natural selection. As Darwin observes, "I never dreamed that islands 50 or 60 miles apart, and most of them in sight of each other, formed of precisely the same rocks, placed under a quite similar climate, rising to nearly equal height, would have been differently tenanted."

1836   *2 October*   Darwin's five-year voyage ends when the *Beagle* docks in England. Soon thereafter, he begins work on his account of the voyage, which later appears as *Journal of Researches* and as the appealing *The Voyage of the Beagle*. In *Journal of Researches*, Darwin notes that finches on the Galápagos appeared as if "one species had been taken and modified for different ends," but he isn't yet ready to say how this might have happened.

1837   Swiss naturalist Louis Agassiz proposes the glacial (Ice Age) theory to explain geological features believed caused by the biblical flood. Agassiz, who later becomes the most famous scientist in America, rejects Darwin's theory throughout his entire life.

July   Darwin becomes an evolutionist as he begins writing the first of several notebooks about the "species question." Darwin knows that species change, but he can't yet explain why.

1838   Mathias Schleiden publishes a new botany book in which he champions the idea that all plants are made of cells. The following year, Theodor Schwann extends this view to animals.

28 September   While reading "for amusement" the sixth edition of Malthus's *Essay on the Principle of Population*, Darwin discovers his theory of natural selection. He uses Malthus's ideas to create natural selection; it is competition, not deliberate selection, that steers evolution. As Darwin observes, "Being well prepared to appreciate the struggle for existence . . . it at once struck me that under these circumstances favourable variations would tend to be preserved and unfavourable ones destroyed. The result of this would be the formation of a new species." To Darwin, natural selection is the force that constantly adjusts the traits of future generations. Darwin's ideas about evolution differ significantly from other such ideas, in which individuals not fit for survival died and left the survivors unchanged and in the form they were created.

1839   *29 January*   Charles Darwin marries Emma Wedgwood. Like Marx and Freud, Darwin exploits the security of a happy marriage to develop his ideas.

1842   *May*   Just before moving from "dirty odious London" to Downe, Darwin completes a thirty-five-page handwritten summary of natural selection.

Darwin publishes *Structure and Distribution of Coral Reefs*.

1844   Darwin expands his earlier summary of natural selection into a 230-page essay. Darwin leaves instructions that his essay should be published in the event of his unexpected death. In a letter to his friend Joseph Hooker, Darwin rejects the immutability of species, adding that he has discovered "the simple way by which species become exquisitely adapted to various ends." Darwin confesses to Hooker that believing in evolution seems like confessing to a murder.

October   Publisher and amateur scientist Robert Chambers anonymously publishes his grandly titled and popular *Vestiges of the Natural History of Creation*, a best-selling book that (1) tries to reconcile the Bible with uniformitarianism, (2) claims that Earth was not specifically created by God but formed by laws that expressed the Creator's will, and (3) presents evolution via unknown laws as a steady upward progression. Chambers writes, "How can we suppose that the august Being . . . was to interfere personally and on every occasion when a new shell-fish or reptile was ushered into existence? . . . The idea is too ridiculous for a moment to be entertained." Chambers emphasizes that the "races of mankind are simply representations of particular stages in the development of the highest or 'Caucasian type.'" *Vestiges* is denounced by scientists and theologians alike (geologist Adam Sedgwick wrote a damning eighty-five-page review), but it shows Darwin some of the obstacles he will have to overcome if his theory of evolution is to gain acceptance.

November Darwin publishes *Geological Observations on Volcanic Islands.*

1845 John Murray publishes the second edition of Darwin's *Journal of Researches*. The book is profitable. Fourteen years later, Murray will publish Darwin's *On the Origin of Species.*

Unwilling to abandon their views supporting slavery, Baptists in the South meet in Augusta, Georgia, and decide to split from the Baptist General Convention and form the Southern Baptist Convention. Southern Baptists become leaders in the antievolution movement. Many, such as J. Frank Norris, use creationism to support their ideas about racial discrimination.

1847 French customs officer Jacques Boucher de Crèvecoeur de Perthes reports deposits in northern France that contain stone tools and the remains of now-extinct animals. Perthes's discovery shows that humans existed at least as early as these extinct creatures, as well as much earlier than scientists believed. His book *Antiquités celtiques et antédiluviennes* attracts little attention for the next decade but is rediscovered in 1858, when English geologists William Pengelly and Hugh Falconer make similar findings.

1856 Darwin begins work on his "big book," which will become the monumental *On the Origin of Species by Means of Natural Selection.*

Alfred Russel Wallace (a naturalist working in Southeast Asia) begins corresponding with Charles Darwin.

The first remains of a Neanderthal skeleton are discovered in a limestone cave in Germany's Neander valley. Neanderthals date back about 300,000 years ago.

1857   Ralph Waldo Emerson writes in his journal that, "The religion that is afraid of science dishonors God and commits suicide."

1858   German pathologist Rudolf Virchow champions the idea that all cells come from preexisting cells. Virchow's claim puts the cell theory into an evolutionary context; ever since the first cells appeared on Earth, all cells—and, basically, all organisms—on Earth have come from one another.

18 June   Darwin receives a letter from Alfred Wallace, accompanied by a twelve-page manuscript titled "On the Tendency of Varieties to Depart Indefinitely from the Original Type," which describes Wallace's ideas about natural selection—ideas that strongly resemble those of Darwin—and which hastens Darwin's work on *On the Origin of Species.* As Darwin notes, "I never saw a more striking coincidence. All my originality, whatever it may amount to, will be smashed." Darwin sends Wallace's manuscript to Charles Lyell.

1 July   Alfred Wallace and Charles Darwin make a joint presentation to the Linnaean Society of London announcing their theory of natural selection. The presentation includes Wallace's paper, a letter from Darwin to botanist Asa Gray from 1857 discussing whether natural selection inevitably makes species diverge, and an extract from Darwin's essay written in 1844. The clear implication is that Darwin has a prior claim on the idea. Darwin does not attend the presentation because one of his sons (Charles Waring, born 6 December 1856) had died two days earlier of scarlet fever. The presentation attracts little interest and produces no controversy; at year's end, the Linnaean Society president reports that "the year . . . has not, indeed, been marked by any of those striking discoveries which at once revolutionize, so to speak, the department of science on which they bear."

20 July   Darwin begins the actual writing of the book that would become *On the Origin of Species*.

20 August   The joint Darwin/Wallace paper titled "On the Tendency of Species to Form Varieties; and On the Perpetuation of Varieties and Species by Natural Means of Selection" is published in the Linnaean Society's *Journal of Proceedings*.

1859   Charles Lyell suggests to publisher John Murray that his house might want to publish Darwin's "important new work." Murray agrees.

19 March   Darwin finishes the last chapter of *On the Origin of Species*.

25 May   Darwin begins correcting proofs of *On the Origin of Species*.

10 October   Darwin finishes correcting proofs of *On the Origin of Species*. He offers to pay for the large number of corrections he feels obliged to make.

24 November   Darwin's 502-page *On the Origin of Species by Means of Natural Selection: Or, The Preservation of Favoured Races in the Struggle for Life* is rushed into print and introduces historicity into science. Darwin tells readers who do "not admit how vast have been the past periods of time [that they] may at once close this volume." All 1,250 copies of the book sell (for 15 shillings) to booksellers on the first day after publication. Darwin modeled *Origin* after Lyell's *Principles of Geology*. Compared with other revolutionary books in science, *Origin* is straightforward and contains relatively little jargon. Darwin, "half-killed" with exhaustion after writing his "accursed book" in thirteen months and ten days of "hard labour," takes a vacation and waits for the upcoming controversy. *Origin*, which gets mixed reviews, will eventually go through six editions, the last of which appears in 1872. The day after *Origin* becomes public, Darwin begins writing letters using the term *creationist* to refer to anti-evolutionists.

December   Famed Harvard botanist Asa Gray receives a copy of Darwin's *Origin.* Four months later, Gray publishes a review of the book that greatly influences scientists throughout the United States.

1860   *7 January*   The second edition of *On the Origin of Species* (3,000 copies) is published.

18 February   Having seen a draft of Gray's upcoming review of *Origin,* Darwin calls Gray's review "by far the best which I have read. . . . No one person understands my views and has defended them so well as A. Gray; though he does not by any means go all the way with me."

March   Gray publishes the extensive and widely read review of Darwin's *Origin* in the *American Journal of Science and Arts* (for which Gray served as senior editor), the leading science periodical in the United States at the time. Gray provides a clear discussion of Darwin's ideas, notes that Darwin's theory is not necessarily atheistic, contrasts Darwin's ideas with those of ardent creationist Louis Agassiz, and predicts that the debate will be primarily between those who accept Darwin's ideas (such as Gray himself) and those who continue to believe in the special creationism of scholars such as Louis Agassiz and Georges Cuvier.

19 March   William Jennings Bryan is born in Salem, Illinois.

27 March   The American Academy of Arts and Sciences holds a special meeting to discuss Darwin's ideas.

July   Famed Harvard biologist Louis Agassiz, writing in the *American Journal of Science and Arts,* describes Darwin's theory as a collection of "mere guesses" that is "a scientific mistake, untrue in its facts, unscientific in its methods, and mischievous in its tendency."

October   Asa Gray publishes a widely read article in *Atlantic Monthly* claiming that Darwin's ideas work best with theism, not atheism. Gray tells readers that nature is filled with "unmistakable and irresistible indications of design," an idea of which Darwin is not convinced.

1861   Explorer Paul Belloni Du Chaillu stages an exhibition of stuffed gorillas in London—the first time gorillas have been seen outside of Africa. The exhibit generates much excitement but causes many people to recoil at the notion of evolution.

The discovery of a fossil of genus *Archaeopteryx*, a transitional life-form between birds and reptiles, supports the idea that species change gradually over time.

Herbert Spencer, in his book titled *First Principles*, writes that, "We have unmistakable proof that throughout all past time, there has been a ceaseless devouring of the weak by the strong."

April   The third edition of *On the Origin of Species* (2,000 copies) is published.

1862   Louis Pasteur refutes the idea of spontaneous generation.

15 May   Charles Darwin publishes *On the Various Contrivances by Which British and Foreign Orchids Are Fertilized by Insects.*

1863   Thomas Henry Huxley's *Evidence as to Man's Place in Nature* uses comparative data to argue for the simian ancestry of humans.

Ellen G. White establishes the Seventh-Day Adventists' opposition to evolution by proclaiming that "when men leave the word of God in regard to the history of creation, and seek to account for God's creative works upon natural principles, they are upon a boundless ocean of uncertainty. . . . The genealogy of our race, as given by inspiration, traces back its origins, not to a line of developing germs, mollusks, and quadrupeds, but to the great Creator."

Benjamin Disraeli asks, "Is man an ape or an angel? I, my lord, I am on the side of the angels. I repudiate with indignation and abhorrence those newfangled theories."

In his *Principles of Biology*, English philosopher Herbert Spencer coins the phrase *survival of the fittest* to describe a way of understanding Darwin's theory and natural selection. Spencer will also suggest that natural selection implies that the weakest, most useless members should be allowed to die off.

30 November Darwin is awarded the Copley Medal by the Royal Society of London.

1866 Gregor Mendel publishes a forty-eight-page paper in the *Proceedings of the Brünn Society for the Study of Natural Science* that details his ideas about inheritance in the garden pea (*Pisum sativum*), which ultimately revolutionize genetics. Mendel's work is not widely recognized until it is "rediscovered" in 1900 by Karl Correns, Erich Tschermak, and Hugo Marie de Vries.

15 December The fourth edition of *On the Origin of Species* (1,250 copies) is published.

1868 The first skeletal remains of Cro-Magnon man are found in France. Cro-Magnons date back to about 200,000 years ago.

30 January Darwin publishes *The Variation of Animals and Plants under Domestication* (1,500 copies). In this book, Darwin announces that "however much we may wish it, we can hardly follow Professor Asa Gray in his belief" in divinely guided evolution.

20 February Reprint of *Variation* (1,500 copies) is published.

1869 The American Museum of Natural History is founded.

7 August The fifth edition of *On the Origin of Species* (2,000 copies) is published.

THE

DESCENT OF MAN,

AND

SELECTION IN RELATION TO SEX.

By CHARLES DARWIN, M.A., F.R.S., &c.

IN TWO VOLUMES.—Vol. I.

WITH ILLUSTRATIONS.

LONDON:
JOHN MURRAY, ALBEMARLE STREET.

In The Descent of Man, *Charles Darwin applied his ideas about evolution to humans. Not surprisingly, the book was quite controversial. (Library of Congress)*

1871 *24 February* Darwin's *The Descent of Man* (2,500 copies and a reprint of 5,000 copies) is published. The book, which generates much controversy, eliminates the possibility that evolution does not apply to humans.

1872 In *Alice Through the Looking Glass* by Lewis Carroll, the Red Queen says to Alice, "Here, you see, it takes all the running you can do, to keep in the same place." This becomes the evolutionary principle known as the Red Queen Hypothesis, which states that because the environment is constantly changing, organisms must constantly change to remain as fit for the environment as they had been before.

19 February The sixth and final edition of Darwin's *On the Origin of Species* (3,000 copies) appears. This edition, unlike others, contains an additional chapter dealing with objections that have been raised about Darwin's theory.

26 November Darwin's *The Expression of the Emotions in Man and Animals* (7,000 copies) is published.

1874 Darwin publishes the second edition of *The Descent of Man.*

June Darwin publishes the second edition of *Structure and Distribution.*

1875 Darwin publishes the second edition of *Variation.*

2 July Darwin publishes *Insectivorous Plants.*

September Darwin publishes *Climbing Plants.*

1876 Asa Gray (with his collaborator, theologian Frederick Wright) publishes *Darwiniana*, a collection of essays and reviews that had appeared over the past fifteen years. *Darwiniana*, a clear delineation of a middle position in the Darwinian debate, includes a new essay by Gray titled "Evolutionary Teleology" and again moves Gray into a prominent position in the evolution/creationism debate.

5 December   Darwin publishes *Effects of Cross and Self Fertilisation in the Vegetable Kingdom.*

1877   *January*   Darwin publishes the second edition of *On the Various Contrivances.*

9 July   Darwin publishes *Different Forms of Flowers on Plants of the Same Species.*

1878   American astronomer Simon Newcomb simplifies the reason for favoring evolution over creationism, stating that, "We are not to call in a supernatural cause to account for a result which could have been produced by the action of the known laws of nature."

In *Methods of Study in Natural History*, famed biologist Louis Agassiz concludes that "species were created by God." Agassiz remains a staunch creationist until his death.

May   Vanderbilt University fires geologist Alexander Winchell "for holding questionable views on Genesis." Winchell claims that humans existed before Adam and that Earth is much older than indicated in Genesis.

1879   British social theorist and philosopher Herbert Spencer, who introduced the phrase *survival of the fittest* into biology, publishes *Principles of Ethics.*

19 November   Darwin publishes *Life of Erasmus Darwin.*

1880   *22 November*   Darwin publishes *Power of Movement in Plants.*

1881   The British Museum of Natural History opens.

10 October   Darwin publishes *Formation of Vegetable Mould through the Action of Worms.* Like his other books, this book supports Darwin's ideas about evolution. For example, the burrowing of worms is seemingly trivial but can be dramatic if it persists for a long time. Similarly, slight modifications of a species, if continued long enough, can change the species dramatically.

1882   Frederick Wright's *Studies in Science and Religion* argues that scientists accept evolution because it agrees with observed facts, just as does Christianity. The work of Wright and Asa Gray helps calm many people's fears about evolution.

19 April   Charles Robert Darwin dies at his home in Downe.

26 April   Despite having been denounced by the church, Charles Darwin is buried a few feet from Sir Isaac Newton in Westminster Abbey in London. Pallbearers include Alfred Wallace and Joseph Hooker; the service is attended by representatives from France, Germany, Italy, Spain, and Russia. The inscription on his tombstone is simple: CHARLES ROBERT DARWIN, BORN 12 FEBRUARY 1809, DIED 19 APRIL 1882.

1884   *May*   Professor James Woodrow of the Columbia Presbyterian Theological Seminary—an English-born scientist-cleric, uncle of future president Woodrow Wilson, and former student of Louis Agassiz—presents his proevolution ideas to the alumni and directors of the seminary and publishes them two months later in the July issue of *Southern Presbyterian Review*. Woodrow's opponents have him tried before the Synod of South Carolina, which passes a resolution disapproving of his teaching of evolution and asks him to resign. Woodrow refuses, thereby beginning a series of hearings in the Presbyterian government that spans four years.

1886   After a hearing before the Synod of South Carolina, Woodrow is fired for claiming that evolution is compatible with Christianity.

1888   Geologist Joseph LeConte, a student of Louis Agassiz, publishes *Evolution and Its Relation to Religious Thought*, which merges neo-Lamarckism and traditional arguments for design. LeConte rejects explanations based on natural selection.

May The Presbyterian General Assembly votes 139–31 to support the earlier dismissal of James Woodrow. Church doctrine declares that Adam was formed from the dust of the ground and "without any natural animal parentage of any kind."

1890   Enrollment in U.S. high schools reaches 360,000 students, which represents 6.7 percent of fourteen- to seventeen-year-olds in the country.

Reverend Thomas Howard MacQuery, influenced by Le Conte's attempts to reconcile science and religion, publishes *The Evolution of Man and Christianity*, an attempt to reconcile evolution and religion. The book is praised by *Popular Science Monthly*, but it outrages the Episcopal Church and leads to the first trial for heresy in the history of that denomination. The following year, MacQuery is tried and removed as minister.

1892   George McCready Price produces the first of many publications attacking evolution, claiming that evolution and socialism are destroying morality, proclaiming the Advent of Christ, and advocating the biblical flood as the cause of geological formations. Price insists that deviations from James Ussher's chronology are "the devil's counterfeit" and "theories of Satanic origin." Price, like William Bell Riley, claims that evolutionary biologists are Communists.

1894   The first skeletal remains of *Homo erectus* are discovered in Java. *Homo erectus* dates back to about 1.5 million years ago.

1896   *August* William Jennings Bryan electrifies the Democratic National Convention in Chicago with his "Cross of Gold" speech, delivered in defiance of Grover Cleveland, the party's conservative leader. In the speech, Bryan demands an alternative silver-based currency to help people who are struggling under deflation caused by reliance on limited gold-backed currency. Bryan wins the party's presidential nomination. Clarence Darrow is a delegate at that convention. In November, Bryan loses the national election. Before his death in 1925, he will lose two more as the Democrat's nominee for president.

1900 Gregor Mendel's work is "rediscovered" by Hugo Marie de Vries, Karl Correns, and Erich Tschermak.

3 August John Thomas Scopes is born in Paducah, Kentucky. Twenty-five years later, Scopes will volunteer to be the doomed defendant in the infamous Scopes "Monkey Trial."

1902 The Bible League of North America is founded to combat "current destructive teachings" and to restore faith by means of a "common sense and rational, or true scientific, method." The league is critical of new discoveries in biology and begins publishing the *Bible Student and Teacher* (later known as the *Bible Champion*), which includes articles by fundamentalists such as William Bell Riley. Most fundamentalists pay little attention to the league, which disappears after 1930.

1904 William Jennings Bryan first publishes his views of evolution in *The Prince of Peace*, telling scientists, "you shall not connect me with your family tree [of monkeys] without more evidence." Bryan heartened and strengthened fundamentalists with his prestige and eloquence.

24 November Mark Twain comments that "Our Heavenly Father invented man because he was disappointed in the monkey."

1906 While working as a handyman at a Seventh-Day Adventist sanitarium in southern California, George McCready Price develops his scientific views into a small book titled *Illogical Geology: The Weakest Point in the Evolution Theory*. Price argues that Darwin's theory is "a most gigantic hoax." Decades later, Price's ideas become the foundation for "scientific creationism."

1908 Godfrey H. Hardy and Wilhelm Weinberg independently develop a mathematical proof illustrating how genes behave in populations and that sexual reproduction alone cannot cause evolutionary change. This finding, which becomes known as the "Hardy-Weinberg law," shows that evolution is not a self-generating process.

1909   The popular *Scofield Reference Bible* includes an annotation claiming that Genesis 1:1 "refers to the dateless past, and gives scope for all the geological ages." This annotation supports the *gap theory* of creation, which was popularized by Presbyterian preacher Harry Rimmer.

In his *The Finality of Higher Criticism*, Minneapolis preacher William Bell Riley claims that evolution gives humans "a slime sink for origin and an animal ancestry" whereas Christianity makes humans "the creature and child of the most high."

1910   Enrollment in U.S. high schools reaches 1.1 million students, which represents 15.4 percent of fourteen- to seventeen-year-olds in the country.

1910–1915   *The Fundamentals*, a series of pamphlets that proclaims biblical literalism as the antidote to "modernism," is published. The series is distributed widely; each pressrun averages 250,000 copies per volume. These pamphlets, written by respected Bible teachers and theologians such as Benjamin Warfield and James Orr, give rise to the term *fundamentalists* to describe biblical literalists.

1912   Alfred L. Wegener's theory of continental drift helps explain the distribution of organisms across present-day landmasses.

Near Piltdown in southeastern England, amateur archaeologist Charles Dawson unearths pieces of jaw and skull from a gravel bed. A banner headline in the *New York Times* proclaims, "Darwin Theory is Proved True." However, Dawson's discovery, which becomes known as "Piltdown man," is at odds with other discoveries. Piltdown man, which has a massive brain but otherwise primitive features, is declared a fraud in 1953; the skull was from a human, but the jaw and teeth came from an orangutan.

1913   George McCready Price publishes *Fundamentals of Geology*, one of his most important books. Price again argues that geological features are best explained by a Noachian flood.

1914	The American Book Company publishes George Hunter's *A Civic Biology: Presented in Problems*, the textbook that John Scopes will use when he serves as a substitute biology teacher in Dayton, Tennessee, in 1925.
1915	Thomas Hunt Morgan's work is disseminated widely in *The Mechanism of Mendelian Heredity*. Morgan and his colleagues discuss a new theory of heredity that helps revitalize Darwinism and later becomes a basis for the "modern synthesis" in biology.
	November The Ku Klux Klan is "reborn" atop Stone Mountain near Atlanta, Georgia. The Klan becomes an influential organization that strongly endorses creationism and, in 1925, becomes the first organization to urge that creationism and evolution be given equal time in public schools.
1916	James Henry Leuba, a professor of psychology at Bryn Mawr, publishes *The Belief in God and Immorality*, a study showing that college students had lost faith after being exposed to modern ideas. Leuba's book, which is cited often by William Jennings Bryan in his antievolution speeches, helps convince Bryan to become involved in the antievolution campaign.
	The National Education Association endorses the teaching of evolution in biology courses.
1917	Stanford University zoologist Vernon Kellogg claims that German officers used Darwin's doctrine to justify their instigation of World War I.
	Calls begin in Kentucky to ban the teaching of evolution in public schools.
	William Bell Riley's *The Menace of Modernism* attacks intellectuals and educators who are questioning fundamentalists' worldview. Riley claims that liberal preachers, university officials, and teachers show their loyalty to modernism by "their insistence on Darwinism."
	George McCready Price publishes *Q.E.D.: Or, New Light on the Doctrine of Creation*. Although Price is hailed by believ-

ers as a true scientist who has avoided the speculation typical of evolutionists, his work has little impact on scientists.

1918   William Bell Riley meets with A. C. Dixon and six biblicists at R. A. Torrey's summer home to discuss forming a new organization to promote fundamentalism.

Benjamin Kidd publishes *The Science of Power*, a book that helps convince William Jennings Bryan that German militarists used evolutionary theory to justify their actions and lead people away from Christianity.

1919   *May* William Jennings Bryan speaks at a high school graduation ceremony in his hometown of Salem, Illinois. Among the graduates who attend the ceremony and meet Bryan is John Scopes.

25 May William Bell Riley founds the World's Christian Fundamentals Association at a meeting in Philadelphia attended by 6,000 people. Riley describes the gathering as "an event of more historical moment than the nailing up, at Wittenberg, of Martin Luther's ninety-five theses." By 1920, the association has organized more than 100 "Conferences on Christian Fundamentals" throughout the United States and Canada. In 1925, the association will send William Jennings Bryan to Dayton, Tennessee, to help prosecute John Scopes.

1920   William Bell Riley intensifies his efforts to ban the teaching of evolution in public schools.

Enrollment in U.S. high schools reaches 2.5 million students, which represents 32.3 percent of fourteen- to seventeen-year-olds in the country.

William Jennings Bryan, giving a speech titled "Brother or Brute?" to the World Brotherhood Congress, claims that Friedrich Nietzsche had carried Darwinism to its ultimate conclusion and that Darwinism is "the most paralyzing influence with which civilization has had to contend." Bryan argues that if Darwinism is true, humans cannot overcome their animal nature, and therefore all prospects for reform are pointless.

Antievolution efforts begin that ultimately result in the formation of the Baptist Bible Union. In association with John Roach Straton in New York, the union begins publishing *The Fundamentalist* magazine. Its leadership is combative, however, and by 1928, its impact is negligible.

The National Civil Liberties Bureau (which will later become the American Civil Liberties Union) is founded in New York. In 1925, the ACLU will sponsor the defense of John Scopes in Dayton, Tennessee. The ACLU will also become involved in several other later court cases associated with the evolution/creationism controversy.

1921   The National Federation of Fundamentalists of the Northern Baptists is formed and begins occasional attacks on evolution by claiming that evolution is "false." The federation spends most of its time searching for instances of evolution being taught in church-related schools.

The Research Science Bureau is founded by Harry Rimmer and begins to try to abolish evolution with documentable evidence instead of with authoritarian proclamations. The bureau is never very influential; by 1926, it will have only 200 members. However, Rimmer will remain popular (especially throughout the 1930s) with his "Bible and Science" lectures.

Truman J. Moon's best-selling *Biology for Beginners* states in its preface that biology is "based on the fundamental idea of evolution" and avers that "both man and ape are descended from a common ancestor." Five years later, the word *evolution* disappears from the text and Charles Darwin's portrait is replaced by a cartoon.

William Bell Riley organizes twenty-two antievolution meetings in Kentucky and, aided by subsequent appearances by William Jennings Bryan, galvanizes support for a ban on the teaching of evolution in the state's public schools. Kentucky's antievolution campaign peaks in 1926, when three bills sponsored by fundamentalists die in the legislature.

William Jennings Bryan's attacks on evolution establish him

as the national leader of the antievolutionists. Bryan delivers for the first time his "Menace of Evolution" speech, in which he says his primary concern is to protect "man from the demoralization involved in accepting a brute ancestry." This speech evolves into a book titled *In His Image* that is published the following year.

The South Carolina legislature considers a rider to an annual appropriation bill that will ban state funds from going to any school that teaches the "cult known as 'Darwinism.'" The rider has considerable support but is removed by a joint committee. The next antievolution bill in South Carolina will not appear until 1927; that bill, like the one in 1921, fails.

The Kentucky Baptist Board of Missions demands that the state ban the teaching of the "false and degrading theory of evolution." The Baptists' cause is supported by William Jennings Bryan, who is invited to address a joint session of the Kentucky General Assembly. The resolution passed by the Kentucky Baptist Board of Missions inspires Bryan's crusade against the teaching of evolution.

December   Speaking at the annual meeting of the American Association for the Advancement of Science in Toronto, British biologist William Bateson describes the origin and nature of species as "utterly mysterious." Bateson's comments are reported throughout the world as the "collapse of Darwinism" and imply that Bateson supports religious and political efforts to ban the teaching of evolution.

1922   A Kentucky couple refuses to allow their child to attend a school where a teacher said that the Earth is round. The teacher is fired.

Columbia University philosopher John Dewey notes that "the campaign of William Jennings Bryan against science and in favor of obscurantism and intolerance is worthy of serious study. It demands more than the mingled amusement and irritation which it directly evokes."

The AAAS passes a resolution supporting the teaching of evolution.

William Jennings Bryan publishes *In His Image*, a book in which he attacks Darwinism as irreligious and unscientific. Bryan argues that "if it is contended that an instructor has a right to teach anything he likes, . . . [then] the parents who pay the salary have a right to decide what shall be taught. . . . A man can believe anything he pleases but he has no right to teach it against the protest of his employers."

The World's Christian Fundamentals Association, meeting at the Bible Institute of Los Angeles, announces its first official support of the antievolution movement by passing a resolution stating that "as taxpayers we have a perfect right to demand of public schools that they cease from giving to our children pure speculation in the name of science, and we have an equal right to demand the removal of any teacher who attempts to undermine . . . the Christian faith of pupils."

The Southern Baptists, meeting in Jacksonville, Florida, proclaim that "no man can rightly understand evolution's claim as set forth in the textbooks of today, and at the same time understand the Bible."

North Dakota's Governor Ragnvald A. Nestos congratulates William Jennings Bryan on his work to condemn professors who teach evolution. Soon thereafter, Nestos helps draft an antievolution bill for North Dakota, but it generates little support.

Wild-eyed preacher J. Frank Norris exposes the teaching of evolution at Baylor University and elsewhere. Norris will become a leading figure in the antievolution movement.

Representative John W. Butler from Tennessee takes up the antievolution cause in his state when a preacher tells him of a woman whose faith has been shaken by a professor's lecture about evolution. Butler's crusade leads to the passage of the nation's most famous antievolution law—the Butler Law—which is used to prosecute John Scopes in 1925.

January   William Jennings Bryan tells the Kentucky legislature to "have this heresy [evolution], this anti-Bible teaching, thrown out, too." The next day, Representative George

W. Ellis introduces a bill to ban the teaching of the "false and degrading" theory of evolution "as it pertains to man" and provides fines, imprisonment, and the revocation of a school's charter to violators. A few days later, J. R. Rach presents a milder version of the bill to the Kentucky Senate.

February University of Kentucky President Frank McVey defies public opinion and risks losing money for his institution when he fights antievolution legislation.

9 March In the nation's first legislative vote to ban the teaching of evolution, the Kentucky General Assembly defeats (by a vote of 42–41) Ellis's proposal to ban the teaching of the theory of evolution. Soon thereafter, the antievolution bill introduced in January by Rach fails by two votes. Seventy-seven years later, Kentucky will delete the word *evolution* from its state educational guidelines.

November The Oklahoma Baptist Convention calls for legislation to ban the teaching of evolution in the state's public schools. The next year, Oklahoma becomes the first state to pass an antievolution law.

1923   George McCready Price publishes his 726-page magnum opus, *The New Geology*, in which he argues that the Noachian flood explains most of the observed geological phenomena, including fossil-containing rocks. *The New Geology*, which dismisses the chronological data underlying evolutionary research, is a Genesis-based book that inspires generations of creationists. *New Geology* becomes a classic of creation science.

William Jennings Bryan addresses the Georgia and West Virginia legislatures and he claims that "the hand that writes the pay check rules the school." However, subsequent antievolution proposals in those states generate little support. Bryan again blames evolution for World War I and claims that the teaching of evolution is "poison."

The AAAS passes another resolution supporting the teaching of evolution.

Baptist preacher T. T. Martin publishes his *Hell and the*

High Schools: Christ or Evolution—Which?, a diatribe in which he argues that the acceptance of evolution dooms high school students to hell. Martin later becomes active in the Anti-Evolution League of America and the Bible Crusaders of America; and in 1926, he helps secure passage of an antievolution law in Mississippi.

A widely read editorial in *Manufacturers' Record* claims that "evolution has well-nigh wrecked every land that has adopted it."

The Southern Baptist Convention, meeting in Kansas City, affirms biblical literalism. T. T. Martin's *Hell and the High Schools* is a best-seller at the convention. Baptists in Arkansas demand that no Baptist institution employ anyone who believes in Darwinism.

The World's Christian Fundamentals Association meets in J. Frank Norris's Baptist church in Fort Worth, Texas, where Norris stages sensational trials of Texas biology professors who teach evolution.

The Tennessee legislature considers an antievolution bill, but it is abandoned in the legislature's rush to adjourn. Two years later, the legislature will pass the Butler Law, which leads to the Scopes trial.

At the urging of Southern Baptist firebrand J. Frank Norris, the Texas legislature debates a bill that will censor textbooks that include evolution. The most convincing argument for the legislation is William Jennings Bryan's claim that citizens do not want evolution to be taught to their children, so it is therefore inappropriate to use tax money to teach the theory. Energized by Representative J. A. Dodd's claim that the state shows students "the road to hell through teaching them the hellish infidelity of evolution," the bill passes the Texas House by a 71–34 vote, but it dies without a vote in the Senate. A similar bill will fail two years later.

Legislatures in Alabama, Georgia, and Tennessee reject antievolution bills.

Kentucky Wesleyan College suspends five professors who claim that evolution does not contradict the Scriptures.

William Bell Riley visits Tennessee but fails to convince the legislature to consider an antievolution bill. Riley goes home to Minneapolis, where he and three other preachers form the Anti-Evolution League of Minnesota. The league soon becomes the Anti-Evolution League of America, which campaigns vigorously against the teaching of evolution.

The Oklahoma legislature adds a rider to a free-textbook bill that bans the use of any textbook that promotes "a materialistic conception of history, that is, the Darwin theory of evolution versus the Bible theory of creation." The legislation easily passes the House, but it survives in the Senate by only four votes.

24 March Oklahoma becomes the first state to circumspect the teaching of evolution when Governor John Walton signs legislation offering free textbooks to public schools whose teachers will not mention evolution and banning the use of books promoting Darwinism. The Oklahoma Baptist Convention congratulates the governor and legislature for their work. This law—America's first antievolution law—is repealed in 1925 after Walton is impeached.

25 May The Florida legislature, following an address by William Jennings Bryan, passes a joint resolution saying that it is "improper and subversive" for any teacher at a public school "to teach Atheism or Agnosticism, or to teach as true Darwinism, or any other hypothesis that links man in blood relationship to any other form of life." The law has little opposition but goes unnoticed; it has virtually no impact on instruction in Florida. Two years later, the Florida legislature fails to transcribe this resolution into law.

4 July When the *Chicago Tribune* publishes an editorial criticizing William Jennings Bryan's attempts to proscribe the theory of evolution, Clarence Darrow responds with a long, terse letter and a list of questions for Bryan that are published on the front pages of the *Tribune* and other newspapers. Darrow uses many of these questions when he questions Bryan at the Scopes trial on 20 July 1925.

1924   The California Board of Education instructs public school teachers to present evolution "as a theory only." Similar demands will be made by many state legislatures throughout the country in the decades that follow.

Zoologist H. H. Newman writes in *Outlines of General Zoology* that evolution has triumphed over creationism, noting that "there is no rival hypothesis to evolution except the outworn and completely refuted one of special creation, now retained only by the ignorant, dogmatic, and the prejudiced."

The Committee on Freedom of Teaching in Science of the American Association of University Professors issues a report stressing that it is inappropriate to rely on popular votes or legislative action to determine what science is to be taught in classrooms. The committee declares that experts are the best people to decide what should be taught.

William Bell Riley visits North Carolina to help T. T. Martin's North Carolina Anti-Evolution League campaign for an antievolution law. Soon thereafter, D. Scott Poole is elected to the state legislature based on his successful antievolution campaign platform. Governor Cameron Morrison then persuades the state's Board of Education to reject as "unsafe" two proevolution biology books that had been approved by a subcommittee charged with reviewing textbooks. Governor Morrison proclaims that he doesn't want his "daughter or anybody's daughter to have to study a book that prints pictures of a monkey and a man on the same page. . . . I don't believe in any missing links. If there were any such things as missing links, why don't they keep on making them?" The ban on these two books will be the only victory for the antievolution forces in North Carolina.

The AAAS examines the role of William Jennings Bryan in the burgeoning antievolution campaign.

The Georgia legislature debates an antievolution bill, but it dies in the House.

William Jennings Bryan expands his indictment of evolution by claiming that the teaching of evolution in schools is responsible for "all the ills from which America suffers."

A national committee of educators recommends that evolution be one of nine major units covered in high school biology textbooks.

Meeting in San Francisco, the Science League of America establishes itself as the leader of the scientific opposition to William Jennings Bryan and the antievolution campaign. An overflow crowd hears talks by prominent scientists such as Luther Burbank.

As part of a national speaking tour, William Jennings Bryan gives a speech titled "Is the Bible True?" in Nashville, as Tennessee legislators discuss the evolution/creationism controversy. Bryan sends copies of his lectures to public officials; the lectures capture the public's attention.

May   John W. Summers, a U.S. representative from Washington, introduces an amendment to the District of Columbia's appropriation bill stating that no money be used to pay the salary of anyone who permits the teaching of "disrespect of the Holy Bible." The amended bill passes without debate. The following year, administrator Loren H. Wittner uses this bill to try to stop paying two education officials who permit evolution to be taught in their schools.

17 December   Tennessee state legislator John Butler, worried that his children will be corrupted by the teaching of evolution in the public schools, makes good on a campaign promise by spending his birthday drafting an antievolution law (House Bill 185: "An Act Prohibiting the Teaching of the Evolution Theory . . .") that would become known as the "Butler Law." Seven months later, the Butler Law will be used in Dayton, Tennessee, to prosecute John Scopes in the infamous "Monkey Trial."

1925   The Florida House of Representatives passes legislation making its 1923 joint resolution a law (i.e., making it against the law "to teach as true Darwinism, or any other hypothesis that links man in blood relationship to any other form of life"). However, the bill dies in the Florida Senate, leaving Florida with no legal restrictions on the teaching of evolution.

Loren Wittner uses a little-noted amendment to the District of Columbia's appropriation bill to sue two district education officials who permit evolution to be taught in their schools. The suit fails on technical grounds.

Anatomy professor Raymond Dart discovers in Africa a skeleton of *Australopithecus africanus*, a humanlike organism with an upright stance but a far smaller brain than humans. Dart's discovery is not accepted until the 1940s.

While the Tennessee legislature debates banning the teaching of evolution in its public schools, the Mississippi legislature rejects antievolution legislation.

J. Frank Norris focuses the attention of the Southern Baptist Convention on evolution.

The California Board of Education appoints a committee of nine college presidents to determine if the teaching of evolution discredits religion.

After the state legislature rejects an antievolution law, Mississippi's superintendent of schools issues an order that temporarily bans the teaching of evolution.

The West Virginia legislature debates an antievolution bill, but it dies without a vote.

The Texas legislature again considers a bill banning textbooks that discuss evolution, but the bill fails.

The Georgia House defeats an antievolution bill that is attached as an amendment to an appropriation bill.

In his book *Concerning Evolution*, biologist J. A. Thomson claims that creationism is a thing of the past, adding that "we do not know of any competent naturalist who has any hesitation in accepting evolution."

January Fundamentalists in Tennessee publish and distribute to state legislators an antievolution pamphlet based on William Jennings Bryan's "Is the Bible True?" speech.

20 January Senator John A. Shelton introduces to the Tennessee legislature a bill banning the teaching of evolution. Shelton's bill is rejected by the Senate Education Committee by one vote, on the basis that it would be inappropriate to pass a law dealing with religious beliefs.

21 January John Butler introduces to the Tennessee legislature House Bill 185, banning the teaching of evolution "to protect our children from infidelity." Butler's bill will become the most famous of all antievolution statutes.

23 January The Tennessee House Education Committee recommends passage of Butler's legislation.

28 January The Tennessee House of Representatives passes Butler's bill by a vote of 71–5.

29 January The Tennessee Senate Judiciary Committee votes 5–4 to reject the antievolution bill introduced by Senator Shelton, citing its tampering with "the question of religious belief."

February Fiery evangelist Billy Sunday conducts an eighteen-day crusade in Memphis, during which he denounces evolution, declares that Darwin is an "infidel," and claims that education is "chained to the devil's throne." Sunday's spectacular crusade, attended by many legislators and more than 10 percent of Tennessee's residents, helps ensure the passage of the Butler Law in the Tennessee Senate the following month.

4 February The Tennessee Senate Judiciary Committee rejects Butler's antievolution legislation.

10 February The Tennessee Senate calls up Butler's bill as a special order of business but refers it and Shelton's bill back to the Judiciary Committee to resolve differences in the two bills. The General Assembly adjourns for a four-week recess before the Judiciary Committee submits its report.

19 February Following a week of debate, Representative Poole's bill to ban the teaching of evolution in North Carolina is endorsed by the House Committee on Education but is defeated by a vote of 67–46 when considered by the full House. Instrumental in the bill's defeat is opposition by University of North Carolina President Harry W. Chase, Wake Forest University President William L. Poteat, and the North Carolina Association for Science. Soon thereafter, however, several schools ban the teaching of evolution and give their administrators the authority to remove all books that discuss evolution from their libraries. The North Carolina Education Association remains silent during the controversy.

March Ohio Wesleyan zoologist (and AAAS vice-president) Edward L. Rice publishes an essay in *Science* magazine claiming that William Jennings Bryan's opposition to the teaching of evolution "is due to Mr. Bryan's simple ignorance of the facts."

10 March The Judiciary Committee of the Tennessee Senate, sensing the public's support of an antievolution bill, reverses itself and recommends passage of the Butler bill by a vote of 7–4.

13 March After several hours of debate spiced with numerous proclamations of faith, the Tennessee Senate passes the Butler bill by a vote of 24–6. In contrast to their colleagues in Kentucky and North Carolina (where antievolution bills were rejected by state legislatures), Tennessee's educational leaders (e.g., Harcourt A. Morgan, president of the University of Tennessee) urge faculty to remain silent about the Butler bill as it moves through the legislature. They do.

21 March Under pressure from fellow Baptists, Tennessee Governor Austin Peay ("The Maker of Modern Tennessee") signs John Butler's legislation into law because of the bill's popularity and his "deep and widespread belief that something is shaking the fundamentals of the country, both in religion and morals. . . . An abandonment of the old-fashioned faith and belief in the Bible is our trouble in large degree. . . . The people have the right and must have the right to regulate what is taught in their schools." The Butler Law makes it a crime to teach human evolution in Tennessee and leads to the prosecution of John Scopes in Dayton four months later. There is no opposition to the Butler bill before it becomes law. William Jennings Bryan immediately sends a congratulatory telegram to Peay applauding his actions and stressing that parents in Tennessee owe Peay "a debt of gratitude for saving their children from the poisonous influence of an unproven hypothesis." The World's Christian Fundamentals Association commends the legislature and governor of Tennessee for passing the Butler Law. The Butler Law is not repealed until 1967.

22 March Lucile Milner, an employee at the obscure and newly renamed ACLU, reads a newspaper article with the headline TENNESSEE BANS THE TEACHING OF EVOLUTION, which describes the recently passed antievolution law in Tennessee. Milner gives the article to Roger Baldwin, the executive director of the ACLU, who gets his board's backing for raising money to finance a test case to challenge the law. The ACLU later sends Arthur Garfield Hays to head its delegation at the trial.

April The California Board of Education upholds the teaching of evolution, insists that the idea be taught "only as a theory," and bans textbooks that present evolution as fact. At a subsequent hearing, Maynard Shipley argues that evolution is a fact, but William Bell Riley of Minnesota argues that "evolution has never been proved and never can be."

23 April John Scopes, serving as a substitute teacher in a science class, tells his students to read the chapter in *Civic Biology* about evolution for discussion the next day. Ironically, Scopes is ill the next day and misses class.

4 May The ACLU places an ad on the front page of the *Chattanooga Daily Times* and other Tennessee newspapers, "looking for a Tennessee teacher who is willing to accept our services in testing [the Butler] law in the courts." Dr. George Rappleyea, a thirty-one-year-old engineer and businessman in Dayton, goes to Robinson's Drugstore, where he, Walter White, Wallace Haggard, and the Hicks brothers decide to recruit a local coach—John Scopes—to test the law as a means of boosting Dayton's economy. Scopes reluctantly agrees to be charged with the crime; "Bryan's majority" will sit in judgment.

5 May   Judge John Raulston convenes a special meeting of the grand jury to indict John Scopes for violating the recently passed Butler Law. Although questions are later raised about the indictment's validity (which requires that Scopes be reindicted before his trial), this indictment secures for Dayton one of the most famous trials in U.S. history. Scopes is the only teacher to be indicted for violating an antievolution law.

7 May   Scopes is charged with violating Tennessee's Butler Law.

10 May   Following a preliminary hearing, Scopes is arraigned and bound over to a grand jury under a $1,000 bond.

13 May   Ignoring pleas from his wife, William Jennings Bryan announces that he'll participate in the Scopes trial. Clarence Darrow soon follows suit, setting the stage for their epic confrontation. Darrow volunteers his services directly to Scopes and therefore can't be replaced by his critics at the ACLU.

28 May   The American Medical Association unanimously condemns the prosecution of John Scopes and the restrictions on the teaching of evolution.

June   Scopes and one of his attorneys, John R. Neal (who lives in Spring City, 17 miles north of Dayton), visit New York to discuss Scopes's case with ACLU officials.

25 June   William Jennings Bryan writes to Dayton's Chief Commissioner A. P. Haggard that "Darrow's attitude on religious questions will offset his ability." One month later, Darrow will question and embarrass Bryan on the stand at the Scopes trial.

30 June   The American Federation of Teachers, meeting in Chicago, passes a resolution supporting John Scopes and denouncing Tennessee's Butler Law as "unenlightened legislative dictatorship."

George Rappleyea claims that there is "absolutely no foundation" for a report that he originated the Scopes trial for publicity purposes.

1 July   Lela V. Scopes, John Scopes's sister, is told by the Paducah, Kentucky, school board that her "services will not be desired unless she renounces the theory of evolution." Ms. Scopes responds by telling the board that she endorses her brother's views "in their entirety." Ms. Scopes is refused a job in the school district.

The National Education Association, meeting in Indianapolis, remains silent about the Butler Law and the upcoming trial of John Scopes. U. W. Lamkin, chairman of the group, says that it is "inadvisable" to express an opinion on the subjects. The Tennessee Academy of Science also remains silent.

John Butler reaffirms his belief that his legislation will "protect our children from infidelity."

2 July   Scopes's defense team, meeting in New York, decides to broaden the trial to pit science against fundamentalism and to sacrifice Scopes's acquittal for a chance to appeal the verdict to a higher court.

3 July   Over the objections of Dudley Field Malone and John Neal, Clarence Darrow announces in Chicago that he will try to get the trial of John Scopes moved to a federal court in either Knoxville or Chattanooga. Community leaders in Dayton, fearing lost revenues generated by the trial, protest the announcement. Meanwhile, Scopes returns to Dayton after a vacation in Kentucky, and Tennessee's superintendent of schools, Walter White, announces that he has invited evangelist Billy Sunday to participate in the trial as a witness for the prosecution.

6 July   In Cookeville, Tennessee, Federal Judge John J. Gore refuses two petitions asking that Scopes's trial be moved out of Dayton. Gore does not address the constitutionality of the Tennessee statute under which Scopes was indicted.

Billy Sunday announces that although he won't attend the Scopes trial, he endorses any views that will be expressed there by William Jennings Bryan.

7 July William Jennings Bryan, serving as a special prosecutor and attorney for the World's Christian Fundamentals Association, arrives in Dayton from Miami, Florida, by train to help prosecute John Scopes. Bryan is greeted by a cheering crowd of almost 1,000 people (about half Dayton's population). At a dinner honoring Bryan sponsored by the Progressive Dayton Club that evening (and attended by John Scopes), Bryan renews his proposal for a constitutional amendment to ban the teaching of evolution and emphasizes that supporters of the teaching of evolution are a small minority in the United States. Bryan concludes his talk by saying that "the contest between evolution and Christianity is a duel to the death . . . the two cannot stand together."

8 July Judge John Raulston arrives in Dayton, Tennessee, for the Scopes trial. Raulston announces that he's ready to preside at the "evolution case" even if the task requires "all summer."

9 July Clarence Darrow and Thomas Scopes (John Scopes's father) arrive in Dayton for the trial. Bryan announces that John Scopes is harming teachers throughout the country, but John Butler says that his reading of Darwin's books "didn't hurt me."

10 July The World's Christian Fundamentals Association again denounces "the teaching of the unscientific, anti-Christian, atheistic, anarchistic, pagan rationalistic evolutionary theory."

State of Tennessee v. John Thomas Scopes opens at 10:00 A.M. in Dayton's Rhea County Courthouse with a fundamentalist prayer. Scopes's trial—one of the most influential events of the twentieth century—is the original "trial of the century." The Scopes trial marks the beginning of the most active period of the evolution/creationism controversy; the trial will influence the debate for many decades.

11 July In the most famous of his articles about the Scopes trial, journalist H. L. Mencken uses the front page of the *Baltimore Sun* to describe the trial as a "religious orgy."

12 July William Jennings Bryan preaches "an old fashioned sermon" on the lawn of the Rhea County Courthouse. Elsewhere, Reverend Howard Byrd of Dayton's Methodist Episcopal Church (where George Rappleyea teaches Sunday school) resigns when his congregation threatens violence if Reverend Charles Potter, a member of Scopes's defense team, gives a sermon in the church about evolution.

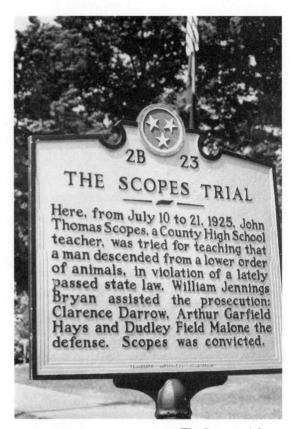

The Scopes trial *(State of Tennessee v. John Thomas Scopes) remains the most famous event in the history of the evolution-creation controversy. This monument stands outside the Rhea County Courthouse in Dayton, TN, the site of the trial. (Courtesy of Randy Moore)*

15 July Biologist Maynard Metcalf tells people attending the Scopes trial that "the fact of evolution is as fully established as the fact that the earth revolves around the sun."

16 July Dudley Malone asks, "Are we to have our children know nothing about science except what the church says they shall know?"

18 July Darrow tells reporters that he's an agnostic, adding that "it is hard to understand how an intelligent man can believe that a photograph of a human being needs only to be enlarged to give us a picture of God."

20 July In one of the most famous events in courtroom history, Clarence Darrow examines the religious beliefs of William Jennings Bryan during the Scopes trial.

21 July After deliberating for nine minutes, a jury convicts John Scopes of the crime of teaching human evolution. Judge Raulston fines Scopes $100 plus court costs, the minimum allowed, and the *Des Moines Register* proclaims that

John Thomas Scopes being sentenced for the crime of teaching human evolution, 21 July 1925. (Bryan College)

Scopes "is on his way to a place beside Dred Scott on the shelf of lasting fame." Scopes's conviction will be overturned in 1927, but the state's antievolution law will remain in effect until 1967.

25 July William Jennings Bryan tells a reporter, "If I should die tomorrow, I should feel that much has been accomplished in the greatest cause for enlightening humanity ever known. I believe that on the basis of the accomplishments of the past few weeks, I could truthfully say, 'Well done.'"

26 July After a trip to Winchester, Tennessee (the home of John Raulston and A. Thomas Stewart) and working on his response to Clarence Darrow, William Jennings Bryan dies of apoplexy after a service at the First Southern Methodist Church in Dayton. Sue Hicks, Wallace Haggard, Herbert Hicks, and Gordon McKenzie watch over Bryan's body through the night. Bryan's funeral services are later broadcast throughout the United States and Canada. Bryan's death leaves the fundamentalists without a national leader, and their zeal for the antievolution cause soon begins to fade.

27 July H. L. Mencken describes the late William Jennings Bryan as "a charlatan, a mountebank, a zany without shame or dignity."

The 5,000 delegates to the International Walther League of Lutherans, meeting in San Francisco, pass a resolution opposing the teaching of evolution and declaring it "part of a movement for the overthrow of orderly government."

28 July William Jennings Bryan's *Last Message*—which Bryan has touted as "the mountain peak of my life's efforts"—is given to the media. In that message, Bryan demands, among other things, that one can accept either Christianity or evolution, but not both. This statement is embraced by many future creationists.

31 July After being taken from Dayton to Washington, D.C., via train, William Jennings Bryan is buried in a late-

William Jennings Bryan became a martyr for creationists when he died five days after the Scopes trial in Dayton, TN. He is buried (in Grave 31210 in Section 4 of Arlington National Cemetery) beneath the inscription "He Kept the Faith." (Courtesy of Randy Moore)

afternoon ceremony in Arlington National Cemetery under the inscription HE KEPT THE FAITH. By order of President Calvin Coolidge, flags in Washington, D.C., are displayed at half-mast. Newspaper headlines throughout the United States are similar to this one that appeared in the *Des Moines Register* : "Capital Bows in Tribute to the Commoner." Bryan becomes a martyr for the creationists' cause, and the creationists lose a distinguished leader who is never replaced. Following Bryan's death, fundamentalism is often viewed as little more than a rural, anti-intellectual movement.

Chapters of the Ku Klux Klan burn crosses at memorial services for William Jennings Bryan. At Toledo, Ohio, a cross is inscribed, "In memory of the greatest Klansman." Although Bryan was not a member of the Klan, he often defended their goals.

August   The Rhea County School Board offers a new contract to John Scopes (at a salary of $150 per month), provided he adhere "to the spirit of the evolution law." Scopes rejects the offer and leaves town to ponder his future. The following month, he enrolls in graduate school at the University of Chicago, on a scholarship funded by scientists and reporters who attended his trial. Scopes, who will return to Dayton again only twice in the next forty years, is content to let his hour of fame pass without regrets; indeed, he rejects several lucrative offers to cash in on his accidental fame. He is never again involved significantly in the evolution/creationism controversy.

Rhea County natives Oren Metzger and William Hilleary publish *The World's Most Famous Court Trial*, the stenographer's transcript of the Scopes trial. By the next spring, they have sold more than 20,000 copies to customers as far away as China, Russia, Japan, and South Africa.

The House of Delegates of the American Medical Association approves a resolution to support the teaching of evolution in public schools. The resolution closes by stating that "any restriction of the proper study of scientific fact in regularly established scientific institutions [should] be considered inimical to the progress of science and to the public welfare."

Thirty thousand members of the Ku Klux Klan, meeting in Washington, D.C., pay tribute to William Jennings Bryan as the Klan becomes the first national organization to call for "equal time" for creationism and evolution in public schools. This demand will be renewed by creationists in the 1970s and 1980s and will culminate in *McLean v. Arkansas Board of Education* (1982) and *Edwards v. Aguillard* (1987), which stipulate that laws requiring "equal time" and "balanced treatment" for creationism are unconstitutional.

September   Phi Beta Kappa passes a resolution opposing antievolution laws.

October Texas Governor Miriam A. "Ma" Ferguson, who heads the Texas Textbook Commission, bans high school textbooks that teach the theory of evolution. Teachers who use the banned textbooks face prosecution and dismissal. The state's Subcommittee for the Modification of Textbooks formalizes agreements with several publishers to produce sanitized textbooks.

The Bryan Bible League becomes one of the few antievolution organizations to originate on the West Coast. The league, endorsed by William Jennings Bryan's widow, publishes the *Bryan Broadcaster* but accomplishes little.

November The Tennessee Academy of Science condemns the Butler Law, eight months after the law was passed. University officials, however, either support the law or remain silent, as do such newspapers as the *Nashville Tennessean* and Memphis' *Commercial Appeal.*

The Bible Crusaders of America is formed in Florida by George Washburn.

25 December The well-financed Bible Crusaders of America publishes the first issue of *Crusaders' Champion* magazine. *Champion*, which absorbed John Roach Straton's *Fundamentalist* and T. T. Martin's *Conflict*, attacks the teaching of evolution.

1925–1935   Various antievolution groups, often supported by religious fundamentalists and groups such as the Ku Klux Klan, form throughout the South. Within a few years, however, organized interest in the cause fades and the organizations disappear.

1926   U.S. Representative Bill G. Lowrey (MS) introduces an antievolution amendment to a District of Columbia appropriation bill. The bill fails. Soon thereafter, Senator Coleman Blease (SC) tries to amend the Radio Control Bill to enable government officials "to make and enforce regulations to censor and prohibit all discourses broadcast from stations under its control regarding the subject of evolution." The bill fails.

Ohio Wesleyan zoologist Edward Rice uses a widely read article in *Current History* to emphasize the parallels between the Scopes trial and the prosecution of Galileo. Rice claims that the antievolution movement is due largely to the public's ignorance of evolution.

The Southern Baptist Convention meets in Houston, Texas, and passes a resolution repudiating "as unscriptural and scientifically false every claim of evolution that declares or implies that man evolved to his present state from some lower order of life. . . . [We] accept Genesis as teaching that man was the special creation of God, and reject every theory, evolution or other, which teaches that man originated in, or came by way of, a lower animal ancestry."

Several attempts to remove proevolution books from Kansas' public schools fail. The Kansas legislature is never presented with an antievolution bill.

Via a written plea, the ACLU appeals to members of the AAAS to pay the remainder of its debt generated by the Scopes trial.

The superintendent of education in Cleveland, Ohio, bans the use of some proevolution biology books in schools under his jurisdiction.

An antievolution bill in Virginia is withdrawn without a vote, prompting an administrator at the University of Virginia to praise the governor and legislature for having "kept faith with the child of Thomas Jefferson."

Responding to pressure from the Bible Crusaders, the Louisiana House of Representatives passes an antievolution bill; the only opposition comes from the president of Louisiana State University, Thomas D. Boyd. On the morning of the Senate vote, the *Times-Picayune* describes the bill as "an unwise and futile undertaking" and the Senate postpones further consideration of the legislation.

Gerald Winrod creates the Defenders of the Christian Faith to fight evolution and promote his versions of racial and religious prejudice. By 1927, the Defenders have 3,000 members and publish *Defender* magazine. Within a few years, however, the organization shifts most of its criticisms to modernism and the "Negro menace."

The Texas Senate kills another antievolution bill that has passed the Texas House.

The Louisiana Baptist Convention demands that the State Board of Education abolish the teaching of evolution. A subsequent antievolution bill passes the House 52–43, but the Senate refuses to consider it.

The word *evolution* disappears from high school biology textbooks as they are sanitized in response to the Scopes trial. Evolution remains absent from most biology books for several decades.

January After the Mississippi House Education Committee votes 10–4 to reject an antievolution bill (modeled after Tennessee's Butler Law) that has been introduced by Representative L. Walter Evans (a Church of God minister), the Bible Crusaders of America dispatch T. T. Martin and two assistants to Mississippi to help pass the legislation. Martin addresses a joint session of the legislature, after which Evans's bill passes the House by a vote of 76–32. The Senate Education Committee rejects the bill, but the full Senate passes the bill by a vote of 29–16 and sends the nation's newest antievolution statute to Governor Henry L. Whitfield for his signature. Only after the bill reaches Governor Whitfield does Chancellor Alfred Hume of the University of Mississippi announce his opposition to the legislation, while also adding that the university is a Christian institution "shot through and through with the teaching of our Lord." During the next two years, the Bible Crusaders of America disappears as the nation becomes relatively indifferent to the evolution controversy.

Edward Young Clarke, who had earlier rebuilt the Ku Klux Klan, founds the Supreme Kingdom in Atlanta, Georgia, to fight the teaching of evolution. The Supreme Kingdom resembles the Klan in structure and membership. By 1928, however, the Kingdom disappears.

The ACLU files a brief with the Tennessee Supreme Court in Nashville to appeal the conviction of John Scopes. Scopes plays no role in the appeal; his only knowledge of it comes from newspapers and reporters who contact him for information.

In Kentucky, preacher Andrew Johnson announces plans to ban the teaching of evolution in all schools (including colleges and universities) in the state, leading Representative Grover Cleveland Johnson to introduce a bill (House Bill 96) that would enact this ban. Johnson's bill fails, as do two subsequent antievolution bills the same year. Thereafter, Kentucky considers no more attempts to ban the teaching of evolution in its public schools.

February   The Atlanta Board of Education bans the teaching of evolution in its public schools. When faced with legal questions, the board again states its opposition to the teaching of evolution but rescinds its earlier ban.

12 March   Governor Henry Whitfield signs the Mississippi antievolution legislation. Soon thereafter, George Rappleyea moves to Mississippi in hopes of helping the ACLU find someone to challenge the law, but there are no volunteers. The Mississippi law, which will become the last surviving antievolution law, is not declared unconstitutional until 1970.

4 May   In North Carolina, more than 300 antievolutionists meet in Charlotte and form the Committee of One Hundred (also known as the North Carolina Bible League), which tries to combat "heresies contrary to the Bible." The committee supports "useful arts and science" but hires a "Christian lawyer" to help state Representative Poole again draft antievolution legislation. Poole's bill punishes universities that contradict or deny "the divine origin of man or of the universe, as taught in the Holy Bible."

31 May   John Scopes's defense team, led by Clarence Darrow, argues to the Tennessee Supreme Court that Scopes's individual freedoms have been violated by the Butler Law. The state argues that the Butler Law is reasonable and that

Scopes, a state employee, is bound by state guidelines. The arguments end in early June, but the court doesn't announce its decision for six months.

September Kirtley Mather, one of the expert witnesses at the Scopes trial, publishes "The Psychology of the Anti-Evolutionist" in the *Harvard Graduates' Magazine.* Mather points out the many inconsistencies of the antievolutionists' arguments, paying special attention to their willingness to accept the evolution of plants and lower animals but not humans.

5 November Groundbreaking ceremonies for William Jennings Bryan University (later Bryan College) occur in Dayton, Tennessee, before a crowd of 10,000 onlookers, including Governor Austin Peay. Ten of the original nineteen incorporators of Bryan College (e.g., John Raulston, A. Thomas Stewart, Ben McKenzie) have direct connections to the Scopes trial.

December Arkansas state Representative Astor L. Rotenberry releases his proposed antievolution bill to the press. The bill contains no references to Genesis, but it makes it illegal (and fines violators $1,000) to teach evolution and use texts that claim that humans descended from a lower order of animals.

In hopes of fending off legislation that is pending in seventeen states, the American Association of University Professors and the American Association for the Advancement of Science pass a joint resolution opposing antievolution laws.

1927 Bob Jones Sr. opens Bob Jones University in Florida. Bob Jones University, like Bryan College in Dayton, stresses the fundamentalist belief in biblical inerrancy. The racist, fundamentalist university moves to Greenville, South Carolina, in 1947, where it later becomes the largest fundamentalist school in the world.

Maynard Shipley, who heads the Science League of America, publishes *The War on Modern Science: A Short History of the Fundamentalist Attacks on Evolution and Modernism.*

Shipley notes that "the armies of ignorance are being organized, literally by the millions, for a combined political assault upon modern science. . . . For the first time in our history, organized knowledge has come into open conflict with organized ignorance."

Herbert W. Armstrong, who will found the Worldwide Church of God in 1934, decides that "evolution [cannot] honestly be reconciled with the first chapter of Genesis" and that it "stands disproved—an error—a false theory."

The World's Christian Fundamentals Association, meeting in Atlanta, begins to formulate an antievolution bill to present to legislatures in every state as well as in Europe, China, South America, and Europe. This meeting is the high-water mark of the association, for membership begins to drop hereafter. By 1930, the group's convention will include no scheduled speeches about evolution.

The Methodists, who have not formed any organizations to fight the teaching of evolution, pass resolutions opposing restrictions on teaching and reject a proposal stating that the group disagrees "with the agnostic Darrow."

California Representative S. L. Heisinger introduces legislation to ban the teaching of evolution in the state's public schools. The bill dies in the House Education Committee in May.

William Bell Riley helps introduce an antievolution bill in the Minnesota legislature. The bill generates strong opposition and dies. Although Riley claims that 83 percent of the public endorses his work, he never presents another antievolution bill to the legislature.

Legislatures in Maine, New Hampshire, Delaware, Missouri, Oklahoma, West Virginia, and elsewhere consider and defeat antievolution bills.

The Tennessee legislature decisively rebuffs attempts to repeal the Butler Law.

The Louisiana superintendent of schools bans the teaching of evolution in the state's public schools.

The South Carolina legislature considers an antievolution bill, but the bill is withdrawn without a vote.

The Alabama House Committee on Education defeats an antievolution bill sponsored by the Supreme Kingdom.

January The House Education Committee of the North Carolina legislature rejects Representative Poole's antievolution bill by a vote of 25–11. This vote convinces creationists in the legislature that there is fading support for the antievolution cause.

12 January Representative T. P. Atkins introduces the first antievolution legislation in Arkansas.

13 January Representative Rotenberry introduces another antievolution bill (House Bill 34) to the Arkansas legislature. When Reverend Ben Bogard announces that he prefers Rotenberry's bill, Atkins withdraws his legislation. Subsequent hearings before the House Education Committee are poorly attended.

15 January Chief Justice Grafton Green announces that the Tennessee Supreme Court, in a split decision (*John Thomas Scopes v. State of Tennessee*), upholds the Butler Law as constitutional but reverses Scopes's conviction on a technicality. The court recommends that Scopes not be tried again ("We see nothing to be gained by prolonging the life of this bizarre case"), and he is not. Scopes plays no role in the appeal and does not return to Tennessee for the trial or decision.

28 January Hearings begin on Rotenberry's antievolution bill in Arkansas.

2 February Only four of the thirteen members of the Arkansas House Education Committee attend a hearing on Rotenberry's bill. The next day, the committee votes 5–2 to recommend that the House reject the bill.

9 February   The Arkansas House of Representatives brings up Rotenberry's bill as a special order of business. The bill passes by a vote of 50–47.

10 February   The Arkansas Senate tables consideration of the Rotenberry bill, thereby killing the legislation. Bogard begins a petition drive to mandate a public referendum on the teaching of evolution.

11 April   Florida Representative Leo Stalnaker of Tampa introduces a bill to ban the teaching of evolution and proevolution textbooks in the state's public schools.

19 April   The Florida House Judiciary Committee rejects Stalnaker's bill by a vote of 19–18, prompting antievolutionists to draft a substitute measure banning the teaching of evolution "as a fact."

17 May   The Florida House of Representatives passes (by a vote of 67–24) a bill banning the teaching of evolution in the state's public schools, but the bill dies in the Senate as the legislative session ends.

June   At its annual meeting in Seattle, the National Education Association passes a resolution opposing the antievolution laws.

November   Thanks to the efforts of Baptist preacher Ben Bogard, petitions for a public referendum to ban the teaching of evolution are circulating throughout Arkansas.

1928   The American False Anti-Science League and Home-Church State Protective Association is formed in California in honor of antievolution activist John Roach Straton. The association fails to generate much support.

The annual meeting of the Southern Baptist Convention includes no mention of evolution.

British microbiologist Fred Griffith discovers that transformations are inherited.

Reverend Bogard creates the American Anti-Evolution Association and continues gathering signatures in Arkansas for an antievolution law modeled after Tennessee's Butler Law.

6 June   Bogard files petitions with the Arkansas secretary of state containing signatures of more than 19,000 voters (8 percent of the state's eligible voters) supporting a ban on the teaching of evolution in Arkansas. These signatures ensure that legislation to ban the teaching of evolution in Arkansas' public schools (Initiated Act No. 1) will be decided by a popular vote by the state's citizens in November.

31 October   While campaigning for passage of Initiated Act No. 1, Bogard tells Arkansas voters that "Tennessee has taken on new life since the evolution bill became law. People of the right sort want to live in a state where the faith of their children will not be attacked in the free schools."

November   Almost two-thirds (108,991 for, 63,406 against) of the voters of Arkansas vote to ban the teaching of evolution in the state's public schools, thereby making the Arkansas antievolution law the only such law to be approved by a popular vote. Only five counties in the state vote against the act. Soon after the law's passage, the State Department of Education withdraws proevolution textbooks from public schools. The Arkansas antievolution law is the last statewide antievolution law that is passed (Tennessee and Mississippi had passed such laws earlier). The antievolution laws will not be overturned until 1968 by *Epperson v. Arkansas*.

A high school principal in Tennessee is forced to resign because he opposes the Butler Law.

1929   The Texas Senate kills another antievolution bill that has passed its House.

The Tennessee legislature again decisively rebuffs attempts to repeal the state's Butler Law.

A poll reports that 63 percent of Baptist preachers believe in the literal truth of Genesis.

1930	William Jennings Bryan University opens its temporary headquarters in the old high school where John Scopes allegedly taught evolution in 1925. In 1958, the university will be renamed William Jennings Bryan College; this name will be shortened to Bryan College in 1993.
	The Oklahoma legislature rejects a bill similar to Tennessee's Butler Law.
	Enrollment in U.S. high schools reaches 4.8 million students, which represents 51.4 percent of fourteen- to seventeen-year-olds in the country.
	The antievolution movement temporarily fades; at the annual meeting of the World's Christian Fundamentals Association, none of the scheduled speeches addresses evolution.
	English biologist Ronald Fisher's *The Genetical Theory of Natural Selection* reestablishes Darwin's theory of evolution by arguing that natural selection controls the direction of evolution by eliminating harmful mutations and perpetuating useful ones.
1931	Julian Huxley, grandson of Darwin's advocate Thomas Huxley, declares the antievolution movement to be "dull, but dead." Like those before and after him to make such claims, Huxley is wrong.
1932	After a seven-year search, the ACLU abandons its attempt to find another volunteer to challenge an antievolution law. The various antievolution laws remain unchallenged until 1965.
	Sewall Wright describes his "adaptive landscape" metaphor for evolution. Wright points out that not all genetic changes in species are adaptive.
	The transmission electron microscope enables scientists to see the internal structure of cells.
1933	Fundamentalists' claims are bolstered by a survey attempting to measure the degree of religious belief among U.S.

scientists. The survey finds that (1) believers tend to associate with less prominent scientists, (2) there are fewer believers than there were in an earlier survey conducted in 1914, and (3) education causes many people to reject traditional beliefs.

1935   George McCready Price and others form the Religion and Science Association to oppose the teaching of evolution. The association claims that God does not necessarily follow the laws of nature.

An attempt to repeal Tennessee's Butler Law fails by a vote of 67–20 in the Tennessee House of Representatives.

1936   Russian biologist Aleksandr Oparin argues in *The Origin of Life* that life originated through chemical evolution enhanced by increasingly complex organization of preliving organisms. Oparin claims that a type of natural selection acted on complex molecules in Earth's "primordial soup" and, in the process, eventually created life.

Russian émigré Theodosius Dobzhansky is invited to give a prestigious series of lectures in New York. Dobzhansky uses these lectures as the basis for his famous book, *Genetics and the Origin of Species*, which is released the following year.

1 January   Oscar Riddle of the Carnegie Institution of Washington reports to the AAAS that the antievolution movement has remained alive because of poor textbooks, the failure of biologists to educate the public about evolution, and poor teaching. Riddle argues forcefully that "the presumption that for making a teacher of biology there is any substitute for long-continued training under our best college biological departments is an expensive fraud, and the extent to which that presumption is being enforced in one or another guise is now an educational disgrace."

March   At the first meeting of the Religion and Science Association, moderate creationists alienate George McCready Price and other biblical literalists. Soon thereafter, the association disintegrates, prompting Price and his followers to form the Deluge Geology Society two years later.

| 1937 | Dobzhansky's *Genetics and the Origin of Species* helps biologists reconcile the fieldwork of naturalists with the mathematical ideas of population geneticists and, in the process, initiates a flurry of work that helps establish the "modern synthesis" in biology during the next decade. *Genetics* is described as "perhaps the most influential single book on evolutionary biology during the period from 1937 through the 1950s." |

An attempt to repeal the Arkansas antievolution law dies in committee without coming to a vote.

| 1938 | Self-described geologist and biblical literalist George McCready Price founds the Deluge Geology Society. The society lasts for seven years and publishes twenty issues of its *Bulletin of Deluge Geology and Related Sciences*. In 1970, Price's ideas will be updated, renamed "scientific creationism," and become the basis for a revival of creationism in the United States. |

Oparin's *The Origin of Life* is translated into English; the book stimulates a flurry of work and debate about the origin of life.

In another widely read essay published in *Science*, Oscar Riddle energizes scientists fighting for the acceptance of evolution by asking, "Shall the public that decides the fate of our democracy conceive nature and man as research discloses them or as uninformed and essentially ignorant masses can variously imagine them?"

In one of the few bright spots for evolutionists, Ella Smith's *Exploring Biology* (published by Harcourt, Brace, and Company) supports evolution, noting that "no one has discovered a single fact to disprove the theory of evolution, and the facts that establish its truth are abundant. . . . Evolution is a fact. Plants and animals do change and have been changing." However, virtually all other textbooks continue to ignore or downplay evolution; some, such as George Hunter and F. W. Hunter's *Biology in Our Lives* (published in 1949), even advocate creationism.

13 March   Famed attorney Clarence Darrow dies in Chicago at the age of eighty. His body is cremated and his ashes spread off of Clarence Darrow Bridge into Jackson Park Lagoon in Chicago.

1940s   Biologists complete the revolution started by Charles Darwin by confirming the importance of gradualism, natural selection, inheritance, paleontology, and population structure in evolution. This merger, based primarily on the work of Thomas Hunt Morgan, George Gaylord Simpson, Ronald Fisher, J. B. S. Haldane, Sewall Wright, Ernst Mayr, and Theodosius Dobzhansky, stimulates discussions that ultimately produce the "modern synthesis" in biology. Mayr describes the modern synthesis as "the most decisive event in the history of evolutionary biology since the publication of the *Origin of Species* in 1859." No longer is Darwinian evolution by natural selection one of several competing versions of evolution. Indeed, by the late 1950s, the modern synthesis is the guiding force in biology.

1940   Will Houghton, president of the Moody Bible Institute, writes a widely read article in the *Moody Monthly* arguing that Nazism (a "great mechanical monster") is based on evolution and materialism. According to Houghton, universities are responsible for the fact that modernism has replaced orthodox faith with Darwinism and Marxism.

1941   Chromatography is introduced as a way of separating chemical substances according to their structural properties and molecular weights.

Writer Irving Stone describes the Scopes trial as the "death blow" to creationism.

A national survey reports that one-third of teachers in public schools are "afraid to express acceptance of evolution" publicly.

September   At the invitation of the president of the Moody Bible Institute, a group of five evangelical Christian scientists meet in Chicago and establish the American Scientific Affiliation (ASA). The group initially opposes evolution and wants to unify evangelical Christianity and science by correlating "the facts of science and the Holy Scriptures." The affiliation, which tries to show that Christianity and science are not necessarily incompatible, delays its first meeting until after World War II. The ASA is never very influential. In 1963, several disgruntled members depart to form the Creation Research Society, which will become the leading creationist society of the late twentieth century.

1942   A national survey shows that less than half of high school biology teachers in the United States teach evolution.

Julian Huxley publishes *Evolution: The Modern Synthesis.* Huxley's review of evolutionary theory, which includes much evidence unavailable to Darwin, reenergizes Darwin's ideas. Huxley's book is reprinted with a new introduction in 1963.

After gaining insights from Dobzhansky's *Genetics and the Origin of Species*, Ernst Mayr publishes his masterwork, *Systematics and the Origin of Species*, which helps establish the evolutionary significance of geographic isolation and small selective advantages. Mayr's work, like that of Dobzhansky, plays a critical role in the formulation of the "modern synthesis" during the upcoming two decades.

1943   *The Teaching of the Basic Sciences*, a report from the commissioner of education, argues that the nonscientific emphasis of science education in the United States results primarily from the poor preparation of science teachers.

1944   George Gaylord Simpson, heavily influenced by Dobzhansky's *Genetics and the Origin of Species*, publishes his *Tempo and Mode in Evolution.* Simpson's book, delayed somewhat by the war, bridges paleontology and genetics, thereby solidifying the modern synthesis in biology. Later in the year, however, Simpson comments that there is a "regular absence of transitional forms" in the fossil record. For years, creationists will use this statement to discredit the theory of evolution.

Oswald T. Avery and his colleagues show that DNA is the hereditary molecule.

1945	As had occurred earlier in Price's *Religion and Science Association*, the Deluge Geology Society becomes influenced by old-Earth creationists and abandons biblical literalism. Soon thereafter, the society declines rapidly.
1946	The ASA has its first formal meeting, at which it decides to begin publishing a journal.
	Influential creationist Henry Morris publishes his antievolution book titled *That You Might Believe*, in which he claims that the teaching of evolution could damage students.
1947	In *Everson v. Board of Education*, the U.S. Supreme Court announces that states cannot legitimately help religion in any form. Justice Hugo Black's majority opinion reaffirms the concept of a "wall of separation" between church and state.
	The journal *Evolution* is founded.
1948	The ASA publishes the first issue of *Modern Science and Christian Faith*. Members of the affiliation, who increasingly hold advanced degrees in science, reject Price's flood geology.
	In *Illinois ex rel. McCollum v. Board of Education*, the U.S. Supreme Court emphasizes the importance of public schools to American culture: "The public school is at once the symbol of our democracy and the most pervasive means for promoting our common destiny. In no activity of the state is it more vital to keep out divisive forces than in its schools."
	The Soviet Communist Party declares that natural selection and Mendelian genetics are erroneous, allowing Russian botanist Trofim Lysenko to introduce his own version of Lamarckism in their place. The results are disastrous.
1949	The ASA begins publishing a nondoctrinal periodical that later becomes the *Journal of the American Scientific Affiliation*. The journal publishes a variety of viewpoints.
1950	G. L. Stebbins publishes *Variation and Evolution in Plants*.

Pope Pius XII's *Humani generis* declares that "the teaching of the Church leaves the doctrine of evolution an open question."

1950–1955   A variety of surveys of biology teachers shows that at least 30 percent of respondents do not discuss evolution in their courses.

1951   George Gaylord Simpson makes his famous observation: "Evolution has no purpose; man must supply this for himself."

1952   Alfred Hershey and Martha Chase show that genes are made of DNA.

Rosalind Franklin makes the first X-ray diffraction photographs of DNA.

Another attempt to repeal Tennessee's Butler Law fails, thanks largely to the efforts of Bryan College.

1953   Stanley Miller and Richard Urey confirm many of Aleksandr Oparin's claims about the early atmosphere and the origin of life. Miller and Urey pass a spark through Oparin's re-created early atmosphere and produce amino acids. Miller's work encourages biologists to study the origin of life on Earth.

In a famous article in *Nature*, James Watson and Francis Crick announce the double-helix structure of DNA.

J. S. Weiner and his colleagues show that the Piltdown man is a hoax; the skull and jaw belong to two different creatures.

Henry Morris meets John C. Whitcomb Jr. at a meeting of the ASA. The two begin discussions that ultimately lead to their monumental book, *The Genesis Flood*.

1955   Biologist John W. Klotz publishes *Genes, Genesis, and Evolution*, which typifies many creationists' demands for capitulation rather than examination of evidence. Klotz knew enough about biology to wish that he didn't have to defend creationism and a worldwide flood, but he felt he had no choice because "Scripture speaks and that settles it for me."

Jerome Lawrence and Robert E. Lee publish the screenplay of *Inherit the Wind.* Five years later, the movie version of *Inherit the Wind*—albeit fictitious—informs the world about the trial of John Scopes in 1925.

The American Institute of Biological Sciences forms an Education and Professional Recruitment Committee to develop a program in biology education. The committee recommends that evolution be included in all biology programs.

10 January   *Inherit the Wind* opens at the Dallas Theater on Broadway. In the popular play the Scopes Trial, then safely a generation in the past, is used to highlight the threat to intellectual freedom presented by the anti-Communist hysteria of the McCarthy era. Most people consider the play and subsequent movie versions of the play to be accurate depictions of the Scopes trial. When its Broadway run ends in 1957, *Inherit the Wind* is the most successful and longest running drama in U.S. history. In the play and in the movies, Bryan is depicted as the vanquished fool and the voice of majoritarian oppression, whereas Darrow is depicted as the voice of freedom.

1956   President Dwight D. Eisenhower and the U.S. Congress increase the budget of the National Science Foundation by 256 percent.

29 January   H. L. Mencken dies and is buried in Loudon Park Cemetery in Baltimore, Maryland.

1957   Jerrold Zacharias and a group of physicists form the Physical Science Study Committee, which receives a grant of $303,000 from the NSF to develop materials to teach physics to high school students. The NSF makes similar grants for math, chemistry, biology, and the social sciences. By 1975, the NSF will have provided $101,207,000 to fund fifty-three projects.

Arthur Garfield Hays, one of Scopes's defenders, notes that he can hardly believe that "religious views of the Middle

Ages" could persist in the age of "railroads, steamboats, the telephone, the radio, the airplane, all the great mechanistic discoveries."

4 October   The Soviet Union successfully launches *Sputnik I*, the first orbiting artificial satellite. This launch, combined with the failure of the American *Vanguard* satellite a few weeks later, triggers widespread concern that the United States is lagging behind the Soviet Union in science and technology. This concern ultimately prompts the NSF to implement the first significant reforms in science education, one of which is the creation of the Biological Sciences Curriculum Study (BSCS) in 1959 at the University of Colorado.

December   Henry Morris and John Whitcomb begin writing *The Genesis Flood*. The book, which will not appear until 1961, promotes flood geology and becomes a landmark in the creationism movement in the United States.

1958   Congress passes the National Defense Education Act, which encourages the National Science Foundation to fund and develop state-of-the-art science textbooks. This results in a $143,000 grant from the NSF to establish the BSCS.

Biologists learn that DNA controls cell operations by directing the synthesis of RNA, which in turn directs the synthesis of proteins.

November   In a talk presented at the annual meeting of the Central Association of Science and Mathematics Teachers, Nobel laureate Hermann J. Muller tells attendees that "one hundred years without Darwin are enough." In a subsequent essay that is widely publicized, Muller challenges biology teachers to do a better job of teaching evolution.

1959   The American Scientific Affiliation publishes zoologist Russell Mixter's *Evolution and Christian Thought*, a collection of essays that marks a clear departure from biblical literalism, which insists on the ideas of a young Earth and a worldwide flood.

Another attempt to repeal the Arkansas antievolution law

fails. The leader of the attempt, Willie Oates, is branded an atheist and withdraws her bill. Oates loses her next bid for reelection.

Biologist Oscar Riddle notes that "biology is still pursued by long shadows from the Middle Ages, shadows screening from our people that our science has learned of human origins . . . a science sabotaged because its central and binding principle displaces a hallowed myth."

The Middle Tennessee State University chapter of the American Association of University Professors petitions the state legislature to repeal the Butler Law. The Rutherford County Court condemns the "freethinking" educators and says that the "God-fearing men" of the court oppose action against the law.

Hermann Muller writes that biology in public schools is dominated by "antiquated religious traditions."

February The Biological Sciences Curriculum Study is created with equal numbers of professional biologists and high school teachers and begins work on several biology textbooks that emphasize evolution, human reproduction, and laboratory work. Among the contributors are Hermann Muller and George Gaylord Simpson. The BSCS books "put evolution back in the biology curriculum" and, as a result, revive the evolution/creationism controversy.

November As part of the Darwin Centennial Celebration at the University of Chicago, the NSF convenes sixty-three of the leading high school biology teachers at the National Conference of High School Biology Teachers. The teachers criticize the poor coverage of evolution in textbooks but are hesitant to endorse evolution as a "fact."

1960   The BSCS decides to refer to its three upcoming textbooks not by the books' foci (e.g., cell biology), but instead by their color (e.g., yellow) so that it doesn't imply that the texts are specialized for advanced biology courses or that the BSCS is trying to establish a national curriculum for biology.

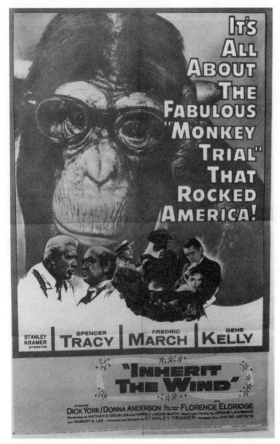

Although factually inaccurate, the movie version of Inherit the Wind *popularized the legend of the Scopes trial. The movie garnered four Academy Awards nominations. Among the film's many highlights is Spencer Tracy's 11-minute summation, which was filmed in a single take to heighten the tension of the movie's climax. (Courtesy of Randy Moore)*

21 July   The movie version of *Inherit the Wind* has its world premiere during the thirty-fifth anniversary of the Scopes trial in Dayton, Tennessee. John Scopes attends the premiere and is honored with a parade and a key to the city. One of the writers of the screenplay, Nedrick Young, had been blacklisted by Joseph McCarthy and wrote under the pseudonym Nathan E. Douglas; Young's credits are restored in 1997.

1961

The BSCS continues work on biology textbooks that stress evolution as the unifying theme of biology. Some states accept the BSCS books, but education officials in Texas insist that the publisher delete statements such as, "To biologists there is no longer any reasonable doubt that evolution occurs." The publisher accepts these revisions, which appear in subsequent editions of the blue version. Within a few years after being released, the BSCS books are being used in nearly half of all high school biology courses in the United States. Publishers of competing books soon begin producing books similar to the BSCS books.

In a footnote to the *Torcaso v. Watkins* case, U.S. Supreme Court Justice Hugo Black lists "Secular Humanism" as a religion that does not "teach what would generally be considered a belief in the existence of God." In subsequent years, such creationists as William Willoughby claim that the teaching of evolution promotes the religion of secular humanism.

Marshall Nirenberg's discovery that the nucleotide triplet of uracil codes for the amino acid phenylalanine begins the challenge of cracking the genetic code. The code is finally deciphered in 1968.

A survey of 1,000 high school teachers reveals that two-thirds of the teachers believe that they can teach biology effectively without accepting evolution. Another survey later in the decade shows that more than 60 percent of biology teachers believe that evolution is a theory and therefore cannot be said to have definitely occurred.

March John Whitcomb and Henry Morris publish *The Genesis Flood: The Biblical Record and Its Scientific Implications*, a book that becomes a creation science classic and a flash point in creationists' subsequent demands for "equal time" in the classroom. *The Genesis Flood*, which includes photos of the bed of the Paluxy River to claim that humans lived with dinosaurs, presents George McCready Price's flood geology as the only acceptable interpretation of Genesis. Whitcomb and Morris present two complementary ideas: (1) natural phenomena can be explained by principles of biblical inerrancy (e.g., "the fossil record, no less than the present taxonomic classification system, and the nature of genetic mutation mechanism, shows exactly what the Bible teaches"), and (2) flood geology is the central paradigm of creationism. Whitcomb and Morris announce creationism as truth by claiming that humans cannot know and should not speculate about the details of creation. The authors stress their indoctrination-based ideas with statements such as, "The fully instructed Christian knows that the evidence for full divine inspiration of Scripture is far weightier than the evidences for any fact of science." *The Genesis Flood*, which challenges the theistic evolution that typified organizations such as the American Scientific Affiliation, rescues antievolutionary thought from thirty-five years of obscurity.

The Genesis Flood *popularized "creation science" and revived the anti-evolution crusade. (Institute for Creation Research)*

1962   The preparation of the BSCS books goes smoothly despite a cutback in support from the National Science Foundation.

Early results indicate that students who use BSCS books do better on a variety of tests than do students who use other books.

January Mormon leaders in Phoenix, Arizona, demand that drafts of the BSCS books that are being tested there be removed from schools because the books come "as close to teaching atheism as one can at the secondary level." Dr. Howard Seymour (superintendent of the Phoenix School System) quells the protest by proclaiming that "students are not expected to believe this [instruction in evolution]."

June In *Engel v. Vitale*, the U.S. Supreme Court bans compulsory state-sponsored prayer in public schools.

1963   Henry Morris and like-minded creationists (most of whom are dissatisfied members of the ASA) organize the Creation Research Society, which becomes the leading creationist organization of the late twentieth century. The Creation Research Society is a Christian-only organization. Geneticist Walter Lammerts is named the society's first president. By 1973, the society has almost 2,000 members. Morris claims that evolution is guided by Satan and that it produces communism.

In Phoenix, Southern Baptist preacher Aubrey Moore claims that the teaching of evolution is "the first step in communism" and demands that it be removed from the curriculum. Moore warns school board members that if they "won't do it, we're going to get people together who will do something about it." When Superintendent Howard Seymour rejects Moore's demands, Moore begins trying to gather 55,000 signatures to force a public referendum about his antievolution message. The bombastic Moore tries to gather signatures by telling citizens that "there is nothing in the [B]ible about a fish turning into a man." Moore fails to gather enough signatures to force a public referendum.

John Scopes retires as a geologist and begins granting more interviews about his famous trial.

The BSCS publishes three high school biology textbooks

(i.e., blue, green, yellow); within seven years of their publication, the books are used in almost half of all U.S. high schools, including those in the three southern states that have had antievolution laws.

The NSF provides funding (which will eventually amount to $4.8 million) for the MACOS (Man: A Course of Study) curriculum, an introduction to evolution and the behavioral and social sciences for elementary school students. When it is finally released years later, MACOS creates a nationwide controversy.

Walter Lang, a Lutheran preacher in Caldwell, Idaho, founds the Bible Science Association in Minneapolis, "to stimulate an exchange of ideas on Bible-Science relationships," and begins publishing the mimeographed *Bible-Science Newsletter*. The association produces a variety of books for grades K–12 and sponsors tours, seminars, films, radio programs, and meetings. The association, which eventually boasts 15,000 members, focuses its ministry in southern California through the work of Nell Segraves and Jean Sumrall.

Tennessee passes legislation requiring all biology textbooks to include a disclaimer stating that any idea about "the origin and creation of man and his world . . . is not represented to be scientific fact." Legislators make the Bible exempt from this disclaimer.

In *School District of Abington Township v. Schempp*, the U.S. Supreme Court declares that it is unconstitutional for states to require Bible reading and the recitation of the Lord's Prayer in public schools. Many people upset by the decision describe it as an attempt to "outlaw God."

Creationists and self-appointed textbook censors Mel and Norma Gabler begin examining textbooks and testifying at meetings of the Texas Board of Education. A decade later, the Gablers devote all their time to the creationism cause and found Education Research Analysts, which tries to ban textbooks that "eliminate coming to Christ for forgiveness of sin."

May   Unable to convince the Orange County Board of Education to ban the teaching of evolution, Nell Segraves and Jean Sumrall (who later help create the Creation Science Research Center) petition the California Board of Education to require that evolution be taught as theory rather than fact. Segraves and Sumrall believe that the teaching of evolution promotes atheism and is therefore unfair to Christian children. Soon thereafter, conservative Superintendent of Public Instruction Max Rafferty orders that all textbooks in California be so labeled.

1964   Graduate student William D. Hamilton proposes his theory of kin selection. Hamilton argues that altruism is beneficial if the organisms being helped bear the same genes as oneself.

January   The California Board of Education hears Segraves and Sumrall claim that "atheistic and agnostic" evolution should be referred to as a theory instead of a fact in state-approved biology textbooks. Segraves and Sumrall's argument is based on the recent *School District of Abington Township v. Schempp* decision, in which the U.S. Supreme Court declared that mandated Bible reading in public schools is not religiously neutral because it violates the rights of nonbelievers. Segraves and Sumrall argue that if it is unconstitutional "to teach God in the school," then it must also be unconstitutional "to teach the absence of God." The Board of Education unanimously rejects the request that textbooks be rewritten to accommodate creationists' concerns.

June   Claiming that the BSCS's textbooks are the "most vicious attack we have ever seen on the Christian religion," Church of Christ preacher Reuel Gordon Lemmons of Austin begins a campaign to block the adoption of proevolution textbooks in Texas. Like Segraves and Sumrall in California, Lemmons demands that evolution be taught "as a theory" and is helped by antievolution groups (e.g., the Creation Research Society) and by Mel and Norma Gabler. The Gablers believe that the humanistic emphasis of the textbooks leads to the rejection of traditional morality.

September   Susan Epperson, the daughter of a biology professor, begins teaching biology at Little Rock Central High

School in Arkansas. Epperson teaches evolution in her biology course.

15 October   The Texas Textbook Commission rejects claims that the five biology textbooks recommended for adoption in the state's schools promote atheism. The textbooks include the three books produced by the BSCS. The commission's decision is supported by J. W. Edgar, the state's education commissioner.

9 November   The Texas Board of Education endorses the State Textbook Commission's recommendation about textbooks but insists that evolution be referred to as a theory rather than a fact.

1965   NBC produces and broadcasts a new version of *Inherit the Wind.*

The California State Advisory Committee on Science Education, which includes members such as Jacob Bronowski of the Salk Institute, begins drafting new curriculum recommendations for its public schools. The committee's recommendations, which will appear in the fall of 1969 as *The Scientific Framework for California Public Schools, Kindergarten–Grades One through Twelve,* trigger lawsuits and controversy.

Trofim Lysenko is removed as director of the Soviet Institute of Genetics, but it takes years to repair the damage that his policies have inflicted in Russia. Lysenko's removal helps return Soviet biological thought to the mainstream of international scientific ideas.

Nobel laureate James D. Watson says that "the theory of evolution is an accepted fact for everyone but a fundamentalist minority, whose objections are based not on reasoning but on doctrinaire adherence to religious principles."

Another attempt to repeal the Arkansas antievolution law, this one led by Nathan Schoenfeld, fails.

John Scopes claims that "restrictive legislation on academic freedom is forever a thing of the past."

The Creation Research Society bans old-Earth ideas from its publications and commits itself to publishing a creationism-based biology textbook. Those efforts culminate in 1970 with the publication of *Biology: A Search for Order in Complexity.*

February House Bill 301 banning the teaching of evolution in Arizona's public schools is introduced in the Arizona Senate, but it dies in the Senate Education Committee.

September Forrest Rozzell calls a press conference in Little Rock, Arkansas, to issue a "personal position" statement emphasizing the importance of understanding nature and recommending the repeal of the 1928 Arkansas antievolution law.

Biology teacher Susan Epperson sued in 1965 to overturn Arkansas' ban on teaching evolution in public schools. (AP Photo)

November High school teacher Susan Epperson meets with representatives of the Arkansas Education Association to discuss challenging the state's antievolution law. Epperson agrees to test the 1928 law because of her "concept of responsibilities as a teacher of biology and as an American citizen." The ACLU offers legal assistance to Epperson and the AEA, but it is declined because of the negative connotations that the entrance of the ACLU would produce.

4 December The AEA's Board of Directors authorizes a legal challenge of Arkansas' antievolution law.

6 December The AEA files a lawsuit on behalf of Susan Epperson in the Pulaski County Chancery Court challenging the Arkansas antievolution law. Wanting to avoid a "Scopes fiasco," Epperson asks for a declaratory judgment that the teaching of evolution represents a constitutional right and that obeying the 1928 law will force her to ignore "the obligations of a responsible teacher of biology." Epperson's challenge is later joined by Hubert Blanchard, who argues that the state's antievolution law damages his sons. Epperson's case is the first challenge of an antievolution law since the trial of John Scopes in 1925.

1966   Henry Morris describes his strict creationist ideas in his book *Studies in the Bible and Science.* Morris claims that if anyone wants to know about creation, the "sole source of true information is . . . divine revelation. God was there when it happened . . . [the Bible] is our textbook on the science of Creation!"

Encouraged by Max Rafferty, California's superintendent of public instruction, Segraves and Sumrall ask the California Board of Education to mandate equal time for creationism in classrooms and textbooks. The board refuses the request.

5 March   John Wright, the last of the Scopes jurors, dies at age eighty-four.

1 April   Susan Epperson's case is heard in a two-hour proceeding without a jury in chancery court in Arkansas. Attorney General Bruce Bennett, after proclaiming that he "intends to defend" the Bible, invokes the memory of William Jennings Bryan by claiming that evolution is atheistic and that the state has the right to determine what is taught in its public schools. Judge Murray Reed later rules that the Arkansas antievolution statute is unconstitutional.

November   Arkansas voters oust Bennett and several other segregationists in general elections.

1967   Henry Morris emphasizes his belief in truth by indoctrination when he tells believers that "the final and conclusive evidence against evolution is the fact that the Bible denies it," that the Bible contains "all the known facts of science," and that "there neither is, nor can be, any proof of evolution. . . . Only the Creator—God himself—can tell us what is the truth about the origin of all things. And this He has done, in the Bible, if we are willing simply to believe that He has told us. . . . If we expect to learn anything more than this about the Creation, then God above can tell us."

13 January   Knoxville attorney Martin Southern files a lawsuit in the name of his fourteen-year-old son, Thomas, in Knox County Chancery Court to test the validity of Tennessee's Butler Law. Southern claims that the law has "limited" his son's education and asks for a declaratory judgment to overturn the law. Chancellor Len G. Broughton takes the matter under advisement.

1 March   A coalition of legislators from Nashville and Memphis introduces House Bill 48 to repeal Tennessee's Butler Law. The following day, the bill is sent to the Judiciary Committee, whose chairperson (Charles Galbreath) had cosponsored the bill.

12 April   The Tennessee House of Representatives begins debating whether to repeal the Butler Law. When Memphis Democrat D. O. Smith (the bill's cosponsor) asks for the repealer to be brought before the House, the House's sergeant at arms brings a caged monkey to Smith's desk. The debate includes numerous proclamations of faith, after which the House supports the bill by a vote of 59–30.

13 April   Encouraged by a group of fundamentalist preachers, Archie Cotton—a local coal mine operator and member of the Campbell County Board of Education—charges Jacksboro High School science teacher Gary L. Scott with unprofessional conduct, neglect of duty, and violation of Tennessee's Butler Law. At a closed meeting, Cotton convinces the Board of Education to vote unanimously to fire Scott.

14 April   Gary Scott is fired for allegedly teaching evolution. The next day, Scott's story appears on the front page of the *New York Times*. Scott gets little local support. By the end of April, Scott has gained the support of the ACLU and the National Education Association, who arrange for Scott to be represented by William Kunstler.

20 April   The Tennessee Senate's two-hour debate about repealing the Butler Law is broadcast on television. The Senate's vote is a tie (16–16), which defeats the bill. The Senate then votes 23–10 to support Senate Bill 536, which amends the Butler Law to ban the teaching of evolution as "fact." However, the Tennessee House refuses to accept this proposed amendment, thereby leaving as uncertain the fate of the Butler Law.

11 May   Facing bad publicity and high expected costs for

defending the decision to fire Gary Scott, the Campbell County Board of Education votes 7–1 to reinstate Scott and pay him his salary. Scott's reinstatement removes the Campbell County Board of Education as a defendant in the case but doesn't address the constitutionality of the Butler Law.

15 May   Scott's attorneys use a class action suit in federal district court to charge that Tennessee's Butler Law is unconstitutional; the suit includes Scott, two of his students, fifty-nine Tennessee teachers, and the National Science Teachers Association. Scott asks for a permanent injunction to restrain state and local officials from enforcing the Butler Law. Scott's attorneys admit that they will drop Scott's lawsuit if the Tennessee Senate repeals the Butler Law.

16 May   The Tennessee Senate debates House Bill 48 to repeal the Butler Law. After debating for less than three minutes, senators vote 20–13 to repeal the nation's most famous antievolution law.

18 May   Tennessee Governor Buford Ellington signs legislation to repeal the Butler Law, which had been used in 1925 to convict John Scopes of the crime of teaching human evolution. Gary Scott and Martin Southern drop their lawsuits.

27 May   Citing the Scopes trial, Judge Reed issues a nine-page decision declaring that the Arkansas antievolution law is unconstitutional because it tends to "hinder the quest for knowledge, restrict the freedom to learn, and restrain the freedom to teach." Reed's decision makes it legal—at least temporarily—to teach human evolution in Arkansas.

5 June   The Arkansas Supreme Court reverses Judge Reed's decision by ruling that the Arkansas antievolution law is "a valid exercise of the state's power to specify the curriculum in its public schools." The court's one-paragraph opinion again makes it a crime to teach human evolution in Arkansas but does not address larger issues or comment on the validity of evolution. Susan Epperson decides to appeal the decision.

26 July   The Arkansas Supreme Court refuses to reconsider its decision upholding the ban on the teaching of evolution in the state's public schools.

1968   Biologists complete deciphering the genetic code.

4 March   The U.S. Supreme Court agrees to hear Susan Epperson's challenge of the Arkansas antievolution law.

16 October   *Epperson v. Arkansas* is argued before the U.S. Supreme Court. Epperson's principal brief to the Court closes with a dramatic reference to "the famous *Scopes* case" and to the "darkness in that jurisdiction" that followed it. The state counters by appealing to the authority of the *Scopes* case and closes with excerpts from the Tennessee Supreme Court's opinion in that case.

12 November   The U.S. Supreme Court rules unanimously in *Epperson v. Arkansas* that banning the teaching of evolution is unconstitutional. This decision is subsequently applied in a variety of other decisions, including those involving censorship of textbooks, Bible readings in public schools, and academic freedom. After *Epperson v. Arkansas*, only Mississippi retained an antievolution law. John Scopes later notes that the controversy "will go on with other actors and other plays."

1969   Acting on behalf of her daughter Frances, Mrs. Arthur G. Smith of Jackson, Mississippi, sues in state court for an injunction against the enforcement of the state's antievolution law. Smith argues that her daughter is being denied a proper education and, citing *Epperson v. Arkansas*, that the antievolution law is unconstitutional. The lower court later dismisses Smith's lawsuit and claims that the state's antievolution law is constitutional, despite the U.S. Supreme Court's ruling to the contrary in the *Epperson* case. Smith appeals the decision to the Mississippi Supreme Court.

More than forty years after his famous trial, John Scopes receives an average of one letter per day about his trial.

Mel and Norma Gabler celebrate their first major success

when the Texas Board of Education deletes BSCS textbooks—the only biology textbooks that cover evolution thoroughly—from its list of state-approved books.

The $10 million provided by the National Science Foundation and other agencies to the BSCS has contributed significantly to the improvement of biology education in the United States. BSCS director Arnold B. Grobman announces that "it appears now that the major storms are over. There is every indication that the teaching of evolution is generally accepted in America and will become far more commonplace that it ever was before." Grobman, like those before him who made similar predictions, is wrong.

October Following a heated discussion, the California Board of Education sends *The Scientific Framework* guidelines to the State Department of Education for revision. Soon thereafter, Superintendent Rafferty announces that the guidelines will be rewritten to include creationism.

13 November Led by aerospace engineer and ASA member Vernon Grose, creationists file a 13-page memorandum that convinces the California Board of Education (of which seven members had been appointed by Governor Ronald Reagan) to vote unanimously to include scientific creationism in the state's 205-page *Scientific Framework*. Publishers change their textbooks to accommodate the new recommendations.

4 December Outraged members of the California State Advisory Committee on Science Education issue a statement drafted by Stanford University's Paul DeHart Hurd opposing the changes made in *The Scientific Framework* by Grose and his creationist colleagues.

1970   The scanning electron microscope enables biologists to see a high-resolution image of the surfaces of structures.

Proponents of George McCready Price's "flood geology"—most notably, Henry Morris—repackage his ideas as "creation science" and "scientific creationism" and start a revival of creationism in the United States. The creation science movement will later become immensely popular.

Thanks largely to the work of Morris, strict creationism— once a minority point of view among creationists—becomes the movement's dominant view.

The Education Development Center publishes the NSF-backed MACOS introductory curriculum for elementary school students. Within four years, 1,700 school districts in 47 states adopt the award-winning and acclaimed program, but soon thereafter nationwide opposition by parents and teachers cuts sales dramatically. In response, several members of Congress, led by Representative John Conlan and Senator Jesse Helms, pressure the NSF to limit funding for proevolution projects. To avoid further investigations, the NSF becomes cautious in its treatment of evolution-related projects. In 1980, presidential candidate Ronald Reagan uses MACOS as an example of the federal government's endorsement of subversive values.

January While on a sabbatical from Virginia Polytechnic Institute, Henry Morris meets Baptist preacher Tim LaHaye at the Torrey Memorial Bible Conference in Los Angeles. Morris later resigns his faculty position in Virginia and moves to California to help LaHaye establish the fundamentalist Christian Heritage College in San Diego; while teaching a course there, Morris unveils the phrase *creation science*. All students attending the conservative college are required to take six semester hours of scientific creationism.

Prompted by the California textbook controversies in the late 1960s, Nell Segraves convinces Henry Morris to merge her chapter of the Bible Science Association with the research branch of the college to create a new organization; thus, they, along with Kelly Segraves, found the Creation Science Research Center, which will be directed by Morris. Soon thereafter, Morris's Creation Research Society produces *Biology: A Search for Order in Complexity*, a procreationism and antievolution textbook that claims that "there is no way to support the doctrine of evolution" and promotes what comes to be known as the "two-model approach"— that is, a "creation model" (which mirrors Genesis and no other creation myth) and an "evolution model." The textbook, which is published by Zondervan (a Christian publishing house) after more than five years in development, is used at several public and many private schools. The Creation Research Society uses royalties from sales of *Biology* to promote creation science.

21 January   Mississippi legislators begin debating a bill to repeal the state's antievolution law. The effort to repeal the law fails by a vote of 70–42, leaving the fate of the law to the state's courts.

1 April   During a two-day visit to Peabody College in Nashville, John Scopes makes his final public appearance and his first appearance in a Tennessee classroom in forty-five years. Scopes says that, "It is the teacher's business to decide what to teach. It is not the business of the federal courts nor of the state." *Time* magazine notes that "history has treated Scopes well and he was greeted like a returning hero."

13 July   Russell Artist, a biology professor and ardent creation scientist at Nashville's David Lipscomb College, and a delegation of believers convince the Tennessee Textbook Commission to approve *Biology: A Search for Order in Complexity* as a supplemental textbook, but no school system buys the book. However, by the mid-1970s, the Creation Research Science Education Foundation convinces education officials in nine states to approve *Biology* for use in their schools.

21 October   John Scopes dies at age seventy and is buried in a family plot in Oak Grove Cemetery in Paducah, Kentucky, not far from Loan Oak School, where he first learned about evolution. Scopes is buried beneath the inscription A MAN OF COURAGE.

November   The *American Biology Teacher* publishes an article by Duane Gish titled "A Challenge to Neo-Darwinism" that stresses familiar antievolution arguments (e.g., there are no intermediate life-forms) while claiming that many scientists question evolution. Gish pleads for teachers to give a "balanced presentation" of the evidence. These calls for fairness and equal time will become increasingly popular in coming decades.

John Scopes died on 21 October 1970 and was buried in Lot 104, Section 7 of Oak Grove Cemetery in Paducah, New York, beneath the inscription "A Man of Courage." At the foot of John's grave is the gravestone of his sister Lela, who was fired as a math teacher when she would not renounce the theory of evolution. (Courtesy of Randy Moore)

Leona Wilson sues the Houston Independent School District in federal district court on behalf of her daughter, Rita Wright, and other students on the basis that their constitutional rights are being violated by the teaching of evolution as fact and without referring to other theories of origin. The resulting lawsuit (*Wright v. Houston Independent School District*) is the first suit initiated by creationists.

21 December In a ruling on Mrs. Arthur Smith's appeal of a lower court's decision to uphold the state's antievolution law, the Mississippi Supreme Court rules in *Smith v. State* that Mississippi's antievolution law—the last surviving law of its kind—is "void." The state does not appeal. Within a span of three years, legislatures and courts have rejected all of the antievolution laws.

| 1971 | Wilson Riles, the new superintendent of public instruction in California, appoints scientists to a new Curriculum Committee that will make textbook recommendations for the state's public schools. |

The discovery of restriction enzymes enables scientists to build the first recombinant DNA by combining DNA fragments from two different viruses.

The Michigan legislature considers a bill requiring "equal time" for creationism. After references to the Bible are removed from the bill, the legislation is supported by the House of Representatives. However, the bill reaches the Senate too late to be considered.

The Board of Education in Columbus, Ohio, passes a resolution encouraging teachers to present creationism and evolution in their science classes.

| 1972 | The National Academy of Sciences, the National Science Teachers Association, and the National Association of Biology Teachers—spurred into action by creationists' victories in California—begin campaigns to oppose requirements that biology teachers include creationism in their courses. |

Biologists Niles Eldredge and Stephen J. Gould challenge the traditional view of gradual evolution and announce their theory of punctuated equilibrium, which states that evolution proceeds through relatively short bursts of rapid change followed by long periods of stasis.

A poll shows that 75 percent of students at Rhea County High School—the school at which John Scopes taught—are creationists who believe that evolution produces corruption, lust, greed, drug addiction, war, and genocide.

Jack Chick publishes *Big Daddy?*, a comic-book tract that is probably the most popular and widely distributed piece of creationist literature ever. In *Big Daddy?*, a college student teaches a professor about creationism.

The NABT, which publishes the journal *American Biology*

Teacher, establishes its Fund for Freedom in Science Teaching to help combat creationists. The fund receives $12,000 in donations, but the NABT's campaign also triggers a strong backlash from creationist biologists protesting the existence of the fund.

Still smarting over how creationists used his 1944 comment about the "absence of transitional forms" to discredit evolution, George Gaylord Simpson points out that biologists have discovered "literally thousands of transitional forms" and that "anyone who cites me or my work in opposition [to evolution] is either woefully ignorant or willfully misrepresenting the facts."

Henry Morris emphasizes his belief that evolution is the anti-God conspiracy of Satan by noting that "the peculiar rings of Saturn, the meteorite swarms . . . reflect some kind of heavenly catastrophe associated either with Satan's primeval rebellion or his continuing battle with Michael and the angels."

February Colorado state legislators introduce House Concurrent Resolution 1011 requiring "equal time" for creationism as an amendment to the state Constitution. Thanks to the efforts of William Mayer (director of the BSCS) and others, the bill dies in the Judiciary Committee.

April The Creation Science Research Center votes 8–4 to split from Christian Heritage College. Nell and Kelly Segraves take control of the CSRC while most of the rest of the staff (including Duane Gish, Henry Morris, and Harold Slusher) remain with the college. The latter group, still funded by the college, becomes the Institute for Creation Research, which will promote Morris's "young-Earth" beliefs. In *The Remarkable Birth of Planet Earth*, Morris presents scientific evidence of divine creation while blaming evolution "for our present-day social, political, and moral problems."

May The California Board of Education ignores the pro-science recommendations of the state's Curriculum Committee and restores creationist textbooks to its list of approved books. Soon thereafter, the board dissolves the Curriculum

Committee and replaces it with the Curriculum Development and Supplemental Materials Commission, which is staffed with creationists. The commission's subcommittee outrages many members of the State Board of Education when it refuses to recommend creationist textbooks.

June   Judge Woodrow B. Seals dismisses *Wright v. Houston Independent School District*, ruling that the free exercise of religion is not accompanied by a right to be insulated from scientific findings incompatible with one's beliefs.

August   William Willoughby, religion editor of the *Washington Evening Star*, sues H. Guyton Stever (director of the National Science Foundation) and the Board of Regents of the University of Colorado "in the interest of forty million evangelistic Christians in the United States." The NSF had provided funds for the development of the BSCS's textbooks; Willoughby wants the NSF to spend the same amount of money "for the promulgation of the creationist theory of the origin of man."

September   Prompted by the controversy in California, *Science* magazine editor William Bevan warns that creationists' victories could politicize the nation's classrooms, noting that "if the state can dictate the content of a science, it makes little difference that its motivation is religious rather than political."

October   To placate its many members who are creationists, the NABT sponsors a creationism session at its annual meeting; it is the best-attended session at the meeting. Bill Mayer of the BSCS condemns the NABT for acquiescing to creationists' demands.

November   The California Baptist Convention and other creationist groups pass resolutions calling for the California Board of Education to implement its original decision requiring the inclusion of creation science in textbooks.

9 November   The California Board of Education, meeting to examine creation science, hears testimonials from creationists such as Duane Gish, Vernon Grose, and Nell Segraves. The board agrees on a compromise that emphasizes the speculative nature of Darwinian evolution but does not mention God or Genesis.

December The California Board of Education accepts the texts recommended by the Curriculum Development and Supplemental Materials Commission. When Reverend David Hubbard of Pasadena complains about the dogmatism of scientists, the board votes 7–1 to remove dogmatism in explanations of origins in state-approved textbooks. The board appoints a committee of four creationists to oversee implementation of the new policy.

1973   Surveys indicate that in some parts of California, more than 80 percent of the residents favor the teaching of both creationism and evolution in public schools.

The Wisconsin and Michigan legislatures consider bills requiring "balanced treatment" for creationism and evolution, but the bills die in committee.

Biologists clone genes for the first time.

Creationist Henry Morris tells teachers to "present as many theories as possible and give the child the right to choose the one that seems most logical to him. We are working to have students receive a fair shake."

The Oregon School Board requires school libraries to include creationist materials and tells teachers to urge students to "weigh the information and arrive at their own conclusions."

The Georgia legislature holds public hearings on an equal-time law.

The Fifth Circuit Court of Appeals upholds Judge Seals's dismissal of *Wright v. Houston Independent School District*, declaring that the request for equal time is "an unwarranted intrusion into the authority of public school systems to control the academic curriculum."

American Biology Teacher publishes articles by Duane Gish

and John N. Moore proclaiming the tenets of creationism. The articles are prefaced by a statement saying that biologists reject creationism. In the same volume, the journal publishes an article by Theodosius Dobzhansky containing his now famous quotation, "Nothing in biology makes sense except in the light of evolution."

February   Duane Gish appears at Seattle-area churches and schools in hopes of mobilizing support for an equal-time bill in the state legislature. That bill (House Bill 1021) is killed by the House Education Committee. When the Committee for the Initiative on Creation and Evolution tries to gather enough signatures to force a referendum on the issue (Initiative 47) the following year, it falls far short of the 118,000 signatures needed to transmit the measure to the legislature.

March   The California Board of Education votes 7–3 to accept the recommendations of creationists that weaken the presentation in textbooks. Few scientists object.

26 March   Russell Artist convinces Tennessee Senator Milton Hamilton and several of his colleagues to introduce Senate Bill 394, which calls for "balanced treatment" of evolution and creationism. The bill, which becomes known as the "Genesis Act," requires (1) all textbooks to claim that discussions of origins are not scientific facts and (2) equal numbers of words, space, and emphasis for "other theories, including, but not limited to, the Genesis account in the Bible." The following day, the bill is referred to the Committee on Education, whose eleven members include all five cosponsors of the bill.

April   The Kanawha County (West Virginia) School Board adopts *Biology: A Search for Order in Complexity* and other texts produced by creationist publishers. The following year, residents of the county threaten violence and go on strike over books that question fundamentalism.

3 April   A coalition of seven representatives, including Tennessee's Speaker of the House Ned Ray McWherter (who went on to become governor of Tennessee from 1986 to 1994), introduces the innocuously titled "Act to Amend

Tennessee Code Annotated, Section 49–2008, Relative to Selection of Textbooks." This bill is similar to the equal-time bill introduced the previous week in the Tennessee Senate.

18 April   Despite the Tennessee attorney general's opinion that the Genesis Act is probably unconstitutional, the Tennessee Senate begins debating the act. When a group of Tennessee professors claims that the legislation is "utterly repugnant to the American idea of democracy," Senator Milton Hamilton responds with, "This is not a Ph.D. bill. It is a people's bill." The Senate votes 29–1 in favor of the Genesis Act (Senate Bill 394), after which the House of Representatives accepts the Senate bill in lieu of its own.

26 April   The Tennessee House of Representatives amends Senate Bill 394 to (1) require a literal reading of Genesis in the state's biology classroom and (2) declare that the Bible is a textbook rather than a reference book. The amended legislation passes by a vote of 69–15.

30 April   The Tennessee Senate approves the amended Senate Bill 394 and forwards the legislation to Republican Governor Winfield Dunn for his signature. When Dunn refuses to veto the legislation within five days of receiving it, Tennessee has a new antievolution law. Soon thereafter, the law is challenged in Davidson County Chancery Court by a group of biology teachers, parents, students, and the Nashville chapter of Americans United for Separation of Church and State.

May   *Willoughby v. Stever* is dismissed by the U.S. District Court in Washington, D.C., on the grounds that (1) books supported by taxes allocated to the National Science Foundation disseminate scientific findings, not religion, and (2) the First Amendment does not allow the state to require that teaching be tailored to particular religious beliefs. Willoughby appeals his case to the U.S. Supreme Court.

The Georgia Board of Education approves *Biology: A Search for Order in Complexity* for adoption in the state's public schools. Soon thereafter, the Institute for Creation Research sponsors a symposium at an Atlanta Baptist church at which Henry Morris urges attendees to organize and pass an antievolution law. The people form CAVE (Citizens for Another Voice in Education), but the group is not influential.

28 December   The NABT and several science teachers join the challenge to Tennessee's Genesis Act in federal district court in Nashville.

1974

Henry Morris states the basis of scientific creationism by proclaiming, "The Bible is a book of science." Later, Morris claims that Satan invented evolution at the Tower of Babel.

The Tennessee legislature fails to remove the most blatant aspects of fundamentalism from its Genesis Act. The fate of the law rests in the courts.

Don Johanson discovers in Ethiopia one of the most complete australopithecine skeletons. Its owner, nicknamed "Lucy," was a little bigger than a chimp and had a brain about one-third the size of that of modern humans. Lucy, a member of the species *Australopithecus afarensis*, died about 3 million years ago.

The Texas Education Policy Act adopts Mel and Norma Gabler's recommendation that all biology textbooks include a prominent statement that evolution is a theory rather than a fact and is only one of several explanations of human origins. Soon afterward, and despite the protests of some scientists, the Texas Board of Education uses the new policy to reject all three of the BSCS textbooks.

Citizens of Kanawha County, West Virginia, erupt when they discover that the English and biology textbooks used in local schools question fundamentalist beliefs. Coal miners go on strike to protest the books, preachers vilify the books from their pulpits, teachers are threatened, snipers fire on school buses and on police escorting the teachers, and terrorists dynamite three cars, attack school buses, and vandalize the Board of Education building. The board responds by adopting creationist materials for the entire school district, stipulating that students must be excused from reading any book that their parents find objectionable.

Henry Morris, several members of the ICR, Scott Memorial Church, and Christian Heritage College establish Creation-Life Publishers in San Diego. One of the company's first books is *Scientific Creationism*, a "reference book" that appears in two editions: one for public schools and another for church-related schools.

26 February   A three-judge panel hears the challenge to Tennessee's Genesis Act. The judges accept the state's argument for abstention, after which attorneys for the plaintiffs appeal the decision to the circuit court of appeals.

14 March   The California Board of Education reverses its 1969 decision and eliminates creationism from state-adopted textbooks.

The influential Scientific Creationism *appeared in two editions: one for public schools (shown here) and one for church-related schools. The book, written by Henry Morris and other creationists, promotes the "two-model" approach—a Genesis-based "creation model" and an "evolution model." (Institute for Creation Research)*

1975

June   The U.S. Supreme Court refuses to review *Wright v. Houston Independent School District*, thereby ending the first lawsuit initiated by creationists.

17 June   The Atlanta Board of Education accepts its textbook commission's recommendation to reject *Biology: A Search for Order in Complexity*, noting that the book "contains numerous errors."

9 September   As the federal lawsuit spawned by Tennessee's Genesis Act moves toward circuit court, Chancellor Ben H. Cantrell of Tennessee state court declares the Genesis Act to be unconstitutional because it advances religion.

November   Professors and high school teachers who oppose Tennessee's Genesis Act file their brief in the Sixth Circuit Court of Appeals in Cincinnati, Ohio. The NABT joins the lawsuit. The state argues that the federal court should not interfere with Tennessee's policies.

Controversy created by the NSF-sponsored MACOS project

prompts the U.S. House of Representatives to pass the Bauman Amendment, which gives Congress direct supervision and veto power over every project funded by the NSF. The bill later dies in the Senate.

E. O. Wilson publishes *Sociobiology: The New Synthesis.* Wilson views sociobiology as a product of evolutionary ecology.

Henry Morris again reminds his followers that "Satan himself is the originator of the concept of evolution." In the preface to Morris's *The Troubled Waters of Evolution,* Tim LaHaye claims that evolution is the basis for socialism, humanism, and communism.

In Texas, one of the nation's largest purchasers of textbooks, 80 percent of biology textbooks in use do not mention evolution.

Robert Kohfal and Kelly Segraves publish the popular and overtly religious *The Creation Explanation: A Scientific Alternative to Evolution.* Not surprisingly, the authors laud biblical catastrophism while dismissing evolution and much of science (e.g., Einstein's theory of relativity is "under strong criticism"). After being informed that ice floats because "the Creator designed it that way," readers are told that they must choose between creation and evolution. Faith in biblical literalism will "redeem an individual . . . from the destructive effects of the evolutionary faith."

California Attorney General Evelle J. Younger rules that the California Board of Education's elimination of creationism from the state's guidelines is constitutional.

February   The U.S. Supreme Court refuses to hear the appeal of *Willoughby v. Stever,* which ends the case.

10 April   In a 2–1 decision, the Sixth Circuit Court of Appeals announces in *Daniel v. Waters* that Tennessee's 1973 Genesis Act is "patently unconstitutional" because it is little more than a revised edition of the Butler Law that led to the Scopes trial in 1925. Circuit Court Judge George Edwards notes that the law is clearly intended to displace evolution

with biblical teachings. Tennessee refuses to appeal the decision. The demise of the Genesis Act causes several other equal-time bills to die quietly in several state legislatures.

July   The California Board of Education, with several of its members having been replaced by appointees of Governor Jerry Brown, approves no social science textbooks that include creationist explanations.

20 August   The Tennessee Supreme Court and the U.S. District Court use the argument made by the Sixth Circuit Court of Appeals to agree that the Genesis Act is unconstitutional. One of the district judges notes that the demand for equal time for all theories of creation is "patently unreasonable."

Biologist Richard Dawkins, the author of The Selfish Gene *and other books explaining evolution, is one of today's most vocal critics of creationism. (Courtesy of Michael Ruse)*

1976   Indiana's West Clark Community Schools adopt the pro-creationism *Biology: A Search for Order in Complexity* as the only approved textbook for their biology classes. Within a few months, this adoption is challenged in court.

Richard Dawkins publishes the provocative and flamboyant *The Selfish Gene.*

Arizona Republican Congressman John Conlan sponsors an amendment to the National Defense Education Act that would "prohibit federal funding of any curriculum project with evolutionary content or implications." The amendment passes by a vote of 222–174, but it is narrowly defeated by the U.S. Senate.

Sales of the award-winning MACOS proevolution program drop by 70 percent in response to nationwide protest.

Kentucky passes a law stipulating that teachers who cover evolution in their classes can also teach "the theory of creationism as presented in the Bible" and that students who adhere to the biblical account should get credit on all exams.

1977   Stephen J. Gould publishes his best-selling *Ever Since Darwin.*

The Rhea County Courthouse, built in 1891, is designated a national historic landmark by the National Park Service. Two years later, a $1 million grant restores the courthouse and produces the Scopes Trial Museum in the courthouse basement. Today, the courtroom contains the original judge's-bench, four tables, dais rail, jury chairs, and spectator seats.

Creationists' complaints cause publishers to again reduce their coverage of evolution in biology textbooks. For example, between 1974 and 1977, a section about Charles Darwin in one best-selling book is cut from 1373 words to 45 words, and discussions of fossil formation and geology disappear completely.

Henry Morris tells believers, "There is . . . really no way of proving scientifically any assumed evolutionary phylogeny, as far as the fossil record is concerned. . . . There neither is, nor can be, any proof of evolution." Morris urges schools to become extensions of the church and the home and bewails the folly of teaching "human wisdom."

January Trustees of the Dallas Independent School District vote 6–3 to approve *Biology: A Search for Order in Complexity* for adoption, to purchase sixty copies as reference books, and to train teachers to use the book.

February The Indiana Civil Liberties Union sues in an Indianapolis court on behalf of parent Jon Hendren and others to ban the use of *Biology: A Search for Order in Complexity* in the state's public schools because, among other things, it advances religion. Despite the testimonies of scientists that creationism is a scientifically useless idea, the textbook commission upholds its original recommendation that the book is acceptable. Soon thereafter, the ICLU returns to court to challenge the decision.

19 April In *Hendren v. Campbell*, Marion, Indiana, Superior Court Judge Michael T. Dugan rules that the use of *Biology: A Search for Order in Complexity* in the state's public schools violates constitutional bans on the advancement of religion. The state textbook commission removes *Biology* from its list of approved texts and does not appeal Dugan's decision. Soon afterward, school board officials in Dallas remove *Biology* from classrooms.

1978   Paul Ellwanger founds the Citizens for Fairness in Education, which bases its legislative efforts for equal time for creationism on Wendell Bird's upcoming publication for the ICR's "Impact" series. Ellwanger's bill is defeated in the South Carolina legislature, but within one year, it appears in the legislatures of eight other states.

Duane Gish proclaims that "not for a moment do I believe that the theory of evolution can be reconciled with the Bible. Theistic evolution is bankrupt both biblically and scientifically. It's bad science and it's bad theology. You really cannot believe the Bible and the theory of evolution both."

Creation-Life Publishers produces a public school edition of Duane Gish's book *Evolution? The Fossils Say No!* Gish repeats creationists' familiar criticisms of evolution ("Evolution theory is indeed no less religious nor more scientific than creation") while claiming that creationism is not a religious doctrine. Because he uses the word *Creator* instead of *God*, Gish believes that he has avoided religious statements.

January   Yale law student and creationist Wendell Bird publishes an award-winning legal justification in *Yale Law Journal* for teaching evolution and creation science in public schools. Bird argues that creationism is as scientific as evolution and that evolution is as religious as creationism. The proposal soon becomes the foundation for creationists' demands for "equal time" and "balanced treatment" in classrooms.

11 April   After Congress provides almost $500,000 for an exhibit titled "The Emergence of Man: Dynamics of Evolution" at the Museum of Natural History at the Smithsonian Institution, Dale Crowley Jr. sues to either close the exhibit or force the Smithsonian to provide equal space and money for an exhibit addressing the biblical story of creation.

11 December   In *Crowley v. Smithsonian Institution*, a

lawsuit attempting to ban the federally funded evolution-based exhibit at the Smithsonian's Museum of Natural History, District Judge Barrington D. Parker rejects the claim that the Smithsonian should give equal time to the biblical story of creation. Parker rules that providing the remedy requested by Crowley would violate the Establishment Clause of the U.S. Constitution, as noted in *Epperson v. Arkansas* and *Daniel v. Waters.*

1979   Kelly Segraves and the Creation Science Research Center sue in California to stop the distribution of *The Scientific Framework* and to end presentations of evolution as fact in California's public schools. The petition is denied.

In Cobb County, Georgia, the school board allows students to ignore the biology requirement for graduation from high school if they have religious objections to evolution.

Stephen J. Gould and Richard Lewontin argue that much in biology has little or no direct connection to adaptive advantage. Gould and Lewontin also argue that developmental constraints often mold organisms in nonadaptive ways.

Legislatures in nearly a dozen states begin considering equal-time bills. One such bill, if passed in Georgia, would reap $2 million in creationist textbooks sales for the Institute for Creation Research. All of the bills fail.

May   The Smithsonian Institution's Museum of Natural History opens its contested "Emergence of Man" exhibit.

Wendell Bird's four-page "Resolution for Balanced Presentation of Evolution and Scientific Creationism" is published in the Institute for Creation Research's "Impact" series; the ICR distributes thousands of copies. Bird's resolution is prefaced by an editorial advising that the resolution should be used with local school boards, not as a model for legislation. Bird and other creationists are encouraged by a Gallup poll indicating that half of Americans believe in a literal version of the biblical story of Adam and Eve as the beginning of the human race.

1980   Texas declares that evolution must be presented as "only one of several explanations of the origin of mankind." Other states will soon do the same.

Stephen J. Gould declares that the "synthetic theory" of Theodosius Dobzhansky and his colleagues is "effectively dead."

The American Humanist Association begins producing *Creation/Evolution*, a journal that tries to counter the political activities of creationists.

Various state legislatures continue to debate equal-time legislation based on Paul Ellwanger's model. Iowa's equal-time bill, which is opposed by the Iowa Academy of Science and is estimated to cost taxpayers more than $6 million, is referred to the House Finance Committee, where it dies. Nevertheless, students in many Iowa schools, as well as elsewhere, continue to be taught creationism in their science classes. Many teachers, often with the approval of students and parents alike, discuss both creationism and evolution before declaring creationism to be the best explanation.

Scientists organize to form "committees of correspondence" to challenge creationists.

Paul Ellwanger removes the major weaknesses (e.g., superior being, worldwide flood) from his equal-time model for legislation and changes its name to "Unbiased Presentation of Creation-Science and Evolution-Science Bill."

The U.S. District Court for the District of Columbia supports the earlier ruling in *Crowley v. Smithsonian Institution*—namely, that the Smithsonian Institution is not required to provide equal time to the biblical story of creation. The U.S. Supreme Court later refuses to review the case.

Presidential candidate Ronald Reagan cites MACOS as an example of the federal government's support of subversive values and asks why the National Science Foundation did not instead develop curricular materials supporting Christian values. Needing votes from fundamentalists, Reagan tells reporters that he questions evolution and wants "the Biblical theory of creation" taught in public schools.

A *Science* reporter estimates that textbook commissions in almost thirty states are under "heavy pressure" to include creationists' materials on their lists of approved books.

Cobb County (GA) teachers threaten to go on strike unless the local school board rescinds an earlier order to include creation science in the curriculum.

The Institute for Creation Research separates from Christian Heritage College and establishes a graduate college to educate creationists. Henry Morris announces that Jesus was a creationist.

January A poll finds that almost half of the readers of the *American School Board Journal* favor teaching both evolution and creationism; 25 percent believe that evolution should be the only explanation that is presented; 19 percent want only biblical discussions to be presented; and 8 percent want to avoid teaching anything about the origin of humans.

October The ICR begins a public relations campaign to promote its creation science agenda. During the next four years, Baptist churches and other Baptist organizations account for 30 percent of the sites of the ICR's public appearances, more than any other kind of church organization.

December Teachers in junior high schools in Little Rock, Arkansas, begin reviewing science textbooks for adoption. Creationist and math teacher Larry Fisher, wanting the alleged shortcomings of evolution to be included in science textbooks, sends the ICR's resolution to the superintendent of the Pulaski County Special School District. Fisher tells the superintendent that the district will reap a public relations bonanza because "about 80%" of people support the resolution. Fisher's activities ultimately lead to *McLean v. Arkansas Board of Education*, in which Judge William R. Overton rules that creation science has no scientific merit.

1981   With the help of Richard Turner, a former legal aide to Ronald Reagan, Kelly Segraves alleges in a lawsuit that California is violating his children's religious rights because evolution is being taught in a dogmatic way. In *Segraves v.*

State of California, the Sacramento Superior Court does not overturn *The Scientific Framework* or order major changes, but it does require the California Board of Education to recommend a less dogmatic presentation of evolution. The judge praises the nondogmatism policy as necessary for a pluralistic society and requires that copies of the policy be sent to all school districts in the state.

Braswell Deen, Chief Justice of the Georgia Circuit Court of Appeals, proclaims that "This monkey mythology of Darwin is the cause of permissiveness, promiscuity, pills, prophylactics, perversions, pregnancies, abortions, pornotherapy, pollution, poisoning, and the proliferation of crimes of all types."

The Pro-Family Forum of Fort Worth, Texas, produces and distributes tens of thousands of copies of "Can America Survive the Fruits of Atheistic Evolution?" The pamphlet, which claims that evolution will destroy America by producing Nazism, communism, abortion, divorce, and venereal disease, is cited by several groups trying to force creationism into public schools.

Wayne Moyer, executive director of the National Association of Biology Teachers, admits that "we have done a botched job of teaching evolutionary theory." Chemist Russell Doolittle delivers a stronger indictment, noting that science education in the United States is "simply, sadly, awful." Few disagree.

Thanks to the *McLean* decision (see below) and local opposition, legislatures defeat creationist bills in Florida, Georgia, Kansas, Mississippi, South Dakota, Kansas, Maryland, West Virginia, and elsewhere.

G. L. Stebbins and Francisco Ayala (a student of Theodosius Dobzhansky) publish a widely read paper showing that natural selection can produce all of the changes posited by Stephen J. Gould.

After a poll shows that almost 75 percent of parents and teachers accept the teaching of creationism in public schools, the Tampa (FL) School Board requires equal time for creationism and evolution. This decision, opposed by many science teachers, makes the study of creationism mandatory for Tampa's 115,000 students. Soon thereafter, a debate in the city that involves Henry Morris is attended by 1,700 spectators and is covered by seven radio stations, six television stations, and numerous newspapers.

Republican Representative William Dannemeyer asks Congress to review and limit funding for the Smithsonian Institution's exhibit titled "The Emergence of Man: Dynamics of Evolution," which had already been the topic of an earlier lawsuit (*Crowley v. Smithsonian Institution*). Dannemeyer claims that the exhibit promotes the religion of secular humanism, but his request gathers little support.

The Alabama House Education Committee supports an equal-time bill, but the bill is killed by a filibuster by Representative Robert Albright, a former biology teacher.

Jerry Falwell, leader of the Moral Majority, wages a campaign to have creationism taught in public schools, and warns his followers not to read books other than the Bible. However, Falwell distributes Henry Morris's *The Remarkable Birth of Planet Earth* after Morris appears on his *Old-Time Gospel Hour* to promote creationism.

A poll shows that half of all Californians accept the teaching of creationism and evolution in public schools.

Henry Morris announces that more than 1 million copies of the books produced by his Institute for Creation Research are in circulation. Morris again states that only God can tell us about the origins of life.

The not-for-profit and religiously neutral National Center for Science Education forms and becomes the only national organization devoted primarily to opposing creationism. By 2001, the organization has about 4,000 members.

Biologist Richard C. Lewontin urges scientists "to state clearly that evolution is a fact, not theory. . . . Birds arose from nonbirds and humans from nonhumans. No person who pretends to any understanding of the natural world can deny these facts any more than she or he can deny that the earth is round, rotates on its axis, and revolves around the sun."

The American Association of University Professors passes a resolution asking state governments to "reject creation-science legislation as utterly inconsistent with the principles of academic freedom."

Louisiana Senator William Keith introduces a bill for balanced treatment that is based on Paul Ellwanger's model. Soon thereafter, the Academic Freedom Legal Defense Fund (formerly known as the Creation Science Legal Defense Fund) is founded to defend Keith's legislation. The defense ultimately fails (*Edwards v. Asuillard*).

January The American Association for the Advancement of Science, meeting in Toronto, sponsors a session to discuss creationism and warn of its harmful effects to science education.

The Pulaski County School Board [Arkansas], recently lobbied by the Moral Majority and FLAG (Family Life, America, and God), hears Larry Fisher argue that scientific creationism must be presented in science classrooms. In response, the board creates a Creation Science Curriculum Committee to study Fisher's proposal.

Reverend W. A. Blount convinces the Greater Little Rock Evangelical Fellowship to begin lobbying the Arkansas legislature for a creationism bill. Blount and his colleagues start their work by asking Paul Ellwanger for an updated copy of his balanced-treatment resolution (a modification of the resolution drafted originally by Wendell Bird). Senator James Holsted, a born-again Christian, meets with Republican Governor Frank White before introducing his creationism bill. White, supported heavily by the Moral Majority, promises his support for the creationism bill.

24 February Senator Holsted introduces his balanced

treatment for scientific creationism bill (Act 590) without consulting with scientists, science educators, the Arkansas attorney general, or the Arkansas Department of Education. Holsted's bill is referred to the Judiciary Committee, which includes Holsted as a member and is chaired by born-again Christian Max Howell. Howell gains the committee's endorsement by claiming that the bill stresses "fairness" and "freedom of choice."

2 March   The nonjury trial involving Kelly Segraves's petition, often referred to as "Scopes II," opens in Sacramento, California, with Judge Irving Perluss presiding. By the second day of the trial, creationists abandon their demand for equal time and their claim that the teaching of evolution is a state-sponsored establishment of religion. Having thereby changed the trial to a discussion of the phrasing in *The Scientific Framework*, Segraves tells Judge Perluss that he will accept the removal of dogmatic statements about evolution from the guidelines.

6 March   Judge Perluss decides that *The Scientific Framework* prohibits dogmatic statements about human evolution and orders the California Department of Education to disseminate its policies more widely. Future violations regarding the *Framework* are to be handled by local school boards. Soon after Perluss's decision, Nell Segraves demands that creationists get "50% of the curriculum and the content. . . . We want 50% of the tax dollars used for education. . . . We have a lot to undo."

13 March   After a twenty-minute debate and no hearings, the Arkansas Senate passes Act 590 by a vote of 22–2.

17 March   After voting to suspend parliamentary rules, the Arkansas House of Representatives, lobbied by the Moral Majority and FLAG, passes the balanced-treatment act by a vote of 69–18 on the day before adjourning.

19 March   Arkansas Governor Frank White pays his debt to the Moral Majority by signing Act 590 into law, despite the fact that he hasn't read the legislation. White justifies his actions by asking, "If we're going to teach evolution in the public school system, why not teach scientific creationism? Both of them are theories."

24 March   Despite the efforts of Wendell Bird and others, the Colorado Senate Education Committee kills an equal-time bill with only one dissenting vote.

April   Arkansas' Moral Majority, led by Reverend Roy McLaughlin, forms Arkansas Citizens for Balanced Education in Origins to promote the enactment of Act 590. When the ACLU announces its plans to challenge the law, creationists begin raising money to hire Wendell Bird and John Whitehead to defend the law.

May   The graduate school of the Institute for Creation Research is accredited by California.

27 May   The ACLU sues in federal district court to declare Arkansas' Act 590 unconstitutional because it establishes religion. Arkansas Attorney General Steve Clark excludes Wendell Bird from the state's defense team. Bird later claims that Clark did "an inadequate job" of defending the law, and television preacher Pat Robertson tells his followers that Clark previously supported the ACLU.

June   After the Louisiana Senate Education Committee amends Senator Keith's balanced-treatment bill (e.g., making balanced treatment a local option, eliminating the "findings of fact"), the Louisiana Senate passes the legislation by a vote of 26–12 with little discussion and dissent.

6 July   Following the defeat of several amendments that would have weakened the balanced-treatment bill, the Louisiana House of Representatives passes the bill by a vote of 71–19.

8 July   Senator Keith tells his colleagues that "evolution is no more than a fairy tale about a frog that turns into a prince," after which the Louisiana Senate approves the House version of the balanced-treatment bill, which requires the balanced treatment of evolution and creationism in public schools.

19 July   Louisiana Governor David Treen reluctantly signs Keith's balanced-treatment bill, thereby making it law.

20 July   The ACLU challenges the constitutionality of Louisiana's newly passed balanced-treatment law. This challenge ultimately reaches the U.S. Supreme Court, which declares the law unconstitutional in 1987 in *Edwards v. Aguillard.*

October   The National Academy of Sciences and the National Association of Biology Teachers pass a joint resolution urging scientists to challenge creationists at the local level, but they stress the futility of public debates with creationists.

An Associated Press–*NBC News* poll indicates that more than 75 percent of the U.S. population believes that both evolution and creationism should be taught in public schools.

2 December   Before the ACLU can challenge Louisiana's balanced-treatment law, Wendell Bird sues in Baton Rouge federal district court (on behalf of Senator Keith and fifty-four other plaintiffs) for a declaratory judgment to force Louisiana's schools to comply with the newly passed law. The lawsuit (*Keith v. Louisiana*) will be dismissed six months later.

3 December   The ACLU and other groups sue in federal district court in New Orleans to challenge the constitutionality of Louisiana's balanced-treatment law. In the trial that follows, the ACLU's defense follows that used in *McLean v. Arkansas Board of Education*. Judge Adrian Duplantier postpones the suit (*Aguillard v. Treen*) until a decision is rendered in the creationists' lawsuit (*Keith v. Louisiana*) filed the previous day.

7 December   *McLean v. Arkansas Board of Education* opens in federal district court in Little Rock, Arkansas, with Judge William Overton presiding.

17 December   The in-court proceedings of *McLean v.*

Arkansas Board of Education end with the state's case all but destroyed.

1982   Books such as Philip Kitcher's *Abusing Science: The Case against Creationism* and Niles Eldredge's *The Monkey Business: A Scientist Looks at Creationism* refute creationists' claims. In *The Monkey Business: A Scientist Looks at Creationism*, American paleontologist Eldredge describes creationists as "liars" with a "peculiarly myopic view of the natural world."

John Maynard Smith uses "game theory" to show how selection can promote equilibrium situations where competing participants get the most that is possible.

Isaac Asimov speaks for many scientists when he says that, "To those trained in science, creationism seems like a bad dream, a sudden reliving of a nightmare, a renewed march of an army of the night risen to challenge free thought and enlightenment."

In a widely read editorial published in *Christianity Today*, geologist Edwin Olsen says that creationists are intolerant, simplistic, and less honest than evolutionists about their own failings, adding that "in its isolation and inflexibility, 'creationism' . . . is doing more harm than good."

5 January   In *McLean v. Arkansas Board of Education*, Judge Overton rules that (1) Arkansas' equal-time law is unconstitutional, (2) creation science is religion, not science, and (3) scientific creationism has no scientific significance. Overton describes Wendell Bird's resolution as a "student note," the argument of which "has no legal merit." Overton's blunt and devastating decision destroys creationists' hopes of using "creation science" as a means of forcing their religion into the science classes of public schools. Overton's decision is not appealed. The nation's first balanced-treatment law has lasted less than one year.

Mississippi enacts its "Balanced Treatment for Creation Science and Evolution Science Act."

February In Arizona, state Republican Representative Jim Cooper (chair of the House Education Committee) introduces legislation to ban the teaching of evolution in ways that "foster the belief in a religion or cause disbelief in religion." Cooper wants violators to be fined $10,000 and face up to a year in prison. Cooper's bill receives little support, but a similar bill passes both the Senate and the House the following year.

4 February Arkansas Attorney General Clark decides not to appeal Overton's decision in *McLean v. Arkansas Board of Education*.

19 February *Science* publishes Overton's opinion from *McLean v. Arkansas Board of Education*.

June District Judge Frank Polozola dismisses *Keith v. Louisiana* because it doesn't raise a federal question.

July The Illinois Board of Education approves what it touts as world-class standards for science education, but the standards do not mention evolution. The standards, strongly influenced by the Illinois Christian Coalition, also do not mention human sexuality and multicultural studies.

2 November Judge Duplantier rules in favor of the ACLU by deciding that Louisiana's balanced-treatment law usurps the authority of the Louisiana Board of Elementary and Secondary Education. Louisiana Attorney General William Guste appeals Duplantier's decision to the Louisiana Supreme Court. Thereafter, the lawsuit is known as *Edwards v. Aguillard*, since the state and its governor (Edwin Edwards) are now the plaintiffs.

1983

April The Arizona House and Senate pass a bill similar to that proposed the preceding year by Representative Cooper, which bans the teaching of evolution in ways that promote or cause disbelief in religion.

29 April Arizona Governor Bruce Babbitt vetoes legislation that would ban the teaching of evolution in ways that promote or cause disbelief in religion. Babbitt's veto is sustained.

September   The Texas Board of Education issues rules requiring, among other things, that "textbooks presented for adoption which treat the subject of evolution substantively in explaining the historical origins of man . . . must carry a statement on an introductory page that any material on evolution . . . is clearly presented as theory rather than verified."

October   Texas Senator Oscar Mauzy (chair of the Senate Jurisprudence Committee) asks Texas Attorney General Jim Mattox for an opinion about the constitutionality of the state's 1974 procreationism guidelines (i.e., that evolution be identified as a theory rather than as a fact, that evolution be identified in textbooks "as only one of several explanations of the origins of humankind"). Mattox won't issue the opinion for almost five months.

17 October   The Louisiana Supreme Court, in a vote of 4–3, overturns Judge Adrian Duplantier's decision, concluding that the legislature can mandate the teaching of creation science. In response, the ACLU revives its original lawsuit challenging the Arkansas law as a violation of the First Amendment. This decision returns the case challenging Louisiana's balanced-treatment law to Judge Duplantier's court.

1984   Henry Morris's *History of Modern Creationism* vilifies scientists and tells his followers that the creationism movement is "far too widespread . . . for the evolutionists ever to regain the obsequious submission of the public which they used to enjoy and abuse."

Morris denounces the American Scientific Affiliation, claiming that it has "capitulated to theistic evolution."

Tennessee Democratic Representative Pete Drew introduces "The Balanced Treatment for Creation-Science and Evolution-Science Act." Drew's bill attracts little attention, so he decides to introduce it again the following year.

Tennessee Governor Ned Ray McWherter announces during

a news conference that he will "vigorously pursue" the superconducting supercollider; at the same conference, he advocates equal time for evolution and creationism in science classes. Texas is chosen as the site for the supercollider.

A survey of 2,400 science students shows that whereas almost 40 percent reject evolution, 80 percent believe that creationism and evolution should be taught in public schools.

March Texas Attorney General Jim Mattox uses Judge William Overton's decision in *McLean v. Arkansas Board of Education* to rule that Texas' procreationism textbook guidelines (enacted in 1974) are unconstitutional because they are motivated by "religious sensibilities, rather than a dedication to scientific truth."

April The Texas Board of Education repeals the state's 1974 procreationism guidelines for textbooks. When the guidelines are formally repealed in June, state education officials demand better coverage of evolution in textbooks. Publishers, hoping to secure some of the state's $80 million textbook market, quickly comply.

1985   Mel and Norma Gabler publish *Scientific Creationism Handbook #10* in which they claim that neither creation nor evolution is scientific, but creation-science is superior. The Gablers claim that communists worked on the BSCS textbooks. Norris Anderson, who worked with BSCS, claims in *Scientific Creationism* that BSCS writers admitted that there was no evidence for human evolution.

Proclaiming that "we need teaching that puts God back in the classroom," Representative Pete Drew reintroduces his "Balanced Treatment for Creation-Science and Evolution-Science Act" in the Tennessee House of Representatives. Nashville Democrat Steve Cobb's recommendation that the bill be deferred indefinitely passes by a vote of 15–4.

In *Creation and the Modern Christian*, Henry Morris again calls his followers to war against the spread of evolution. Morris claims that creationism is the source of "Americanism" and that evolution produces racism, communism, and other ills.

10 January   U.S. District Court Judge Adrian Duplantier issues a summary judgment ruling that the Louisiana balanced-treatment law is unconstitutional because, among other things, "creation science" is an attempt to advance religion. Duplantier notes that the defendants could produce more evidence on collateral issues, but is "convinced that whatever that evidence, it could not affect the outcome." Senator Bill Keith condemns Duplantier, and Wendell Bird convinces Louisiana Attorney General Guste to appeal Duplantier's decision to the Fifth Circuit Court of Appeals.

July   The California Curriculum Committee begins hearings on science textbooks. The committee recommends that all of the science textbooks submitted for seventh and eighth grades be rejected.

8 July   Citing the Scopes trial, the Fifth Circuit Court of Appeals votes 8–7 to support Judge Duplantier's ruling that the Louisiana balanced-treatment law is unconstitutional. Louisiana's attorney general asks for a rehearing before the entire fifteen-member court.

September   The California Curriculum Committee's recommendation to reject seventh- and eighth-grade science textbooks is supported by the State Board of Education. The board asks publishers to improve their discussion of evolution. Although the ten revised textbooks are criticized by scientists, they are adopted by a vote of 7–2 by the board.

December   The Fifth Circuit Court votes 8–7 to deny Attorney General Guste's request for a rehearing before the entire court. Guste announces that Louisiana will appeal the decision to the U.S. Supreme Court.

1986   New Mexico's State Board of Education votes to retain its disclaimer that "evolution is a theory" and encourages local school boards to consider presenting "multiple theories of origin."

Humanlike footprints found near dinosaur tracks in Glen Rose, Texas, are shown to be either "inept carvings" from the 1930s or dinosaur tracks that have not weathered like other tracks. These findings convince some creationists to stop showing the *Footprints in Stone* film.

5 May The U.S. Supreme Court announces that it will hear the appeal of Judge Duplantier's decision on the Louisiana balanced-treatment law. A dozen amicus curiae briefs supporting the lower courts' decisions are filed by organizations such as the National Academy of Sciences and a group of seventy-two Nobel Prize winners.

10 December The U.S. Supreme Court hears opening arguments in *Edwards v. Aguillard*, the case testing Louisiana's balanced-treatment law. Wendell Bird argues the creationists' case; ACLU attorney Jay Topkis argues that the law is unconstitutional.

1987 Oxford zoologist Richard Dawkins defends evolution and refutes intelligent design in his popular book *The Blind Watchmaker: Why the Evidence of Evolution Reveals a Universe Without Design*.

A national study shows that 45 percent of science teachers support the inclusion of creationism in the classroom.

In *Mozert v. Hawkins*, the U.S. Sixth Circuit Court of Appeals rules that students do not have a right to be excused from classroom activities that expose them to competing ideas, even if some of those ideas are contrary to their religious beliefs.

19 June Citing the Scopes trial, the U.S. Supreme Court rules 7–2 in *Edwards v. Aguillard* that Louisiana's balanced-treatment law is unconstitutional. The *Edwards* case signals the end of most laws demanding equal time and balanced treatment for creationism in public schools. In response, some creationists begin to abandon Henry Morris's ideas and, in their place, repackage creationism as "intelligent design." Television preacher Pat Robertson calls the Supreme Court's decision an "intellectual scandal."

1988	California's antidogmatism policy is replaced by a statement that lacks antievolution features.
	The California Board of Education, despite strong opposition, requires in Proclamation No. 65 that evolution be explained in approved textbooks.
	A study documents the poor scientific literacy in the United States; for example, only 12 percent of the respondents believe that astrology is "not at all scientific." Meanwhile, a survey of 400 biology teachers shows that only 25 percent have biology degrees. Half of the teachers believe that "some races of people are more intelligent than others" (or were not sure), and one-third believe that humans and dinosaurs lived at the same time (or were not sure).
	Another of the many remakes of *Inherit the Wind* is broadcast on network television.
	7 December Bill Honig, California's new superintendent of public instruction, announces that the ICR can no longer offer graduate degrees in science. Honig schedules a second review of the ICR's programs for the following summer.
1989	The National Science Foundation (NSF) approves a grant for a project conducted by the Biological Sciences Curriculum Study (BSCS) titled "Advances in Evolution: Biological and Geological Perspectives." NSF asks BSCS director Joseph McInerney to remove the word *evolution* from the title of the project because some members of Congress will be unhappy to see that NSF has funded an educational project on evolution. McInerney responds by making the word *evolution* the most prominent word on the cover of the three books and the videodisk that result from the project.
	Percival Davis and Dean Kenyon publish *Of Pandas and People*, a creationism book that is adopted by many schools. The slim and illustrated *Pandas* uses six case studies to support its claims of presenting a balanced treatment of evolution and "intelligent-design theory." The book reads as if it were engineered to try to promote creationism while avoiding the restrictions imposed by *McLean v. Arkansas Board of Education* and *Edwards v. Aguillard*.

In addition to educational programs and other "outreach" activities, the Institute for Creation Research sponsors a variety of field trips and workshops promoting creation science. (Institute for Creation Research)

In *The Long War Against God*, Henry Morris claims that the evolution/creationism controversy has its roots in the original rebellion of Satan against God. Morris again claims that evolution is responsible for everything evil in the world and that special creation is the most certain truth of science.

January The Texas Education Agency proposes in Proclamation No. 66 that biology textbooks include the "scientific theory of evolution" and "scientific evidence of evolution." The recommendation does not mention scientific creationism or alternative theories. The slightly modified proclamation is approved two months later by a vote of 12–3.

The California Board of Education decides to strengthen the teaching of evolution in its public schools.

July   The California Board of Education, despite its announcement in January that it will strengthen the teaching of evolution, deletes the claim that evolution is a "scientific fact" from its guidelines. The board also removes from its guidelines quotes from the U.S. Supreme Court's *Edwards v. Aguillard* decision and the National Academy of Sciences book *Science and Creationism*.

1990s   Creationists in several states begin to abandon legal challenges to evolution and focus instead on school boards, which set the curricula and teaching standards in public schools. Creationists also begin to demand that science teachers present the supposed "evidence against evolution."

Gallup polls show that, as in previous decades, the U.S. public overwhelmingly supports the inclusion of creationism in science classes of public schools.

Republican parties in several states adopt platforms calling for the teaching of creationism in public schools.

1990   Readers of *Scientific American* learn of the clash between the magazine and science writer Forrest M. Mims III, a creationist. *Scientific American* editor Jonathan Piel prints three more of Mims's columns (the last of which appears in October) but does not hire him to edit the magazine's "Amateur Scientist" column. Piel's decision prompts a variety of responses.

Conservative philosopher Larry Azar claims in *Twentieth Century in Crisis: Foundations of Totalitarianism* that evolutionism was the force behind the totalitarianism of Adolf Hitler.

John Morris of the Institute for Creation Research tells believers that, "If evolution is right, if the earth is old, if fossils date from before man's sin, then Christianity is wrong," and that "evolution and salvation are mutually exclusive concepts."

The Human Genome Project begins. It will be completed in 2001.

A survey reports that 57 percent of newspaper editors disagree strongly with the statement that "every word in the Bible is true," and 41 percent disagree strongly with the statement that "Adam and Eve were actual people"— roughly the same proportions that occur in the general population. When editors devote space to the controversy, 75 percent give equal or more space to creation science than to evolution. Meanwhile, of the roughly 1,600 daily newspapers published in the United States, about 1,400 publish daily astrology columns, fewer than 50 of which print disclaimers (e.g., that the columns are not scientific and are only for entertainment).

Ray Webster, a junior high social science teacher in New Lenox, Illinois, is told by his superintendent to stop teaching creation science. Webster sues the school district, claiming that it has violated his right to free speech.

Defying *Edwards v. Aguillard* and other court decisions, Kentucky reenacts its 1976 law stipulating that teachers who cover evolution in their classes can also teach "the theory of creationism as presented in the Bible" and that students who adhere to the biblical account of creation should get credit on all exams. The state decides that gun control, evolution, and other similar topics may not be suitable for inclusion on the state's assessment exams. Meanwhile, education officials in Louisiana group evolution with the occult, witchcraft, and drug use as topics inappropriate for the state's exit exams.

January California's Superintendent Honig receives a forty-eight-page report recommending that the ICR's graduate programs in science be closed.

March When Honig revokes the license of ICR to offer graduate science degrees, the institute files suits in state and federal courts, claiming that its First Amendment rights have been violated.

The Texas Board of Education adopts guidelines that mandate the inclusion of "other valid scientific theories" in addition to evolution.

June Honig restores the ICR's license for graduate science programs and gives the decision about the institute's accreditation to the newly formed Council for Private Post-Secondary and Vocational Education Agency.

November The Texas Board of Education rescinds its March decision and votes 11–4 to approve eight new biology textbooks that thoroughly cover evolution. The board rejects creationist books and ranks two BSCS textbooks that had been banned from Texas schools for twenty years as the top two textbooks for biology classes.

In *Webster v. New Lenox School District #122*, the Seventh Circuit Court of Appeals declares that (1) a teacher does not have a First Amendment right to teach creationism in a public school and (2) a school district can ban a teacher from teaching creationism.

1991   In *Bishop v. Aranov* (1991 926 F. 2d 1066; 1991 U.S. App. Lexis 4118), Phillip A. Bishop, a professor of exercise physiology at the University of Alabama, loses his bid to use optional class meetings to tell students about religion. Bishop's proselytizing had often included discussions of "intelligent design theory" and "evidence of God in human physiology." When university administrators told Bishop to stop witnessing in class and to quit having optional classes in which he discussed religion, Bishop sued on free speech and academic freedom grounds. He won at the federal district court level but lost on appeal. The appeals court rules that a classroom, during instructional time, is not an open forum and that the university can reasonably restrict Bishop's speech during that time.

University of California law professor Phillip Johnson publishes *Darwin on Trial*, a popular book that rejects evolution while promoting intelligent-design creationism. Johnson searches for evidence of God but does not advocate Morris's ideas about creation science.

A national study concludes that "over a quarter—and perhaps as many as half—of the nation's high school students get educations shaped by creationist influences."

In Orange County, California, parents and teachers complain that Capistrano High School biology teacher John Peloza is teaching creationism and proselytizing for conservative Christianity. When Peloza is reprimanded and told by the district to stop teaching creationism and to follow California's guidelines for teaching evolution, Peloza sues. Peloza argues that the district is violating his right to free speech and forcing him to teach the religion of evolution.

In Morton, Illinois, the school board decides that too much evolution is in the curriculum and orders staff to develop a creationism-based curriculum to balance the current curriculum. Administrators at nearby schools speak out in favor of teaching creationism. Many biology teachers respond by not mentioning evolution in their classes.

Phillip Johnson, a Berkeley law professor and proponent of "intelligent design." Early in his career, Johnson was a law clerk for U.S. Chief Justice Earl Warren. (Courtesy of Phillip Johnson)

1992   Creationists in Minnesota's Anoka-Hennepin School District ask that the curriculum include "evidence against evolution." This strategy, which will become increasingly popular in upcoming years, prompts even more teachers to avoid the topic of evolution.

January   Federal Judge David W. Williams dismisses John Peloza's lawsuit, ruling that the district acted appropriately in prohibiting teachers from teaching creationism. Williams emphasizes that a teacher cannot teach his or her own curriculum that violates the state's educational guidelines. Peloza appeals Williams's decision.

31 January   The California Board of Education and the Institute for Creation Research announce an out-of-court agreement that gives the ICR $225,000 and allows it to continue to teach creation science.

31 October   Pope John Paul II admits that Galileo was treated "unfairly" by the Catholic Church.

| 1993 | Creationist Henry Morris tells people that, "The data of true science . . . must agree with the testimony of Scripture." |
| | |

1993   Creationist Henry Morris tells people that, "The data of true science . . . must agree with the testimony of Scripture."

The American Association for the Advancement of Science's "Benchmarks for Science Literacy" cites evolution as an integral part of the science curriculum.

1994   In *John E. Peloza v. Capistrano Unified School District*, the Ninth Circuit Court of Appeals declares that requiring a teacher to teach evolution is not a violation of the Establishment Clause of the U.S. Constitution.

Answers in Genesis opens for business in Kentucky and begins discrediting evolution and promoting fundamentalism. By 2001, the organization has a $5 million budget and a staff of 55 people. Answers in Genesis claims that all animals were originally vegetarians and there was no death, disease, or bloodshed. When Adam sinned, death and suffering became commonplace and God punished the world with a flood. Bones of animals killed in the flood are reminders of God's judgment of sin.

The American Museum of Natural History reports that 45 percent of Americans agree that "human beings evolved from earlier species of animals."

The Tennessee Senate again considers legislation to restrict the teaching of evolution in its public schools. The Senate Education Committee approves the legislation by a vote of 8–1, but it is defeated in the Senate by a vote of 20–13.

19 April   The Tangipahoa [Louisiana] Parish Board of Education adopts a resolution by a vote of 5–4 disclaiming the endorsement of evolution. The resolution requires elementary and high school teachers to read a disclaimer to students before teaching evolution; the resolution states that the teaching of evolution is "not intended to influence or dissuade the Biblical version of Creation or any other concept."

7 November   Three parents of children in Tangipahoa Parish sue in U.S. District Court for the Eastern District of

Louisiana, challenging the validity of the disclaimer under the U.S. and Louisiana Constitutions barring laws "respecting an establishment of religion."

1995   Creationist Duane Gish tells people that "the stifling stranglehold that Darwinism has exerted over our educational system must be loosened."

Phillip Johnson's *Reason in the Balance: The Case against Naturalism in Science, Law, and Education* continues his criticism of naturalistic evolution because it excludes theistic factors as possible explanations of natural events.

November   Alabama's Board of Education adopts science content standards calling for evolution to be taught as a "theory" rather than a "fact." Following a suggestion by Textbook Commission members who complained about textbooks treating evolution as "fact," Alabama requires that biology textbooks used in its public schools include a disclaimer stating, among other things, that evolution is a "theory, not fact."

1996   Biochemist Michael Behe's popular book *Darwin's Black Box: The Biochemical Challenge to Evolution* claims that complex biochemical pathways arose as a result of "intelligent design."

The Georgia legislature votes down an amendment to an education bill that would "provide that local boards of education may establish optional courses in creationism."

School administrators in Draffenville, Kentucky, recall text-

---

A MESSAGE FROM THE ALABAMA STATE BOARD OF EDUCATION

This textbook discusses evolution, a controversial theory some scientists present as a scientific explanation for the origin of living things, such as plants, animals and humans.

No one was present when life first appeared on earth. Therefore, any statement about life's origins should be considered as theory, not fact.

The word "evolution" may refer to many types of change. Evolution describes changes that occur within a species. (White moths, for example, may "evolve" into gray moths.) This process is microevolution, which can be observed and described as fact. Evolution may also refer to the change of one living thing to another, such as reptiles into birds. This process, called macroevolution, has never been observed and should be considered a theory. Evolution also refers to the unproven belief that random, undirected forces produced a world of living things.

There are many unanswered questions about the origin of life which are not mentioned in your textbook, including:

- Why did the major groups of animals suddenly appear in the fossil record (known as the "Cambrian Explosion")?
- Why have no new major groups of living things appeared in the fossil record for a long time?
- Why do major groups of plants and animals have no transitional forms in the fossil record?
- How did you and all living things come to possess such a complete and complex set of "Instructions" for building a living body?

<u>Study hard and keep an open mind.</u> Someday, you may contribute to the theories of how living things appeared on earth.

This disclaimer appears in all state-approved biology textbooks used in Alabama. (Courtesy of Randy Moore)

books from classrooms and glue together the pages that discuss the "big bang."

A survey reports that 30 percent of U.S. biology teachers reject the theory of evolution.

Republican parties in seven states adopt platforms that endorse the teaching of creationism in public schools.

Senator Tommy Burks of Tennessee introduces legislation (Senate Bill 3229) requiring that evolution be taught as a scientific theory and that anyone who teaches evolution as a fact could be fired. Zane Whitson, the bill's sponsor in the state's House of Representatives, proclaims that people who oppose the legislation "aren't believers like I am. . . . The atheists are opposed to this bill." The bill passes Education Committee votes in both the House and Senate, but it is rejected by the full Senate in March.

February The "National Science Education Standards" are published by the National Research Council. These standards present evolution as one of the "unifying concepts and processes" and list it prominently in the content standards for grades 9–12.

March Alabama Governor Fob James uses discretionary funds to send all biology teachers in Alabama a copy of Johnson's antievolution book *Darwin on Trial.*

28 March The Tennessee Senate rejects Senate Bill 3229 by a vote of 20–13.

May The Education Committee of the Ohio Senate votes down (by a vote of 12–8) legislation requiring that the teaching of evolution be accompanied by discussions of the "arguments against evolution."

The NSF reports that 44 percent of Americans accept that "human beings as we know them today developed from earlier species of animals."

24 October Pope John Paul II describes evolution as "more than a hypothesis" and announces that he sees no conflict between religious teachings and the theory of evolution. The pope's statement enrages many creationists.

1997   Pope John Paul II issues a papal letter accepting modern evolutionary theory.

Legislatures in four states begin debating procreationism legislation. The bills fail.

Famed creationist Henry Morris tells his followers that "A 'Christian evolutionist' . . . is an oxymoron."

A Gallup poll reports that 68 percent of Americans believe that "creationism should be taught along with evolution" in public schools. Meanwhile, a creationist poll shows that 56 percent of science teachers either disagree or are undecided about evolution being a scientific fact.

July   The Illinois Board of Education quietly deletes the word *evolution* from its education standards and science tests. The "evolutionless" standards are approved by the state's superintendent of education, many educators, and an official representing a teachers' union.

8 August   In *Freiler v. Tangipahoa Parish Board of Education*, U.S. District Court Judge Marcel Livaudais Jr. rules that (1) it is unlawful to require teachers to read aloud disclaimers saying that the biblical version of creation is the only concept "from which students [are] not to be dissuaded" and (2) proposals for teaching "intelligent design" are equivalent to proposals for teaching "creation science." The court awards $49,444.50 to Herb Freiler's attorneys.

1998   Several schools adopt the Bible as a textbook for history courses.

Money floods the coffers of antievolution organizations. For example, the budget of Answers in Genesis for 1998 is $3,702,800 and that of the Institute for Creation Research is $4,167,547. For comparison, the National Center for Science Education—an organization that advocates the teaching of evolution and the banishment of creationism from science classes—reports revenues of $258,957.

A survey of 500 high school biology teachers shows that 40 percent of respondents spend little or no time teaching evolution.

A Gallup poll reports that 47 percent of Americans believe that "God created man pretty much in his present form at one time within the last 10,000 years."

8 April   The National Academy of Sciences reaffirms its belief that evolution is "the most important concept to modern biology" and that "there is no debate within the scientific community over whether evolution has occurred, and there is no evidence that evolution has not occurred."

30 June   A committee of twenty-seven scientists and science educators, appointed by the state's commissioner on education, starts writing new science standards for Kansas.

November   Don Aguillard tells teachers attending the annual meeting of the NABT that "the fight [for the teaching of evolution] has shifted from people like Susan Epperson and myself to you. The task has shifted from constitutional challenges to grass-roots efforts."

1999   U.S. Representative and Republican Whip Tom DeLay links the teaching of evolution with abortion and school violence.

Harvard paleontologist Stephen J. Gould warns people that "we may laugh at a marginal movement like young-earth creationism, but only at our peril—for history features the principle that visible stalking horses, if unchecked at the starting gate, often grow into powerful champions of darkness."

Encouraged by Governor Cecil Underwood, the Kanawha County School Board in West Virginia debates a proposal to begin teaching the biblical story of creation. The proposal is defeated, but a poll shows that almost 60 percent of the state's residents believe that the biblical story of creation is probably the "actual explanation for the origin of human life on earth."

The Arizona House of Representatives debates equal-time legislation. The legislation dies in committee.

Scientific American reports that less than 10 percent of the members of the National Academy of Sciences believe in God. By contrast, 90 percent of Americans believe in God and claim that God played at least some role in creation.

Baylor University quietly opens the Michael Polanyi Center, which promotes intelligent design.

January   Public hearings begin on the draft of the new science standards in Kansas.

May   In *Rodney LeVake v. Independent School District #656*, science teacher Rodney LeVake sues the Faribault (MN) School District when he is reassigned for refusing to stop promoting the alleged "evidence against evolution" in his science classes. LeVake claims that evolution is "impossible," that there is an "amazing lack of transitional forms in the fossil record," that evolution violates the second law of thermodynamics, and that evolution is not science. LeVake, who believes that accepting evolution is as absurd as believing that Earth is the center of the universe, demands that the school pay him $50,000 plus court costs. LeVake is represented by the American Center for Law and Justice, a spin-off of television preacher Pat Robertson's Christian Coalition.

August   The ICR announces a "five-year plan" to "remove" radioisotope dating from science.

1 August   The Kansas Board of Education eliminates virtually all mention of evolution in the state's science standards. If the board's changes are upheld, the state's assessment tests in 2001 and thereafter will not include any questions about evolution. The AAAS describes the decision as "a serious disservice to students and teachers," and Kansas Governor Bill Graves calls the action "terrible, tragic, embarrassing." Soon after the Kansas decision, the Kentucky Department of Education deletes the word *evolution* from its educational guidelines.

13 August A three-judge panel of the U.S. Fifth Circuit Court of Appeals affirms the *Freiler v. Tangipahoa Parish Board of Education* decision (1997), stating that (1) a school board cannot require that a disclaimer be read immediately before the teaching of evolution in elementary and secondary classes and (2) the Board's disclaimer promotes religion. However, the panel does not rule out the possibility that a school board can require some type of disclaimer stating that evolution is not the only accepted explanation of the origin of life.

The ACLU of Kansas and western Missouri notifies Kansas school districts that it will consider legal action if the districts teach "creation science."

23 August *Time* magazine, in an article that outrages creationists, publishes "Up from the Apes," which begins by stating, "Despite the protests of creationists . . . science has long taught that human beings are just another kind of animal."

September The Tangipahoa Parish Board of Education proposes an alternative disclaimer. The plaintiffs reject this new disclaimer, and the board asks for a hearing by all fifteen members of the Fifth Circuit Court.

23 September Presidents of the American Association for the Advancement of Science and the National Science Teachers Association and the chair of the National Research Council issue a joint statement denying the Kansas Board of Education copyright permission to reference or use text from their documents in Kansas' revised science standards.

October *George* magazine rates the Scopes trial as fourth in a list of the "one hundred greatest defining political moments" of the twentieth century.

9 October The New Mexico Board of Education makes its standards match national standards by mandating the teaching of evolution as part of its science curriculum.

11 November The Oklahoma Textbook Commission votes

to place a disclaimer in biology textbooks used in the state's public schools. The disclaimer instructs readers to consider evolution "as theory, not fact" because "no one was present when life first appeared on earth." Oklahoma Attorney General Drew Edmondson later rules that the disclaimer is unconstitutional because the textbook commission does not have the authority to make such a decision. Legislators respond by proposing bills that require science textbooks to acknowledge the existence of God, but these bills die in process. Oklahoma will not again review science textbooks until 2005.

December   The Idaho Curricular Materials Selection Committee votes not to adopt the creationist text *Of Pandas and People*.

A study published in *Science Teacher* reports that only 57 percent of science teachers consider evolution to be a unifying theme in biology and that almost half of science teachers believe that there is much scientific evidence for creationism. Large percentages of biology teachers believe that creationism should be taught in public schools.

2000   The Showtime cable TV network produces and broadcasts another version of *Inherit the Wind*.

Paleontologist Niles Eldredge warns people that "the integrity of science education in the United States and abroad is directly threatened by [creationists'] nonsense."

National Heritage Academies, a chain of state-funded charter schools, experience rapid growth. Science classes at these schools are based on creationism.

The Kentucky legislature debates legislation that bans the teaching of human evolution.

12 January   The South Carolina Board of Education unanimously approves the state's proevolution science standards.

24 January   The full Fifth Circuit Court denies by a vote of 8–7 the appeal of the Tangipahoa Parish Board of Education, noting that the board's disclaimer "is not sufficiently neutral to be constitutionally permissible."

February   Antievolution legislation introduced in the Indiana legislature is defeated in committee.

The Tangipahoa Parish Board of Education votes 5–4 against further appeals. Two members of the board later change their votes, prompting the issue to be placed on the agenda for the board's meeting later in the month.

3 February   Oklahoma Attorney General Edmondson rules that the state textbook commission has no authority to require an evolution disclaimer in all new biology books.

22 February   After reconsidering its earlier vote, Louisiana's Tangipahoa Parish School Board votes 7–2 to ask the U.S. Supreme Court to consider hearing an appeal of a lower court's rulings opposing its controversial evolution disclaimer.

March   A national survey shows that 79 percent of the population wants creationism taught in public schools and that half believe evolution is "far from being proven scientifically." Only 57 percent of science teachers consider evolution to be a unifying theme in biology, and almost half of all science teachers believe that there is as much evidence for creationism as there is for evolution.

Students at Thomas Jefferson High School in Lafayette, Indiana, petition the school board to have "special creation" taught in their biology classes. The board tells students that creationism is not part of the state's science curriculum and therefore will not be taught.

April   The Faculty Senate at Baylor University votes 26–2 to dissolve its Michael Polanyi Center, an intelligent-design think tank directed by creationist William Dembski.

A bill introduced into the Kentucky House of Representatives that would ban the teaching of human evolution fails to become law.

7 April　The Tangipahoa Parish School Board files an appeal of the lower court's decision about its textbook disclaimer.

May　John McIntosh, a science teacher at Colton (CA) High School, is instructed to stop using his search for Noah's ark as a way to teach the scientific method to his students.

10 May　Supporters of intelligent design (e.g., Michael Behe, Phillip Johnson) present a three-hour briefing before Congress on the evidence for the origin and development of life and the universe as the work of an intelligent designer. Presenters also debunk Darwinian evolutionary theory and point out the alleged negative social impact of Darwinism. Senator Sam Brownback (R-Kansas) compares the current controversy about evolution to the one spawned by abolitionist John Brown.

19 June　The U.S. Supreme Court (by a vote of 6–3) affirms a lower court's decision (in *Freiler v. Tangipahoa Parish Board of Education*) that ruled unconstitutional the Tangipahoa Parish School Board's policy of requiring teachers to read aloud a disclaimer whenever they teach evolution. Creationists on the board warn, "The war isn't over."

20 June　District Court Judge Bernard E. Borene issues a summary judgment dismissing *Rodney LeVake v. Independent School District #656*. LeVake had argued for the right to teach "evidence both for and against the theory" of evolution. Borene concludes that LeVake's right to free speech does not override the right of the school district to set its curriculum.

26 June　Scientists announce the completion of a "working draft" of the human genome. The draft covers about 85 percent of the genome's coding regions.

24 July　LeVake files an appeal of Judge Borene's decision.

August　Senator Robert Byrd (D-WV) announces that he's not bothered by having evolution taught in schools, but then asks, "Why not teach the creation in the book of Genesis, which was the greatest scientific thesis that was ever written?"

1 August Kansas voters repudiate the State Board of Education's removal of human evolution from the state's science standards by voting all but one of the antievolution candidates out of office in the state's primary elections. The creationists blame their defeats on elites from Washington, D.C., on the National Academy of Sciences, and on other science groups. Creationist Phillip Johnson blames the defeats on "very heavy-handed intimidation," and a Kansas student adds a factual observation with a postmodern twist, noting that "no one was there that's still alive today that actually witnessed creation or evolution. It's just what a person believes. I mean, we have no right to say what exactly is true."

September Alabama Judge Roy S. Moore, already famous for having defied a federal circuit court's order to remove the Ten Commandments from the wall of his courtroom and stop opening his court sessions with prayer, rejects evolution. Moore claims that the solution to the education issue is the fear of God. In November, Moore is elected Chief Justice of the Alabama Supreme Court with 55 percent of the vote.

Ohio State Representative Ron Hood and several cosponsors reintroduce Hood's 1996 bill requiring teachers to present evidence for and against evolution. Hood's bill dies in committee. In November, Hood loses his seat to Democrat John Boccieri in a close race.

The Thomas B. Fordham Foundation publishes Lawrence Lerner's *Good Science, Bad Science: Teaching Evolution in the States.* Lerner reports that (1) thirty-one states do an adequate-to-excellent job of treating evolution in their science standards, (2) nineteen states do a weak-to-reprehensible job of treating evolution in their science standards, (3) twelve states shun the word *evolution* in their standards, and (4) four states avoid teaching evolution altogether.

26 September The Southern Baptist Convention announces that it was not going to "go away on [the evolution] subject" and that Southern Baptists are "more aware of weaknesses" in evolution.

19 October   After much controversy, creationist Michael Dembski is removed as director of Baylor University's intelligent-design think tank. Dembski accuses the university of "intellectual McCarthyism."

29 October   Canada's *Ottawa Citizen* reports that a new curriculum designed to avoid controversy will ensure that most students in Ontario will go through elementary and high school without being taught about evolution.

November   Virtually all major candidates for president of the United States declare their support for teaching creationism. The election is won by George W. Bush, who says that "the jury is still out" on evolution.

Hundreds of believers (including John Whitcomb, coauthor of *The Genesis Flood*) gather in northern Kentucky to dedicate land for the future home of the $14 million Creation Museum and Family Discovery Center. The creationism complex, which will be sponsored by Answers in Genesis and will cover 47 acres, is scheduled to open in the summer of 2002.

25 November   The *Ottawa Citizen* reports that 38 percent of Canadians support teaching creationism in public schools.

December   A national survey reports that only 57 percent of science teachers consider evolution to be a unifying theme in biology, that almost half believe that there is as much evidence for creationism as for evolution, that almost half fear raising controversy by teaching evolution, and that large percentages of biology teachers are creationists.

2001   Attacks on evolution intensify in Wisconsin, Connecticut, Indiana, West Virginia, Washington, Montana, Georgia, Michigan, and elsewhere. Creationists continue to disguise their efforts with euphemisms such as "intelligent-design theory" and "abrupt appearance theory."

January   Geoff Stevens, a lecturer with Answers in Genesis, says that a lion killing and eating a water buffalo "is what sin looks like."

14 February   The Kansas Board of Education votes 7–3 to restore evolution to the state's science curriculum, eighteen months after excising all references to the origin of man and the age of the Earth at the urging of conservative Christians. Throughout the state, where more than 25 percent of the biology teachers are creationists, creationists vow to continue their efforts to include creationism in the state's science classes.

March   Proponents of intelligent design ask the National School Board Association to include creationism in science classrooms. Meanwhile, Henry Morris announces that, "Bible-believing Christians should take the Genesis record literally if we want to honor God."

The Michigan House of Representatives begins considering House Bill 4382, which would require science standards to refer to evolution as an unproven theory and to give equal time to "the theory that life is the result of the purposeful, intelligent design of the creator."

April   Louisiana Representative Sharon Weston Broome, worried that evolution "has provided the main rationale for racism," introduces a resolution linking evolution and Darwin with racism, Hitler, and eugenics. In May, the resolution is amended and reference to evolution and Darwin are removed, leaving only a condemnation of racism. The amendment passed by a vote of 65–28. She makes the typical creationist argument: "If you are going to teach [evolution] in our schools, you have to make children aware of the weaknesses in the theory."

8 May   Colin Dovichin, a science teacher in northwestern Minnesota, alleges that he's being fired for teaching evolution and not giving in to pressure from parents to teach creationism. Administrators dispute Dovichin's claim.

The Minnesota Appeals Court rejects the appeal of Rodney LeVake to teach "evidence against evolution," thereby supporting the summary judgment dismissal of *Rodney LeVake v. Independent School District #656*. The Appeals Court rules that "the established curriculum and LeVake's responsibility as a public school teacher to teach evolution in the manner prescribed by the curriculum overrides his First Amendment rights as a public citizen."

13 June   The U.S. Senate adopts a "Sense of the Senate" amendment to the Elementary and Secondary Education Authorization Bill, S.1, stating, "It is the sense of the Senate that (1) good science education should prepare students to distinguish the data or testable theories of science from philosophical or religious claims that are made in the name of science, and (2) where biological evolution is taught, the curriculum should help students to understand why the subject generates so much continuing controversy, and should prepare the students to be informed participants in public discussions regarding he subject." The amendment (Amendment #799) is proposed by Senator Rick Santorum (R-PA) and shaped by "intelligent design" advocate Phillip Johnson. On the following day, the overall bill passes the Senate 91–8.

July   Answers in Genesis proclaims that the Bible "is the only 100 percent accurate history book in the world" and that evolution is "the anti-God religion of death."

BIBLIOGRAPHY

Abbott, James Francis. 1914. *The Elementary Principles of General Biology.* New York: Macmillan.

ACLU Executive Committee. 1925. "Minutes, 3 August 1925." In *ACLU Archives* 279 (3 August).

Affannato, F. 1986. "A Survey of Biology Teachers' Opinions about the Teaching of Evolutionary Theory and/or the Creation Model in the United States in Public and Private Schools." Ph.D. dissertation, University of Iowa, Ames.

Agassiz, Louis. 1878. *Methods of Study in Natural History.* Boston: Osgood.

Aguillard, Don. 1989. "Foreword." In Haig A. Bosmajian, ed., *Academic Freedom* (pp. xiii–xv), First Amendment in the Classroom Series, no. 4. New York: Neal-Schuman Publishers.

———. 1999. "Evolution Education in Louisiana Public Schools: A Decade Following *Edwards v. Aguillard.*" *American Biology Teacher* 61: 182–188.

Aldrich, K. J. 1999. "Teachers' Attitudes toward Evolution and Creationism in Kansas Biology Classrooms, 1991." *Kansas Biology Teacher* 81: 20–21.

Alexander, Charles C. 1965. *The Ku Klux Klan in the Southwest.* Lexington: University of Kentucky Press.

Allem, W. 1959. "Backgrounds of the Scopes Trial at Dayton, Tennessee." Master's thesis, University of Tennessee, Knoxville.

Amicus Curiae Brief of Seventy-two Nobel Laureates, Seventeen State Academies of Science, and Seven Other Scientific Organizations, in Support of Appellees, Submitted to the Supreme Court of the United States, October Term, 1986, as Edwin W. Edwards, in His Official Capacity of Governor of Louisiana, et al., Appellants v. Don Aguillard et al., Appellees. Available at http://www.talkorigins.org/faqs/edwards-v-aguillard/amicus1.html

Ammerman, Nancy Tatom. 1990. *Baptist Battles: Social Change and Religious Conflict in the Southern Baptist Convention.* New Brunswick, NJ: Rutgers University Press.

"Antievolution in Arkansas—A History." 1966. *Arkansas Gazette*, 24 April.

"Antievolution Law Is Good, Faubus Says." 1966. *Arkansas Gazette*, 5 April.

"Arkansas 'Monkey' Battle." 1966. *Oakland Tribune*, 30 March, p. A21.

Armstrong, Herbert W. 1967. *The United States and Britain in Prophecy*. Pasadena, CA: Worldwide Church of God.

"As Expected, Bryan Wins." 1925. *Chicago Tribune*, 22 July, p. 7.

Ashby, LeRoy. 1987. *William Jennings Bryan: Champion for Democracy*. Boston: Twayne Publishers.

"Attempts Thwarted to Limit Testimony." 1981. *Arkansas Gazette*, 8 December, p. E10.

Austin, Steve A. 1994. *Grand Canyon: Monument to Catastrophe*. Santee, CA: Institute for Creation Research.

Azar, Larry. 1990. *Twentieth Century in Crisis: Foundations of Totalitarianism*. Dubuque, IA: Kendall Hunt.

Bailey, Kenneth K. 1964. *Southern White Protestantism in the Twentieth Century*. New York: Harper and Row.

Baker, A. O., and L. N. Mills. 1933. *Dynamic Biology*. Chicago: Rand McNally.

"Balanced Treatment for Creation Science and Evolution Science, Act 590." 1981. *Arkansas Statutes, Annotated*, 580–1663 Supp.

"Baptist Cleric Says Evolution Is 'Impossible.'" 1965. *Arkansas Gazette*, 1 November.

"Baptists Seek 'Monkey Law' Enforcement." 1965. *Arkansas Gazette*, 5 November.

Behe, Michael J. 1996. *Darwin's Black Box: The Biochemical Challenge to Evolution*. New York: The Free Press.

Bennetta, W. 1986. "Looking Backwards." In W. Bennetta, ed., *Crusade of the Credulous: A Collection of Articles about Contemporary Creationism and the Effects of That Movement on Public Education*. San Francisco: California Academy of Science Press.

Bentley, G. 1966. "Bennett Is Accused of 'Making a Joke' of Evolution Case." *Arkansas Gazette*, 19 March.

Berman, E. H. 1997. "Fundamentalists, the Schools, and Cultural Politics." *Educational Foundations* (Fall 1997): 1–12.

Bernard, J. D. 1926. "The Baptists." *American Mercury*, pp. 135–146.

Bird, Wendell. 1978. "Freedom of Religion and Science Indoctrination in Public Schools." *Yale Law Journal* 87: 516–517.

———. 1979. "Resolution for Balanced Presentation of Evolution and Scientific Creationism." ICR Impact Series, no. 71. San Diego, CA: Institute for Creation Research.

———. 1989. *The Origin of Species Revisited*. El Cajon, CA: Institute for Creation Research.

Blessing, W. L. 1952. *White Supremacy*. Denver, CO: House of Worship for All People.

Broad, W. 1981. "Creationists Limit Scope of California Case." *Science* 211: 1331–1332.

Brooks, P., D. Crowley Jr., D. Griffin, and H. Schieber. 1990. *Freedom or Slavery?* Fletcher, NC: New Puritan Library.

Brummett, John. 1981a. "'Creation-Science' Bill Prompted by Religious Beliefs, Sponsor Says." *Arkansas Gazette*, 22 March, p. A1.

———. 1981b. "He Hasn't Read It, but White Signs Bill on 'Creation.'" *Arkansas Gazette*, 20 March, p. 1.

"Bryan and Darrow Wage War of Words in Trial Interlude." 1925. *New York Times*, 19 July, p. 1.

"Bryan Here Saturday." 1924. *American Forum: The Klan Paper for Province Number 5, Realm of Texas, Knights of the Ku Klux Klan* 25 (52): 1.

Bryan, William Jennings. 1925. *The Last Message of William Jennings Bryan: A Reprint Commemorating the Fiftieth Anniversary of Bryan College.* Dayton, TN: Bryan College.

Bull, J., and H. Wichman. 1998. "A Revolution in Evolution." *Science* 281: 1959.

Burbank, Luther, to John Haynes Holmes (letter). 1925. *ACLU Archives* 274 (29 July).

Butler, John W. 1925. "For Heaven's Sake!" *Commercial Appeal* (Memphis), 19 July, p. 3.

Campbell, Ernest Q., and Thomas F. Pettigrew. 1959. *Christians in Racial Crisis: A Study of Little Rock's Ministry.* Washington, DC: Public Affairs Press.

Carlesen, W. S. 1991. "Effects of New Biology Teachers' Subject-Matter Knowledge on Curricular Planning." *Science Education* 756: 631–647.

Carr, S. 2000. "Bob Jones U. Offers Its Controversial Curriculum to High-School Students Online." *Chronicle of Higher Education* 10 March, p. A47.

Carroll, Charles. 1900. *The Negro a Beast: Or, In the Image of God.* St. Louis, MO: American Book and Bible House.

Cash, Wilbur Joseph. 1941. *The Mind of the South.* New York: Knopf.

Cauchon, R. 2000. "College Ascribes Its Ways to Christian Beliefs." *USA Today,* 3 March, p. A4.

Cavanaugh, M. 1985. "Scientific Creationism and Rationality." *Nature* 315: 185–189.

Chalmers, David Mark. 1965. *Hooded Americanism: The History of the Ku Klux Klan.* New York: Franklin Watts.

Chambers, Robert. 1844. *Vestiges of the Natural History of Creation, with a Sequel.* New York: Harper and Bros.

Cherny, Robert W. 1985. *A Righteous Cause: The Life of William Jennings Bryan.* Boston: Little, Brown.

Christensen, J. 1998. "Teachers Fight for Darwin's Place in U.S. Classrooms." *New York Times*, 24 November, p. B3.

Church, D. M. 1925. "News of Dayton Trial Spreads." *Nashville Banner,* 7 June, sec. 2, p. 7.

Clapper, Raymond. 1925. "Bryan Turns Guns on Scopes." *Des Moines Register*, 17 July, p. 1.

Clouse, R. G. 1995. "Evangelicalism before and after the Scopes Trial." In *Creation of an Evolving Controversy: A Symposium on the 70th Anniversary of the Scopes Evolution Trial*, ed. Richard M. Cornelius, (pp. 11–16). Dayton, TN: Bryan College.

Cole, H., and E. Scott. 1982. "Creation Science and Scientific Research." *Phi Beta Kappan* 63: 557–558.

Coletta, Paolo E. 1964–1969. *William Jennings Bryan*. 3 vols. Lincoln: University of Nebraska Press.

———. 1969. *Political Puritan, 1915–1925*. Vol. 3 of *William Jennings Bryan*. Lincoln: University of Nebraska Press.

Cornelius, Richard M. 1981. "Science at Scopes' School Today." *Eternity* 32 (June): 17.

———. 1990. "The Trial That Made Monkeys Out of the World." *USA Today Magazine* 119 (November): 88–90.

———. 1991. "World's Most Famous Court Trial." In B. J. Broyles, ed., *History of Rhea County, Tennessee* (pp. 66–71). Dayton, TN: Rhea County Historical and Genealogical Society.

———. 1995. "Their Stage Drew All the World: A New Look at the Scopes Evolution Trial." In R. M. Cornelius and J. D. Morris, eds., *Scopes: Creation on Trial* (pp. 2–21). El Cajon, CA: Institute for Creation Research. Note: Much of this text also appears in *Tennessee Historical Quarterly* 40 (Summer 1981): 129–143.

———. 1997. *William Jennings Bryan, the Scopes Trial, and* Inherit the Wind. Dayton, TN: Bryan College.

———. 1998. "Selected Bibliography of Recordings Featuring the Campaign Songs and Speeches of William Jennings Bryan, Scopes Trial Songs, and Other Songs about Evolution and Monkeys." *Arts and Letters* 6: 23–27.

Cowen, R. 1986. "Creationism and the Science Classroom." *California Science Teacher's Journal* 16 (5): 8–15.

"Creation Science Act Improper, Challenger of Anti-Evolution Law Says." 1981. *Arkansas Gazette*, 18 May, p. A1.

"Creationism in Schools: The Decision in *McLean v. Arkansas Board of Education*." 1982. *Science* 215: 937.

Cross, W. C. 1925. "Bryan, Noted Orator, in Favor at Dayton." *Knoxville Journal* 10 July, p. 1.

Culliton, B. 1978. "Science's Restive Public." *Daedalus* 107: 147–156.

Cuvier, Georges. 1813. *Essay on the Theory of the Earth*. Edinburgh, Scotland: W. Blackwood.

Dalhouse, Mark T. 1996. *An Island in the Lake of Fire: Bob Jones University, Fundamentalism, and the Separatist Movement*. Athens: University of Georgia Press.

Darrow, Clarence. 1932. *The Story of My Life*. New York: Scribner's.

"Darrow Likens Bryan to Nero." 1925. *Nashville Banner*, 18 May, p. 1.

"Darrow Loud in His Protest." 1925. *Nashville Banner,* 8 July, p. 1.

"Darrow's Statement." 1925. *Commercial Appeal* (Memphis), 19 July, p. 1.

Darwin, Charles. 1859. *On the Origin of Species by Means of Natural Selection: Or, The Preservation of Favoured Races in the Struggle for Life.* London: John Murray.

———. 1871. *The Descent of Man and Selection in Relation to Sex.* London: John Murray.

"A Darwinism Ban in Arkansas Ends." 1968. *New York Times,* 13 November, pp. 1, 4.

Daughtrey, L. 1973. "Dunn Signature Withheld, but Genesis Bill Now Law." *Nashville Tennesseean,* 9 May, p. 1.

Davis, Percival William, and Dean H. Kenyon, eds. 1989. *Of Pandas and People: The Central Question of Biological Origins.* Dallas, TX: Haughton.

Dawkins, Richard. 1986. *The Blind Watchmaker: Why the Evidence of Evolution Reveals a Universe Without Design.* New York: Norton.

"Dayton Keyed Up for Opening Today of Trial of Scopes." 1925. *New York Times,* 10 July, p. 1.

"Dayton Says It'd Convict Scopes Still." 1968. *Arkansas Gazette,* 14 November.

"Dayton's 'Amazing' Trial." 1925. *Literary Digest,* 25 July, p. 7.

de Camp, Lyon Sprague. 1968. *The Great Monkey Trial.* Garden City, NY: Doubleday.

———. 1969. "The End of the Monkey War." *Scientific American* 220: 15–21.

"Defendants' Trial Brief." 1981. *McLean v. Arkansas,* 529 F. Supp. 1225 (ED Ark. 1982, pp. 23–27).

"Defies Ban on Teaching Evolution." 1966. *Pacific Stars and Stripes,* 4 April.

Denton, Michael. 1986. *Evolution: A Theory in Crisis.* Bethesda, MD: Adler & Adler.

Destiny Publishers. 1967. *In the Image of God.* Merrimac, MA: Destiny Publishing.

Dickey, C. R. 1958. *The Bible and Segregation.* Merrimac, MA: Destiny Publishing.

"A Dignified Trial of Law on Evolution." 1966. *Arkansas Gazette,* 3 April.

Dobzhansky, Theodosius. 1973. "Nothing in Biology Makes Sense Except in the Light of Evolution." *American Biology Teacher* 35: 125–129.

Donaldson, K. 1988. "The Creationism Controversy: It's Only the Beginning." *School Library Journal* 34 (7): 107–113.

Dowsett, F. W. 1991. "Kingdom Identity." *Christian Patriot Crusader* 7: 3–6.

Eckberg, D., and A. Nesterenko. 1985. "For and against Evolution: Religion, Social Class, and the Symbolic Universe." *Social Science Journal* 22: 1–17.

"Editorial." 1992. *Atlanta Constitution,* 6 August.

"Educators Criticize Creationism Bill." 1981. *Arkansas Gazette,* 3 May, p. A8.

Eldredge, Niles. 1982. *The Monkey Business: A Scientist Looks at Creationism.* New York: Washington Square.

Elliott, E. N., ed. 1860. *Cotton Is King, and Pro-Slavery Arguments.* Augusta, GA: Pritchard, Abbott, and Loomis.

Encyclopedia of Southern Baptists. 1958. Nashville, TN: Broadman Press.

"Ended at Last." 1925. *New York Times,* 22 July, p. 18.

Evans, H. W. 1925. "The Klan: Defender of Americanism." *Forum* 74: 813.

Eve, Raymond, and Francis Harrold. 1991. *The Creationist Movement in Modern America.* Boston: Twayne Publishers.

"Explanations of Origin Differ on Age, Method." 1981. *Oregonian,* March 22, p. G12.

Falwell, Jerry, ed. 1981. *The Fundamentalist Phenomenon: The Resurgence of Conservative Christianity.* Garden City, NY: Doubleday.

"Famous Trials in American History: Tennessee v. John Scopes, the 'Monkey Trial.'" Available at: http://www.law.umkc.edu/ftrials/scopes/scopes/htm.

Fecher, Charles A. 1978. *Mencken: A Study of His Thought.* New York: Knopf.

"Federal Judge Denies Arkansas Creation Law." 1982. *Moral Majority Report,* 25 January, p. 3.

Feldman, Glen. 1999. *Politics, Society, and the Klan in Alabama, 1915–1949.* Tuscaloosa: University of Alabama Press.

"First Verse of Bible Key to All Scriptures." 1925. *Commercial Appeal* (Memphis, TN), 13 March, p. 11.

Fredrickson, George M. 1981. *White Supremacy: A Comparative Study in American and South African History.* Oxford: Oxford University Press.

Futuyma, Douglas J. 1983. *Science on Trial: The Case for Evolution.* New York: Random House.

Gabler, Mel, and Norma Gabler. 1985a. *What Are They Teaching Our Children?* Wheaton, IL: Victor Books.

———. 1985b. *Scientific Creationism,* Handbook #10. Longview, TX: Educational Research Analysts.

Gallup, G. H., Jr., and F. Newport. 1991. "Belief in Paranormal Phenomena among Adult Americans." *Skeptical Inquirer* 2: 137–147.

Georgia House Journal. 1923, pp. 1001–1002.

Gieryn, T. R., G. M. Bevins, and S. C. Zehr. 1985. "Professionalization of American Scientists: Public Science in the Creation/Evolution Trials." *American Sociological Review* 50: 393–407.

Gilkey, Langdon, ed. 1985. *Creationism on Trial: Evolution and God at Little Rock.* New York: Harper and Row.

Gillis, A. M. 1994. "Keeping Creationism Out of the Classroom." *Bioscience* 44: 650–656.

Ginger, Ray. 1958. *Six Days or Forever? Tennessee vs. John Thomas Scopes.* Oxford: Oxford University Press.

Gish, Duane T. 1972. *Evolution? The Fossils Say No!* San Diego, CA: Creation-Life Publishers.

———. 1988. "Creation, Evolution, and the Historical Evidence" (pp. 266–283). In

M. Ruse, ed., *But Is It Science?* Buffalo, NY: Prometheus Books.

Glanz, J. 2000. "79% Back Creationism in Schools." *The Denver Post*, 11 March, pp. 1A, 7A.

Gorman, J. 1980. "Creationism on the Rise." *Discover* (October): 92–94.

Gould, Stephen J. 1977a. *Ever Since Darwin*. New York: W. W. Norton.

———. 1977b. *Ontogeny and Phylogeny*. Cambridge, MA: Harvard University Press.

———. 1980. *The Panda's Thumb*. New York: W. W. Norton.

———. 1981. The *Mismeasure of Man*. New York: W. W. Norton.

———. 1983. *Hen's Teeth and Horse's Toes*. New York: W. W. Norton.

———. 1985. The *Flamingo's Smile*. New York: W. W. Norton.

———. 1993. *Eight Little Piggies*. New York: W. W. Norton.

Grabiner, J. V., and P. D. Miller. 1974. "Effects of the Scope Trial." *Science* 185: 832–836.

Graham, F. P. 1968. "Court Ends Darwinism Ban." *New York Times*, 12 November, p. 1.

Gray, Asa. 1857. *First Lessons in Botany and Vegetable Physiology*. New York: Ivison.

Greenwood, M. R. C., and K. K. North. 1999. "Science through the Looking Glass: Winning the Battles but Losing the War?" *Science* 286: 2071–2079.

Griffee, C. 1981a. "Creation Act Is Unconstitutional, Lawsuit Charges." *Arkansas Gazette*, 28 May, pp. D7–D8.

———. 1981b. "Creationism Is Not New to Instructor: He's Been Teaching It since 1968." *Arkansas Gazette*, 12 December, p. E8.

Griffin, Larry J., and Don H. Doyle. 1995. *The South as an American Problem*. Athens: University of Georgia Press.

Grobman, Arnold B. 1969. *The Changing Classroom: The Role of the Biological Science Curriculum Studies*. Garden City, NY: Doubleday.

Grose, Vernon. 1974. "Second Thoughts about Textbooks on Sexism." *Science and Scripture*, 4 January, p. 14.

Haller, John S. 1971. *Outcasts from Evolution: Scientific Attitudes of Racial Inferiority, 1859–1900*. Urbana: University of Illinois Press.

Halliburton, R., Jr. 1973. "Mississippi's Contribution to the Anti-Evolution Movement." *Journal of Mississippi History* 35: 177.

Ham, Ken. 1987. *The Lie: Evolution*. El Cajon, CA: Master Books.

Harp, L. 1999. "The Evolution Debate: Even Today, the 'E-Word' Divides." *Courier-Journal* (Louisville, KY), 3 October, pp. A1, A10.

Hasskarl, G. C. H. 1898. *The Missing Link: Or, The Negro's Ethnological Status*. Chambersburg, PA: Democratic News.

Hays, A. 1983. "The Scopes Trial." In Gail Kennedy, ed., *Evolution and Religion: The Conflict between Science and Religion in Modern America*. Boston: D. C. Heath.

Hays, Arthur Garfield. 1925. "The Strategy of the Scopes Defense." *Nation*, 5 August, p. 158.

Hazen, R. M., and J. Trefil. 1991. "Quick! What's a Quark?" *New York Times Magazine*, 13 January, pp. 24–26.

Heard, Alex. 1982. "Creationism Movement Appears to Be Slowed by Loss in Arkansas." *Education Week*, 17 February, p. 4.

Hebel, S., and P. Schmidt. 2000. "Bob Jones U. Shifts Its Policies on Interracial Dating by Students." *Chronicle of Higher Education*, 17 March, p. A39.

Hernstein, Richard J., and C. Murray. 1996. *The Bell Curve: Intelligence and Class Structure in American Life.* Detroit, MI: Free Press.

Hodgman, Stephen A. 1884. *Moses and the Philosophers.* Philadelphia: Ferguson Bros.

Holden, C. 1999. "Breakdown of the Year: Creationists Win in Kansas." *Science* 286: 2242.

Holtzman, R., and D. Klasfeld. 1983. "The Arkansas Creationism Trial: An Overview of the Legal and Scientific Issues" (pp. 94–107). In M. La Follette, ed., *Creationism, Science, and the Law: The Arkansas Case.* Cambridge, MA: MIT Press.

Horowitz, J. 1981. "Battle Lines Drawn over Scientific Creationism in the Classroom." *Los Angeles Times*, 6 March, pp. 5–6.

"House Act Fails to Stir Scopes." 1967. *Nashville Tennessean*, 13 April, p. 1.

Huba, S. 1998. "Creationists Plan Clubs for Students." *Cincinnati Post*, 12 October, p. A4.

Humber, P. G. 1987. "The Ascent of Racism." ICR Impact Series, no. 164. El Cajon, CA: Institute for Creation Research.

Hunter, George William. 1907. *Elements of Biology.* Chicago: American Book Co.

———. 1911. *Essentials of Biology.* Chicago: American Book Co.

———. 1914. *A Civic Biology: Presented in Problems.* New York: American Book Co.

———. 1926. *New Civic Biology.* Chicago: American Book Co.

———. 1941. *Life Sciences—A Social Biology.* Chicago: American Book Co.

Hutchinson, W. 1926. "Darrow Makes Fervid Plea." *Nashville Banner*, 1 June, p. 1.

Ipsen, D. C. 1973. *Eye of the Whirlwind: The Story of John Scopes.* Reading, MA: Addison-Wesley.

Irons, Peter. 1988. *The Courage of Their Convictions.* New York: Free Press.

Irons, Peter, and Stephanie Guitton. 1993. *May It Please the Court: The Most Significant Oral Arguments before the Supreme Court since 1955.* New York: New Press.

Johnson, Phillip E. 1993. *Darwin on Trial.* Downers Grove, IL: Intervarsity Press.

———. 1995. *Reason in the Balance: The Case Against Naturalism in Science, Law, and Education.* Downers Grove, IL: Intervarsity Press.

Katz, William Loren. 1986. *The Invisible Empire.* Washington, DC: Open Hand Publishing.

Kazan, C. 1966a. "Arkansas 'Monkey Trial' Starts Today." *Charlotte Observer*, 1 April, p. A20.

———. 1966b. "Trial of '66 Has Its Opening in Little Rock Today." *Washington Post*, 1 April.

———. 1966c. "'Antievolution' in Arkansas—A History." *Arkansas Gazette*, 24 April, p. E1.

Keienburg, J. W., III. 1978. "Epperson v. Arkansas: A Question of Control over Curriculum and Instruction Decision Making in the Public Schools." Ph.D. dissertation, Texas A&M University, College Station, Texas.

Kennedy, D. 1998. "Helping Schools to Teach Evolution." *Chronicle of Higher Education*, 7 August, p. A48.

Kennedy, J. 1992. "Teaching of Creationism Splits Louisville Parents." *Repository*, 30 September, p. B4.

Kenyon, R. 1981. "Trial Zeroes In on Fundamentalist Christian Beliefs." *Milwaukee Journal*, 12 December, p. A4.

Kitcher, Philip. 1982. *Abusing Science: The Case against Creationism*. Cambridge, MA: MIT Press.

Kofahl, Robert E. 1977. *Handy Dandy Evolution Refuter*. San Diego, CA: Beta.

Kuh, F. 1925. "Ape Case Loosens Up Tongue of Einstein." *Pittsburgh Sun*, 22 June, p. 10.

La Follette, M., ed. 1983. *Creationism, Science, and the Law: The Arkansas Case*. Cambridge, MA: MIT Press.

Lane, J. 1982. "Letter." *Physics Today* 35 (15): 103.

Larson, Edward J. 1989. *Trial and Error: The American Controversy over Creation and Evolution*. Updated ed. New York: Oxford University Press.

———. 1997. *Summer for the Gods: The Scopes Trial and America's Continuing Debate over Science and Religion*. New York: Basic Books.

Larson, Edward J., and L. Witham. 1998. "Leading Scientists Still Reject God." *Nature* 394: 313.

Lauden, L. 1983. "Commentary on Ruse: Science at the Bar—Causes for Concern." In M. La Follette, ed. *Creationism, Science, and the Law: The Arkansas Case*. Cambridge, MA: MIT Press.

"Law on Creation Theory Proves Boon for Governor of Arkansas." 1981. *New York Times*, 22 March, p. A26.

Lawrence, Jerome, and Robert E. Lee. 1955. *Inherit the Wind*. New York: Bantam Books.

Lessl, T. 1988. "Heresy, Orthodoxy, and the Politics of Science." *Quarterly Journal of Speech* 74: 18–34.

Levy, Leonard Williams. 1986. *The Establishment Clause: Religion and the First Amendment*. New York: Macmillan.

Lewis, J. 1962. *Man and Evolution*. New York: International Publications.

Lewis, R. 1997. "To Effectively Discuss Evolution, First Define 'Theory.'" *Scientist* 12 May, pp. 13–14.

Lienesch, Michael. 1993. *Redeeming America: Piety and Politics in the New Christian Right.* Chapel Hill: University of North Carolina Press.

Lightfoot, John. 1642. *A Few, and New Observations, Upon the Book of Genesis, The Most of Them Certain, the Rest Probable, All Harmless, Strange, and Rarely Heard of Before.* London: T. Badger.

Linville, Henry. 1923. *The Biology of Man and Other Organisms.* New York: Harcourt, Brace.

Lutholtz, M. William. 1991. *Grand Dragon: D. C. Stephenson and the Ku Klux Klan in Indiana.* West Lafayette, IN: Purdue University Press.

Luxenberg, S. 1981. "The Arkansas Creationist Story Actually Has Its Origin in S.C." *Sun* (Baltimore), 10 December, pp. C13–C14.

Maclean, Nancy. 1994. *Behind the Mask of Chivalry: The Making of the Second Ku Klux Klan.* New York: Oxford University Press.

Magne, C. L. 1970. *The Negro and the World Crisis.* Hollywood, CA: New Christian Crusade Church.

"Maintaining One's Ideas Requires Courage." 1965. *Tiger* (Little Rock Central High School) 71 (7): 1.

Marks, J. 1998. "How Can We Interject Human Evolution into More Museums?" *Chronicle of Higher Education*, 4 December, p. B9.

Marsden, George M. 1980. *Fundamentalism and American Culture: The Shaping of Twentieth Century Evangelicalism, 1870–1925.* Oxford: Oxford University Press.

Martin, William C. 1996. *With God on Our Side: The Rise of the Religious Right in America.* New York: Broadway Books.

Matsumura, M. V. 1995. "Tennessee Upset: 'Monkey Bill' Law Defeated." *NCSE* [National Center for Science Education] *Reports* 15: 6–7.

———. 1998. "How to Fight Creationism/Evolution Battles." *Free Inquiry* (Spring): 37–38.

McDonald, K. 1986. "Pervasive Belief in 'Creation Science' Dismays and Perplexes Researchers." *Chronicle of Higher Education*, 10 December, pp. 5, 6, 10.

McIver, T. 1994. "The Protocols of Creationism." *Skeptic* 2: 76–87.

McLester, R. L. 1966. "Teaching Unproven Theory as Fact." *Arkansas Gazette*, 7 April.

McLoughlin, William G. 1955. *Billy Sunday Was His Real Name.* Chicago: University of Chicago Press.

McLoughlin, William G., and Robert N. Bellah. 1968. *Religion in America.* Boston: Houghton Mifflin.

Mecklin, John M. 1924. *The Ku Klux Klan: A Study of the American Mind.* New York: Harcourt, Brace.

"Memorandum Brief." 1966. Chancery Court of Pulaski County, Arkansas. No. 131575.

"Memorandum Opinion." 1966. Chancery Court of Pulaski County, Arkansas. No. 131575.

Mencken, H. L. 1925. "Art." *Chattanooga News*, 18 September.

Mercer, T. C. 1978. "Introduction." In reprint ed. of "Trial Transcript" (1925), in *The World's Most Famous Court Trial: Tennessee Evolution Case* (pp. xiii–xv). Dayton, TN: Bryan College.

Metzger, G. O. 1978. "Looking Back to the Original Publication." In reprint ed. of "Trial Transcript" (1925), in *The World's Most Famous Court Trial: Tennessee Evolution Case* (pp. xvii–xix). Dayton, TN: Bryan College.

Miller, J. 1987. "Scientific Literacy in the United States." In David Evered and Maeve O'Connor, eds., *Communicating Science to the Public* (pp. 19–40). New York: Wiley.

Miller, K. 1983. "Answers to the Standard Creationist Arguments." In J. Peter Zetterberd, ed., *Science versus Creationism* (pp. 249–262). Phoenix: Oryx Press.

"A Minister Says Negroes Have No Souls." 1899. *Cleveland Gazette*, 3 June, p. 1.

"Monkey Law Bill May Be Decided." 1967. *Nashville Tennessean*, 13 April, p. 8.

"Monkey Trial Seen in Suit over Act 590." 1981. *Arkansas Gazette*, 29 July, p. A1.

Monsour, T. 1997. "Evolution Getting Short Shrift in Class." *Saint Paul Pioneer Press* 149 (167): 1, 6.

Moon, Truman J. 1921. *Biology for Beginners*. New York: Holt; rev. ed. 1926.

Moon, Truman J., Paul Mann, and James H. Otto. 1965. *Modern Biology*. New York: Holt.

Moore, John N. 1974. *Biology: A Search for Order in Complexity*. Grand Rapids, MI: Zondervan.

Moore, Randy. 1997. "The Persuasive Mr. Darwin." *BioScience* 47(2): 107–114.

———. 1998a. *In the Light of Evolution*. Reston, VA: National Association of Biology Teachers.

———. 1998b. "Creationism in the United States. V. The *McLean* Decision Destroys the Credibility of Creation Science." *The American Biology Teacher* 61(2): 92–101.

———. 1998c. "Creationism in the United States. VI. Demanding 'balanced treatment.'" *The American Biology Teacher* 61(3): 175–180.

———. 2001a. "Racism, Creationism, and the Confederate Flag." *Negro Educational Review* 52(1–2): 19–28.

———. 2001b. "The Lingering Impact of the Scopes Trial on High School Biology Textbooks." *BioScience* 51(9): 791–797.

Morris, Henry M. 1974. *Scientific Creationism*. El Cajon, CA: Master Books.

———. 1975. *The Troubled Waters of Evolution*. San Diego, CA: Creation Life Publishers.

———. 1984. *History of Modern Creationism*. San Diego, CA: Master Books.

———. 1985. *Creation and the Modern Christian*. El Cajon, CA: Master Books.

———. 1989. *The Long War against God: The History and Impact of the Creation/Evolution Conflict*. Grand Rapids, MI: Baker.

Morris, Henry M., and J. D. Morris. 1989. *Science, Scripture, and the Young Earth*. El Cajon, CA: Institute for Creation Research.

Morris, John D. 1994. *The Young Earth*. Colorado Springs, CO: Creation Life Publishers.

"Mr. DeLay's Power Play." 1999. *New York Times Week in Review*, 20 June, p. 14.

Murrow, Edward R. 1950. *I Can Hear It Now*. Vol. 3. New York: Columbia Records.

Myers, E. 1990. "The Impact of Modern Theories of Evolution upon Western Intellectual Thought." *Creation Research Society Quarterly* 26: 150–152.

National Academy of Sciences. 1984. *Science and Creationism: A View from the National Academy of Sciences*. Washington, DC: National Academy Press.

National Science Board. 1996. *Science and Engineering Indicators—1996*. Washington, DC: U.S. Government Printing Office.

Nelkin, Dorothy. 1976. "Science or Scripture: The Politics of 'Equal Time.'" In Gerald Holton and William Blanpied, eds., *Science and Its Public: The Changing Relationship* (pp. 209–228). Dordrecht, Holland: Reidel Publishers.

———. 1982. *The Creation Controversy: Science or Scripture in the Schools?* New York: W. W. Norton.

Nelson, Thomas H. 1925. "The Real Issue in Tennessee." *Moody Bible Institute Monthly* (September).

"New Poll Points to Increase in Paranormal Belief." *Skeptical Inquirer* (September–October): 9–10.

"New 'Scopes Trial' Opens in Arkansas." 1966. *New York Times*, international ed., 2–3 April.

"No Help Needed on Act 590." 1981. *Arkansas Gazette*, 3 June, p. A3.

Nott, Josiah C., and George R. Gliddon. 1854. *Types of Mankind*. Philadelphia: Lippincott, Grambo.

Novik, Jack D. 1983. "Litigating the Religion of Creation Science." *Federation of American Societies for Experimental Biology Proceedings* 42: 3041–3042.

Numbers, Ronald L. 1992. *The Creationists: The Evolution of Scientific Creationism*. Berkeley: University of California Press.

———. 1998. *Darwinism Comes to America*. Cambridge, MA: Harvard University Press.

O'Brien, T. E. 1974. *Proof: God's Chosen Are White Adamic Christians*. Metairie, LA: New Christian Crusade Church.

Odeneal, W. C. 1958. *Segregation: Sin or Sensible?* Merrimac, MA: Destiny Publishing.

Olson, LaDonna R. 1995. *Legacy of Faith: The Story of Bryan College*. Hayesville, NC: Schoettle Publishing.

"One Case: A Step-by-Step Account of Its Progress through the Supreme Court." 1987. *Life* 10 (Fall): 114–115.

"One Legislator's Vote Made Sure Kentucky Had No Monkey Trial." 1999. *Courier Journal* (Louisville, KY), 4 October, p. A7.

Orfield, Gary. 1969. *The Reconstruction of Southern Education*. New York: Wiley Interscience.

Otten, H. J. 1989. "Christians Defend the Truth—Reject All Hoaxes." *Christian News* 278: 6–22.

———. 1990. "The Holocaust—History or Hollywood?" *Christian News* 278: 20–29.

Otto, James, and Albert Towle. 1965. *Modern Biology*. New York: Holt, Rinehart, and Winston.

"An Overdue Rescue from a Law of Ignorance." 1968. *Arkansas Gazette*, 14 November, p. A6.

Overton, W. R. 1985. "Memorandum Opinion of United States District Judge William R. Overton in *McLean v. Arkansas*, 5 January 1982." In Langdon Gilkey, ed., *Creationism on Trial: Evolution and God at Little Rock*. New York: Harper and Row.

Padian, K. 1997. "Creationist Geology and Intuition: Isn't Science Just Common Sense?" *NCSE Reports* 17: 28–29.

Paterson, Frances R. A., and Lawrence F. Rossow. 1999. "'Chained to the Devil's Throne': Evolution and Creation Science as a Religio-Political Issue." *American Biology Teacher* 61: 358–364.

Payne, Buckner H. "Ariel." 1867. *The Negro: What Is His Ethnological Status?* Cincinnati: Privately published.

Peabody, James E., and Arthur E. Hunt. 1913. *Elementary Biology: Animal and Human*. New York: Macmillan.

———. 1924. *Biology and Human Welfare*. New York: Macmillan.

Peay, Austin. 1929. "The Passing of William Jennings Bryan." In Austin Peay, ed., *A Collection of State Papers and Political Addresses*. Kingsport, TN: Southern.

Pennock, Robert T. 1999. *Tower of Babel: The Evidence Against the New Creationism*. Cambridge, MA: MIT Press.

Pickover, C. A. 1998. "Paranormal Web Sites Proliferate." *Skeptical Inquirer* (May–June): 12.

Pigliucci, Massimo. 1998. "Summer for the Gods" (book review). *Bioscience* 48: 406–407.

Poovey, B. 1998. "Alabama Governor Wins GOP Primary Runoff." *Courier Journal* (Louisville, KY), 1 July, p. A6.

Pope, J. 1981. "It's No Monkey Trial, but It Can Get a Little Hairy." *Times-Picayune* (New Orleans), 14 December, p. 1.

———. 1982. "Creationism Isn't Dead Yet." *Times-Picayune* (New Orleans), 6 January, p. A1.

Prelli, Lawrence J. 1989. "Practicing Rhetorical Invention: Creating Scientifically Reasonable Claims." In *A Rhetoric of Science: Inventing Scientific Discourse*. Columbia: University of South Carolina Press.

"The *Press-Scimitar* Blitzes the Tennessee Anti-Evolution Law." 1967. *Scripps-Howard News*, (August): 9.

Prewitt, K. 1983. "Scientific Illiteracy and Democratic Theory." *Daedalus* 112: 49–64.

Price, George McCready. 1929. "Bringing Home the Bacon." *Bible Champion* 35: 205.

"Proceedings of the Democratic National Convention." 1924. *New York Times*, 29 June, pp. 1–8.

Puente, M. 1999. "The Century's Biggest News: List Ranks Headlines as History." *USA Today*, 24 February, pp. D1–D2.

"Putting 'Creation-Science' to Rest." 1984. *Arkansas Gazette*, 7 January, p. A1.

Recer, P. 1998. "Americans Lack Knowledge but Are Tops as Science Fans." *Courier Journal* (Louisville, KY), 4 July, p. A11.

"Republican Candidate Picks Fight with Darwin." 1980. *Science* 12: 1214.

Rice, Arnold S. 1962. *The Ku Klux Klan in American Politics*. Washington, DC: Public Affairs Press.

Riddle, Oscar. 1938. "Educational Darkness and Luminous Research." *Science* 7: 375–380.

Rosenberg, Ellen M. 1989. *The Southern Baptists: A Subculture in Transition*. Knoxville: University of Tennessee Press.

Roy, Ralph L. 1953. *Apostles of Discord: A Study of Organized Bigotry and Disruption on the Fringes of Protestantism*. Boston: Beacon Press.

Ruse, M. 1998. "Answering the Creationists." *Free Inquiry* (Spring): 28–32.

"Same Evidence Begets Different Conclusions." 1981. *Sun* (Baltimore), 6 December, p. G2.

Sanders, A. L. 1987. "Memories of the Monkey Trial." *Time* 129 (26): 54.

Scanlon, L., and G. L. Uy. 1999. "The Evolution Debate: Private and Church Schools' Approaches Vary Widely." *Courier-Journal* (Louisville, KY), 3 October, p. A10.

Schmertz, Herb, and William Novak. 1986. *Goodbye to the Low Profile: The Art of Creative Confrontation*. Boston: Brown.

Schmidt, P. 2000. "Caught in the Crossfire of Presidential Campaign, Bob Jones U. Stands Firm." *Chronicle of Higher Education*, 10 March, p. A37.

Scopes, Jack. 1989. "The Man Who Put the Monkey on Dayton's Back." *Chattanooga Life and Leisure*, 5 July, pp. 12–15, 19, 21.

Scopes, John T. 1961. "The Trial That Rocked the Nation." *Readers' Digest* (March 1961): 136–144.

———. 1965. "Reflections: Forty Years Later." In J. R. Tompkins, *D-Days at Dayton: Reflections on the Scopes Trial* (pp. 17–31). Baton Rouge: Louisiana State University Press.

Scopes, John T., and James Presley. 1967. *Center of the Storm: Memoirs of John T. Scopes*. New York: Holt, Rinehart, and Winston.

"Scopes Goes Free, but Law Is Upheld." 1927. *New York Times*, 16 January, p. 1.

"Scopes Rests Hope in U.S. Constitution and Supreme Court." 1925. *Washington Post*, 13 June, p. 1.

"The Scopes Trial." 1925. *Baptist Monthly Magazine* (August).

Scott, E. C. 1994. "The Struggle for the Schools." *Natural History* 7 (94): 10–13.

——. 1995. "State of Alabama Distorts Science, Evolution." *NCSE Reports* 15: 10–11.

——. 1996a. "Close Ohio Vote Scuttles Evidence against Evolution Bill." *NCSE Reports* 16: 18.

——. 1996b. "Creationism, Ideology, and Science." In Paul R. Gross, Norman Levitt, and Martin W. Lewis, eds., *The Flight from Science and Reason* (pp. 505–522). Baltimore, MD: Johns Hopkins University Press.

——. 1997. "Antievolution and Creationism in the United States." *Annual Review of Anthropology* 26: 263–289.

Scott, E. C., and H. Cole. 1985. "The Elusive Basis of Creation Science." *Quarterly Review of Biology* 60: 21–30.

Segraves, Kelly, and Robert Kohfal. 1975. *The Creation Explanation: A Scientific Alternative to Evolution.* San Diego, CA: Creation Science Research Center.

Sehlstedt, A. 1981. "In the Beginning . . . What? When? How? Questions Split Creationists and Scientists." *Sun* (Baltimore), 6 December, pp. G3–G5.

"Seventy-Five News Organizations Register to Cover Trial." 1981. *Arkansas Gazette*, 20 December, p. A2.

"Shaw and Coleman on Scopes Trial." 1925. *New Leader*, 25 July, p. 6.

Shearer, Benjamin F., and Barbara S. Shearer. 1994. *State Names, Seals, Flags, and Symbols.* London: Greenwood Press.

Shermer, Michael. 1997. *Why People Believe Weird Things: Pseudoscience, Superstition, and Other Confusions of Our Time.* New York: W. H. Freeman.

Shipley, Maynard. 1927. *The War on Modern Science: A Short History of the Fundamentalist Attacks on Evolution and Modernism.* New York: Knopf.

Sinclair, A., and M. P. Pendarvis. 1998. "Evolution vs. Conservative Religious Beliefs: Can Biology Instructors Assist Students with Their Dilemma?" *Journal of College Science Teaching* 27: 167–170.

Skoog, G. 1979. "The Topic of Evolution in Secondary School Biology Textbooks, 1900–1977." *Science Education* 63: 621–640.

Smith, Ella T. 1949. *Exploring Biology: The Science of Living Things.* Chicago: Harcourt, Brace; originally published 1938.

Smith, S. D. 1965. "The Great Monkey Trial." *New York Times*, 4 July.

Smith, W. H. 1975. *The Social and Religious Thought of William Jennings Bryan.* Lawrence, KS: Coronado Press.

Spain, Rufus B. 1961. "Attitudes and Reactions of Southern Baptists to Certain Problems of Society, 1865–1900." Ph.D. dissertation, Vanderbilt University, Nashville, Tennessee.

——. 1967. *At Ease in Zion: Social History of the Southern Baptists, 1865–1900.* Nashville, TN: Vanderbilt University Press.

"Sponsor Sees Victory in End of Act." 1982. *Arkansas Gazette*, 6 January, p. A1.

Stanton, William R. 1960. *The Leopard's Spots: Scientific Attitudes toward Race in America, 1815–1859.* Chicago: University of Chicago Press.

Stuart, R. 1981. "U.S. Court to Hear Arguments on Creationism." *New York Times,* 7 December, pp. A4, A21.

"Supreme Court Hears Scopes Case." 1926. *Nashville Banner,* 31 May, p. 1.

Swatos, William H., Jr. 1998. *Encyclopedia of Religion and Society.* Walnut Creek, CA: Altamira Press.

Sweeney, L. T. 1966. "The Anti-Evolution Movement in Arkansas." Master's thesis, University of Arkansas, Fayetteville.

Taylor, C. A. 1992. "Of Audience, Expertise, and Authority: The Evolving Creationism Debate." *Quarterly Journal of Speech* 78: 277–295.

Taylor, C. A., and C. M. Condit. 1988. "Objectivity and Elites: A Creation Science Trial." *Critical Studies in Mass Communication* 5: 293–312.

"Teacher in Tennessee Is Fired for Teaching Evolution; Test Likely." 1967. *Arkansas Gazette,* 15 April.

"Teacher's Challenge: New Scopes Trial." 1965. *San Francisco Examiner,* 12 December.

"Tennessee House Votes to Repeal Antievolution Law; Bill Goes to Senate." 1967. *Arkansas Gazette,* 13 April, p. A13.

Thompson, B. 1981. *Can America Survive the Fruits of Atheistic Evolution?* Fort Worth, TX: Pro-Family Forum.

Tompkins, Jerry R. 1965. "John Thomas Scopes: A Profile." In Jerry R. Tompkins, *D-Days at Dayton: Reflections on the Scopes Trial* (pp. 7–16). Baton Rouge: Louisiana State University Press.

———. 1966. "Anti-Evolution Law Tested." *Science News Letter* (January): 7.

"Top 100 Works of Journalism in the United States in the 20th Century." 2001. New York University, Department of Journalism and Mass Communications. Available at http://www.nyu.edu/gsas/dept/journal/dept_news/news_stories/990301_topjourn.htm.

Torbet, Robert G. 1963. *A History of the Baptists.* Valley Forge, PA: Judson.

Tracy, S. 1925. "Malone Wins Cheers from Dayton People on Answering Bryan." *Commercial Appeal* (Memphis), 17 July, p. 1.

Trafton, Gilbert H. 1923. *Biology of Home and Community.* New York: Macmillan.

Traylor, Jack W. 1990. "William Jennings Bryan College: A Brief History." In reprint ed. of "Trial Transcript" (1925), in The *World's Most Famous Court Trial: Tennessee Evolution Case* (pp. vii–xii). Dayton, TN: Bryan College.

"Trial of 1966 Has Its Opening in Little Rock Today." 1966. *Washington Post,* 1 April.

"Trial Transcript." 1925. In *The World's Most Famous Court Trial: Tennessee Evolution Case.* Dayton, TN: Bryan College.

Trimble, M. 1981. "Keeps Trial Moving: Mother Was a Teacher." *Arkansas Gazette,* 18 December, p. F8.

"A Try, Finally, to Test Evolution Law." 1965. *Arkansas Gazette,* 8 December.

Tucker, Richard K. 1991. *The Dragon and the Cross: The Rise and Fall of the Ku Klux Klan in Middle America.* Hamden, CT: Archon.

"A Typical Southern Jury." 1925. *Pittsburgh American,* 17 July, p. 4.

Untitled article. 1997. *NCSE Reports* 17: 29.

"Updates." 1998. *NCSE Reports* 18 (1): 9.

Virginia Council on Human Relations. 1966. *Newsletter* (July): 3–4.

Wade, Wyn C. 1987. *The Fiery Cross: The Ku Klux Klan in America.* New York: Simon and Schuster.

Webb, George E. 1994. *The Evolutionary Controversy in America.* Lexington: University Press of Kentucky.

Weber, T. P. 1990. "William Bell Riley." In T. George and D. Dockery, eds., *Baptist Theologians* (pp. 351–365). Nashville, TN: Broadman Press.

Weisman, C. A. 1990. *The Origin of Race and Civilization: As Studied and Verified from Science History and the Holy Scriptures.* Burnsville, MN: Privately published.

Weld, J., and J. C. McNew. 1999. "Attitudes Toward Evolution." *The Science Teacher* 66(9): 27–31.

Wells, G. 1981. "Testimony Ends: Ruling Promised as Soon as Possible." *Arkansas Gazette,* 18 December, pp. E10–E11.

———. 1984. "Made Decision on Ruling in 'Creation-Science' Case Early, Overton Indicates." *Arkansas Gazette,* 4 February, p. A1.

Werner, Morris R. 1929. *Bryan.* New York: Harcourt, Brace.

Whitcomb, John, Jr., and Henry M. Morris. 1961. *The Genesis Flood: The Biblical Record and Its Scientific Implications.* Philadelphia: Presbyterian and Reformed Publishing.

"Will Ask Court to Rehear Case." 1927. *Nashville Banner,* 17 January, p. 1.

Willard, Charles A. 1996. *Liberalism and the Problem of Knowledge: A New Rhetoric for Modern Democracy.* Chicago: University of Chicago Press.

"William Jennings Bryan Here Saturday." 1924. *The American Forum, Recognized by the Great Titan as the Klan Paper for Province Number 5, Realm of Texas, Knights of the Ku Klux Klan,* 31 January, p. 1.

Wilson, Charles R. 1980. *Baptized in Blood: The Religion of the Lost Cause, 1865–1920.* Athens: University of Georgia Press.

Winchell, Alexander. 1870. *Sketches of Creation: A Popular View of Some of the Grand Conclusions of the Sciences in Reference to the History of Matter and Life.* New York: Harper and Bros.

———. 1880. *Preadamites: Or, A Demonstration of the Existence of Man before Adam.* 2d ed. Chicago: S. C. Griggs.

Wise, D. L. 1998. "Creationism's Geological Time Scale." *American Scientist* 86 (March–April): 160–173.

Witham, L. 1997. "Many Scientists See God's Hand in Evolution." *Washington Times,* 11 April, p. A8.

Wood, Forrest G. 1990. *The Arrogance of Faith: Christianity and Race in America from the Colonial Era to the Twentieth Century.* New York: Knopf.

Ziman, J. 1991. "Public Understanding of Science." *Science, Technology, and Human Values* 39: 111–121.

Zimmerman, M. 1987. "The Evolution-Creation Controversy: Opinions of Ohio High School Biology Teachers." *Ohio Journal of Science* 87: 115–125.

———. 1989. "Hiding at the National Science Foundation." *Newsletter of the Ohio Center for Center for Science Education* (April): 4–5.

DOCUMENTS

JOHN THOMAS SCOPES V. THE STATE

The "Monkey Trial" of John Scopes in 1925 remains the most famous event in the history of the creationism/evolution controversy and one of the most famous events of the twentieth century. Scopes was convicted of the misdemeanor of teaching human evolution, but his lawyers appealed the decision to the Tennessee Supreme Court. That court's decision ended the celebrated case with a whimper and left many issues unanswered.

SUPREME COURT of TENNESSEE

JOHN THOMAS SCOPES v. THE STATE

(*Nashville*, December Term, 1926.)

Opinion filed January 17, 1927.

Appeal from the Criminal Court of Rhea County; HON. J. T. RAULSTON, Judge.

JOHN R. NEAL, CLARENCE DARROW, ARTHUR G. HAYES, DUDLEY FIELD MALONE, WILLIAM T. THOMAS, and FRANK B. MCELWEE, for plaintiff in error.

THOMAS H. MALONE and HENRY E. COLTON *amici curiae* for appellant.

FRANK M. THOMPSON, Attorney-General, ED. T. SEAY, and K. T. MCCONNICO, for defendant in error.

CHIEF JUSTICE GREEN delivered majority opinion; JUDGE CHAMBLISS concurring opinion, and JUSTICE COOK concurred; JUDGE COLIN P. MCKINNEY, opinion dissenting, and JUDGE SWIGGART did not participate.

Scopes was convicted of a violation of chapter 27 of the Acts of 1925, for that he did teach in the public schools of Rhea county a certain theory that denied the story of the divine creation of man, as taught in the Bible, and did teach instead thereof that man had descended from a lower order of animals. After a verdict of guilty by the jury, the trial judge imposed a fine of $100, and Scopes brought the case to this court by an appeal in the nature of a writ of error.

The bill of exceptions was not filed within the time fixed by the court below, and, upon motion of the state, at the last term, this bill of exceptions was stricken from the record. *Scopes v. State*, 152 Tenn. 424. . . .

When the draftsman came to express this purpose in the body of the Act, he first forbade the teaching of "any theory that denies the story of the divine creation of man, as taught in the Bible"—his conception evidently being that to forbid the denial of the Bible story would ban the teaching of evolution. To make the purpose more explicit, he added that it should be unlawful to teach "that man had descended from a lower order of animals." . . .

It thus seems plain that the Legislature in this enactment only intended to forbid teaching that men descended from a lower order of animals. The denunciation of any theory denying the Bible story of creation is restricted by the caption and by the final clause of section 1. . . .

It is contended that the Statute violates section 8 of article 1 of the Tennessee Constitution, and section 1 of the Fourteenth Amendment of the Constitution of the United States—the Law of the Land clause of the state Constitution, and the Due Process of Law clause of the Federal Constitution, which are practically equivalent in meaning.

We think there is little merit in this contention. The plaintiff in error was a teacher in the public schools of Rhea County. He was an employee of the State of Tennessee or of a municipal agency of the State. He was under contract with the State to work in an institution of the State. He had no right or privilege to serve the State except upon such terms as the State prescribed. His liberty, his privilege, his immunity to teach and proclaim the theory of evolution, elsewhere than in the service of the State, was in no wise touched by this law. . . .

Since the State may prescribe the character and the hours of labor of the employees on its works, just as freely may it say what kind of work shall be performed in its service, what shall be taught in its schools, so far at least as section 8 of article 1 of the Tennessee Constitution, and the Fourteenth Amendment to the Constitution of the United States, are concerned. . . .

If the Legislature thinks that, by reason of popular prejudice, the cause of education and the study of Science generally will be promoted by forbidding the teaching of evolution in the schools of the State, we can conceive of no ground to justify the court's interference. The courts cannot sit in judgment on such Acts of the legislature or its agents and determine whether or not the omission or addition of a particular course of study tends "to cherish Science."

The last serious criticism made of the Act is that it contravenes the provision of section 3 of article 1 of the Constitution, "that no preference shall ever be given, by law, to any religious establishment or mode of worship." . . .

We are not able to see how the prohibition of teaching the theory that man has descended from a lower order of animals gives preference to any religious establishment or mode of worship. So far as we know, there is no religious establishment or organized body that has in its creed or confession of faith any article denying or affirming such a theory. So far as we know, the denial or affirmation of such a theory does not enter into any recognized mode of worship. Since this cause has been pending in this court, we have been favored, in addition to briefs of counsel and various *amici curiae*, with a multitude of resolutions, addresses, and communications from scientific bodies, religious factions, and individuals giving us the benefit of their views upon the theory of evolution. Examination of these contributions indicates that Protestants, Catholics, and Jews are divided among themselves in their beliefs, and that there is no unanimity among the members of any religious establishment as to this subject. Belief or unbelief in the theory of evolution is no more a characteristic of any religious establishment or mode of worship than is belief or unbelief in the wisdom of the prohibition laws. It would appear that members of the same churches quite generally disagree as to these things.

Furthermore, chapter 277 of the Acts of 1925 *requires* the teaching of nothing. It only *forbids* the teaching of evolution of man from a lower order of animals. Chapter 102 of the Acts of 1915 requires that ten verses from the Bible be read each day at the opening of every public school, without comment, and provided the teacher does not read the same verses more than twice during any session. It is also provided in this Act that pupils may be excused from the Bible readings upon the written request of their parents.

As the law thus stands, while the theory of evolution of man may not be taught in the schools of the State, nothing contrary to that theory is required to be taught. It could scarcely be said that the statutory scriptural reading just mentioned would amount to teaching of a contrary theory. . . .

This record disclosed that the jury found the defendant below guilty, but did not assess the fine. The trial judge himself undertook to impose the minimum fine of $100 authorized by the Statute. This was error. Under section 14 of article 6 of the Constitution of Tennessee, a fine in excess of $50 must be assessed by a jury. The Statute before us does not permit the imposition of a smaller fine than $100.

Since a jury alone can impose the penalty this Act requires, and as a matter of course no different penalty can be inflicted, the trial judge exceeded his jurisdiction in levying this fine, and we are without power to correct his error. The judgment must accordingly be reversed. *Upchurch v. State*, 153 Tenn. 198.

The Court is informed that the plaintiff in error is no longer in the service of the State. We see nothing to be gained by prolonging the life of this bizarre case. On the contrary, we think the peace and dignity of the State, which all criminal prosecutions are brought to redress, will be better conserved by the entry of a *nolle prosequi* herein. Such a course is suggested to the Attorney-General. . . .

EPPERSON V. ARKANSAS

In 1928, Arkansas voters overwhelmingly approved a law banning the teaching of human evolution in public schools. That law went unchallenged until 1965, when Susan Epperson—a young biology teacher at Little Rock's Central High School—challenged the law to resolve a dilemma she faced: she wanted to include evolution in her biology course, but she knew that she'd be committing a crime if she did. Epperson's lawsuit was the first challenge to an antievolution law since State of Tennessee v. John Thomas Scopes *in 1925. Her case generated much publicity and reached the U.S. Supreme Court in 1968. Here are excerpts from the Court's decision:*

SUSAN EPPERSON et al., Appellants, v. STATE OF ARKANSAS
393 US 97, 21 L Ed 2d 228, 89 S Ct 266

[No.7]

Argued October 16, 1968. Decided November 12, 1968.

SUMMARY

A public school biology teacher in Arkansas, faced with the dilemma that if she used a new textbook she would presumably teach a chapter therein on the Darwinian theory of evolution and thus be subject to dismissal for committing a criminal offense in violation of the Arkansas statute prohibiting any teacher in the state schools from teaching such theory, instituted an action in the state Chancery Court seeking a declaration that such statute was void and enjoining the state officials from dismissing her for violation of the statute. A parent of children attending the public schools intervened in support of the action. The Chancery Court held that the statute violated the Fourteenth Amendment to the United States Constitution, but on appeal the Supreme Court of Arkansas reversed, sustaining the statute as an exercise of the state's power to specify the curriculum in public schools, while expressing no opinion on whether the statute prohibited any explanation of the theory of evolution or merely prohibited teaching that the theory was true. (242 Ark 922, 416 SW2d 322.)

On appeal, the United States Supreme Court reversed. In an opinion by FORTAS, J., it was held, expressing the views of seven members of the court, that the statute was contrary to the mandate of the First, and in violation of the Fourteenth, Amendment, as conflicting with the constitutional prohibition of state laws respecting an establishment of religion or prohibiting the free exercise thereof.

BLACK, J., concurred in the result, but expressed the view that it was doubtful whether the case presented a justiciable controversy, and that, assuming that it did, either the statute should be struck down as too vague to enforce, or the case should be remanded to the Arkansas Supreme Court for clarification of its holding and opinion.

HARLAN, J., concurred in the result and in so much of the court's opinion as held that the statute constituted an "establishment of religion" forbidden to the states by the Fourteenth Amendment, but disapproved, as obscuring the holding, the court's extended discussion of the issues of vagueness and freedom of speech despite its conclusion that it was unnecessary to decide such issues.

STEWART, J., concurred in the result, expressing the view that the statute was so vague as to be invalid under the Fourteenth Amendment.

Appearances of Counsel

Eugene R. Warren argued the cause for appellants. Don Langston argued the cause for appellee. Briefs of Counsel, p 832, infra.

Opinion of THE COURT

Mr. Justice Fortas delivered the opinion of the Court.

[393 US 98]

I.

This appeal challenges the constitutionality of the "anti-evolution" statute which the State of Arkansas adopted in 1928 to prohibit the teaching in its public schools and universities of the theory that man evolved from other species of life. The statute was a product of the upsurge of "fundamentalist" religious fervor of the twenties. The Arkansas statute was an adaptation of the famous Tennessee "monkey law" which that State adopted in 1925.*(1)* The constitutionality of the Tennessee law was upheld by the Tennessee Supreme Court in the celebrated Scopes case in 1927.*(2)*

The Arkansas law makes it unlawful for a teacher in any state-supported school or university "to teach the theory or doctrine that mankind ascended or descended from a lower order of animals," or "to adopt or use in any such institution a text-book that teaches" this theory. Violation is a misdemeanor and subjects the violator to dismissal from his position.*(3)* [393 US 99]

The present case concerns the teaching of biology in a high school in Little Rock. According to the testimony, until the events here in litigation, the official text-book furnished for the high school biology course did not have a section on the Darwinian Theory. Then, for the academic year 1965–1966, the school administration, on recommendation of the teachers of biology in the school system, adopted and pre-scribed a textbook which contained a chapter setting forth "the theory about the origins of man from a lower form of animal." [393 US 100]

Susan Epperson, a young woman who graduated from Arkansas' school system and then obtained her master's degree in zoology at the University of Illinois, was employed by the Little Rock school system in the fall of 1964 to teach 10th grade biology at Central High School. At the start of the next academic year, 1965, she was confronted by the new textbook (which one surmises from the record was not un-welcome to her). She faced at least a literal dilemma because she was supposed to use the new textbook for classroom instruction and presumably to teach the statu-torily condemned chapter; but to do so would be a criminal offense and subject her to dismissal.

She instituted the present action in the Chancery Court of the State, seeking a declaration that the Arkansas statute is void and enjoining the State and the defen-dant officials of the Little Rock school system from dismissing her for violation of the statute's provisions. H. H. Blanchard, a parent of children attending the public schools, intervened in support of the action.

The Chancery Court, in an opinion by Chancellor Murray O. Reed, held that the statute violated the Fourteenth Amendment to the United States Constitution.*(4)* The court noted that this Amendment encompasses the prohibitions upon state in-terference with freedom of speech and thought which are contained in the First Amendment. Accordingly, it held that the challenged statute is unconstitutional be-cause, in violation of the First Amendment, it "tends to hinder the quest for knowl-edge, restrict the freedom to learn, and restrain the freedom to teach."*(5)* In this per-spective, the Act, it held, was an unconstitutional and void restraint upon the freedom of speech guaranteed by the Constitution. [393 US 101]

On appeal, the Supreme Court of Arkansas reversed.*(6)* Its two-sentence opin-ion is set forth in the margin.*(7)* It sustained the statute as an exercise of the State's power to specify the curriculum in public schools. It did not address itself to the competing constitutional considerations.

[1] Appeal was duly prosecuted to this Court under 2 USC § 1257 (2). Only Arkansas and Mississippi have such "anti-evolution" or "monkey" laws on their books.*(8)* There is no record of any prosecutions in Arkansas under its statute. It is possible that the statute is presently more of a curiosity than a vital fact of life in these States.*(9)* Nevertheless, the present case was brought, the appeal as of right is properly here, and it is our duty to decide the issues presented. [393 US 102]

II.

At the outset, it is urged upon us that the challenged statute is vague and uncertain and therefore within the condemnation of the Due Process Clause of the Fourteenth Amendment. The contention that the Act is vague and uncertain is supported by language in the brief opinion of Arkansas' Supreme Court. That court, perhaps reflecting the discomfort which the statute's quixotic prohibition necessarily engenders in the modern mind, *(10)* stated that it "expresses no opinion" as to whether the Act prohibits "explanation" of the theory of evolution or merely forbids "teaching that the theory is true." Regardless of this uncertainty, the court held that the statute is constitutional.

On the other hand, counsel for the State, in oral argument in this Court, candidly stated that, despite the State Supreme Court's equivocation, Arkansas would interpret the statute "to mean that to make a student aware of the theory; just to teach that there was such a theory" would be grounds for dismissal and for prosecution under the statute; and he said "that the Supreme Court of Arkansas' opinion should be interpreted in that manner." He said: "If Mrs. Epperson would tell her students that 'Here is Darwin's theory, that man ascended or descended from a lower form of being,' then I think she would be under this statute liable for prosecution." [393 US 103]

[2] In any event, we do not rest our decision upon the asserted vagueness of the statute. On either interpretation of its language, Arkansas' statute cannot stand. It is of no moment whether the law is deemed to prohibit mention of Darwin's theory, or to forbid any or all of the infinite varieties of communication embraced within the term "teaching." Under either interpretation, the law must be stricken because of its conflict with the constitutional prohibition of state laws respecting an establishment of religion or prohibiting the free exercise thereof. The overriding fact is that Arkansas' law selects from the body of knowledge a particular segment which it proscribes for the sole reason that it is deemed to conflict with a particular religious doctrine; that is, with a particular interpretation of the Book of Genesis by a particular religious group.*(11)*

III.

The antecedents of today's decision are many and unmistakable. They are rooted in the foundation soil of our Nation. They are fundamental to freedom.

[3] Government in our democracy, state and national, must be neutral in matters of religious theory, doctrine, and practice. It may not be hostile to any religion or to the advocacy of no religion; and it may not aid, foster, or promote one religion or religious theory against another or even against the militant opposite. The First Amendment mandates governmental neutrality between religion and religion, and between religion and nonreligion.*(12)* [393 US 104] . . .

[4, 5] Judicial interposition in the operation of the public school system of the Nation raises problems requiring care and restraint. Our courts, however, have not failed to apply the First Amendment's mandate in our educational system where essential to safeguard the fundamental values of freedom of speech and inquiry and of belief. By and large, public education in our Nation is committed to the control of state and local authorities. Courts do not and cannot intervene in the resolution of conflicts which arise in the daily operation of school systems and which do not directly and sharply implicate basic constitutional values.*(13)* On the other hand, "[t]he vigilant protection of constitutional freedoms is nowhere more vital than in the community of American schools," *Shelton v Tucker*, 364 US 479, 487, 5 L Ed 2d 231, 236, 81 S Ct 247 (1960). . . .

The earliest cases in this Court on the subject of the impact of constitutional guarantees upon the classroom were decided before the Court expressly applied the specific prohibitions of the First Amendment to the States. But as early as 1922, the Court did not hesitate to condemn under the Due Process Clause "arbitrary" restrictions upon the freedom of teachers to teach and of students to learn. In that year, the Court, in an opinion by Justice McReynolds, held unconstitutional an Act of the State of Nebraska making it a crime to teach any subject in any language other than English to pupils who had not passed the eighth grade.*(14)* The State's purpose in enacting the law was to promote civic cohesiveness by encouraging the learning of English and to combat the "baneful effect" of permitting foreigners to rear and educate their children in the language of the parents' native land. The Court recognized these purposes, and it acknowledged the State's power to prescribe the school curriculum, but it held that these were not adequate to support the restriction upon the liberty of teacher and pupil. The challenged statute, it held, unconstitutionally interfered with the right of the individual, guaranteed by the Due Process Clause, to engage in any of the common occupations of life and to acquire useful knowledge. . . .

[3, 6] There is and can be no doubt that the First Amendment does not permit the State to require that teaching and learning must be tailored to the principles or prohibitions of any religious sect or dogma. In Everson v Board of Education, this Court, in upholding a state law to provide free bus service to school children, including those attending parochial schools, said: "Neither [a State nor the Federal Government] can pass laws which aid one religion, aid all religions, or prefer one religion, or prefer one religion over another." 330 US 1, 15, 91 L Ed 711, 723, 67 S Ct 504, 168 ALR 1392 (1947).

[7–9] At the following Term of Court, in *McCollum v Board of Education*, 333 US 203, 92 L Ed 649, 68 S Ct 461, 2 ALR2d 1338 (1948), the Court held that Illinois could not release pupils from class to attend classes of instruction in the school buildings in the religion of their choice. This, it said, would involve the State in using tax-supported property for religious purposes, thereby breaching the "wall of separation" which, according to Jefferson, the First Amendment was intended to erect between church and state . . . . While study of religions and of the Bible from a literary and historic view-point, presented objectively as part of a secular program of education, need not collide with the First Amendment's prohibition, the State may not adopt programs or practices in its public schools or colleges which "aid or oppose" any religion. Id., at 225, 10 L Ed 2d at 860. This prohibition is absolute. It forbids alike the preference of a religious doctrine or the prohibition of theory which is deemed antagonistic to a particular dogma. As Mr. Justice Clark stated in *Joseph Burstyn, Inc. v Wilson*, "the state has no legitimate interest in protecting any or all religions from views distasteful to them . . ." 343 US 495, 505, 96 L Ed 1098, 1108, 72 S Ct 777 (1952). The test was stated as follows in *Abington School District v Schempp*, supra, at 222, 10 L Ed 2d at 858: "[W]hat are the purpose and the primary effect of the enactment? If, either is the advancement or inhibition of religion then the enactment exceeds the scope of legislative power as circumscribed by the Constitution." [393 US 107]

[10] These precedents inevitably determine the result in the present case. The State's undoubted right to prescribe the curriculum for its public schools does not carry with it the right to prohibit, on pain of criminal penalty, the teaching of a scientific theory or doctrine where that prohibition is based upon reasons that violate the First Amendment. It is much too late to argue that the State may impose upon the teachers in its schools any conditions that it chooses, however restrictive they may be of constitutional guarantees. . . .

In the present case, there can be no doubt that Arkansas has sought to prevent its teachers from discussing the theory of evolution because it is contrary to the belief of some that the Book of Genesis must be the exclusive source of doctrine as to the origin of man. No suggestion has been made that Arkansas' law may be justified by considerations of state policy other than the religious views of some of its citizens.*(15)* It is clear that fundamentalist sectarian conviction was and is the law's reason for existence.*(16)* Its antecedent, Tennessee's "monkey law," candidly stated its purpose: to make it unlawful "to teach any theory that denies the story of the Divine Creation of man as taught in the Bible, and to teach instead that man has descended from a lower order of animals."*(17)* Perhaps the sensational publicity attendant upon the Scopes trial induced Arkansas to adopt less explicit language.*(18)* It eliminated Tennessee's reference to "the story of the Divine Creation of man" as taught in the Bible, but there is no doubt that the motivation for the law was the same: to suppress the teaching of a theory which, it was thought, "denied" the divine creation of man. [393 US 108] [393 US 109]

[2] Arkansas' law cannot be defended as an act of religious neutrality. Arkansas did not seek to excise from the curricula of its schools and universities all discussion of the origin of man. The law's effort was confined to an attempt to blot out a particular theory because of its supposed conflict with the Biblical account, literally read. Plainly, the law is contrary to the mandate of the First, and in violation of the Fourteenth Amendment to the Constitution.

The judgment of the Supreme Court of Arkansas is reversed.

Separate Opinions
Mr. Justice Black, concurring.

I am by no means sure that this case presents a genuinely justiciable case or controversy. Although Arkansas Initiated Act No. 1, the statute alleged to be unconstitutional, was passed by the voters of Arkansas in 1928, we are informed that there has never been even a single attempt by the State to enforce it. And the pallid, unenthusiastic, even apologetic defense of the Act presented by the State in this Court indicates that the State would make no attempt to enforce the law should it remain on the books for the next century. Now, nearly 40 years after the law has slumbered on the books as though dead, a teacher alleging fear that the State might arouse from its lethargy and try to punish her has asked for a declaratory judgment holding the law unconstitutional. She was subsequently joined by a parent who alleged his interest in seeing that his two then school-age sons "be informed of all scientific theories and hypotheses . . . ." . . . The textbook adopted for use in biology classes in Little Rock includes an entire chapter dealing with evolution. There is no evidence that this chapter is not being freely taught in the schools that use the textbook and no evidence that the intervenor's sons, who were 15 and 17 years old when this suit was brought three years ago, are still in high school or yet to take biology. Unfortunately, however, the State's languid interest in the case has not prompted it to keep this Court informed concerning facts that might easily justify dismissal of this alleged lawsuit as moot or as lacking the qualities of a genuine case or controversy. [393 US 110] . . .

It seems to me that in this situation the statute is too vague for us to strike it down on any ground but that: vagueness. Under this statute as construed by the Arkansas Supreme Court, a teacher cannot know whether he is forbidden to mention Darwin's theory at all or only free to discuss it as long as he refrains from contending that it is true. It is an established rule that a statute which leaves an ordinary man so doubtful about its meaning that he cannot know when he has violated it denies him the first essential of due process. . . .

The Court, not content to strike down this Arkansas Act on the unchallengeable ground of its plain vagueness, chooses rather to invalidate it as a violation of the Establishment of Religion Clause of the First Amendment. I would not decide this case on such a sweeping ground for the following reasons, among others.

1. In the first place I find it difficult to agree with the Court's statement that "there can be no doubt that Arkansas has sought to prevent its teachers from discussing the theory of evolution because it is contrary to the belief of some that the Book of Genesis must be the exclusive source of doctrine as to the origin of man." It may be instead that the people's motive was merely that it would be best to remove this controversial subject from its schools; there is no reason I can imagine why a State is without power to withdraw from its curriculum any subject deemed too emotional and controversial for its public schools. . . .

2. A second question that arises for me is whether this Court's decision forbidding a State to exclude the subject of evolution from its schools infringes the religious freedom of those who consider evolution an anti-religious doctrine. If the theory is considered anti-religious, as the Court indicates, how can the State be bound by the Federal Constitution to permit its teachers to advocate such an "anti-religious" doctrine to schoolchildren? The very cases cited by the Court as supporting its conclusion hold that the State must be neutral, not favoring one religious or anti-religious view over another. The Darwinian theory is said to challenge the Bible's

story of creation; so too have some of those who believe in the Bible, along with many others, challenged the Darwinian theory. Since there is no indication that the literal Biblical doctrine of the origin of man is included in the curriculum of Arkansas schools, does not the removal of the subject of evolution leave the State in a neutral position toward these supposedly competing religious and anti-religious doctrines? Unless this Court is prepared simply to write off as pure nonsense the views of those who consider evolution an anti-religious doctrine, then this issue presents problems under the Establishment Clause far more troublesome than are discussed in the Court's opinion.

3. I am also not ready to hold that a person hired to teach schoolchildren takes with him into the classroom a constitutional right to teach sociological, economic, political, or religious subjects that the school's managers do not want discussed. . . . I question whether it is absolutely certain, as the Court's opinion indicates, that "academic freedom" permits a teacher to breach his contractual agreement to teach only the subjects designated by the school authorities who hired him. [393 US 114]

Certainly the Darwinian theory, precisely like the Genesis story of the creation of man, is not above challenge. In fact the Darwinian theory has not merely been criticized by religionists but by scientists, and perhaps no scientist would be willing to take an oath and swear that everything announced in the Darwinian theory is unquestionably true. The Court, it seems to me, makes a serious mistake in bypassing the plain, unconstitutional vagueness of this statute in order to reach out and decide this troublesome, to me, First Amendment question. However wise this Court may be or may become hereafter, it is doubtful that, sitting in Washington, it can successfully supervise and censor the curriculum of every public school in every hamlet and city in the United States. I doubt that our wisdom is so nearly infallible.

I would either strike down the Arkansas Act as too vague to enforce, or remand to the State Supreme Court for clarification of its holding and opinion.

Mr. Justice Harlan, concurring.

I think it deplorable that this case should have come to us with such an opaque opinion by the State's highest court. With all respect, that court's handling of the case savors of a studied effort to avoid coming to grips with this anachronistic statute and to "pass the buck" to this Court. This sort of temporizing does not make for healthy operations between the state and federal judiciaries. Despite these observations, I am in agreement with this Court's opinion that, the constitutional claims having been properly raised and necessarily decided below, resolution of the matter by us cannot properly be avoided. *(19)* . . .

I concur in so much of the Court's opinion as holds that the Arkansas statute constitutes an "establishment of religion" forbidden to the States by the Fourteenth Amendment. . . .

Mr. Justice Stewart, concurring in the result.

The States are most assuredly free "to choose their own curriculums for their own schools." A State is entirely free, for example, to decide that the only foreign language to be taught in its public school system shall be Spanish. But would a State be constitutionally free to punish a teacher for letting his students know that other languages are also spoken in the world? I think not. [393 US 116]

It is one thing for a State to determine that "the subject of higher mathematics, or astronomy, or biology" shall or shall not be included in its public school curriculum. It is quite another thing for a State to make it a criminal offense for a public school teacher so much as to mention the very existence of an entire system of respected human thought. That kind of criminal law, I think, would clearly impinge upon the guarantees of free communication contained in the First Amendment, and made applicable to the States by the Fourteenth.

The Arkansas Supreme Court has said that the statute before us may or may not be just such a law. The result, as Mr. Justice Black points out, is that "a teacher cannot know whether he is forbidden to mention Darwin's theory at all." Since I believe that no State could constitutionally forbid a teacher "to mention Darwin's theory at all," and since Arkansas may, or may not, have done just that, I conclude that the statute before us is so vague as to be invalid under the Fourteenth Amendment. See *Cramp v Board of Pub. Instruction*, 368 US 278, 7 L Ed 2d 285, 82 S Ct 275.

Footnotes:

1. Chapter 27, Tenn Acts 1925; Tenn Code Ann § 49–1922 (1966 Repl Vol).

2. *Scopes v State*, 154 Tenn 105, 289 SW 363 (1927). The Tennessee court, however, reversed Scopes's conviction on the ground that the jury and not the judge should have assessed the fine of $100. Since Scopes was no longer in the State's employ, it saw 'nothing to be gained by prolonging the life of this bizarre case.' It directed that a nolle prosequi be entered, in the interests of 'the peace and dignity of the State.' 154 Tenn, at 121, 289 SW, at 367.

3. Initiated Act No. 1, Ark Acts 1929; Ark Stat Ann §§ 80–1627, 80–1628 (1960 Repl Vol). The text of the law is as follows:

§ 80–1627; Doctrine of ascent or descent of man from lower order of animals prohibited. It shall be unlawful for any teacher or other instructor in any University, College, Normal, Public School, or other institution of the State, which is supported in whole or in part from public funds derived by State and local taxation to teach the theory or doctrine that mankind ascended or descended from a lower order of animals and also it shall be unlawful for any teacher, textbook commission, or other authority exercising the power to select textbooks for above mentioned educational institutions to adopt or use in any such institution a textbook that teaches the doctrine or theory that mankind descended or ascended from a lower order of animals.

§ 80–1628. Teaching doctrine or adopting textbook mentioning doctrine. Penalties: Positions to be vacated. Any teacher or other instructor or textbook commissioner who is found guilty of violation of this act by teaching the theory or doctrine mentioned in section 1 hereof, or by using, or adopting any such textbooks in any such educational institution shall be guilty of a misdemeanor and upon conviction shall be fined not exceeding five hundred dollars; and upon conviction shall vacate the position thus held in any educational institutions of the character above mentioned or any commission of which he may be a member.

4. The opinion of the Chancery Court is not officially reported.

5. The Chancery Court analyzed the holding of its sister State of Tennessee in the Scopes case sustaining Tennessee's similar statute. It refused to follow Tennessee's 1927 example. It declined to confine the judicial horizon to a view of the law as merely a direction by the State as employer to its employees. This sort of astigmatism, it held, would ignore overriding constitutional values, and 'should not be followed,' and it proceeded to confront the substance of the law and its effect.

6. 42 Ark 922, 416 SW2d 322 (1967).

7. Per Curiam. Upon the principal issue, that of constitutionality, the court holds that Initiated Measure No. 1 of 1928, Ark Stat Ann § 80–1627 and § 80–1628 (Repl 1960), is a valid exercise of the state's power to specify the curriculum in its public schools. The court expresses no opinion on the question whether the Act prohibits any explanation of the theory of evolution or merely prohibits teaching that the theory is true; the answer not being necessary to a decision in the case, and the issue not having been raised.

'The decree is reversed and the cause dismissed.

'Ward, J., concurs. Brown, J., dissents.

'Paul Ward, Justice, concurring. I agree with the first sentence in the majority opinion.

'To my mind, the rest of the opinion beclouds the clear announcement made in the first sentence.'

8. Miss Code Ann, §§ 6798, 6799 (1942). Ark Stat Ann, 1947, §§ 80–1627, 80–1628 (1960 Repl Vol). The Tennessee law was repealed in 1967. Oklahoma enacted an anti-evolution law, but it was repealed in 1926. The Florida and Texas Legislatures, in the period between 1921 and 1929, adopted resolutions against teaching the doctrine of evolution. In all, during that period, bills to this effect were introduced in 20 States. American Civil Liberties Union (ACLU), The Gag on Teaching 8 (2d ed., 1937).

9. Clarence Darrow, who was counsel for the defense in the Scopes trial, in his biography published in 1932, somewhat sardonically pointed out that the States with anti-evolution laws did not insist upon the fundamentalist theory in all respects. He said: 'I understand that the States of Tennessee and Mississippi both continue to teach that the earth is round and that the revolution on its axis brings the day and night, in spite of all opposition.' The Story of My Life 247 (1932).

10. R. Hofstadter & W. Metzger, in The Development of Academic Freedom in the United States 324 (1955), refer to some of Darwin's opponents as 'exhibiting a kind of phylogenetic snobbery [which led them] to think that Darwin had libeled the [human] race by discovering simian rather than seraphic ancestors.'

11. In *Scopes v State*, 154 Tenn 105, 126, 289 SW 363, 369 (1927), Judge Chambliss, concurring, referred to the defense contention that Tennessee's anti-evolution law gives a 'preference' to 'religious establishments which have as one of their tenets or dogmas the instantaneous creation of man.'

12. *Everson v Board of Education*, 330 US 1, 18, 91 L Ed 711, 724, 67 S Ct 504, 168 ALR 1392 (1947); *McCollum v Board of Education*, 333 US 203, 92 L Ed 649, 68 S Ct 461, 2 ALR2d 1338 (1948); *Zorach v Clauson*, 343 US 306, 313–314, 96 L Ed 954, 961, 962, 72 S Ct 679 (1952); *Fowler v Rhode Island*, 345 US 67, 97

L Ed 828, 73 S Ct 526 (1953); *Torcaso v Watkins*, 367 US 488, 495, 6 L Ed 2d 982, 985, 81 S Ct 1680 (1961).

13. See the discussion in Developments in The Law. Academic Freedom, 81 Harv L Rev 1045, 1051–1055 (1968).

14. The case involved a conviction for teaching the subject of reading in the German language to a child of 10 years.

15. Former Dean Leflar of the University of Arkansas School of Law has stated that the same ideological considerations underlie the anti-evolution enactment as underlie the typical blasphemy statute. He says that the purpose of these statutes is an ideological one which involves an effort to prevent (by censorship) or punish the presentation of intellectually significant matter which contradicts accepted social, moral or religious ideas. Leflar, Legal Liability for the Exercise of Free Speech, 10 Ark L Rev 155, 158 (1956). See also R. Hofstadter & T. Metzger, The Development of Academic Freedom in the United States 320–366 (1955) (passim); H. Beale, A History of Freedom of Teaching in American Schools 202–207 (1941); Emerson & Haber, The Scopes Case in Modern Dress, 27 U Chi L Rev 522 (1960); Waller, The Constitutionality of the Tennessee Anti-Evolution Act, 35 Yale L J 191 (1925) (passim); ACLU, The Gag on Teaching 7 (2d ed., 1937); J. Scopes & J. Presley, Center of the Storm 45–53 (1967).

16. The following advertisement is typical of the public appeal which was used in the campaign to secure adoption of the statute:

The Bible or Atheism, Which?
All atheists favor evolution. If you agree with atheism vote against Act No. 1. If you agree with the Bible vote for Act No. 1 . . . Shall conscientious church members be forced to pay taxes to support teachers to teach evolution which will undermine the faith of their children? The Gazette said Russian Bolshevists laughed at Tennessee. True, and that sort will laugh at Arkansas. Who cares? Vote for act no. 1. The Arkansas Gazette, Little Rock, Nov. 4, 1928, p.12, cols. 4–5.

Letters from the public expressed the fear that teaching of evolution would be subversive of Christianity, id., Oct. 24, 1928, p. 7, col. 2; see also id., Nov. 4, 1928, p. 19, col. 4, and that it would cause school children to disrespect the Bible, id., Oct. 27, 1928, p. 15, col. 5. One letter read: "The cosmogony taught by [evolution] runs contrary to that of Moses and Jesus, and as such is nothing, if anything at all, but atheism. Now let the mothers and fathers of our state that are trying to raise their children in the Christian faith arise in their might and vote for this anti-evolution bill that will take it out of our tax supported schools. When they have saved the children, they have saved the state." Id., at cols. 4–5.

17. Arkansas' law was adopted by popular initiative in 1928, three years after Tennessee's law was enacted and one year after the Tennessee Supreme Court's decision in the Scopes case, supra.

18. In its brief, the State says that the Arkansas statute was passed with the holding of the Scopes case in mind. Brief for Appellee 1.

19. Short of reading the Arkansas Supreme Court's opinion to have proceeded on the premise that it need not consider appellants' establishment contention, clearly raised in the state courts and here, in view of its holding that the State possesses plenary power to fix the curriculum in its public schools, I can perceive no tenable basis for remanding the case to the state court for an explication of the purpose and meaning of the statute in question. I am unwilling to ascribe to the Arkansas Supreme Court any such quixotic approach to constitutional adjudication. I take the first sentence of its opinion (ante, at 101, n. 7, 21 L Ed 2d 232) to encompass an overruling of appellants establishment point, and the second sentence to refer only to their vagueness claim.

SEGRAVES V. STATE OF CALIFORNIA

In 1979, Kelly Segraves filed suit to overturn the California Board of Education's Scientific Framework because he believed that it violated his children's rights; Segraves believed that the teaching of evolution was dogmatic and might cause students to question their religious beliefs. Segraves v. State of California, generated much publicity; Segraves described it as "the trial of the century" and "a rerun of the Scopes trial."

In the Superior Court of the State of California in and for the county of Sacramento

Kasey Segraves, Jason Segraves and Kevin Segraves, minors under 14 years of age, by their Guardian ad Litem, Kelly Segraves . . . and Creation Science Research Center, Plaintiffs, vs. State of California, Board of Education of the State of California, Department of Education of the State of California, Department of General Services, . . ., Defendants.

No. 278978 Dept. 14

. . . we are almost unanimous in our views, counsel and I . . . this is a most significant cause because it does involve religious liberty, which is one of our most cherished freedoms, and even more important, and you both touched on this, this involves the sensibilities of a child. And isn't it truly wonderful that in our country we can seek to invoke the awesome authority of the courts to assuage the feelings of a single child, a child. And in the final analysis, I believe that is what this case is all about.

Now, we are concerned with the constitutional guarantee, . . . It is set forth in the First Amendment, "Congress shall make no law respecting an establishment of religion or prohibiting the free exercise thereof." And some people may say, "Well, that is directed toward the Congress, how does the State of California get involved with this?" Well, the Supreme Court of the United States has held that both clauses are incorporated in the Fourteenth Amendment, which applies to the states, and accordingly the guarantees also apply to state action. . . .

Now, fortunately—I say "fortunately" because I'm the fellow that has to make the decision—the issues have been narrowed here to the point where we are not faced with such a dilemma, and thus there is on contention here that evolution should not be taught in the public schools. I think you've heard me say on several occasions that if there were, it would be rejected as an impermissible accommodation, for that battle was fought and resolved by the Supreme Court of the United States, in Epperson versus Arkansas.

Now, moreover, the Plaintiffs have disclaimed any interest in an accommodation which would require the teaching of special creation in the public schools. . . .

Now, the issue, simply stated, accordingly, is whether or not the free exercise of religion by Mr. Segraves and his children was thwarted by the instruction in science that children had received in school, and if so, has there been sufficient accommodation for their views? . . .

. . . the Court is prepared to find that the State Board of Education has acted throughout in good faith, just as the Court finds the Plaintiffs herein have acted throughout in good faith. The Court, in addition, is prepared to find and does find that the science framework, as written, and if qualified by the policy of the Board exemplified by Exhibit N, does provide sufficient accommodation for the views of the Plaintiff. . . .

But nevertheless, . . . sometimes . . . we need to be reminded of our responsibilities. It seems to me that what has happened here has developed from a lack of communication from the Board to the school to the classroom teacher. I think it is the emphasis on tolerance and understanding that should be communicated as a fundamental policy of the State Board of Education. This is true not only in science, but it's true throughout the entire public school system. . . .

In the final analysis, ladies and gentlemen, counsel, all that Plaintiffs seek, in the Court's view, presently is contained in Board policy. It appears, however, that this Board policy may not have been communicated to all who should know of it, and who should be guided by that policy. As this is a Court of equity, it seems to the Court that an appropriate remedy may be fashioned.

It will be the order of the Court that there shall be disseminated to all the publishers, institutions, school districts, schools, and persons regularly receiving the science framework a copy of the Board policy. . . . By this, the Court means, insofar as possible, the . . . policy shall be sent to those who have received the framework in the past. It shall be included in the framework disseminated in the future. It follows that if there are violations of this policy when disseminated it becomes a matter of concern for students and parents to adjust with their local teachers, their local schools, and their local school boards. . . .

As I view this case, accordingly, counsel, I really don't believe that either side has lost. I truly believe that both sides have won. I think that we have all won because hopefully what we have achieved in this case is understanding. . . .

MCLEAN V. ARKANSAS BOARD OF EDUCATION

In 1981, Arkansas passed a law mandating equal time for evolution and "creation science" in public schools. The law was immediately challenged by the American Civil Liberties Union (ACLU), which argued that the law violated the First Amendment because it was an attempt to establish religion in public schools. In his decision in the case Judge William Overton addressed a variety of issues and remains the only evolution-related decision to directly address the scientific merits and educational value of "creation science."

McLean v. Arkansas Board of Education

Decision by U.S. District Court Judge William R. Overton

Judgment

Pursuant to the Court's Memorandum Opinion filed this date, judgment is hereby entered in favor of the plaintiffs and against the defendants. The relief prayed for is granted.

Dated this January 5, 1982.

Injunction

Pursuant to the Court's Memorandum Opinion filed this date, the defendants and each of them and all their servants and employees are hereby permanently enjoined from implementing in any manner Act 590 of the Acts of Arkansas of 1981.

It is so ordered this January 5, 1982.

Memorandum Opinion

Introduction

On March 19, 1981, the Governor of Arkansas signed into law Act 590 of 1981, entitled "Balanced Treatment for Creation-Science and Evolution-Science Act." The Act is codified as Ark. Stat. Ann. &80–1663, et seq., (1981 Supp.). Its essential mandate is stated in its first sentence: "Public schools within this State shall give balanced treatment to creation-science and to evolution-science." On May 27, 1981, this suit was filed (1) challenging the constitutional validity of Act 590 on three distinct grounds.

First, it is contended that Act 590 constitutes an establishment of religion prohibited by the First Amendment to the Constitution, which is made applicable to the states by the Fourteenth Amendment. Second, the plaintiffs argue the Act violates a right to academic freedom which they say is guaranteed to students and teachers by the Free Speech Clause of the First Amendment. Third, plaintiffs allege the Act is impermissibly vague and thereby violates the Due Process Clause of the Fourteenth Amendment.

The individual plaintiffs include the resident Arkansas Bishops of the United Methodist, Episcopal, Roman Catholic and African Methodist Episcopal Churches, the principal official of the Presbyterian Churches in Arkansas, other United Methodist, Southern Baptist and Presbyterian clergy, as well as several persons who sue as parents and next friends of minor children attending Arkansas public schools. One plaintiff is a high school biology teacher. All are also Arkansas taxpayers. Among the organizational plaintiffs are the American Jewish Congress, the Union of American Hebrew Congregations, the American Jewish Committee, the Arkansas Education Association, the National Association of Biology Teachers and the National Coalition for Public Education and Religious Liberty, all of which sue on behalf of members living in Arkansas (2).

The defendants include the Arkansas Board of Education and its members, the Director of the Department of Education, and the State Textbooks and Instructional Materials Selecting Committee (3). The Pulaski County Special School District and its Directors and Superintendent were voluntarily dismissed by the plaintiffs at the pre-trial conference held October 1, 1981.

The trial commenced December 7, 1981, and continued through December 17,

1981. This Memorandum Opinion constitutes the Court's findings of fact and conclusions of law. Further orders and judgments will be in conformity with this opinion.

I

There is no controversy over the legal standards under which the Establishment Clause portion of this case must be judged. The Supreme Court has on a number of occasions expounded on the meaning of the clause, and the pronouncements are clear. Often the issue has arisen in the context of public education, as it has here. . . .

Most recently, the Supreme Court has held that the clause prohibits a state from requiring the posting of the Ten Commandments in public school classrooms for the same reasons that officially imposed daily Bible reading is prohibited. *Stone v. Graham*, 449 U.S. 39 (1980). The opinion in *Stone* relies on the most recent formulation of the Establishment Clause test, that of *Lemon v. Kurtzman*, 403 U.S. 602, 612–613 (1971):

First, the statute must have a secular legislative purpose; second, its principal or primary effect must be one that neither advances nor inhibits religion . . . ; finally, the statute must not foster "an excessive government entanglement with religion." [*Stone v. Graham*, 449 U.S. at 40.]

It is under this three part test that the evidence in this case must be judged. Failure on any of these grounds is fatal to the enactment.

II

The religious movement known as Fundamentalism began in nineteenth century America as part of evangelical Protestantism's response to social changes, new religious thought and Darwinism. Fundamentalists viewed these developments as attacks on the Bible and as responsible for a decline in traditional values.

The various manifestations of Fundamentalism have had a number of common characteristics *(4)*, but a central premise has always been a literal interpretation of the Bible and a belief in the inerrancy of the Scriptures. Following World War I, there was again a perceived decline in traditional morality, and Fundamentalism focused on evolution as responsible for the decline. One aspect of their efforts, particularly in the south, was the promotion of statutes prohibiting the teaching of evolution in public schools. In Arkansas, this resulted in the adoption of Initiated Act 1 of 1929 *(5)*.

Between the 1920's and early 1960's, anti-evolutionary sentiment had a subtle but pervasive influence on the teaching of biology in public schools. Generally, textbooks avoided the topic of evolution and did not mention the name of Darwin. Following the launch of the Sputnik satellite by the Soviet Union in 1957, the National Science Foundation funded several programs designed to modernize the teaching of science in the nation's schools. The Biological Sciences Curriculum Study (BSCS), a nonprofit organization, was among those receiving grants for curriculum study and revision. Working with scientists and teachers, BSCS developed a series of biology texts which, although emphasizing different aspects of biology, incorporated the theory of evolution as a major theme. The success of the BSCS effort is shown by the fact that fifty percent of American school children currently use BSCS books directly and the curriculum is incorporated indirectly in virtually all biology texts. (Testimony of Mayer; Nelkin, Px 1) *(6)*.

In the early 1960's, there was again a resurgence of concern among Fundamentalists about the loss of traditional values and a fear of growing secularism in society. The Fundamentalist movement became more active and has steadily grown in numbers and political influence. There is an emphasis among current Fundamentalists on the literal interpretation of the Bible and the Book of Genesis as the sole source of knowledge about origins.

The term "scientific creationism" first gained currency around 1965 following publication of *The Genesis Flood* in 1961 by Whitcomb and Morris. There is undoubtedly some connection between the appearance of the BSCS texts emphasizing evolutionary thought and efforts of Fundamentalist to attach the theory. (Mayer)

In the 1960's and early 1970's, several Fundamentalist organizations were formed to promote the idea that the Book of Genesis was supported by scientific data. The terms "creation science" and "scientific creationism" have been adopted by these Fundamentalists as descriptive of their study of creation and the origins of man. Perhaps the leading creationist organization is the Institute for Creation Research (ICR), which is affiliated with the Christian Heritage College and supported by the Scott Memorial Baptist Church in San Diego, California. The ICR, through the Creation-Life Publishing Company, is the leading publisher of creation science material. Other creation science organizations include the Creation Science Research Center (CSRC) of San Diego and the Bible Science Association of Minneapolis, Minnesota. In 1963, the Creation Research Society (CRS) was formed from a schism in the American Scientific Affiliation (ASA). It is an organization of literal Fundamentalists (7) who have the equivalent of a master's degree in some recognized area of science. A purpose of the organization is "to reach all people with the vital message of the scientific and historical truth about creation." Nelkin, *The Science Textbook Controversies and the Politics of Equal Time*, 66. Similarly, the CSRC was formed in 1970 from a split in the CRS. Its aim has been "to reach the 63 million children of the United States with the scientific teaching of Biblical creationism." *Id.* at 69.

Among creationist writers who are recognized as authorities in the field by other creationists are Henry M. Morris, Duane Gish, G. E. Parker, Harold S. Slusher, Richard B. Bliss, John W. Moore, Martin E. Clark, W. L. Wysong, Robert E. Kofahl, and Kelly L. Segraves. Morris is Director of ICR, Gish is Associate Director and Segraves is associated with CSRC.

Creationists view evolution as a source of society's ills, and the writings of Morris and Clark are typical expressions of that view.

Evolution is thus not only anti-Biblical and anti-Christian, but it is utterly unscientific and impossible as well. But it has served effectively as the pseudo-scientific basis of atheism, agnosticism, socialism, fascism, and numerous other false and dangerous philosophies over the past century. [Morris and Clark, *The Bible Has The Answer*, (Px 31 and Pretrial Px 89) (8)]

Creationists have adopted the view of Fundamentalists generally that there are only two positions with respect to the origins of the earth and life: belief in the inerrancy of the Genesis story of creation and of a worldwide flood as fact, or a belief in what they call evolution.

Henry Morris has stated, "It is impossible to devise a legitimate means of harmonizing the Bible with evolution." Morris, "evolution and the Bible," *ICR Impact Series* Number 5 (undated, unpaged), quoted in Mayer, Px 8, at 3. This dualistic approach to the subject of origins permeates the creationist literature.

The creationist organizations consider the introduction of creation science into the public schools part of their ministry. The ICR has published at least two pamphlets *(9)* containing suggested methods for convincing school boards, administrators and teachers that creationism should be taught in public schools. The ICR has urged its proponents to encourage school officials to voluntarily add creationism to the curriculum *(10)*.

Citizens For Fairness In Education is an organization based in Anderson, South Carolina, formed by Paul Ellwanger, a respiratory therapist who is trained in neither law nor science. Mr. Ellwanger is of the opinion that evolution is the forerunner of many social ills, including Nazism, racism and abortion (Ellwanger Depo. at 32–34). About 1977, Ellwanger collected several proposed legislative acts with the idea of preparing a model state act requiring the teaching of creationism as science in opposition to evolution. One of the proposals he collected was prepared by Wendell Bird, who is now a staff attorney for ICR *(11)*. From these various proposals, Ellwanger prepared a "model act" which calls for "balanced treatment" of "scientific creationism" and "evolution" in public schools. He circulated the proposed act to various people and organizations around the country.

Mr. Ellwanger's views on the nature of creation science are entitled to some weight since he personally drafted the model act which became Act 590. His evidentiary deposition with exhibits and unnumbered attachments (produced in response to a subpoena *duces tecum*) speaks to both the intent of the Act and the scientific merits of creation science. Mr. Ellwanger does not believe creation science is a science. In a letter to Pastor Robert E. Hays he states, "While neither evolution nor creation can qualify as a scientific theory, and since it is virtually impossible at this point to educate the whole world that evolution is not a true scientific theory, we have freely used these terms—the evolution theory and the theory of scientific creationism—in the bill's text." (Unnumbered attachment to Ellwanger Depo., at 2.) He further states in a letter to Mr. Tom Bethell, "As we examine evolution (remember, we're not making any scientific claims for creation, but we are challenging evolution's claim to be scientific . . . " (Unnumbered attachment to Ellwanger Depo. at 1.)

Ellwanger's correspondence on the subject shows an awareness that Act 590 is a religious crusade, coupled with a desire to conceal this fact. In a letter to State Senator Bill Keith of Louisiana, he says, "I view this whole battle as one between God and anti-God forces, though I know there are a large number of evolutionists who believe in God." And further, " . . . it behooves Satan to do all he can to thwart our efforts and confuse the issue at every turn." Yet Ellwanger suggest to Senator Keith, "If you have a clear choice between having grassroots leaders of this statewide bill promotion effort to be ministerial or non-ministerial, be sure to opt for the non-ministerial. It does the bill effort no good to have ministers out there in the public forum and the adversary will surely pick at this point . . . . Ministerial persons can accomplish a tremendous amount of work from behind the scenes, encouraging their congregations to take the organizational and P.R. initiatives. And they can lead their churches in storming Heaven with prayers for help against so tenacious an adversary." (Unnumbered attachment to Ellwanger Depo. at 1.)

Ellwanger shows a remarkable degree of political candor, if not finesse, in a letter to State Senator Joseph Carlucci of Florida:

2. It would be very wise, if not actually essential, that all of us who are engaged in this legislative effort be careful not to present our position and our work in a religious framework. For example, in written communications that might somehow be shared with those other persons whom we may be trying to convince, it would be well to exclude our own personal testimony and/or witness for Christ, but rather, if we are so moved, to give that testimony on a separate attached note. (Unnumbered attachment to Ellwanger Depo. at 1.) . . .

Perhaps most interesting, however, is Mr. Ellwanger's testimony in his deposition as to his strategy for having the model act implemented:

Q. You're trying to play on other people's religious motives.

A. I'm trying to play on their emotions, love, hate, their likes, dislikes, because I don't know any other way to involve, to get humans to become involved in human endeavors. I see emotions as being a healthy and legitimate means of getting people's feelings into action, and . . . I believe that the predominance of population in America that represents the greatest potential for taking some kind of action in this area is a Christian community. I see the Jewish community as far less potential in taking action . . . but I've seen a lot of interest among Christians and I feel, why not exploit that to get the bill going if that's what it takes. (Ellwanger Depo. at 146–147). . . .

Ellwanger's efforts in preparation of the model act and campaign for its adoption in the states were motivated by his opposition to the theory of evolution and his desire to see the Biblical version of creation taught in the public schools. There is no evidence that the pastors, Blount, Thomas, Young, or The Greater Little Rock Evangelical Fellowship were motivated by anything other than their religious convictions when proposing its adoption or during their lobbying efforts in its behalf. Senator Holsted's sponsorship and lobbying efforts in behalf of the Act were motivated solely by his religious beliefs and desire to see the Biblical version of creation taught in the public schools *(14)*.

The State of Arkansas, like a number of states whose citizens have relatively homogeneous religious beliefs, has a long history of official opposition to evolution which is motivated by adherence to Fundamentalist beliefs in the inerrancy of the Book of Genesis. This history is documented in Justice Fortas' opinion in *Epperson v. Arkansas*, 393 U.S. 97 (1968), which struck down Initiated Act 1 of 1929, Ark. Stat. Ann. &&80–1627–1628, prohibiting the teaching of the theory of evolution. To this same tradition may be attributed Initiated Act 1 of 1930, Ark. Stat. Ann. &80–1606 (Repl. 1980), requiring "the reverent daily reading of a portion of the English Bible" in every public school classroom in the State *(15)*. . . .

III

If the defendants are correct and the Court is limited to an examination of the language of the Act, the evidence is overwhelming that both the purpose and effect of Act 590 is the advancement of religion in the public schools.

Section 4 of the Act provides:

Definitions, as used in this Act:

(a) "Creation-science" means the scientific evidences for creation and inferences from those scientific evidences. Creation-science includes the scientific evidences and related inferences that indicate: (1) Sudden creation of the universe, energy, and life from nothing; (2) The insufficiency of mutation and natural selection in bringing about development of all living kinds from a single organism; (3) Changes only within fixed limits of originally created kinds of plants and animals; (4) Separate ancestry for man and apes; (5) Explanation of the earth's geology by catastrophism, including the occurrence of a worldwide flood; and (6) A relatively recent inception of the earth and living kinds.

(b) "Evolution-science" means the scientific evidences for evolution and inferences from those scientific evidences. Evolution-science includes the scientific evidences and related inferences that indicate: (1) Emergence by naturalistic processes of the universe from disordered matter and emergence of life from nonlife; (2) The sufficiency of mutation and natural selection in bringing about development of present living kinds from simple earlier kinds; (3) Emergence by mutation and natural selection of present living kinds from simple earlier kinds; (4) Emergence of man from a common ancestor with apes; (5) Explanation of the earth's geology and the evolutionary sequence by uniformitarianism; and (6) An inception several billion years ago of the earth and somewhat later of life.

(c) "Public schools" means public secondary and elementary schools.

The evidence establishes that the definition of "creation science" contained in 4(a) has as its unmentioned reference the first 11 chapters of the Book of Genesis. Among the many creation epics in human history, the account of sudden creation from nothing, or *creatio ex nihilo*, and subsequent destruction of the world by flood is unique to Genesis. The concepts of 4(a) are the literal Fundamentalists' view of Genesis. Section 4(a) is unquestionably a statement of religion, with the exception of 4(a)(2) which is a negative thrust aimed at what the creationists understand to be the theory of evolution *(17)*.

Both the concepts and wording of Section 4(a) convey an inescapable religiosity. Section 4(a)(1) describes "sudden creation of the universe, energy and life from nothing." Every theologian who testified, including defense witnesses, expressed the opinion that the statement referred to a supernatural creation which was performed by God.

Defendants argue that : (1) the fact that 4(a) conveys idea similar to the literal interpretation of Genesis does not make it conclusively a statement of religion; (2) that reference to a creation from nothing is not necessarily a religious concept since the Act only suggests a creator who has power, intelligence and a sense of design and not necessarily the attributes of love, compassion and justice *(18)*; and (3) that simply teaching about the concept of a creator is not a religious exercise unless the student is required to make a commitment to the concept of a creator.

The evidence fully answers these arguments. The idea of 4(a)(1) are not merely similar to the literal interpretation of Genesis; they are identical and parallel to no other story of creation *(19)*.

The argument that creation from nothing in 4(a)(1) does not involve a supernatural deity has no evidentiary or rational support. To the contrary, "creation out of nothing" is a concept unique to Western religions. In traditional Western religious thought, the conception of a creator of the world is a conception of God. Indeed, creation of the world "out of nothing" is the ultimate religious statement because God is the only actor. As Dr. Langdon Gilkey noted, the Act refers to one who has the power to bring all the universe into existence from nothing. The only "one" who has this power is God *(20)*.

The leading creationist writers, Morris and Gish, acknowledge that the idea of creation described in 4(a)(1) is the concept of creation by God and make no pretense to the contrary *(21)*. The idea of sudden creation from nothing, or *creatio ex nihilo*, is an inherently religious concept. (Vawter, Gilkey, Geisler, Ayala, Blount, Hicks.)

The argument advanced by defendants' witness, Dr. Norman Geisler, that teaching the existence of God is not religious unless the teaching seeks a commitment, is contrary to common understanding and contradicts settled case law. *Stone v. Graham*, 449 U.S. 39 (1980), *Abington School District v. Schempp*, 374 U.S. 203, 222 (1963).

The facts that creation science is inspired by the Book of Genesis and that Section 4(a) is consistent with a literal interpretation of Genesis leave no doubt that a major effect of the Act is the advancement of particular religious beliefs. The legal impact of this conclusion will be discussed further at the conclusion of the Court's evaluation of the scientific merit of creation science.

IV(A)

The approach to teaching "creation science" and "evolution-science" found in Act 590 is identical to the two-model approach espoused by the Institute for Creation Research and is taken almost verbatim from ICR writings. It is an extension of Fundamentalists' view that one must either accept the literal interpretation of Genesis or else believe in the godless system of evolution.

The two-model approach of the creationists is simply a contrived dualism *(22)* which has not scientific factual basis or legitimate educational purpose. It assumes only two explanations for the origins of life and existence of man, plants and animals: it was either the work of a creator or it was not. Application of these two models, according to creationists, and the defendants, dictates that all scientific evidence which fails to support the theory of evolution is necessarily scientific evidence in support of creationism and is, therefore, creation science "evidence" in support of Section 4(a).

IV(B)

The emphasis on origins as an aspect of the theory of evolution is peculiar to the creationist literature. Although the subject of origins of life is within the province of biology, the scientific community does not consider origins of life a part of evolutionary theory. The theory of evolution assumes the existence of life and is directed to an explanation of how life evolved. Evolution does not presuppose the absence of a creator or God and the plain inference conveyed by Section 4 is erroneous (23).

As a statement of the theory of evolution, Section 4(b) is simply a hodgepodge of limited assertions, many of which are factually inaccurate.

For example, although 4(b)(2) asserts, as a tenet of evolutionary theory, "sufficiency of mutation and natural selection in bringing about development of present living kinds from simple earlier kinds," Drs. Ayala and Gould both stated that biologists know that these two processes do not account for all significant evolutionary change. They testified to such phenomena as recombination, the founder effect, genetic drift and the theory of punctuated equilibrium, which are believed to play important evolutionary roles. Section 4(b) omits any reference to these. Moreover, 4(b) utilizes the term "kinds" which all scientists have said is not a word of science and has no fixed meaning. Additionally, the Act presents both evolution and creation science as "package deals." Thus, evidence critical to some aspect of what the creationists define as evolution is taken as support for a theory which includes a worldwide flood and a relatively young earth *(24)*.

IV(C)

In addition to the fallacious pedagogy of the two model approach, Section 4(a) lacks legitimate educational value because "creation-science" as defined in that section is simply not science. Several witnesses suggested definitions of science. A descriptive definition was said to be that science is what is "accepted by the scientific community" and is "what scientists do." The obvious implication of this description is that, in a free society, knowledge does not require the imprimatur of legislation in order to become science.

More precisely, the essential characteristics of science are: (1) It is guided by natural law; (2) It has to be explanatory by reference to nature law; (3) It is testable against the empirical world; (4) Its conclusions are tentative, i.e., are not necessarily the final word; and (5) Its is falsifiable (Ruse and other science witnesses).

Creation science as described in Section 4(a) fails to meet these essential characteristics. First, the section revolves around 4(a)(1) which asserts a sudden creation "from nothing." Such a concept is not science because it depends upon a supernatural intervention which is not guided by natural law. It is not explanatory by reference to natural law, is not testable and is not falsifiable *(25)*.

If the unifying idea of supernatural creation by God is removed from Section 4, the remaining parts of the section explain nothing and are meaningless assertions. . . .

Section 4(a)(5) refers to "explanation of the earth's geology by catastrophism, including the occurrence of a worldwide flood." This assertion completely fails as science. The Act is referring to the Noachian flood described in the Book of Genesis *(27)*. The creationist writers concede that *any* kind of Genesis Flood depends upon supernatural intervention. A worldwide flood as an explanation of the world's geology is not the product of natural law, nor can its occurrence be explained by natural law.

Section 4(a)(6) equally fails to meet the standards of science. "Relatively recent inception" has no scientific meaning. It can only be given in reference to creationist writings which place the age at between 6,000 and 20,000 years because of the genealogy of the Old Testament. See, e.g., Px 78, Gish (6,000 to 10,000); Px 87, Segraves(6,000 to 20,000). Such a reasoning process is not the product of natural law; not explainable by natural law; nor is it tentative.

Creation science as defined in Section 4(a), not only fails to follow the canons of dealing with scientific theory, it also fails to fit the more general descriptions of "what scientists think" and "what scientists do." The scientific community consists of individuals and groups, nationally and internationally, who work independently in such varied fields as biology, paleontology, geology, and astronomy. Their work is published and subject to review and testing by their peers. The journals for publication are both numerous and varied. There is, however, not one recognized scientific journal which has published an article espousing the creation science theory described in Section 4(a). Some of the State's witnesses suggested that the scientific community was "close-minded" on the subject of creationism and that explained the lack of acceptance of the creation science arguments. Yet no witness produced a scientific article for which publication has been refused. Perhaps some members of the scientific community are resistant to new ideas. It is, however, inconceivable that such a loose knit group of independent thinkers in all the varied fields of science could, or would, so effectively censor new scientific thought.

The creationists have difficulty maintaining among their ranks consistency in the claim that creationism is science. The author of Act 590, Ellwanger, said that neither evolution or creationism was science. He thinks that both are religious. . . .

The methodology employed by creationists is another factor which is indicative that their work is not science. A scientific theory must be tentative and always subject to revision or abandonment in light of facts that are inconsistent with, or falsify, the theory. A theory that is by its own terms dogmatic, absolutist, and never subject to revision is not a scientific theory.

The creationists' methods do not take data, weigh it against the opposing scientific data, and thereafter reach the conclusions stated in Section 4(a). Instead, they take the literal wording of the Book of Genesis and attempt to find scientific support for it. The method is best explained in the language of Morris in his book (Px 31) *Studies in The Bible and Science* at page 114:

. . . it is . . . quite impossible to determine anything about Creation through a study of present processes, because present processes are not creative in character. If man wished to know anything about Creation (the time of Creation, the duration of Creation, the order of Creation, the methods of Creation, or anything else) his sole source of true information is that of divine revelation. God was there when it happened. We were not there . . . . Therefore, we are completely limited to what God has seen fit to tell us, and this information is in His written Word. This is our textbook on the science of Creation!

The Creation Research Society employs the same unscientific approach to the issue of creationism. Its applicants for membership must subscribe to the belief that the Book of Genesis is "historically and scientifically true in all of the original autographs" *(28)*. The Court would never criticize or discredit any person's testimony based on his or her religious beliefs. While anybody is free to approach a scientific inquiry in any fashion they choose, they cannot properly describe the methodology as scientific, if they start with the conclusion and refuse to change it regardless of the evidence developed during the course of the investigation.

IV(D)

In efforts to establish "evidence" in support of creation science, the defendants relied upon the same false premise as the two model approach contained in Section 4, i.e., all evidence which criticized evolutionary theory was proof in support of creation science. For example, the defendants established that the mathematical probability of a chance chemical combination resulting in life from non-life is as remote that such an occurrence is almost beyond imagination. Those mathematical facts, the defendants argue, are scientific evidences that life was the product of a creator. While the statistical figures may be impressive evidence against the theory of chance chemical combinations as an explanation of origins, it requires a leap of faith to interpret those figures so as to support a complex doctrine which includes a sudden creation from nothing, a worldwide flood, separate ancestry of man and apes, and a young earth.

The defendants' argument would be more persuasive if, in fact, there were only two theories or ideas about the origins of life and the world. That there are a number of theories was acknowledged by the State's witnesses, Dr. Wickramasinghe and Dr. Geisler. Dr. Wickramasinghe testified at length in support of a theory that life on earth was "seeded" by comets which delivered genetic material and perhaps organisms to the earth's surface from interstellar dust far outside the solar system. The "seeding" theory further hypothesizes that the earth remains under the continuing influence of genetic material from space which continues to affect life. While Wickramasinghe's theory *(29)* about the origins of life on earth has not received general acceptance within the scientific community, he has, at least, used scientific methodology to produce a theory of origins which meets the essential characteristics of science. . . .

The proof in support of creation science consisted almost entirely of efforts to discredit the theory of evolution through a rehash of data and theories which have been before the scientific community for decades. The arguments asserted by the creationists are not based upon new scientific evidence or laboratory data which has been ignored by the scientific community.

It is easy to understand why . . . educators find the creationists' textbook material and teaching guides unacceptable. The materials misstate the theory of evolution in the same fashion as Section 4(b) of the Act, with emphasis on the alternative mutually exclusive nature of creationism and evolution. Students are constantly encouraged to compare and make a choice between the two models, and the material is not presented in an accurate manner. . . .

Biology, A Search For Order in Complexity (31) is a high school biology text typical of creationists' materials. The following quotations are illustrative:

> Flowers and roots do not have a mind to have purpose of their own: therefore, this planning must have been done for them by the Creator. (at page 12)

> The exquisite beauty of color and shape in flowers exceeds the skill of poet, artist, and king. Jesus said (from Matthew's gospel), "Consider the lilies in the field, how they grow; they toil not, neither do they spin. . . ." (Px 129 at page 363)

The "public school edition" texts written by creationists simply omit Biblical references but the content and message remain the same. For example, *Evolution—The Fossils Say No!* *(32)* contains the following:

> Creation. By creation we mean the bringing into being by a supernatural Creator of the basic kinds of plants and animals by the process of sudden, or fiat, creation.
>
> We do not know how the Creator created, what processes He used, *for he used processes which are not now operating anywhere in the natural universe.* This is why we refer to creation as Special Creation. We cannot discover by scientific investigation anything about the creative processes used by the Creator. (page 40)

Gish's book also portrays the large majority of evolutionists as "materialistic atheists or agnostics."

Scientific Creationism (Public School Edition) by Morris, is another text reviewed by Ms. Wilson's committee and rejected as unacceptable. The following quotes illustrate the purpose and theme of the text:

> Forward
>
> Parents and youth leaders today, and even many scientists and educators, have become concerned about the prevalence and influence of evolutionary philosophy in modern curriculum. Not only is the system inimical to orthodox Christianity and Judaism, but also, as many are convinced, to a healthy society and true science as well. (at page iii)
>
> The rationalist of course finds the concept of special creation insufferably naive, even "incredible." Such a judgment, however, is warranted only if one categorically dismisses the existence of an omnipotent God. (at page 17)

. . .The conclusion that creation science has no scientific merit or educational value as science has legal significance in light of the Court's previous conclusion that creation science has, as one major effect, the advancement of religion. The second part of the three-pronged test for establishment reaches only those statutes as having their *primary* effect the advancement of religion. Secondary effects which advance religion are not constitutionally fatal. Since creation science is not science, the conclusion is inescapable that the *only* real effect of Act 590 is the advancement of religion. The Act therefore fails both the first and second portions of the test in *Lemon v. Kurtzman*, 403 U.S. 602 (1971).

IV(E)

Act 590 mandates "balanced treatment" for creation science and evolution science. The Act prohibits instruction in any religious doctrine or references to religious writings. The Act is self-contradictory and compliance is impossible unless the public schools elect to forego significant portions of subjects such as biology, world history, geology, zoology, botany, psychology, anthropology, sociology, philosophy, physics and chemistry. Presently, the concepts of evolutionary theory as described in 4(b) permeate the public textbooks. There is no way teachers can teach the Genesis account of creation in a secular manner.

The State Department of Education, through its textbook selection committee, school boards and school administrators will be required to constantly monitor materials to avoid using religious references. The school boards, administrators and teachers face an impossible task. How is the teacher to respond to questions about a creation suddenly and out of nothing? How will a teacher explain the occurrence of a worldwide flood? How will a teacher explain the concept of a relatively recent age of the earth? The answer is obvious because the only source of this information is ultimately contained in the Book of Genesis.

References to the pervasive nature of religious concepts in creation science texts amply demonstrate why State entanglement with religion is inevitable under Act 590. Involvement of the State in screening texts for impermissible religious references will require State officials to make delicate religious judgments. The need to monitor classroom discussion in order to uphold the Act's prohibition against religious instruction will necessarily involve administrators in questions concerning religion. These continuing involvements of State officials in questions and issues of religion create an excessive and prohibited entanglement with religion. *Brandon v. Board of Education*, 487 F.Supp 1219, 1230 (N.D.N.Y.), *aff'd.*, 635 F.2d 971 (2nd Cir. 1980).

V

These conclusions are dispositive of the case and there is no need to reach legal conclusions with respect to the remaining issues. The plaintiffs raised two other issues questioning the constitutionality of the Act and, insofar as the factual findings relevant to these issues are not covered in the preceding discussion, the Court will address these issues. Additionally, the defendants raise two other issues which warrant discussion.

V(A)

First, plaintiff teachers argue the Act is unconstitutionally vague to the extent that they cannot comply with its mandate of "balanced" treatment without jeopardizing their employment. The argument centers around the lack of a precise definition in the Act for the word "balanced." Several witnesses expressed opinions that the word has such meanings as equal time, equal weight, or equal legitimacy. Although the Act could have been more explicit, "balanced" is a word subject to ordinary understanding. The proof is not convincing that a teacher using a reasonably acceptable understanding of the word and making a good faith effort to comply with the Act will be in jeopardy of termination. Other portions of the Act are arguably vague, such as the "relatively recent" inception of the earth and life. The evidence establishes, however, that relatively recent means from 6,000 to 20,000 years, as commonly understood in creation science literature. The meaning of this phrase, like Section 4(a) generally, is, for purposes of the Establishment Clause, all too clear.

V(B)

The plaintiffs' other argument revolves around the alleged infringement by the defendants upon the academic freedom of teachers and students. It is contended this unprecedented intrusion in the curriculum by the State prohibits teachers from teaching what they believe should be taught or requires them to teach that which they do not believe is proper. The evidence reflects that traditionally the State Department of Education, local school boards and administration officials exercise little, if any, influence upon the subject matter taught by classroom teachers. Teachers have been given freedom to teach and emphasize those portions of subjects the individual teacher considered important. The limits to this discretion have generally been derived from the approval of textbooks by the State Department and preparation of curriculum guides by the school districts.

Several witnesses testified that academic freedom for the teacher means, in substance, that the individual teacher should be permitted unlimited discretion subject only to the bounds of professional ethics. The Court is not prepare to adopt such a broad view of academic freedom in the public schools.

In any event, if Act 590 is implemented, many teachers will be required to teach materials in support of creation science which they do not consider academically sound. Many teachers will simply forego teaching subjects which might trigger the "balanced treatment" aspects of Act 590 even though they think the subjects are important to a proper presentation of a course.

Implementation of Act 590 will have serious and untoward consequences for students, particularly those planning to attend college. Evolution is the cornerstone of modern biology, and many courses in public schools contain subject matter relating to such varied topics as the age of the earth, geology and relationships among living things. Any student who is deprived of instruction as to the prevailing scientific thought on these topics will be denied a significant part of science education. Such a deprivation through the high school level would undoubtedly have an impact upon the quality of education in the State's colleges and universities, especially including the pre-professional and professional programs in the health sciences.

V(C)

The defendants argue in their brief that evolution is, in effect, a religion, and that by teaching a religion which is contrary to some students' religious views, the State is infringing upon the student's free exercise rights under the First Amendment. Mr. Ellwanger's legislative findings, which were adopted as a finding of fact by the Arkansas Legislature in Act 590, provides:

> Evolution-science is contrary to the religious convictions or moral values or philosophical beliefs of many students and parents, including individuals of many different religious faiths and with diverse moral and philosophical beliefs. Act 590, &7(d).

The defendants argue that the teaching of evolution alone presents both a free exercise problem and an establishment problem which can only be redressed by giving balanced treatment to creation science, which is admittedly consistent with some religious beliefs. This argument appears to have its genesis in a student note written by Mr. Wendell Bird, "Freedom of Religion and Science Instruction in Public Schools," 87 Yale L.J. 515 (1978). The argument has no legal merit.

If creation science is, in fact, science and not religion, as the defendants claim, it is difficult to see how the teaching of such a science could "neutralize" the religious nature of evolution.

Assuming for the purposes of argument, however, that evolution is a religion or religious tenet, the remedy is to stop the teaching of evolution, not establish another religion in opposition to it. Yet it is clearly established in the case law, and perhaps also in common sense, that evolution is not a religion and that teaching evolution does not violate the Establishment Clause, *Epperson v. Arkansas, supra, Willoughby v. Stever*, No. 15574–75 (D.D.C. May 18, 1973); *aff'd.* 504 F.2d 271 (D.C. Cir. 1974), *cert. denied*, 420 U.S. 924 (1975); *Wright v. Houston Indep. School Dist.*, 366 F. Supp. 1208 (S.D. Tex 1978), *aff.d.* 486 F.2d 137 (5th Cir. 1973), *cert. denied* 417 U.S. 969 (1974).

V(D)

The defendants presented Dr. Larry Parker, a specialist in devising curricula for public schools. He testified that the public school's curriculum should reflect the subjects the public wants in schools. The witness said that polls indicated a significant majority of the American public thought creation science should be taught if evolution was taught. The point of this testimony was never placed in a legal context. No doubt a sizeable majority of Americans believe in the concept of a Creator or, at least, are not opposed to the concept and see nothing wrong with teaching school children the idea.

The application and content of First Amendment principles are not determined by public opinion polls or by a majority vote. Whether the proponents of Act 590 constitute the majority or the minority is quite irrelevant under a constitutional system of government. No group, no matter how large or small, may use the organs of government, of which the public schools are the most conspicuous and influential, to foist its religious beliefs on others.

The Court closes this opinion with a thought expressed eloquently by the great Justice Frankfurter:

We renew our conviction that "we have stake the very existence of our country on the faith that complete separation between the state and religion is best for the state and best for religion." *Everson v. Board of Education*, 330 U.S. at 59. If nowhere else, in the relation between Church and State, "good fences make good neighbors." [*McCollum v. Board of Education*, 333 U.S. 203, 232 (1948)]

An injunction will be entered permanently prohibiting enforcement of Act 590. It is ordered this January 5, 1982.

—William R. Overton *in the U.S. District Court, Eastern District of Arkansas, Western Division*

Notes

1. The complaint is based on 42 U.S.C. &1983, which provides a remedy against any person who, acting under color of state law, deprives another of any right, privilege or immunity guaranteed by the United States Constitution or federal law. This Court's jurisdiction arises under 28 U.S.C. 1331, 1343(3) and 1343(4). The power to issue declaratory judgments is expressed in 28 U.S.C. &&2201 and 2202.

2. The facts necessary to establish the plaintiff's standing to sue are contained in the joint stipulation of facts, which is hereby adopted and incorporated herein by reference. There is no doubt that the case is ripe for adjudication.

3. The State of Arkansas was dismissed as a defendant because of its immunity from suit under the Eleventh Amendment. *Hans v. Louisiana*, 134 U.S. 1 (1890).

4. The authorities differ as to generalizations which may be made about Fundamentalism. For example, Dr. Geisler testified to the widely held view that there are five beliefs characteristic of all Fundamentalist movements, in addition, of course, to the inerrancy of Scripture: (1) belief in the virgin birth of Christ, (2) belief in the deity of Christ, (3) belief in the substitutional atonement of Christ, (4) belief in the second coming of Christ, and (5) belief in the physical resurrection of all departed souls. Dr. Marsden, however, testified that this generalization, which has been common in religious scholarship, is now thought to be historical error. There is no doubt, however, that all Fundamentalists take the Scriptures as inerrant and probably most take them as literally true.

5. Initiated Act 1 of 1929, Ark. Stat. Ann. &80–1627 *et seq.*, which prohibited the teaching of evolution in Arkansas schools, is discussed *infra* at text accompanying note 26.

6. Subsequent references to the testimony will be made by the last name of the witness only. References to documentary exhibits will be by the name of the author and the exhibit number.

7. Applicants for membership in the CRS must subscribe to the following statement of belief: "(1) The Bible is the written Word of God, and because we believe it to be inspired thruout [*sic*], all of its assertions are historically and scientifically true in all of the original autographs. To the student of nature, this means that the account of origins in Genesis is a factual presentation of simple historical truths. (2) All basic types of living things, including man, were made by direct creative acts of God during Creation Week as described in Genesis. Whatever biological changes have occurred since Creation have accomplished only changes within the original created kinds. (3) The great Flood described in Genesis, commonly referred to as the Noachian Deluge, was an historical event, worldwide in its extent and effect. (4) Finally, we are an organization of Christian men of science, who accept Jesus Christ as our Lord and Savior. The account of the special creation of Adam and Eve as one man and one woman, and their subsequent Fall into sin, is the basis for our belief in the necessity of a Savior for all mankind. Therefore, salvation can come only thru [*sic*] accepting Jesus Christ as our Savior." (Px 115)

8. Because of the voluminous nature of the documentary exhibits, the parties were directed by pre-trial order to submit their proposed exhibits for the Court's convenience prior to trial. The numbers assigned to the pre-trial submissions do not correspond with those assigned to the same documents at trial and, in some instances, the pre-trial submissions are more complete.

9. Px 130, Morris, *Introducing Scientific Creationism Into the Public Schools* (1975), and Bird, "Resolution for Balanced Presentation of Evolution and Scientific Creationism." *ICR Impact Series* No. 71, App. 14 to Plaintiff's Pretrial Brief.

10. The creationists often show candor in their proselytization. Henry Morris has stated, "Even if a favorable statute or court decision is obtained, it will probably be declared unconstitutional, especially if the legislation or injunction refers to the Bible account of creation." In the same vein he notes, "The only effective way to

get creationism taught properly is to have it taught by teachers who are both willing and able to do it. Since most teachers now are neither willing nor able, they must first be both persuaded and instructed themselves." Px 130, Morris, *Introducing Scientific Creationism Into the Public Schools* (1975)(unpaged).

11. Mr. Bird sought to participate in this litigation by representing a number of individuals who wanted to intervene as defendants. The application for intervention was denied by this Court. *McLean v. Arkansas*, ____ F.Supp. _____, (E.D. Ark. 1981), aff'd. *per curiam*, Slip Op. No. 81–2023 (8th Cir. Oct. 16, 1981).

12. The model act had been revised to insert "creation science" in lieu of creationism because Ellwanger had the impression people thought that creationism was too religious a term. (Ellwanger Depo. at 79)

13. The original model act had been introduced in the South Carolina Legislature, but had died without action after the South Carolina Attorney General had opined that the act was unconstitutional.

14. Specifically, Senator Holsted testified that he holds to a literal interpretation of the Bible; that the bill was compatible with his religious beliefs; that the bill does favor the position of literalists; that his religious convictions were a factor in his sponsorship of the bill; and that he stated publicly to the *Arkansas Gazette* (although not on the floor of the Senate) contemporaneously with the legislative debate that the bill does presuppose the existence of a divine creator. There is no doubt that Senator Holsted knew he was sponsoring the teaching of a religious doctrine. His view was that the bill did not violate the First Amendment because, as he saw it, it did not favor one denomination over another.

15. This statute is, of course, clearly unconstitutional under the Supreme Court's decision in *Abington School District v. Schempp*, 374 U.S. 203 (1963)

16. The joint stipulation of facts establishes that the following areas are the only *information* specifically required by statute to be taught in all Arkansas schools: (1) the effects of alcohol and narcotics on the human body, (2) conservation of national resources, (3) bird week, (4) fire prevention, and (5) flag etiquette. Additionally, certain specific courses, such as American history and Arkansas history, must be completed by each student before graduation from high school.

17. Paul Ellwanger stated in his deposition that he did not know why Section 4(a)(2) (insufficiency of mutation and natural selection) was included as an evidence supporting creation science. He indicated that he was not a scientist, "but these are postulates that have been laid down by creation scientists." (Ellwanger Depo. at 136.)

18. Although defendants must make some effort to cast the concept of creation in non-religious terms, this effort surely causes discomfort to some of the Act's more theologically sophisticated supporters. The concept of a creator God distinct from the God of love and mercy is closely similar to the Marcion and Gnostic heresies, among the deadliest to threaten the early Christian church. These heresies had much to do with development and adoption of the Apostle's Creed as the official creedal statement of the Roman Catholic Church in the West. (Gilkey.)

19. The parallels between Section 4(a) and Genesis are quite specific: (1) "sudden creation from nothing" is taken from Genesis, 1:1–10 (Vawter, Gilkey); (2) de-

struction of the world by a flood of divine origin is a notion peculiar to Judeo-Christian tradition and is based on Chapters 7 and 8 of Genesis (Vawter); (3) the term "kinds" has no fixed scientific meaning, but appears repeatedly in Genesis (all scientific witnesses); (4) "relatively recent inception" means an age of the earth from 6,000 to 10,000 years and is based on the genealogy of the Old Testament using the rather astronomical ages assigned to the patriarchs (Gilkey and several of the defendants' scientific witnesses); (5) separate ancestry of man and ape focuses on the portion of the theory of evolution which Fundamentalists find most offensive, *Epperson v. Arkansas*, 393 U.S. 97 (1968).

20. "[C]oncepts concerning . . . a supreme being of some sort are manifestly religious . . . . These concepts do not shed that religiosity merely because they are presented as philosophy or as a science . . ." *Malnak v. Yogi*, 440 F. Supp. 1284, 1322 (D.N.J. 1977); *aff'd per curiam*, 592 F.2d 197 (3d Cir. 1979).

21. See, e.g., Px 76, Morris, *et al.*, *Scientific Creationism*, 203 (1980) ("If creation really is a fact, this means there is a *Creator*, and the universe is his creation.") Numerous other examples of such admissions can be found in the many exhibits which represent creationist literature, but no useful purpose would be served here by a potentially endless listing.

22. Morris, the Director of ICR and one who first advocated the two model approach, insists that a true Christian cannot compromises with the theory of evolution and that the Genesis version of creation and the theory of evolution are mutually exclusive. Px 31, Morris, *Studies in the Bible & Science*, 102–103. The two model approach was the subject of Dr. Richard Bliss's doctoral dissertation. (Dx 35). It is presented in Bliss, *Origins: Two Models—Evolution, Creation* (1978). Moreover, the two model approach merely casts in educationalist language the dualism which appears in all creationist literature—creation (i.e., God) and evolution are presented as two alternative and mutually exclusive theories. See, e.g., Px 75, Morris, *Scientific Creationism* (1974) (public school edition); Px 59, Fox, *Fossils: Hard Facts from the Earth*. Particularly illustrative is Px 61, Boardman, *et al.*, *Worlds Without End* (1971) a CSRC publication: One group of scientists, known as creationists, believe that God, in a miraculous manner, created all matter and energy . . .

"Scientists who insist that the universe just grew, by accident, from a mass of hot gases without the direction or help of a Creator are known as evolutionists."

23. The idea that belief in a creator and acceptance of the scientific theory of evolution are mutually exclusive is a false premise and offensive to the religious views of many. (Hicks) Dr. Francisco Ayala, a geneticist of considerable renown and a former Catholic priest who has the equivalent of a Ph.D. in theology, pointed out that many working scientists who subscribe to the theory of evolution are devoutly religious.

24. This is so despite the fact that some of the defense witnesses do not subscribe to the young earth or flood hypotheses. Dr. Geisler stated his belief that the earth is several billion years old. Dr. Wickramasinghe stated that no rational scientist would believe the earth is less than one million years old or that all the world's geology could be explained by a worldwide flood.

25. "We do not know how the Creator created, what processes He used, *for he used processes which are not now operating anywhere in the natural universe*. This

is why we refer to creation as Special Creation. We cannot discover by scientific investigation anything about the creative processes used by God." Px 78, Gish, *Evolution—The Fossils Say No!* (42) (3d ed. 1979) (emphasis in original).

26. The evolutionary notion that man and some modern apes have a common ancestor somewhere is the distant past has consistently been distorted by anti-evolutionists to say that man descended from modern monkeys. As such, this idea has long been more offensive to Fundamentalists. See, *Epperson v. Arkansas*, 393 U.S. 97 (1968).

27. Not only was this point acknowledged by virtually all the defense witnesses, it is patent in the creationist literature. See, e.g., Px 89, Kofahl & Segraves, *The Creation Explanation*, 40: "The Flood of Noah brought about vast changes in the earth's surface, including vulcanism, mountain building, and the deposition of the major part of sedimentary strata. This principle is called 'Biblical catastrophism.'"

28. See n. 7, *supra*, for the full text of the CRS creed.

29. The theory is detailed in Wickramasinghe's book with Sir Fred Hoyle, *Evolution from Space* (1981), which is Dx 79.

30. Ms. Wilson stated that some professors she spoke with sympathized with her plight and tried to help her find scientific materials to support Section 4(a). Others simply asked her to leave.

31. Px 129, published by Zonderman Publishing House (1974), states that it was "prepared by the Textbook Committee of the Creation Research Society." It has a disclaimer pasted inside the front cover stating that it is not suitable for use in public schools.

32. Px 77, by Duane Gish.

33. The passage of Act 590 apparently caught a number of its supporters off guard as much as it did the school district. The Act's author, Paul Ellwanger, stated in a letter to "Dick," (apparently Dr. Richard Bliss at ICR): "And finally, if you know of any textbooks at any level and for any subjects that you think are acceptable to you and are also constitutionally admissible, these are things that would be of *enormous* to these bewildered folks who may be cause, as Arkansas now has been, by the sudden need to implement a whole new ball game with which they are quite unfamiliar." [*sic*] (Unnumbered attachment to Ellwanger depo.)

EDWARDS V. AGUILLARD

In 1981, Louisiana passed a law requiring teachers who teach evolution to also give "balanced treatment" to creationism. In effect, the law required that the biblical version of creationism be taught side-by-side with evolution and that both be taught "as a theory, rather than a proven scientific fact." Don Aguillard, a young biology teacher at Acadiana High School, believed that the law undermined science education; as he said, "We just don't have the money to be spending on bad science." Late in 1981, Aguillard and others challenged the constitutionality of the law. Aguillard's case reached the U.S. Supreme Court in 1987. Here's what the Court said:

**EDWARDS, GOVERNOR OF LOUISIANA, ET AL. *v.* AGUILLARD ET AL.
No. 85–1513**

482 U.S. 578; 107 S. Ct. 2573; 1987 U.S. LEXIS 2729; 96 L. Ed. 2d 510; 55
U.S.L.W. 4860

December 10, 1986, Argued June 19, 1987, Decided

Prior History:

Appeal from the United States Court of Appeals for the Fifth Circuit.

Disposition: 765 F.2d 1251, affirmed.

Syllabus: Louisiana's "Creationism Act" forbids the teaching of the theory of
evolution in public elementary and secondary schools unless accompanied by instruction in the theory of "creation science." The Act does not require the teaching
of either theory unless the other is taught. It defines the theories as "the scientific
evidences for [creation or evolution] and inferences from those scientific evidences."
Appellees, who include Louisiana parents, teachers, and religious leaders, challenged the Act's constitutionality in Federal District Court, seeking an injunction
and declaratory relief. The District Court granted summary judgment to appellees,
holding that the Act violated the Establishment Clause of the First Amendment. The
Court of Appeals affirmed.

Held:

1. The Act is facially invalid as violative of the Establishment Clause of the First
Amendment, because it lacks a clear secular purpose. Pp. 585–594.

(a) The Act does not further its stated secular purpose of "protecting academic
freedom." It does not enhance the freedom of teachers to teach what they choose and
fails to further the goal of "teaching all of the evidence." Forbidding the teaching of
evolution when creation science is not also taught undermines the provision of a
comprehensive scientific education. Moreover, requiring the teaching of creation science with evolution does not give schoolteachers a flexibility that they did not already possess to supplant the present science curriculum with the presentation of
theories, besides evolution, about the origin of life. Furthermore, the contention that
the Act furthers a "basic concept of fairness" by requiring the teaching of all of the
evidence on the subject is without merit. Indeed, the Act evinces a discriminatory
preference for the teaching of creation science and against the teaching of evolution
by requiring that curriculum guides be developed and resource services supplied for
teaching creationism but not for teaching evolution, by limiting membership on the
resource services panel to "creation scientists," and by forbidding school boards to
discriminate against anyone who "chooses to be a creation-scientist" or to teach creation science, while failing to protect those who choose to teach other theories or who
refuse to teach creation science. A law intended to maximize the comprehensiveness
and effectiveness of science instruction would encourage the teaching of all scientific
theories about human origins. Instead, this Act has the distinctly different purpose
of discrediting evolution by counterbalancing its teaching at every turn with the
teaching of creationism. Pp. 586–589.

(b) The Act impermissibly endorses religion by advancing the religious belief
that a supernatural being created humankind. The legislative history demonstrates

that the term "creation science," as contemplated by the state legislature, embraces this religious teaching. The Act's primary purpose was to change the public school science curriculum to provide persuasive advantage to a particular religious doctrine that rejects the factual basis of evolution in its entirety. Thus, the Act is designed *either* to promote the theory of creation science that embodies a particular religious tenet *or* to prohibit the teaching of a scientific theory disfavored by certain religious sects. In either case, the Act violates the First Amendment. Pp. 589–594.

2. The District Court did not err in granting summary judgment upon a finding that appellants had failed to raise a genuine issue of material fact. Appellants relied on the "uncontroverted" affidavits of scientists, theologians, and an education administrator defining creation science as "origin through abrupt appearance in complex form" and alleging that such a viewpoint constitutes a true scientific theory. The District Court, in its discretion, properly concluded that the post-enactment testimony of these experts concerning the possible technical meanings of the Act's terms would not illuminate the contemporaneous purpose of the state legislature when it passed the Act. None of the persons making the affidavits produced by appellants participated in or contributed to the enactment of the law. Pp. 594–596.

COUNSEL: Wendell R. Bird, Special Assistant Attorney General of Georgia, argued the cause for appellants. . . .

Jay Topkis argued the cause for appellees. . . .

Briefs of *amici curiae* urging reversal were filed for the Catholic League for Religious and Civil . . .; for the Christian Legal Society . . . ; and for Concerned Women for America. . . .

Briefs of *amici curiae* urging affirmance were filed . . . for the American Association of University Professors . . . ; for the American Federation of Teachers . . .; for the American Jewish Congress . . . ; for Americans United for Separation of Church and State . . . ; for the Anti-Defamation League of B'nai B'rith . . .; for the National Academy of . . .; for the New York Committee for Public Education and Religious Liberty . . .; for People for the American Way . . .; for the Spartacist League . . .; and for 72 Nobel Laureates et al . . . .

Briefs of *amici curiae* were filed . . . for Reverend Bill McLean et al. . . .

JUDGES: Brennan, J., delivered the opinion of the Court, in which Marshall, Blackmun, Powell, and Stevens, JJ., joined, and in all but Part II of which O'Connor, J., joined. Powell, J., filed a concurring opinion, in which O'Connor, J., joined, post, p. 597. White, J., filed an opinion concurring in the judgment, post, p. 608. Scalia, J., filed a dissenting opinion, in which Rehnquist, C. J., joined, post, p. 610.

OPINION BY: BRENNAN

OPINION: JUSTICE BRENNAN delivered the opinion of the Court.(t)

The question for decision is whether Louisiana's "Balanced Treatment for Creation-Science and Evolution-Science in Public School Instruction" Act (Creationism Act), La. Rev. Stat. Ann. §§ 17:286.1–17:286.7 (West 1982), is facially invalid as violative of the Establishment Clause of the First Amendment.

I

The Creationism Act forbids the teaching of the theory of evolution in public schools unless accompanied by instruction in "creation science." § 17:286.4A. No school is required to teach evolution or creation science. If either is taught, however, the other must also be taught. *Ibid.* The theories of evolution and creation science are statutorily defined as "the scientific evidences for [creation or evolution] and inferences from those scientific evidences." §§ 17.286.3*(2)* and *(3)*.

Appellees, who include parents of children attending Louisiana public schools, Louisiana teachers, and religious leaders, challenged the constitutionality of the Act in District Court, seeking an injunction and declaratory relief *(1)*. Appellants, Louisiana officials charged with implementing the Act, defended on the ground that the purpose of the Act is to protect a legitimate secular interest, namely, academic freedom *(2)*. Appellees attacked the Act as facially invalid because it violated the Establishment Clause and made a motion for summary judgment. The District Court granted the motion. *Aguillard v. Treen*, 634 F.Supp. 426 (ED La. 1985). The court held that there can be no valid secular reason for prohibiting the teaching of evolution, a theory historically opposed by some religious denominations. The court further concluded that "the teaching of 'creation-science' and 'creationism,' as contemplated by the statute, involves teaching 'tailored to the principles' of a particular religious sect or group of sects." *Id.*, at 427 (citing *Epperson v. Arkansas*, 393 U.S. 97, 106 (1968)). The District Court therefore held that the Creationism Act violated the Establishment Clause either because it prohibited the teaching of evolution or because it required the teaching of creation science with the purpose of advancing a particular religious doctrine.

The court of Appeals affirmed. 765 F.2d 1251 (CA5 1985). The court observed that the statute's avowed purpose of protecting academic freedom was inconsistent with requiring, upon risk of sanction, the teaching of creation science whenever evolution is taught. *Id.*, at 1257. The court found that the Louisiana Legislature's actual intent was "to discredit evolution by counterbalancing its teaching at every turn with the teaching of creationism, a religious belief." *Ibid.* Because the Creationism Act was thus a law furthering a particular religious belief, the Court of Appeals held that the Act violated the Establishment Clause. A suggestion for rehearing en banc was denied over a dissent. 778 F.2d 225 (CA5 1985). We noted probable jurisdiction, 476 U.S. 1103 (1986), and now affirm.

II

The Establishment Clause forbids the enactment of any law "respecting an establishment of religion" *(3)*. The Court has applied a three-pronged test to determine whether legislation comports with the Establishment Clause. First, the legislature must have adopted the law with a secular purpose. Second, the statute's principal or primary effect must be one that neither advances nor inhibits religion. Third, the statute must not result in an excessive entanglement of government with religion. *Lemon v. Kurtzman*, 403 U.S. 602, 612–613 (1971) *(4)*. State action violates the Establishment Clause if it fails to satisfy any of these prongs. . . .

The Court has been particularly vigilant in monitoring compliance with the Establishment Clause in elementary and secondary schools. Families entrust public schools with the education of their children, but condition their trust on the understanding that the classroom will not purposely be used to advance religious views that may conflict with the private beliefs of the student and his or her family. Students in such institutions are impressionable and their attendance is involuntary. . . . The State exerts great authority and coercive power through mandatory attendance requirements, and because of the students' emulation of teachers as role models and the children's susceptibility to peer pressure *(5)*. See *Bethel School Dist. No. 403 v. Fraser, supra*, at 683; *Wallace v. Jaffree, supra*, at 81 (O'CONNOR, J., concurring in judgment). Furthermore, "the public school is at once the symbol of our democracy and the most pervasive means for promoting our common destiny. In no activity of the State is it more vital to keep out divisive forces than in its schools. . . ." *Illinois ex rel. McCollum v. Board of Education*, 333 U.S. 203, 231 (1948) (opinion of Frankfurter, J.).

Consequently, the Court has been required often to invalidate statutes which advance religion in public elementary and secondary schools. See, *e.g.*, *Grand Rapids School Dist. v. Ball, supra* (school district's use of religious school teachers in public schools); *Wallace v. Jaffree, supra* (Alabama statute authorizing moment of silence for school prayer); *Stone v. Graham*, 449 U.S. 39 (1980) (posting copy of Ten Commandments on public classroom wall); *Epperson v. Arkansas*, 393 U.S. 97 (1968) (statute forbidding teaching of evolution); *Abington School Dist. v. Schempp, supra* (daily reading of Bible); *Engel v. Vitale*, 370 U.S. 421, 430 (1962) (recitation of "denominationally neutral" prayer).

Therefore, in employing the three-pronged *Lemon* test, we must do so mindful of the particular concerns that arise in the context of public elementary and secondary schools. We now turn to the evaluation of the Act under the *Lemon* test.

III

Lemon's first prong focuses on the purpose that animated adoption of the Act. "The purpose prong of the Lemon test asks whether government's actual purpose is to endorse or disapprove of religion." *Lynch v. Donnelly*, 465 U.S. 668, 690 (1984) (O'CONNOR, J., concurring). A governmental intention to promote religion is clear when the State enacts a law to serve a religious purpose. This intention may be evidenced by promotion of religion in general, see *Wallace v. Jaffree, supra*, at 52–53 (Establishment Clause protects individual freedom of conscience "to select any religious faith or none at all"), or by advancement of a particular religious belief, e.g., *Stone v. Graham, supra*, at 41 (invalidating requirement to post Ten Commandments, which are "undeniably a sacred text in the Jewish and Christian faiths") (footnote omitted); *Epperson v. Arkansas, supra*, at 106 (holding that banning the teaching of evolution in public schools violates the First Amendment since "teaching and learning" must not "be tailored to the principles or prohibitions of any religious sect or dogma"). If the law was enacted for the purpose of endorsing religion, "no consideration of the second or third criteria [of *Lemon*] is necessary." *Wallace v. Jaffree, supra*, at 56. In this case, appellants have identified no clear secular purpose for the Louisiana Act.

True, the Act's stated purpose is to protect academic freedom. La. Rev. Stat. Ann. § 17:286.2 (West 1982). This phrase might, in common parlance, be understood as referring to enhancing the freedom of teachers to teach what they will. The Court of Appeals, however, correctly concluded that the Act was not designed to further that goal *(6)*. We find no merit in the State's argument that the "legislature may not [have] use[d] the terms 'academic freedom' in the correct legal sense. They might have [had] in mind, instead, a basic concept of fairness; teaching all of the evidence." Tr. of Oral Arg. 60. Even if "academic freedom" is read to mean "teaching all of the evidence" with respect to the origin of human beings, the Act does not further this purpose. The goal of providing a more comprehensive science curriculum is not furthered either by outlawing the teaching of evolution or by requiring the teaching of creation science.

III A

While the Court is normally deferential to a State's articulation of a secular purpose, it is required that the statement of such purpose be sincere and not a sham. . . . As JUSTICE O'CONNOR stated in *Wallace:* "It is not a trivial matter, however, to require that the legislature manifest a secular purpose and omit all sectarian endorsements from its laws. That requirement is precisely tailored to the Establishment Clause's purpose of assuring that Government not intentionally endorse religion or a religious practice." 472 U.S., at 75 (concurring in judgment).

It is clear from the legislative history that the purpose of the legislative sponsor, Senator Bill Keith, was to narrow the science curriculum. During the legislative hearings, Senator Keith stated: "My preference would be that neither [creationism nor evolution] be taught." 2 App. E–621. Such a ban on teaching does not promote—indeed, it undermines—the provision of a comprehensive scientific education.

It is equally clear that requiring schools to teach creation science with evolution does not advance academic freedom. The Act does not grant teachers a flexibility that they did not already possess to supplant the present science curriculum with the presentation of theories, besides evolution, about the origin of life. Indeed, the Court of Appeals found that no law prohibited Louisiana public school teachers from teaching any scientific theory. 765 F.2d, at 1257. As the president of the Louisiana Science Teachers Association testified, "[a]ny scientific concept that's based on established fact can be included in our curriculum already, and no legislation allowing this is necessary." 2 App. E–616. The Act provides Louisiana schoolteachers with no new authority. Thus the stated purpose is not furthered by it. . . .

Furthermore, the goal of basic "fairness" is hardly furthered by the Act's discriminatory preference for the teaching of creation science and against the teaching of evolution *(7)*. While requiring that curriculum guides be developed for creation science, the Act says nothing of comparable guides for evolution. La. Rev. Stat. Ann. § 17:286.7A (West 1982). Similarly, resource services are supplied for creation science but not for evolution. § 17:286.7B. Only "creation scientists" can serve on the panel that supplies the resource services. *Ibid.* The Act forbids school boards to discriminate against anyone who "chooses to be a creation-scientist" or to teach "creationism," but fails to protect those who choose to teach evolution or any other non-creation science theory, or who refuse to teach creation science. § 17:286.4C.

If the Louisiana Legislature's purpose was solely to maximize the comprehensiveness and effectiveness of science instruction, it would have encouraged the teaching of all scientific theories about the origins of humankind *(8)*. But under the Act's requirements, teachers who were once free to teach any and all facets of this subject are now unable to do so. Moreover, the Act fails even to ensure that creation science will be taught, but instead requires the teaching of this theory only when the theory of evolution is taught. Thus we agree with the Court of Appeals' conclusion that the Act does not serve to protect academic freedom, but has the distinctly different purpose of discrediting "evolution by counterbalancing its teaching at every turn with the teaching of creationism. . . ." 765 F.2d, at 1257.

III B

Stone v. Graham invalidated the State's requirement that the Ten Commandments be posted in public classrooms. "The Ten Commandments are undeniably a sacred text in the Jewish and Christian faiths, and no legislative recitation of a supposed secular purpose can blind us to that fact." 449 U.S., at 41 (footnote omitted). As a result, the contention that the law was designed to provide instruction on a "fundamental legal code" was "not sufficient to avoid conflict with the First Amendment." *Ibid.* Similarly *Abington School Dist. v. Schempp* held unconstitutional a statute "requiring the selection and reading at the opening of the school day of verses from the Holy Bible and the recitation of the Lord's Prayer by the students in unison," despite the proffer of such secular purposes as the "promotion of moral values, the contradiction to the materialistic trends of our times, the perpetuation of our institutions and the teaching of literature." 374 U.S., at 223.

As in *Stone* and *Abington*, we need not be blind in this case to the legislature's preeminent religious purpose in enacting this statute. There is a historic and contemporaneous link between the teachings of certain religious denominations and the teaching of evolution *(9)*. It was this link that concerned the Court in *Epperson v. Arkansas*, 393 U.S. 97 (1968), which also involved a facial challenge to a statute regulating the teaching of evolution. In that case, the Court reviewed an Arkansas statute that made it unlawful for an instructor to teach evolution or to use a textbook that referred to this scientific theory. Although the Arkansas antievolution law did not explicitly state its predominate religious purpose, the Court could not ignore that "[t]he statute was a product of the upsurge of 'fundamentalist' religious fervor" that has long viewed this particular scientific theory as contradicting the literal interpretation of the Bible. *Id.*, at 98, 106–107 *(10)*. After reviewing the history of antievolution statutes, the Court determined that "there can be no doubt that the motivation for the [Arkansas] law was the same [as other anti-evolution statutes]: to suppress the teaching of a theory which, it was thought, 'denied' the divine creation of man." *Id.*, at 109. The Court found that there can be no legitimate state interest in protecting particular religions from scientific views "distasteful to them," *id.*, at 107 (citation omitted), and concluded "that the First Amendment does not permit the State to require that teaching and learning must be tailored to the principles or prohibitions of any religious sect or dogma," *id.*, at 106.

These same historic and contemporaneous antagonisms between the teachings of certain religious denominations and the teaching of evolution are present in this case. The preeminent purpose of the Louisiana Legislature was clearly to advance the religious viewpoint that a supernatural being created humankind *(11)*. The term "creation science" was defined as embracing this particular religious doctrine by those responsible for the passage of the Creationism Act. Senator Keith's leading expert on creation science, Edward Boudreaux, testified at the legislative hearings that the theory of creation science included belief in the existence of a supernatural creator. See 1 App. E–421—E–422 (noting that "creation scientists" point to high probability that life was "created by an intelligent mind") (12). Senator Keith also cited testimony from other experts to support the creation-science view that "a creator [was] responsible for the universe and everything in it." (13) 2 App. E–497. The legislative history therefore reveals that the term "creation science," as contemplated by the legislature that adopted this Act, embodies the religious belief that a supernatural creator was responsible for the creation of humankind.

Furthermore, it is not happenstance that the legislature required the teaching of a theory that coincided with this religious view. The legislative history documents that the Act's primary purpose was to change the science curriculum of public schools in order to provide persuasive advantage to a particular religious doctrine that rejects the factual basis of evolution in its entirety. The sponsor of the Creationism Act, Senator Keith, explained during the legislative hearings that his disdain for the theory of evolution resulted from the support that evolution supplied to views contrary to his own religious beliefs. According to Senator Keith, the theory of evolution was consonant with the "cardinal principle[s] of religious humanism, secular humanism, theological liberalism, aetheistism [sic]." 1 App. E–312—E–313; see also 2 App. E–499—E–500. The state senator repeatedly stated that scientific evidence supporting his religious views should be included in the public school curriculum to redress the fact that the theory of evolution incidentally coincided with what he characterized as religious beliefs antithetical to his own (14). The legislation therefore sought to alter the science curriculum to reflect endorsement of a religious view that is antagonistic to the theory of evolution.

In this case, the purpose of the Creationism Act was to restructure the science curriculum to conform with a particular religious viewpoint. Out of many possible science subjects taught in the public schools, the legislature chose to affect the teaching of the one scientific theory that historically has been opposed by certain religious sects. As in *Epperson*, the legislature passed the Act to give preference to those religious groups which have as one of their tenets the creation of humankind by a divine creator. The "overriding fact" that confronted the Court in *Epperson* was "that Arkansas' law selects from the body of knowledge a particular segment which it proscribes for the sole reason that it is deemed to conflict with . . . a particular interpretation of the Book of Genesis by a particular religious group." 393 U.S., at 103. Similarly, the Creationism Act is designed *either* to promote the theory of creation science which embodies a particular religious tenet by requiring that creation science be taught whenever evolution is taught *or* to prohibit the teaching of a scientific theory disfavored by certain religious sects by forbidding the teaching of evolution when creation science is not also taught. The Establishment Clause, however, "forbids *alike* the preference of a religious doctrine *or* the prohibition of theory which is deemed antagonistic to a particular dogma." *Id.*, at 106–107 (emphasis added). Because the primary purpose of the Creationism Act is to advance a particular religious belief, the Act endorses religion in violation of the First Amendment.

We do not imply that a legislature could never require that scientific critiques of prevailing scientific theories be taught. Indeed, the Court acknowledged in *Stone* that its decision forbidding the posting of the Ten Commandments did not mean that no use could ever be made of the Ten Commandments, or that the Ten Commandments played an exclusively religious role in the history of Western Civilization. 449 U.S., at 42. In a similar way, teaching a variety of scientific theories about the origins of humankind to schoolchildren might be validly done with the clear secular intent of enhancing the effectiveness of science instruction. But because the primary purpose of the Creationism Act is to endorse a particular religious doctrine, the Act furthers religion in violation of the Establishment Clause *(15)*.

IV

Appellants contend that genuine issues of material fact remain in dispute, and therefore the District Court erred in granting summary judgment. Federal Rule of Civil Procedure 56(c) provides that summary judgment "shall be rendered forthwith if the pleadings, depositions, answers to interrogatories, and admissions on file, together with the affidavits, if any, show that there is no genuine issue as to any material fact and that the moving party is entitled to a judgment as a matter of law." A court's finding of improper purpose behind a statute is appropriately determined by the statute on its face, its legislative history, or its interpretation by a responsible administrative agency. See, e.g., *Wallace v. Jaffree*, 472 U.S., at 56–61; *Stone v. Graham*, 449 U.S., at 41–42; *Epperson v. Arkansas*, 393 U.S., at 103–109. The plain meaning of the statute's words, enlightened by their context and the contemporaneous legislative history, can control the determination of legislative purpose. See *Wallace v. Jaffree, supra*, at 74 (O'CONNOR, J., concurring in judgment); *Richards v. United States*, 369 U.S. 1, 9 (1962); *Jay v. Boyd*, 351 U.S. 345, 357 (1956). Moreover, in determining the legislative purpose of a statute, the Court has also considered the historical context of the statute, e.g., *Epperson v. Arkansas, supra*, and the specific sequence of events leading to passage of the statute, e.g., *Arlington Heights v. Metropolitan Housing Dev. Corp.*, 429 U.S. 252 (1977).

In this case, appellees' motion for summary judgment rested on the plain language of the Creationism Act, the legislative history and historical context of the Act, the specific sequence of events leading to the passage of the Act, the State Board's report on a survey of school superintendents, and the correspondence between the Act's legislative sponsor and its key witnesses. Appellants contend that affidavits made by two scientists, two theologians, and an education administrator raise a genuine issue of material fact and that summary judgment was therefore barred. The affidavits define creation science as "origin through abrupt appearance in complex form" and allege that such a viewpoint constitutes a true scientific theory. See App. to Brief for Appellants A–7 to A–40.

We agree with the lower courts that these affidavits do not raise a genuine issue of material fact. The existence of "uncontroverted affidavits" does not bar summary judgment *(16)*. Moreover, the postenactment testimony of outside experts is of little use in determining the Louisiana Legislature's purpose in enacting this statute. The Louisiana Legislature did hear and rely on scientific experts in passing the bill *(17)*, but none of the persons making the affidavits produced by the appellants participated in or contributed to the enactment of the law or its implementation *(18)*. The District Court, in its discretion, properly concluded that a Monday-morning "battle of the experts" over possible technical meanings of terms in the statute would not illuminate the contemporaneous purpose of the Louisiana Legislature when it made the law *(19)*. We therefore conclude that the District Court did not err in finding that appellants failed to raise a genuine issue of material fact, and in granting summary judgment *(20)*.

V

The Louisiana Creationism Act advances a religious doctrine by requiring either the banishment of the theory of evolution from public school classrooms or the presentation of a religious viewpoint that rejects evolution in its entirety. The Act violates the Establishment Clause of the First Amendment because it seeks to employ the symbolic and financial support of government to achieve a religious purpose. The judgment of the Court of Appeals therefore is

Affirmed.

CONCUR BY: POWELL; WHITE

Notes:

JUSTICE O'CONNOR joins all but Part II of this opinion

1. Appellants, the Louisiana Governor, the Attorney General, the State Superintendent, the State Department of Education and the St. Tammany Parish School Board, agreed not to implement the Creationism Act pending the final outcome of this litigation. . . .

2. The District Court initially stayed the action pending the resolution of a separate lawsuit brought by the Act's legislative sponsor and others for declaratory and injunctive relief. After the separate suit was dismissed on jurisdictional grounds, *Keith v. Louisiana Department of Education*, 553 F.Supp. 295 (MD La. 1982), the District Court lifted its stay in this case and held that the Creationism Act violated the Louisiana Constitution. The court ruled that the State Constitution grants authority over the public school system to the Board of Elementary and Secondary Education rather than the state legislature. On appeal, the Court of Appeals certified the question to the Louisiana Supreme Court, which found the Creationism Act did not violate the State Constitution, *Aguillard v. Treen*, 440 So. 2d 704 (1983). The Court of Appeals then remanded the case to the District Court to determine whether the Creationism Act violates the Federal Constitution. *Aguillard v. Treen*, 720 F.2d 676 (CA5 1983).

3. The First Amendment states: "Congress shall make no law respecting an establishment of religion. . . ." Under the Fourteenth Amendment, this "fundamental concept of liberty" applies to the States. *Cantwell v. Connecticut*, 310 U.S. 296, 303 (1940).

4. The *Lemon* test has been applied in all cases since its adoption in 1971, except in *Marsh v. Chambers*, 463 U.S. 783 (1983), where the Court held that the Nebraska Legislature's practice of opening a session with a prayer by a chaplain paid by the State did not violate the Establishment Clause. The Court based its conclu-

sion in that case on the historical acceptance of the practice. Such a historical approach is not useful in determining the proper roles of church and state in public schools, since free public education was virtually nonexistent at the time the Constitution was adopted. . . .

5. The potential for undue influence is far less significant with regard to college students who voluntarily enroll in courses. "This distinction warrants a difference in constitutional results." *Abington School Dist. v. Schempp, supra*, at 253 (BRENNAN, J., concurring). Thus, for instance, the Court has not questioned the authority of state colleges and universities to offer courses on religion or theology. . . .

6. The Court of Appeals stated that "[a]cademic freedom embodies the principle that individual instructors are at liberty to teach that which they deem to be appropriate in the exercise of their professional judgment." 765 F.2d, at 1257. But, in the State of Louisiana, courses in public schools are prescribed by the State Board of Education and teachers are not free, absent permission, to teach courses different from what is required. Tr. of Oral Arg. 44–46. "Academic freedom," at least as it is commonly understood, is not a relevant concept in this context. Moreover, as the Court of Appeals explained, the Act "requires, presumably upon risk of sanction or dismissal for failure to comply, the teaching of creation-science whenever evolution is taught. Although states may prescribe public school curriculum concerning science instruction under ordinary circumstances, the compulsion inherent in the Balanced Treatment Act is, on its face, inconsistent with the idea of academic freedom as it is universally understood." 765 F.2d, at 1257 (emphasis in original). The Act actually serves to diminish academic freedom by removing the flexibility to teach evolution without also teaching creation science, even if teachers determine that such curriculum results in less effective and comprehensive science instruction.

7. The Creationism Act's provisions appear among other provisions prescribing the courses of study in Louisiana's public schools. These other provisions, similar to those in other States, prescribe courses of study in such topics as driver training, civics, the Constitution, and free enterprise. None of these other provisions, apart from those associated with the Creationism Act, nominally mandates "equal time" for opposing opinions within a specific area of learning. See, *e.g.*, La. Rev. Stat. Ann. §§ 17:261–17:281 (West 1982 and Supp. 1987).

8. The dissent concludes that the Act's purpose was to protect the academic freedom of students, and not that of teachers. *Post*, at 628. Such a view is not at odds with our conclusion that if the Act's purpose was to provide comprehensive scientific education (a concern shared by students and teachers, as well as parents), that purpose was not advanced by the statute's provisions. *Supra*, at 587.

Moreover, it is astonishing that the dissent, to prove its assertion, relies on a section of the legislation that was eventually deleted by the legislature. Compare § 3702 in 1 App. E–292 (text of section prior to amendment) with La. Rev. Stat. Ann. § 17:286.2 (West 1982). The dissent contends that this deleted section—which was explicitly rejected by the Louisiana Legislature—reveals the legislature's "obviously intended meaning of the statutory terms 'academic freedom.'" *Post*, at 628. Quite to the contrary, Boudreaux, the main expert relied on by the sponsor of the Act, cautioned the legislature that the words "academic freedom" meant "freedom to teach science." 1 App. E–429. His testimony was given at the time the legislature was deciding whether to delete this section of the Act.

9. See *McLean v. Arkansas Bd. of Ed.*, 529 F.Supp. 1255, 1258–1264 (ED Ark. 1982) (reviewing historical and contemporary antagonisms between the theory of evolution and religious movements).

10. The Court evaluated the statute in light of a series of antievolution statutes adopted by state legislatures dating back to the Tennessee statute that was the focus of the celebrated *Scopes* trial in 1925. *Epperson v. Arkansas*, 393 U.S., at 98, 101, n. 8, and 109. The Court found the Arkansas statute comparable to this Tennessee "monkey law," since both gave preference to "'religious establishments which have as one of their tenets or dogmas the instantaneous creation of man.'" *Id.*, at 103, n. 11 (quoting *Scopes v. State*, 154 Tenn. 105, 126, 289 S. W. 363, 369 (1927) (CHAMBLISS, J., concurring)).

11. While the belief in the instantaneous creation of humankind by a supernatural creator may require the rejection of every aspect of the theory of evolution, an individual instead may choose to accept some or all of this scientific theory as compatible with his or her spiritual outlook. See Tr. of Oral Arg. 23–29.

12. Boudreaux repeatedly defined creation science in terms of a theory that supports the existence of a supernatural creator. See, *e.g.*, 2 App. E–501—E–502 (equating creation science with a theory pointing "to conditions of a creator"); 1 App. E–153—E–154 ("Creation . . . requires the direct involvement of a supernatural intelligence"). The lead witness at the hearings introducing the original bill, Luther Sunderland, described creation science as postulating "that everything was created by some intelligence or power external to the universe." *Id.*, at E–9—E–10.

13. Senator Keith believed that creation science embodied this view: "One concept is that a creator however you define a creator was responsible for everything that is in this world. The other concept is that it just evolved." *Id.*, at E–280. Besides Senator Keith, several of the most vocal legislators also revealed their religious motives for supporting the bill in the official legislative history. See, *e.g.*, *id.*, at E–441, E–443 (Sen. Saunders noting that bill was amended so that teachers could refer to the Bible and other religious texts to support the creation-science theory); 2 App. E–561—E–562, E–610 (Rep. Jenkins contending that the existence of God was a scientific fact).

14. See, *e.g.*, 1 App. E–74—E–75 (noting that evolution is contrary to his family's religious beliefs); *id.*, at E–313 (contending that evolution advances religions contrary to his own); *id.*, at E–357 (stating that evolution is "almost a religion" to science teachers); *id.*, at E–418 (arguing that evolution is cornerstone of some religions contrary to his own); 2 App. E–763—E–764 (author of model bill, from which Act is derived, sent copy of the model bill to Senator Keith and advised that "I view this whole battle as one between God and anti-God forces. . . . [I]f evolution is permitted to continue . . . it will continue to be made to appear that a Supreme Being is unnecessary . . .").

15. Neither the District Court nor the Court of Appeals found a clear secular purpose, while both agreed that the Creationism Act's primary purpose was to advance religion. "When both courts below are unable to discern an arguably valid

secular purpose, this Court normally should hesitate to find one." *Wallace v. Jaffree*, 472 U.S., at 66 (POWELL, J., concurring). . . .

17. The experts, who were relied upon by the sponsor of the bill and the legislation's other supporters, testified that creation science embodies the religious view that there is a supernatural creator of the universe. See, *supra*, at 591–592.

18. Appellants contend that the affidavits are relevant because the term "creation science" is a technical term similar to that found in statutes that regulate certain scientific or technological developments. Even assuming, arguendo, that "creation science" is a term of art as represented by appellants, the definition provided by the relevant agency provides a better insight than the affidavits submitted by appellants in this case. In a 1981 survey conducted by the Louisiana Department of Education, the school superintendents in charge of implementing the provisions of the Creationism Act were asked to interpret the meaning of "creation science" as used in the statute. About 75 percent of Louisiana's superintendents stated that they understood "creation science" to be a religious doctrine. 2 App. E–798—E–799. Of this group, the largest proportion of superintendents interpreted creation science, as defined by the Act, to mean the literal interpretation of the Book of Genesis. The remaining superintendents believed that the Act required teaching the view that "the universe was made by a creator." *Id.*, at E–799.

JUSTICE POWELL, with whom JUSTICE O'CONNOR joins, concurring.

I write separately to note certain aspects of the legislative history, and to emphasize that nothing in the Court's opinion diminishes the traditionally broad discretion accorded state and local school officials in the selection of the public school curriculum.

I

This Court consistently has applied the three-pronged test of *Lemon v. Kurtzman*, 403 US 602 (1971), to determine whether a particular state action violates the Establishment Clause of the Constitution (1). See, e.g., *Grand Rapids School Dist. v. Ball*, 473 US 373, 383 (1985) ("We have particularly relied on Lemon in every case involving the sensitive relationship between government and religion in the education of our children"). The first requirement of the *Lemon* test is that the challenged statute have a "secular legislative purpose." *Lemon v. Kurtzman, supra*, at 612. See *Committee for Public Education & Religious Liberty v. Nyquist*, 413 US 756, 773 (1973). If no valid secular purpose can be identified, then the statute violates the Establishment Clause.

I A

"The starting point in every case involving construction of a statute is the language itself." . . . The Balanced Treatment for Creation-Science and Evolution-Science Act (Act or Balanced Treatment Act), La. Rev. Stat. Ann. § 17:286.1 *et seq.* (West 1982), provides in part:

"[P]ublic schools within [the] state shall give balanced treatment to creation-science and to evolution-science. Balanced treatment of these two models shall be given in classroom lectures taken as a whole for each course, in textbook materials taken as a whole for each course, in library materials taken as a whole for the sciences and taken as a whole for the humanities, and in other educational programs in public schools, to the extent that such lectures, textbooks, library materials, or educational programs deal in any way with the subject of the origin of man, life, the earth, or the universe. When creation or evolution is taught, each shall be taught as a theory, rather than as proven scientific fact." § 17:286.4(A). . . .

A religious purpose alone is not enough to invalidate an act of a state legislature. The religious purpose must predominate. See *Wallace v. Jaffree*, 472 US 38, 56 (1985); *id.*, at 64 (POWELL, J., concurring); *Lynch v. Donnelly*, 465 U.S. 668, 681, n. 6 (1984). The Act contains a statement of purpose: to "protec[t] academic freedom." § 17:286.2. This statement is puzzling. Of course, the "academic freedom" of teachers to present information in public schools, and students to receive it, is broad. But it necessarily is circumscribed by the Establishment Clause. "Academic freedom" does not encompass the right of a legislature to structure the public school curriculum in order to advance a particular religious belief. *Epperson v. Arkansas*, 393 U.S. 97, 106 (1968). Nevertheless, I read this statement in the Act as rendering the purpose of the statute at least ambiguous. Accordingly, I proceed to review the legislative history of the Act.

I B

In June 1980, Senator Bill Keith introduced Senate Bill 956 in the Louisiana Legislature. The stated purpose of the bill was to "assure academic freedom by requiring the teaching of the theory of creation ex nihilo in all public schools where the theory of evolution is taught." 1 App. E–1 (2) The bill defined the "theory of creation ex nihilo" as "the belief that the origin of the elements, the galaxy, the solar system, of life, of all the species of plants and animals, the origin of man, and the origin of all things and their processes and relationships were created ex nihilo and fixed by God." *Id.*, at E–1a—E–1b. This theory was referred to by Senator Keith as "scientific creationism." Id., at E–2.

While a Senate committee was studying scientific creationism, Senator Keith introduced a second draft of the bill, requiring balanced treatment of "evolution-science" and "creation-science." *Id.*, at E–108. Although the Keith bill prohibited "instruction in any religious doctrine or materials," *id.*, at E–302, it defined "creation-science" to include

"the scientific evidences and related inferences that indicate (a) sudden creation of the universe, energy, and life from nothing; (b) the insufficiency of mutation and natural selection in bringing about development of all living kinds from a single organism; (c) changes only within fixed limits or originally created kinds of plants and animals; (d) separate ancestry for man and apes; (e) explanation of the earth's geology by catastrophism, including the occurrence of a worldwide flood; and (f) a relatively recent inception of the earth and living kinds." *Id.*, at E–298—E–299.

Significantly, the model Act on which the Keith bill relied was also the basis for a similar statute in Arkansas. See *McLean v. Arkansas Board of Education*, 529 F.Supp. 1255 (ED Ark. 1982). The District Court in *McLean* carefully examined this model Act, particularly the section defining creation science, and concluded that "[b]oth [its] concepts and wording . . . convey an inescapable religiosity." Id., at 1265. The court found that "[t]he ideas of [this section] are not merely similar to the literal interpretation of Genesis; they are identical and parallel to no other story of creation." Ibid.

The complaint in *McLean* was filed on May 27, 1981. On May 28, the Louisiana Senate committee amended the Keith bill to delete the illustrative list of scientific evidences. . . .

The legislature then held hearings on the amended bill that became the Balanced Treatment Act under review. The principal creation scientist to testify in support of the Act was Dr. Edward Boudreaux. He did not elaborate on the nature of creation science except to indicate that the "scientific evidences" of the theory are "the objective information of science [that] point[s] to conditions of a creator." 2 id., at E–501—E–502. He further testified that the recognized creation scientists in the United States, who "numbe[r] something like a thousand [and] who hold doctorate and masters degrees in all areas of science," are affiliated with either or both the Institute for Creation Research and the Creation Research Society. Id., at E–503—E–504. . . .

The Institute for Creation Research is an affiliate of the Christian Heritage College in San Diego, California. The Institute was established to address the "urgent need for our nation to return to belief in a personal, omnipotent Creator, who has a purpose for His creation and to whom all people must eventually give account." 1 id., at E–197. A goal of the Institute is "a revival of belief in special creation as the true explanation of the origin of the world." Therefore, the Institute currently is working on the "development of new methods for teaching scientific creationism in public schools." . . . A member must subscribe to the following statement of belief: "The Bible is the written word of God, and because it is inspired throughout, all of its assertions are historically and scientifically true." 2 id., at E–583. To study creation science at the CRS, a member must accept "that the account of origins in Genesis is a factual presentation of simple historical truth." Ibid. *(3)*.

I C

. . . My examination of the language and the legislative history of the Balanced Treatment Act confirms that the intent of the Louisiana Legislature was to promote a particular religious belief. The legislative history of the Arkansas statute prohibiting the teaching of evolution examined in *Epperson v. Arkansas*, 393 U.S. 97 (1968), was strikingly similar to the legislative history of the Balanced Treatment Act. In *Epperson*, the Court found:

"It is clear that fundamentalist sectarian conviction was and is the law's reason for existence. Its antecedent, Tennessee's 'monkey law,' candidly stated its purpose: to make it unlawful 'to teach any theory that denies the story of the Divine Creation of man as taught in the Bible, and to teach instead that man has descended from a lower order of animals.' Perhaps the sensational publicity attendant upon the Scopes trial induced Arkansas to adopt less explicit language. It eliminated Tennessee's reference to 'the story of the Divine creation of man' as taught in the Bible, but there is no doubt that the motivation for the law was the same: to suppress the teaching of a theory which, it was thought, 'denied' the divine creation of man." Id., at 107–109 (footnotes omitted).

Here, it is clear that religious belief is the Balanced Treatment Act's "reason for existence." The tenets of creation science parallel the Genesis story of creation *(4)*, and this is a religious belief. "[N]o legislative recitation of a supposed secular purpose can blind us to that fact." *Stone v. Graham*, 449 U.S. 39, 41 (1980). Although the Act as finally enacted does not contain explicit reference to its religious purpose, there is no indication in the legislative history that the deletion of "creation ex nihilo" and the four primary tenets of the theory was intended to alter the purpose of teaching creation science. Instead, the statements of purpose of the sources of creation science in the United States make clear that their purpose is to promote a religious belief. I find no persuasive evidence in the legislative history that the legislature's purpose was any different. The fact that the Louisiana Legislature purported to add information to the school curriculum rather than detract from it as in *Epperson* does not affect my analysis. Both legislatures acted with the unconstitutional purpose of structuring the public school curriculum to make it compatible with a particular religious belief: the "divine creation of man."

That the statute is limited to the scientific evidences supporting the theory does not render its purpose secular. In reaching its conclusion that the Act is unconstitutional, the Court of Appeals "[did] not deny that the underpinnings of creationism may be supported by scientific evidence." 765 F.2d 1251, 1256 (1985). And there is no need to do so. Whatever the academic merit of particular subjects or theories, the Establishment Clause limits the discretion of state officials to pick and choose among them for the purpose of promoting a particular religious belief. The language of the statute and its legislative history convince me that the Louisiana Legislature exercised its discretion for this purpose in this case.

II

Even though I find Louisiana's Balanced Treatment Act unconstitutional, I adhere to the view "that the States and locally elected school boards should have the responsibility for determining the educational policy of the public schools." *Board of Education, Island Trees Union Free School Dist. No. 26 v. Pico*, 457 U.S. 853, 893 (1982) (POWELL, J., dissenting). A decision respecting the subject matter to be taught in public schools does not violate the Establishment Clause simply because the material to be taught "'happens to coincide or harmonize with the tenets of some or all religions.'" *Harris v. McRae*, 448 U.S. 297, 319 (1980) (*quoting McGowan v. Maryland*, 366 U.S. 420, 442 (1961)). In the context of a challenge under the Establishment Clause, interference with the decisions of these authorities is warranted only when the purpose for their decisions is clearly religious. . . .

III

In sum, I find that the language and the legislative history of the Balanced Treatment Act unquestionably demonstrate that its purpose is to advance a particular religious belief. Although the discretion of state and local authorities over public school curricula is broad, " *Epperson v. Arkansas*, 393 U.S., at 106. Accordingly, I concur in the opinion of the Court and its judgment that the Balanced Treatment Act violates the Establishment Clause of the Constitution.

Notes:

1. As the Court recognizes, *ante*, at 583, n. 4, the one exception to this consis-

tent application of the *Lemon* test is *Marsh v. Chambers*, 463 US 783 (1983).

2. Creation *"ex nihilo"* means creation "from nothing" and has been found to be an "inherently religious concept." *McLean v. Arkansas Board of Education*, 529 F.Supp. 1255, 1266 (ED Ark. 1982). The District Court in *McLean* found:

"The argument that creation from nothing in [§] 4(a)(1) [of the substantially similar Arkansas Balanced Treatment Act] does not involve a supernatural deity has no evidentiary or rational support. To the contrary, 'creation out of nothing' is a concept unique to Western religions. In traditional Western religious thought, the conception of a creator of the world is a conception of God. Indeed, creation of the world 'out of nothing' is the ultimate religious statement because God is the only actor." *Id.*, at 1265.

3. The District Court in *McLean* noted three other elements of the CRS statement of belief to which members must subscribe:

"'[i] All basic types of living things, including man, were made by direct creative acts of God during Creation Week as described in Genesis. Whatever biological changes have occurred since Creation have accomplished only changes within the original created kinds. [ii] The great Flood described in Genesis, commonly referred to as the Noachian Deluge, was an historical event, world-wide in its extent and effect. [iii] Finally, we are an organization of Christian men of science, who accept Jesus Christ as our Lord and Savior. The account of the special creation of Adam and Eve as one man and one woman, and their subsequent Fall into sin, is the basis for our belief in the necessity of a Savior for all mankind. Therefore, salvation can come only thru [*sic*] accepting Jesus Christ as our Savior.'" 529 F.Supp., at 1260, n. 7.

4. After hearing testimony from numerous experts, the District Court in *McLean* concluded that "the parallels between [the definition section of the model Act] and Genesis are quite specific." *Id.*, at 1265, n. 19. It found the concepts of "sudden creation from nothing," a worldwide flood of divine origin, and "kinds" to be derived from Genesis; "relatively recent inception" to mean "an age of the earth from 6,000 to 10,000 years" and to be based "on the genealogy of the Old Testament using the rather astronomical ages assigned to the patriarchs"; and the "separate ancestry of man and ape" to focus on "the portion of the theory of evolution which Fundamentalists find most offensive." *Ibid.* (citing *Epperson v. Arkansas*, 393 U.S. 97 (1968)).

JUSTICE WHITE, concurring in the judgment.

As it comes to us, this is not a difficult case. Based on the historical setting and plain language of the Act both courts construed the statutory words "creation science" to refer to a religious belief, which the Act required to be taught if evolution was taught. In other words, the teaching of evolution was conditioned on the teaching of a religious belief. Both courts concluded that the state legislature's primary purpose was to advance religion and that the statute was therefore unconstitutional under the Establishment Clause.

We usually defer to courts of appeals on the meaning of a state statute, especially when a district court has the same view. Of course, we have the power to disagree, and the lower courts in a particular case may be plainly wrong. But if the meaning ascribed to a state statute by a court of appeals is a rational construction of the statute, we normally accept it. . . .We do so because we believe "that district courts and courts of appeals are better schooled in and more able to interpret the laws of their respective States." . . .

Here, the District Judge, relying on the terms of the Act, discerned its purpose to be the furtherance of a religious belief, and a panel of the Court of Appeals agreed. Of those four judges, two are Louisianians. I would accept this view of the statute. Even if as an original matter I might have arrived at a different conclusion based on a reading of the statute and the record before us, I cannot say that the two courts below are so plainly wrong that they should be reversed. Rehearing en banc was denied by an 8–7 vote, the dissenters expressing their disagreement with the panel decision. The disagreement, however, was over the construction of the Louisiana statute, particularly the assessment of its purpose, and offers no justification for departing from the usual rule counseling against *de novo* constructions of state statutes.

If the Court of Appeals' construction is to be accepted, so is its conclusion that under our prior cases the Balanced Treatment Act is unconstitutional because its primary purpose is to further a religious belief by imposing certain requirements on the school curriculum. Unless, therefore, we are to reconsider the Court's decisions interpreting the Establishment Clause, I agree that the judgment of the Court of Appeals must be affirmed.

JUSTICE SCALIA, with whom the chief justice joins, dissenting.

Even if I agreed with the questionable premise that legislation can be invalidated under the Establishment Clause on the basis of its motivation alone, without regard to its effects, I would still find no justification for today's decision. The Louisiana legislators who passed the "Balanced Treatment for Creation-Science and Evolution-Science Act" (Balanced Treatment Act), La. Rev. Stat. Ann. §§ 17:286.1–17:286.7 (West 1982), each of whom had sworn to support the Constitution (1) were well aware of the potential Establishment Clause problems and considered that aspect of the legislation with great care. After seven hearings and several months of study, resulting in substantial revision of the original proposal, they approved the Act overwhelmingly and specifically articulated the secular purpose they meant it to serve. Although the record contains abundant evidence of the sincerity of that purpose (the only issue pertinent to this case), the Court today holds, essentially on the basis of "its visceral knowledge regarding what *must* have motivated the legislators," 778 F.2d 225, 227 (CA5 1985) (Gee, J., dissenting) (emphasis added), that the members of the Louisiana Legislature knowingly violated their oaths and then lied about it. I dissent. Had requirements of the Balanced Treatment Act that are not apparent on its face been clarified by an interpretation of the Louisiana Supreme Court, or by the manner of its implementation, the Act might well be found unconstitutional; but the question of its constitutionality cannot rightly be disposed of on the gallop, by impugning the motives of its supporters.

I

This case arrives here in the following posture: The Louisiana Supreme Court has never been given an opportunity to interpret the Balanced Treatment Act, State officials have never attempted to implement it, and it has never been the subject of a full evidentiary hearing. We can only guess at its meaning. We know that it forbids instruction in either "creation-science" or "evolution-science" without instruction in the other, § 17:286.4A, but the parties are sharply divided over what creation science consists of. Appellants insist that it is a collection of educationally valuable scientific data that has been censored from classrooms by an embarrassed scientific establishment. Appellees insist it is not science at all but thinly veiled religious doctrine. Both interpretations of the intended meaning of that phrase find considerable support in the legislative history.

At least at this stage in the litigation, it is plain to me that we must accept appellants' view of what the statute means. To begin with, the statute itself *defines* "creation-science" as "the *scientific evidences* for creation and inferences from those *scientific evidences.*" § 17:286.3(2) (emphasis added). If, however, that definition is not thought sufficiently helpful, the means by which the Louisiana Supreme Court will give the term more precise content is quite clear—and again, at this stage in the litigation, favors the appellants' view. "Creation science" is unquestionably a "term of art," see Brief for 72 Nobel Laureates et al. as *Amici Curiae* 20, and thus, under Louisiana law, is "to be interpreted according to [its] received meaning and acceptation with the learned in the art, trade or profession to which [it] refer[s]." La. Civ. Code Ann., Art. 15 (West 1952) *(2)*. The only evidence in the record of the "received meaning and acceptation" of "creation science" is found in five affidavits filed by appellants. In those affidavits, two scientists, a philosopher, a theologian, and an educator, all of whom claim extensive knowledge of creation science, swear that it is essentially a collection of scientific data supporting the theory that the physical universe and life within it appeared suddenly and have not changed substantially since appearing. . . . These experts insist that creation science is a strictly scientific concept that can be presented without religious reference. . . . At this point, then, we must assume that the Balanced Treatment Act does *not* require the presentation of religious doctrine.

Nothing in today's opinion is plainly to the contrary, but what the statute means and what it requires are of rather little concern to the Court. Like the Court of Appeals, 765 F.2d 1251, 1253, 1254 (CA5 1985), the Court finds it necessary to consider only the motives of the legislators who supported the Balanced Treatment Act, *ante*, at 586, 593–594, 596. After examining the statute, its legislative history, and its historical and social context, the Court holds that the Louisiana Legislature acted without "a secular legislative purpose" and that the Act therefore fails the "purpose" prong of the three-part test set forth in *Lemon v. Kurtzman*, 403 U.S. 602, 612 (1971). As I explain below, *infra*, at 636–640, I doubt whether that "purpose" requirement of *Lemon* is a proper interpretation of the Constitution; but even if it were, I could not agree with the Court's assessment that the requirement was not satisfied here.

This Court has said little about the first component of the *Lemon* test. Almost invariably, we have effortlessly discovered a secular purpose for measures challenged under the Establishment Clause, typically devoting no more than a sentence or two to the matter. . . .

Nevertheless, a few principles have emerged from our cases, principles which should, but to an unfortunately large extent do not, guide the Court's application of *Lemon* today. It is clear, first of all, that regardless of what "legislative purpose" may mean in other contexts, for the purpose of the *Lemon* test it means the "actual" motives of those responsible for the challenged action. The Court recognizes this, see *ante*, at 585, as it has in the past, see, *e.g., Witters v. Washington Dept. of Services for Blind, supra*, at 486; *Wallace v. Jaffree, supra*, at 56. Thus, if those legislators who supported the Balanced Treatment Act in fact acted with a "sincere" secular purpose, *ante*, at 587, the Act survives the first component of the *Lemon* test, regardless of whether that purpose is likely to be achieved by the provisions they enacted. . . .

It is important to stress that the purpose forbidden by *Lemon* is the purpose to "advance religion." . . .Our cases in no way imply that the Establishment Clause forbids legislators merely to act upon their religious convictions. We surely would not strike down a law providing money to feed the hungry or shelter the homeless if it could be demonstrated that, but for the religious beliefs of the legislators, the funds would not have been approved. Also, political activism by the religiously motivated is part of our heritage. Notwithstanding the majority's implication to the contrary, *ante*, at 589–591, we do not presume that the sole purpose of a law is to advance religion merely because it was supported strongly by organized religions or by adherents of particular faiths. See *Walz v. Tax Comm'n of New York City, supra*, at 670; cf. *Harris v. McRae*, 448 U.S. 297, 319–320 (1980). To do so would deprive religious men and women of their right to participate in the political process. Today's religious activism may give us the Balanced Treatment Act, but yesterday's resulted in the abolition of slavery, and tomorrow's may bring relief for famine victims.

Similarly, we will not presume that a law's purpose is to advance religion merely because it "'happens to coincide or harmonize with the tenets of some or all religions,'" *Harris v. McRae, supra*, at 319 (quoting *McGowan v. Maryland*, 366 U.S. 420, 442 (1961)), or because it benefits religion, even substantially. We have, for example, turned back Establishment Clause challenges to restrictions on abortion funding, *Harris v. McRae, supra*, and to Sunday closing laws, *McGowan v. Maryland, supra*, despite the fact that both "agre[e] with the dictates of [some] Judaeo-Christian religions," *id.*, at 442. "In many instances, the Congress or state legislatures conclude that the general welfare of society, wholly apart from any religious considerations, demands such regulation." *Ibid.* On many past occasions we have had no difficulty finding a secular purpose for governmental action far more likely to advance religion than the Balanced Treatment Act. See, *e.g., Mueller v. Allen*, 463 U.S., at 394–395 (tax deduction for expenses of religious education); *Wolman v. Walter*, 433 U.S., at 236 (plurality opinion) (aid to religious schools); *Meek v. Pittenger*, 421 U.S., at 363 (same); *Committee for Public Education & Religious Liberty v. Nyquist*, 413 U.S., at 773 (same); *Lemon v. Kurtzman*, 403 U.S., at 613 (same); *Walz v. Tax Comm'n of New York City, supra*, at 672 (tax exemption for church property); *Board of Education v. Allen, supra*, at 243 (textbook loans to students in religious schools). Thus, the fact that creation science coincides with the beliefs of certain religions, a fact upon which the majority relies heavily, does not itself justify invalidation of the Act. . . .

II

II A

We have relatively little information upon which to judge the motives of those who supported the Act. About the only direct evidence is the statute itself and transcripts of the seven committee hearings at which it was considered. Unfortunately, several of those hearings were sparsely attended, and the legislators who were present revealed little about their motives. We have no committee reports, no floor debates, no remarks inserted into the legislative history, no statement from the Governor, and no postenactment statements or testimony from the bill's sponsor or any other legislators. Cf. *Wallace v. Jaffree*, 472 U.S., at 43, 56–57. Nevertheless, there is ample evidence that the majority is wrong in holding that the Balanced Treatment Act is without secular purpose.

At the outset, it is important to note that the Balanced Treatment Act did not fly through the Louisiana Legislature on wings of fundamentalist religious fervor— which would be unlikely, in any event, since only a small minority of the State's citizens belong to fundamentalist religious denominations. See B. Quinn, H. Anderson, M. Bradley, P. Goetting, & P. Shriver, Churches and Church Membership in the United States 16 (1982). The Act had its genesis (so to speak) in legislation introduced by Senator Bill Keith in June 1980. . . .

Senator Keith's statements before the various committees that considered the bill hardly reflect the confidence of a man preaching to the converted. He asked his colleagues to "keep an open mind" and not to be "biased" by misleading characterizations of creation science. *Id.*, at E–33. He also urged them to "look at this subject on its merits and not on some preconceived idea." *Id.*, at E–34; see also 2 *id.*, at E–491. Senator Keith's reception was not especially warm. Over his strenuous objection, the Senate Committee on Education voted 5–1 to amend his bill to deprive it of any force; as amended, the bill merely gave teachers permission to balance the teaching of creation science or evolution with the other. . . .

The legislators understood that Senator Keith's bill involved a "unique" subject, 1 *id.*, at E–106 (Rep. M. Thompson), and they were repeatedly made aware of its potential constitutional problems. . . . Although the Establishment Clause, including its secular purpose requirement, was of substantial concern to the legislators, they eventually voted overwhelmingly in favor of the Balanced Treatment Act: The House approved it 71–19 (with 15 members absent), 2 *id.*, at E–716—E–722; the Senate 26–12 (with all members present), *id.*, at E–741—E–744. The legislators specifically designated the protection of "academic freedom" as the purpose of the Act. La. Rev. Stat. Ann. § 17:286.2 (West 1982). We cannot accurately assess whether this purpose is a "sham," *ante*, at 587, until we first examine the evidence presented to the legislature far more carefully than the Court has done.

Before summarizing the testimony of Senator Keith and his supporters, I wish to make clear that I by no means intend to endorse its accuracy. But my views (and the views of this Court) about creation science and evolution are (or should be) beside the point. Our task is not to judge the debate about teaching the origins of life, but to ascertain what the members of the Louisiana Legislature believed. The vast majority of them voted to approve a bill which explicitly stated a secular purpose;

what is crucial is not their *wisdom* in believing that purpose would be achieved by the bill, but their *sincerity* in believing it would be.

Most of the testimony in support of Senator Keith's bill came from the Senator himself and from scientists and educators he presented, many of whom enjoyed academic credentials that may have been regarded as quite impressive by members of the Louisiana Legislature. To a substantial extent, their testimony was devoted to lengthy, and, to the layman, seemingly expert scientific expositions on the origin of life. . . .

Senator Keith and his witnesses testified essentially as set forth in the following numbered paragraphs:

(1) There are two and only two scientific explanations for the beginning of life *(3)*—evolution and creation science. . . . Both posit a theory of the origin of life and subject that theory to empirical testing. Evolution posits that life arose out of inanimate chemical compounds and has gradually evolved over millions of years. Creation science posits that all life forms now on earth appeared suddenly and relatively recently and have changed little. Since there are only two possible explanations of the origin of life, any evidence that tends to disprove the theory of evolution necessarily tends to prove the theory of creation science, and vice versa. For example, the abrupt appearance in the fossil record of complex life, and the extreme rarity of transitional life forms in that record, are evidence for creation science. . . .

(2) The body of scientific evidence supporting creation science is as strong as that supporting evolution. In fact, it may be *stronger. Id.*, at E–214 (Young statement); *id.*, at E–310 (Sen. Keith); *id.*, at E–416 (Sen. Keith); 2 *id.*, at E–492 (Sen. Keith). The evidence for evolution is far less compelling than we have been led to believe. Evolution is not a scientific "fact," since it cannot actually be observed in a laboratory. Rather, evolution is merely a scientific theory or "guess." 1 *id.*, at E–20—E–21 (Morris); *id.*, at E–85 (Ward); *id.*, at E–100 (Reiboldt); *id.*, at E–328—E–329 (Boudreaux); 2 *id.*, at E–506 (Boudreaux). It is a very bad guess at that. The scientific problems with evolution are so serious that it could accurately be termed a "myth." . . .

(3) Creation science is educationally valuable. Students exposed to it better understand the current state of scientific evidence about the origin of life. 1 *id.*, at E–19 (Sunderland); *id.*, at E–39 (Sen. Keith); *id.*, at E–79 (Kalivoda); *id.*, at E–308 (Sen. Keith); 2 *id.*, at E–513—E–514 (Morris). Those students even have a better understanding of evolution. 1 *id.*, at E–19 (Sunderland). Creation science can and should be presented to children without any religious content. . . .

(4) Although creation science is educationally valuable and strictly scientific, it is now being censored from or misrepresented in the public schools. . . . Teachers have been brainwashed by an entrenched scientific establishment composed almost exclusively of scientists to whom evolution is like a "religion." These scientists discriminate against creation scientists so as to prevent evolution's weaknesses from being exposed. . . .

(5) The censorship of creation science has at least two harmful effects. First, it deprives students of knowledge of one of the two scientific explanations for the origin of life and leads them to believe that evolution is proven fact; thus, their educa-

tion suffers and they are wrongly taught that science has proved their religious beliefs false. Second, it violates the Establishment Clause. The United States Supreme Court has held that secular humanism is a religion. *Id.*, at E–36 (Sen. Keith) (referring to *Torcaso v. Watkins*, 367 U.S. 488, 495, n. 11 (1961)); 1 App. E–418 (Sen. Keith); 2 *id.*, at E–499 (Sen. Keith). Belief in evolution is a central tenet of that religion. 1 *id.*, at E–282 (Sen. Keith); *id.*, at E–312—E–313 (Sen. Keith); *id.*, at E–317 (Sen. Keith); *id.*, at E–418 (Sen. Keith); 2 *id.*, at E–499 (Sen. Keith). Thus, by censoring creation science and instructing students that evolution is fact, public school teachers are now advancing religion in violation of the Establishment Clause. . . .

Senator Keith repeatedly and vehemently denied that his purpose was to advance a particular religious doctrine. At the outset of the first hearing on the legislation, he testified: "We are not going to say today that you should have some kind of religious instructions in our schools. . . . We are not talking about religion today. . . . I am not proposing that we take the Bible in each science class and read the first chapter of Genesis." 1 *id.*, at E–35. At a later hearing, Senator Keith stressed: "[T]o . . . teach religion and disguise it as creationism . . . is not my intent. My intent is to see to it that our textbooks are not censored." *Id.*, at E–280. He made many similar statements throughout the hearings. See, *e.g.*, *id.*, at E–41; *id.*, at E–282; *id.*, at E–310; *id.*, at E–417; see also *id.*, at E–44 (Boudreaux); *id.*, at E–80 (Kalivoda).

We have no way of knowing, of course, how many legislators believed the testimony of Senator Keith and his witnesses. But in the absence of evidence to the contrary *(4)*, we have to assume that many of them did. Given that assumption, the Court today plainly errs in holding that the Louisiana Legislature passed the Balanced Treatment Act for exclusively religious purposes.

II B

Even with nothing more than this legislative history to go on, I think it would be extraordinary to invalidate the Balanced Treatment Act for lack of a valid secular purpose. Striking down a law approved by the democratically elected representatives of the people is no minor matter. "The cardinal principle of statutory construction is to save and not to destroy. We have repeatedly held that as between two possible interpretations of a statute, by one of which it would be unconstitutional and by the other valid, our plain duty is to adopt that which will save the act." *NLRB v. Jones & Laughlin Steel Corp.*, 301 U.S. 1, 30 (1937). . . . The Louisiana Legislature explicitly set forth its secular purpose ("protecting academic freedom") in the very text of the Act. La. Rev. Stat. § 17:286.2 (West 1982). We have in the past repeatedly relied upon or deferred to such expressions . . . .

The Court seeks to evade the force of this expression of purpose by stubbornly misinterpreting it, and then finding that the provisions of the Act do not advance that misinterpreted purpose, thereby showing it to be a sham. The Court first surmises that "academic freedom" means "enhancing the freedom of teachers to teach what they will," ante, at 586—even though "academic freedom" in that sense has little scope in the structured elementary and secondary curriculums with which the Act is concerned. Alternatively, the Court suggests that it might mean "maximiz[ing] the comprehensiveness and effectiveness of science instruction," *ante*, at 588—though that is an exceedingly strange interpretation of the words, and one that is refuted on the very face of the statute. See § 17:286.5. Had the Court devoted to this central question of the meaning of the legislatively expressed purpose a small fraction of the research into legislative history that produced its quotations of religiously motivated statements by individual legislators, it would have discerned quite readily what "academic freedom" meant: *students' freedom from indoctrination.* The legislature wanted to ensure that students would be free to decide for themselves how life began, based upon a fair and balanced presentation of the scientific evidence—that is, to protect "the right of each [student] voluntarily to determine what to believe (and what not to believe) free of any coercive pressures from the State." *Grand Rapids School District v. Ball*, 473 U.S., at 385. The legislature did not care *whether* the topic of origins was taught; it simply wished to ensure that *when* the topic was taught, students would receive "'all of the evidence.'" *Ante* at 586 (quoting Tr. of Oral Arg. 60).

As originally introduced, the "purpose" section of the Balanced Treatment Act read: "This Chapter is enacted for the purposes of protecting academic freedom . . . of *students* . . . and assisting *students* in their search for truth." 1 App. E–292 (emphasis added). Among the proposed findings of fact contained in the original version of the bill was the following: "Public school instruction in only evolution-science . . . *violates the principle of academic freedom because it denies students a choice between scientific models and instead indoctrinates them in evolution science alone.*" *Id.*, at E–295 (emphasis added) *(5)*. Senator Keith unquestionably understood "academic freedom" to mean "freedom from indoctrination." See *id.*, at E–36 (purpose of bill is "to protect academic freedom by providing student choice"); *id.*, at E–283 (purpose of bill is to protect "academic freedom" by giving students a "choice" rather than subjecting them to "indoctrination on origins").

If one adopts the obviously intended meaning of the statutory term "academic freedom," there is no basis whatever for concluding that the purpose they express is a "sham." *Ante*, at 587. To the contrary, the Act pursues that purpose plainly and consistently. It requires that, whenever the subject of origins is covered, evolution be "taught as a theory, rather than as proven scientific fact" and that scientific evidence inconsistent with the theory of evolution (viz., "creation science") be taught as well. La. Rev. Stat. Ann. § 17:286.4A (West 1982). Living up to its title of *"Balanced Treatment* for Creation-Science and Evolution-Science Act," § 17.286.1, it treats the teaching of creation the same way. It does *not* mandate instruction in creation science, § 17:286.5; *forbids* teachers to present creation science "as proven scientific fact," § 17:286.4A; and bans the teaching of creation science unless the theory is (to use the Court's terminology) "discredit[ed] ' . . . at every turn'" with the teaching of evolution. *Ante*, at 589 (quoting 765 F.2d, at 1257). It surpasses understanding how the Court can see in this a purpose "to restructure the science curriculum to conform with a particular religious viewpoint," *ante*, at 593, "to provide a persuasive advantage to a particular religious doctrine," *ante*, at 592, "to promote the theory of creation science which embodies a particular religious tenet," *ante*, at 593, and "to endorse a particular religious doctrine," *ante*, at 594.

The Act's reference to "creation" is not convincing evidence of religious purpose. The Act defines creation science as "*scientific evidenc[e]*," § 17:286.3(2) (emphasis added), and Senator Keith and his witnesses repeatedly stressed that the subject can and should be presented without religious content. See *supra*, at 623. We have no basis on the record to conclude that creation science need be anything other than a collection of scientific data supporting the theory that life abruptly appeared on earth. See n. 4, *supra.* Creation science, its proponents insist, no more must explain *whence* life came than evolution must explain whence came the inanimate materials from which it says life evolved. But even if that were not so, to posit a past creator is not to posit the eternal and personal God who is the object of religious veneration. Indeed, it is not even to posit the "*unmoved* mover" hypothesized by Aristotle and other notably nonfundamentalist philosophers. Senator Keith suggested this when he referred to "a creator *however you define a creator.*" 1 App. E–280 (emphasis added).

The Court cites three provisions of the Act which, it argues, demonstrate a "discriminatory preference for the teaching of creation science" and no interest in "academic freedom." *Ante*, at 588. First, the Act prohibits discrimination only against creation scientists and those who teach creation science. § 17:286.4C. Second, the Act requires local school boards to develop and provide to science teachers "a curriculum guide on presentation of creation-science." § 17:286.7A. Finally, the Act requires the Governor to designate seven creation scientists who shall, upon request, assist local school boards in developing the curriculum guides. § 17:286.7B. But none of these provisions casts doubt upon the sincerity of the legislators' articulated purpose of "academic freedom"—unless, of course, one gives that term the obviously erroneous meanings preferred by the Court. The Louisiana legislators had been told repeatedly that creation scientists were scorned by most educators and scientists, who themselves had an almost religious faith in evolution. It is hardly surprising, then, that in seeking to achieve a balanced, "nonindoctrinating" curriculum, the legislators protected from discrimination only those teachers whom they thought were *suffering* from discrimination. (Also, the legislators were undoubtedly aware of *Epperson v. Arkansas*, 393 U.S. 97 (1968), and thus could quite reasonably have concluded that discrimination against evolutionists was already prohibited.) The two provisions respecting the development of curriculum guides are also consistent with "academic freedom" as the Louisiana Legislature understood the term. Witnesses had informed the legislators that, because of the hostility of most scientists and educators to creation science, the topic had been censored from or badly misrepresented in elementary and secondary school texts. In light of the unavailability of works on creation science suitable for classroom use (a fact appellees concede, see Brief for Appellees 27, 40) and the existence of ample materials on evolution, it was entirely reasonable for the legislature to conclude that science teachers attempting to implement the Act would need a curriculum guide on creation science, but not on evolution, and that those charged with developing the guide would need an easily accessible group of creation scientists. Thus, the provisions of the Act of so much concern to the Court *support* the conclusion that the legislature acted to advance "academic freedom."

The legislative history gives ample evidence of the sincerity of the Balanced Treatment Act's articulated purpose. Witness after witness urged the legislators to support the Act so that students would not be "indoctrinated" but would instead be free to decide for themselves, based upon a fair presentation of the scientific evidence, about the origin of life. See, *e.g.*, 1 App. E–18 (Sunderland) ("all that we are advocating" is presenting "scientific data" to students and "letting [them] make up their own mind[s]"); *id.*, at E–19—E–20 (Sunderland) (Students are now being "indoctrinated" in evolution through the use of "censored school books. . . . All that we are asking for is [the] open unbiased education in the classroom . . . your students deserve"); *id.*, at E–21 (Morris) ("A student cannot [make an intelligent decision about the origin of life] unless he is well informed about both [evolution and creation science]"); *id.*, at E–22 (Sanderford) ("We are asking very simply [that] . . . creationism [be presented] alongside . . . evolution and let people make their own mind[s] up"); *id.*, at E–23 (Young) (the bill would require teachers to live up to their "obligation to present all theories" and thereby enable "students to make judgments themselves"); *id.*, at E–44 (Boudreaux) ("Our intention is truth and as a scientist, I am interested in truth"); *id.*, at E–60—E–61 (Boudreaux) ("[W]e [teachers] are guilty of a lot of brainwashing. . . . We have a duty to . . . [present the] truth" to students "at all levels from grade school on through the college level"); *id.*, at E–79 (Kalivoda) ("This [hearing] is being held I think to determine whether children will benefit from freedom of information or if they will be handicapped educationally by having little or no information about creation"); *id.*, at E–80 (Kalivoda) ("I am not interested in teaching religion in schools. . . . I am interested in the truth and [students] having the opportunity to hear more than one side"); *id.*, at E–98 (Reiboldt) ("The students have a right to know there is an alternate creationist point of view. They have a right to know the scientific evidences which suppor[t] that alternative"); *id.*, at E–218 (Young statement) (passage of the bill will ensure that "communication of scientific ideas and discoveries may be unhindered"); 2 *id.*, at E–514 (Morris) ("Are we going to allow [students] to look at evolution, to look at creationism, and to let one or the other stand or fall on its own merits, or will we by failing to pass this bill . . . deny students an opportunity to hear another viewpoint?"); *id.*, at E–516—E–517 (Young) ("We want to give the children here in this state an equal opportunity to see both sides of the theories"). Senator Keith expressed similar views. See, *e.g.*, 1 *id.*, at E–36; *id.*, at E–41; *id.*, at E–280; *id.*, at E–283.

Legislators other than Senator Keith made only a few statements providing insight into their motives, but those statements cast no doubt upon the sincerity of the Act's articulated purpose. The legislators were concerned primarily about the manner in which the subject of origins was presented in Louisiana schools—specifically, about whether scientifically valuable information was being censored and students misled about evolution. Representatives Cain, Jenkins, and F. Thompson seemed impressed by the scientific evidence presented in support of creation science. See 2 *id.*, at E–530 (Rep. F. Thompson); *id.*, at E–533 (Rep. Cain); *id.*, at E–613 (Rep. Jenkins). At the first study commission hearing, Senator Picard and Representative M. Thompson questioned Senator Keith about Louisiana teachers' treatment of evolution and creation science. See 1 *id.*, at E–71—E–74. At the close of the hearing, Representative M. Thompson told the audience:

"We as members of the committee will also receive from the staff information of what is currently being taught in the Louisiana public schools. We really want to see [it]. I . . . have no idea in what manner [biology] is presented and in what manner the creationist theories [are] excluded in the public school[s]. We want to look at what the status of the situation is." *Id.*, at E–104. . . .

It is undoubtedly true that what prompted the legislature to direct its attention to the misrepresentation of evolution in the schools (rather than the inaccurate presentation of other topics) was its awareness of the tension between evolution and the religious beliefs of many children. But even appellees concede that a valid secular purpose is not rendered impermissible simply because its pursuit is prompted by concern for religious sensitivities. Tr. of Oral Arg. 43, 56. If a history teacher falsely told her students that the bones of Jesus Christ had been discovered, or a physics teacher that the Shroud of Turin had been conclusively established to be inexplicable on the basis of natural causes, I cannot believe (despite the majority's implication to the contrary, see *ante*, at 592–593) that legislators or school board members would be constitutionally prohibited from taking corrective action, simply because that action was prompted by concern for the religious beliefs of the misinstructed students.

In sum, even if one concedes, for the sake of argument, that a majority of the Louisiana Legislature voted for the Balanced Treatment Act partly in order to foster (rather than merely eliminate discrimination against) Christian fundamentalist beliefs, our cases establish that that alone would not suffice to invalidate the Act, so long as there was a genuine secular purpose as well. We have, moreover, no adequate basis for disbelieving the secular purpose set forth in the Act itself, or for concluding that it is a sham enacted to conceal the legislators' violation of their oaths of office. I am astonished by the Court's unprecedented readiness to reach such a conclusion, which I can only attribute to an intellectual predisposition created by the facts and the legend of *Scopes v. State*, 154 Tenn. 105, 289 S. W. 363 (1927)—an instinctive reaction that any governmentally imposed requirements bearing upon the teaching of evolution must be a manifestation of Christian fundamentalist repression. In this case, however, it seems to me the Court's position is the repressive one. The people of Louisiana, including those who are Christian fundamentalists, are quite entitled, as a secular matter, to have whatever scientific evidence there may be against evolution presented in their schools, just as Mr. Scopes was entitled to present whatever scientific evidence there was for it. Perhaps what the Louisiana Legislature has done is unconstitutional because there *is* no such evidence, and the scheme they have established will amount to no more than a presentation of the Book of Genesis. But we cannot say that on the evidence before us in this summary judgment context, which includes ample uncontradicted testimony that "creation science" is a body of scientific knowledge rather than revealed belief. *Infinitely* less can we say (or should we say) that the scientific evidence for evolution is so conclusive that no one could be gullible enough to believe that there is any real scientific evidence to the contrary, so that the legislation's stated purpose must be a lie. Yet that illiberal judgment, that *Scopes*-in-reverse, is ultimately the basis on which the Court's facile rejection of the Louisiana Legislature's purpose must rest. . . .

Because I believe that the Balanced Treatment Act had a secular purpose, which is all the first component of the *Lemon* test requires, I would reverse the judgment of the Court of Appeals and remand for further consideration.

III

. . .We have said essentially the following: Government may not act with the purpose of advancing religion, except when forced to do so by the Free Exercise Clause (which is now and then); or when eliminating existing governmental hostility to religion (which exists sometimes); or even when merely accommodating governmentally uninhibited religious practices, except that at some point (it is unclear where) intentional accommodation results in the fostering of religion, which is of course unconstitutional. . . .

Notes:

1. Article VI, cl. 3, of the Constitution provides that "the Members of the several State Legislatures . . . shall be bound by Oath or Affirmation, to support this Constitution."

2. Thus the popular dictionary definitions cited by JUSTICE POWELL, *ante*, at 598–599 (concurring opinion), and appellees, see Brief for Appellees 25, 26; Tr. of Oral Arg. 32, 34, are utterly irrelevant, as are the views of the school superintendents cited by the majority, *ante*, at 595, n. 18. Three-quarters of those surveyed had "[n]o" or "[l]imited" knowledge of "creation-science theory," and not a single superintendent claimed "[e]xtensive" knowledge of the subject. 2 App. E–798.

3. Although creation scientists and evolutionists also disagree about the origin of the physical universe, both proponents and opponents of Senator Keith's bill focused on the question of the beginning of life.

4. Although appellees and amici dismiss the testimony of Senator Keith and his witnesses as pure fantasy, they did not bother to submit evidence of that to the District Court, making it difficult for us to agree with them. The State, by contrast, submitted the affidavits of two scientists, a philosopher, a theologian, and an educator, whose academic credentials are rather impressive. See App. to Juris. Statement A–17—A–18 (Kenyon); *id.*, at A–36 (Morrow); *id.*, at A–39—A–40 (Miethe); *id.*, at A–46—A–47 (Most); *id.*, at A–49 (Clinkert). Like Senator Keith and his witnesses, the affiants swear that evolution and creation science are the only two scientific explanations for the origin of life, see *id.*, at A–19—A–20 (Kenyon); *id.*, at A–38 (Morrow); *id.*, at A–41 (Miethe); that creation science is strictly scientific, see *id.*, at A–18 (Kenyon); *id.*, at A–36 (Morrow); *id.*, at A–40—A–41 (Miethe); *id.*, at A–49 (Clinkert); that creation science is simply a collection of scientific data that supports the hypothesis that life appeared on earth suddenly and has changed little, see *id.*, at A–19 (Kenyon); *id.*, at A–36 (Morrow); *id.*, at A–41 (Miethe); that hundreds of respected scientists believe in creation science, see *id.*, at A–20 (Kenyon); that evidence for creation science is as strong as evidence for evolution, see *id.*, at A–21 (Kenyon); *id.*, at A–34—A–35 (Kenyon); *id.*, at A–37—A–38 (Morrow); that creation science is educationally valuable, see *id.*, at A–19 (Kenyon); *id.*, at A–36 (Morrow); *id.*, at A–38—A–39 (Morrow); *id.*, at A–49 (Clinkert); that creation science

can be presented without religious content, see *id.*, at A–19 (Kenyon); *id.*, at A–35 (Kenyon); *id.*, at A–36 (Morrow); *id.*, at A–40 (Miethe); *id.*, at A–43—A–44 (Miethe); *id.*, at A–47 (Most); *id.*, at A–49 (Clinkert); and that creation science is now censored from classrooms while evolution is misrepresented as proven fact, see *id.*, at A–20 (Kenyon); *id.*, at A–35 (Kenyon); *id.*, at A–39 (Morrow); *id.*, at A–50 (Clinkert). It is difficult to conclude on the basis of these affidavits—the only substantive evidence in the record—that the laymen serving in the Louisiana Legislature must have disbelieved Senator Keith or his witnesses.

5. The majority finds it "astonishing" that I would cite a portion of Senator Keith's original bill that was later deleted as evidence of the legislature's understanding of the phrase "academic freedom." *Ante*, at 589, n. 8. What is astonishing is the majority's implication that the deletion of that section deprives it of value as a clear indication of what the phrase meant—there and in the other, retained, sections of the bill. The Senate Committee on Education deleted most of the lengthy "purpose" section of the bill (with Senator Keith's consent) because it resembled legislative "findings of fact," which, committee members felt, should generally not be incorporated in legislation. The deletion had absolutely nothing to do with the manner in which the section described "academic freedom." See 1 App. E–314—E–320; *id.*, at E–440—E–442.

6. As the majority recognizes, *ante*, at 592, Senator Keith sincerely believed that "secular humanism is a bona fide religion," 1 App. E–36; see also *id.*, at E–418; 2 *id.*, at E–499, and that "evolution is the cornerstone of that religion," 1 *id.*, at E–418; see also *id.*, at E–282; *id.*, at E–312—E–313; *id.*, at E–317; 2 *id.*, at E–499. The Senator even told his colleagues that this Court had "held" that secular humanism was a religion. See 1 *id.*, at E–36, *id.*, at E–418; 2 *id.*, at E–499. (In *Torcaso v. Watkins*, 367 U.S. 488, 495, n. 11 (1961), we did indeed refer to "Secular Humanism" as a "religio[n].") Senator Keith and his supporters raised the "religion" of secular humanism *not*, as the majority suggests, to explain the source of their "disdain for the theory of evolution," *ante*, at 592, but to convince the legislature that the State of Louisiana was *violating the Establishment Clause* because its teachers were misrepresenting evolution as fact and depriving students of the information necessary to question that theory. 1 App. E–2—E–4 (Sen. Keith); *id.*, at E–36—E–37, E–39 (Sen. Keith); *id.*, at E–154—E–155 (Boudreaux paper); *id.*, at E–281—E–282 (Sen. Keith); *id.*, at E–317 (Sen. Keith); 2 *id.*, at E–499—E–500 (Sen. Keith). The Senator repeatedly urged his colleagues to pass his bill to *remedy* this Establishment Clause violation by ensuring state neutrality in religious matters, see, *e.g.*, 1 *id.*, at E–36; *id.*, at E–39; *id.*, at E–313, surely a permissible purpose under *Lemon.* Senator Keith's argument may be questionable, but nothing in the statute or its legislative history gives us reason to doubt his sincerity or that of his supporters.

7. Professor Choper summarized our school aid cases thusly:

"[A] provision for therapeutic and diagnostic health services to parochial school pupils by public employees is invalid if provided *in* the parochial school, but not if offered at a neutral site, even if in a mobile unit adjacent to the parochial school. Reimbursement to parochial schools for the expense of administering teacher-prepared tests required by state law is invalid, but the state may reimburse parochial schools for the expense of administering state-prepared tests. The state may lend school textbooks to parochial school pupils because, the Court has explained, the books can be checked in advance for religious content and are 'self-policing'; but the state may not lend other seemingly self-policing instructional items such as tape recorders and maps. The state may pay the cost of bus transportation to parochial schools, which the Court has ruled are 'permeated' with religion; but the state is forbidden to pay for field trip transportation visits 'to governmental, industrial, cultural, and scientific centers designed to enrich the secular studies of students.'" Choper, The Religion Clauses of the First Amendment: Reconciling the Conflict, 41 U. Pitt. L. Rev. 673, 680–681 (1980) (footnotes omitted).

Since that was written, more decisions on the subject have been rendered, but they leave the theme of chaos securely unimpaired. See, *e.g.*, *Aguilar v. Felton*, 473 U.S. 402 (1985); *Grand Rapids School District v. Ball*, 473 U.S. 373 (1985).

WEBSTER V. LENOX SCHOOL DISTRICT NO. 122

In 1990, Ray Webster was teaching social science in junior high in New Lenox, IL. Webster included creationism and fundamentalist Christianity in his course. When various people complained, Webster's superintendent instructed him to adhere to the approved curriculum and stop teaching creationism. Webster, believing that his rights were being violated, sued. The court's ruling, which was based largely on Edwards v. Aguillard, was unequivocal. Here's part of the decision:

In the United States Court of Appeals for the Seventh Circuit
No. 89–2317
Ray Webster, *Plaintiff-Appellant*,
v.
New Lenox School District No. 122 and Alex M. Martino, individually and as Superintendent of New Lenox School District No. 122, Defendants-Appellees.
Argued February 27, 1990; Decided November 6, 1990.
Before Flaum, Easterbrook, and Ripple, Circuit Judges.

On appeal from the United States District Court for the Northern District of Illinois, Eastern Division. No. 88 C 2828; George M. Marovich, Judge.

Ripple, *Circuit Judge.*

Summary:

Ray Webster sought injunctive and declaratory relief based on his claim that the New Lenox School District violated his first and fourteenth amendment rights by prohibiting him from teaching a nonevolutionary theory of creation in the classroom. He *appeals* the dismissal of his complaint for failure to state a claim. For the following reasons, we affirm the judgment of the district court.

I

Background

The district court dismissed Mr. Webster's suit for failure to state a claim upon which relief can be granted. See Fed. R. Civ. P. 12(b)(6). The grant of a motion to dismiss is, of course, reviewed *de novo*. . . . It is well settled that, when reviewing the grant of a motion to dismiss, we must assume the truth of all well-pleaded factual allegations and make all possible inferences in favor of the plaintiff. . . .

A complaint should not be dismissed "unless it appears beyond doubt that the plaintiff can prove no set of facts in support of his claim which would entitle him to relief." *Conley v. Gibson*, 355 U. S. 41, 45–46 (1957). This obligation is especially serious when, as here, we deal with allegations involving the freedom of expression protected by the first amendment. See *Stewart v. District of Columbia Armory Bd.*, 863 F.2d 1013, 1017–18 (D.C. Cir. 1988) ("where government action is challenged on first amendment grounds, a court should be especially 'unwilling to decide the legal questions posed by the parties without a more thoroughly developed record of proceedings in which the parties have an opportunity to prove those disputed factual assertions upon which they rely'") (quoting *City of Los Angeles v. Preferred Communications*, 476 U.S. 488, 494 (1986)). . . . With these constraints in mind, we set forth the pertinent facts.

A. Facts

Ray Webster teaches social studies at the Oster-Oakview Junior High School in New Lenox, Illinois. In the spring of 1987, a student in Mr. Webster's social studies class complained that Mr. Webster's teaching methods violated principles of separation between church and state. In addition to the student, both the American Civil Liberties Union and the Americans United for the Separation of Church and State objected to Mr. Webster's teaching practices. Mr. Webster denied the allegations. On July 31, 1987, the New Lenox school board (school board), through its superintendent, advised Mr. Webster by letter that he should restrict his classroom instruction to the curriculum and refrain from advocating a particular religious viewpoint.

Believing the superintendent's letter vague, Mr. Webster asked for further clarification in a letter dated September 4, 1987. In this letter, Mr. Webster also set forth his teaching methods and philosophy. Mr. Webster stated that the discussion of religious issues in his class was only for the purpose of developing an open mind in his students. For example, Mr. Webster explained that he taught nonevolutionary theories of creation to rebut a statement in the social studies textbook indicating that the world is over four billion years old. Therefore, his teaching methods in no way violated the doctrine of separation between church and state. Mr. Webster contended that, at most, he encouraged students to explore alternative viewpoints.

The superintendent responded to Mr. Webster's letter on October 13, 1987. The superintendent reiterated that advocacy of a Christian viewpoint was prohibited, although Mr. Webster could discuss objectively the historical relationship between church and state when such discussions were an appropriate part of the curriculum. Mr. Webster was specifically instructed not to teach creation science, because the teaching of this theory had been held by the federal courts to be religious advocacy.*(1)*

Mr. Webster brought suit, principally arguing that the school board's prohibitions constituted censorship in violation of the first and fourteenth amendments. In particular, Mr. Webster argued that the school board should permit him to teach a nonevolutionary theory of creation in his social studies class.

B. The District Court

The district court concluded that Mr. Webster did not have a first amendment right to teach creation science in a public school. The district court began by noting that, in deciding whether to grant the school district's motion to dismiss, the court was entitled to consider the letters between the superintendent and Mr. Webster because Mr. Webster had attached these letters to his complaint as exhibits. In particular, the district court determined that the October 13, 1987, letter was critical; this letter clearly indicated exactly what conduct the school district sought to proscribe. Specifically, the October 13 letter directed that Mr. Webster was prohibited from teaching creation science and was admonished not to engage in religious advocacy. Furthermore, the superintendent's letter explicitly stated that Mr. Webster could discuss objectively the historical relationship between church and state.

The district court noted that a school board generally has wide latitude in setting the curriculum, provided the school board remains within the boundaries established by the constitution. Because the establishment clause prohibits the enactment of any law "respecting an establishment of religion," the school board could not enact a curriculum that would inject religion into the public schools. U.S. Const. amend. I. Moreover, the district court determined that the school board had the responsibility to ensure that the establishment clause was not violated.

The district court then framed the issue as whether Mr. Webster had the right to teach creation science. Relying on *Edwards v. Aguillard*, 482 U.S. 578 (1987), the district court determined that teaching creation science would constitute religious advocacy in violation of the first amendment and that the school board correctly prohibited Mr. Webster from teaching such material. The court further noted:

Webster has not been prohibited from teaching any nonevolutionary theories or from teaching anything regarding the historical relationship between church and state. Martino's [the superintendent] letter of October 13, 1987, makes it clear that the religious advocacy of Webster's teaching is prohibited and nothing else. Since no other constraints were placed on Webster's teaching, he had no basis for his complaint and it must fail.

Webster v. New Lenox School Dist., Mem. op, at 4–5 (N.D. Ill. May 25, 1989). Accordingly, the district court dismissed the complaint.*(2)*

II

Analysis

At the outset, we note that a narrow issue confronts us: Mr. Webster asserts that he has a first amendment right to determine the curriculum content of his junior high school class. He does not, however, contest the general authority of the school board, acting through its executive agent, the superintendent, to set the curriculum.

This case does not present a novel issue. We have already confirmed the right of those authorities charged by state law with curriculum development to require the obedience of subordinate employees, including the classroom teacher. Judge Wood expressed the controlling principle succinctly in *Palmer v. Board of Educ.*, 603 F.2d 1271, 1274 (7th Cir. 1979), cert. denied, 444 U.S. 1026 (1980), when he wrote:

Parents have a vital interest in what their children are taught. Their representatives have in general prescribed a curriculum. There is a compelling state interest in the choice and adherence to a suitable curriculum for the benefit of our young citizens and society. It cannot be left to individual teachers to teach what they please.

Yet Mr. Webster, in effect, argues that the school board must permit him to teach what he pleases. The first amendment is "not a teacher license for uncontrolled expression at variance with established curricular content." *Id.* at 1273. See also *Clard v. Holmes*, 474 F.2d 928 (7th Cir.) (holding that individual teacher has no constitutional prerogative to override the judgment of his superiors as to proper course content), cert. denied, 411 U.S. 972 (1973). Clearly, the school board had the authority and the responsibility to ensure that Mr. Webster did not stray from the established curriculum by injecting religious advocacy into the classroom. "Families entrust public schools with the education of their children, but condition their trust on the understanding that the classroom will not purposely be used to advance religious views that may conflict with the private beliefs of the student and his or her family." *Edwards v. Aguillard*, 482 U.S. 578, 584 (1987).

A junior high school student's immature stage of intellectual development imposes a heightened responsibility upon the school board to control the curriculum. See *Zykan v. Warsaw Community School Corp.*, 631 F.2d 1300, 1304 (7th Cir. 1980). We have noted that secondary school teachers occupy a unique position for influencing secondary school students, thus creating a concomitant power in school authorities to choose the teachers and regulate their pedagogical methods. *Id.* "The state exerts great authority and coercive power through mandatory attendance requirements, and because of the students' emulation of teachers as role models and the children's susceptibility to peer pressure." *Edwards*, 482 U.S. at 584 (footnote omitted).

It is true that the discretion lodged in school boards is not completely unfettered. For example, school boards may not fire teachers for random classroom comments. *Zykan*, 631 F.2d at 1305. Moreover, school boards may not require instruction in a religiously inspired dogma to the exclusion of other points of view. *Epperson v. Arkansas*, 393 U.S. 97, 106 (1968). This complaint contains no allegation that school authorities have imposed "a pall of orthodoxy" on the offerings of the entire public school curriculum, *Keyishian v. Board of Regents*, 385 U.S. 589, 603 (1967), "which might either implicate the state in the propagation of an identifiable religious creed or otherwise impair permanently the student's ability to investigate matters that arise in the natural course of intellectual inquiry." *Zykan*, 631 F2d at 1306. Therefore, this case does not present the issue of whether, or under what circumstances, a school board may completely eliminate material from the curriculum. *Cf. Zykan*, 631 F.2d at 1305–06 (school may not flatly prohibit teachers from mentioning relevant material). Rather, the principle that an individual teacher has no right to ignore the directives of duly appointed education authorities is dispositive of this case. Today, we decide only that, given the allegations of the complaint, the school board has successfully navigated the narrow channel between impairing intellectual inquire and propagating a religious creed.

Here, the superintendent concluded that the subject matter taught by Mr. Webster created serious establishment clause concerns. *Cf. Edwards*, 482 U.S. at 583–84 ("The Court has been particularly vigilant in monitoring compliance with the Establishment Clause in elementary and secondary schools."); *Epperson*, 393 U.S. at 106 (school may not adopt programs that aid or oppose any religion). As the district court noted, the superintendent's letter is directed to this concern. "[E]ducators do not offend the First Amendment . . . so long as their actions are reasonably related to legitimate pedagogical concerns." *Hazelwood School Dist. v. Kuhlmier*, 484 U.S 260, 278 (1988). Given the school board's important pedagogical interest in establishing the curriculum and legitimate concern with possible establishment clause violations, the school board's prohibition on the teaching of creation science to junior high students was appropriate. See *Palmer v. Board of Educ.*, 603 F.2d 1274 (7th Cir. 1979) (school board has "compelling" interest in setting the curriculum). Accordingly, the district court properly dismissed Mr. Webster's complaint.

Conclusion

For the foregoing reasons, the judgement of the district is affirmed.

Notes

1. In *Edwards V. Aguillard*, 482 U.S. 578, 592 (1987), the Supreme Court determined that creation science, as defined in the Louisiana act in question, was a nonevolutionary theory of origin that "embodies the religious belief that a supernatural creator was responsible for the creation of mankind."

2. The District Court also addressed the claims of another plaintiff, Matthew Dunne. Mr. Dunne was apparently a student in Mr. Webster's social studies class. The district court determined that Mr. Dunne failed to state a cognizable first amendment claim because his desire to obtain information about creation science was outweighed by the school district's compelling interest in avoiding establishment clause violations and in protecting the first amendment rights of other students. Mr. Dunne is not a party to this appeal.

PELOZA V. CAPISTRANO UNIFIED SCHOOL DISTRICT

In the early 1990s, John Peloza was teaching creationism in his biology courses at Capistrano High School in Orange County, CA. When parents and teachers complained, Peloza was reprimanded and told to stop. Peloza believed that his rights were being violated and sued the school district. The court's decision addressed how a school district's right to set a curriculum relates to a teacher's right to religious freedom.

JOHN E. PELOZA V. CAPISTRANO UNIFIED SCHOOL DISTRICT
Nos. 92–55228, 92–55644.
United States Court of Appeals, Ninth Circuit.
Argued and Submitted June 9, 1993. Filed July 25, 1994.
Opinion Withdrawn Sept. 20, 1994. Decided Oct. 4, 1994.
SUMMARY

High school biology teacher brought action against school district, its board of trustees, and various personnel at high school, challenging school district's requirement that he teach evolutionism, as well as school district order barring him from discussing his religious beliefs with students. The United States District Court, Central District of California, David W. Williams, J., 782 F.Supp. 1412, dismissed and awarded attorney fees to school district. Teacher appealed. The Court of Appeals held that: (1) teacher failed to state claim for violation of establishment clause of First Amendment in connection with school district's requiring him to teach evolution, i.e., that higher life forms evolved from lower ones; (2) school district's restriction on teacher's right of free speech in prohibiting teacher from talking with students about religion during school day, including times when he was not actually teaching class, was justified by school district's interest in avoiding establishment clause violation; (3) teacher's allegations of injury to his reputation as result of allegedly defamatory statements made to and about him were insufficient to support claim for deprivation of liberty interest under § 1983; but (4) teacher's complaint was not entirely frivolous, precluding award of costs and attorney fees under Rule 11 and § 1988.

Affirmed in part; reversed in part.

John E. Peloza, Plaintiff-Appellant Cyrus Zal, Folsom, CA, for plaintiff-appellant.

Appeal from the United States District Court for the Central District of California.

Before: FLETCHER, POOLE AND THOMPSON, Circuit Judges.

Per Curiam; Partial Concurrence and Partial Dissent by Judge POOLE.

PER CURIAM:

John E. Peloza is a high school biology teacher. He sued the Capistrano Unified School District and various individuals connected with the school district under 42 U.S.C. § 1983. He alleges in his complaint that the school district requires him to teach "evolutionism" and that evolutionism is a religious belief system. He alleges this requirement violates his rights under the (1) Free Speech Clause of the First Amendment; (2) Establishment Clause of the First Amendment; (3) Due Process Clause of the Fourteenth Amendment; and (4) Equal Protection Clause of the Fourteenth Amendment.*(1)*

He also alleges the defendants conspired to violate these constitutional rights and attempted by harassment and intimidation to force him to teach evolutionism. He alleges they did this because they have a class-based animus against practicing Christians, a class of which he is a member, in violation of 42 U.S.C. § 1985(3).

He also alleges state law claims for violation of California's Tom Bane Civil Rights Act, Cal.Civ.Code § 52.1 (which provides a cause of action for interference with an individual's enjoyment of rights secured by the United States or California Constitution or by federal or state law), and for intentional infliction of emotional distress.

The district court dismissed the federal claims for failure to state a claim upon which relief could be granted. Fed.R.Civ.P. 12(b)(6). The court then dismissed the state claims for lack of jurisdiction. The court also determined that the action was frivolous. Relying on Rule 11 of the Federal Rules of Civil Procedure and 18 U.S.C.

§ 1988, the court ordered Peloza and his attorney to pay approximately $32,000 to the defendants for their attorney fees and costs.

Peloza appeals. We have jurisdiction under 28 U.S.C. § 1291. We affirm, except as to attorneys' fees.

THE ALLEGATIONS OF THE COMPLAINT

The following summarizes the allegations of Peloza's complaint:

Peloza is a biology teacher in a public high school, and is employed by the Capistrano Unified School District. He is being forced by the defendants (the school district, its trustees and individual teachers and others) to proselytize his students to a belief in "evolutionism" "under the guise of [its being] a valid scientific theory." Evolutionism is an historical, philosophical and religious belief system, but not a valid scientific theory. Evolutionism is one of "two world views on the subject of the origins of life and of the universe." The other is "creationism" which also is a "religious belief system." "The belief system of evolutionism is based on the assumption that life and the universe evolved randomly and by chance and with no Creator involved in the process. The world view and belief system of creationism is based on the assumption that a Creator created all life and the entire universe." Peloza does not wish "to promote either philosophy or belief system in teaching his biology class." "The general acceptance of . . . evolutionism in academic circles does not qualify it or validate it as a scientific theory." Peloza believes that the defendants seek to dismiss him due to his refusal to teach evolutionism. His first amendment rights have been abridged by interference with his right "to teach his students to differentiate between a philosophical, religious belief system on the one hand and a true scientific theory on the other."

Peloza further alleges he has been forbidden to discuss religious matters with students the entire time that he is on the school campus even if a conversation is initiated by a student and the discussion is outside of class time.

He also alleges that the defendants have conspired to destroy and damage his professional reputation, career and position as a public school teacher. He has been reprimanded in writing for proselytizing students and teaching religion in the classroom. His inquiries as to whether he is being required to teach evolution as "fact" or "as the only valid scientific theory" have not been answered directly. He has not taught creationism in his classroom. He has been wrongly accused in the school newspaper and in the public press of teaching religion in his science class. He has been harassed by the defendant teachers and has received a formal written reprimand from defendant Thomas R. Anthony, the school principal, wrongly accusing him of proselytizing his students and teaching religion in the classroom, directing him to teach evolution as the only valid scientific theory, and forbidding him from teaching creationism as a valid scientific theory. Anthony further directed him not to discuss religion or attempt to convert students to Christianity while on campus. He has been criticized in a petition signed by faculty members for threatening litigation over the rights of faculty members to speak fully to the news media and each other. . . .

DISCUSSION
I. The Section 1983 Claim
A. The Establishment Clause
[1] . . .

Peloza's complaint alleges that the school district has violated the Establishment Clause "by pressuring and requiring him to teach evolutionism, a religious belief system, as a valid scientific theory." Complaint at 19–20. Evolutionism, according to Peloza, "postulates that the 'higher' life forms . . . evolved from the 'lower' life forms . . . and that life itself 'evolved' from non-living matter." Id. at 2. It is therefore "based on the assumption that life and the universe evolved randomly and by chance and with no Creator involved in the process." Id. at 1. Peloza claims that evolutionism is not a valid scientific theory because it is based on events which "occurred in the non-observable and non-recreatable past and hence are not subject to scientific observation." Id. at 3. Finally, in his appellate brief he alleges that the school district is requiring him to teach evolutionism not just as a theory, but rather as a fact.

[2] Peloza's complaint is not entirely consistent. In some places he seems to advance the patently frivolous claim that it is unconstitutional for the school district to require him to teach, as a valid scientific theory, that higher life forms evolved from lower ones. At other times he claims the district is forcing him to teach evolution as fact. Although possibly dogmatic or even wrong, such a requirement would not transgress the establishment clause if "evolution" simply means that higher life forms evolved from lower ones. . . .

[3] . . . Charitably read, Peloza's complaint at most makes this claim: the school district's actions establish a state-supported religion of evolutionism, or more generally of "secular humanism." See Complaint at 24, 20. According to Peloza's complaint, all persons must adhere to one of two religious belief systems concerning "the origins of life and of the universe:" evolutionism, or creationism. Id. at 2. Thus, the school district, in teaching evolutionism, is establishing a state-supported "religion."

We reject this claim because neither the Supreme Court, nor this circuit, has ever held that evolutionism or secular humanism are "religions" for Establishment Clause purposes. Indeed, both the dictionary definition of religion(4) and the clear weight of the case law(5) are to the contrary. The Supreme Court has held unequivocally that while the belief in a divine creator of the universe is a religious belief, the scientific theory that higher forms of life evolved from lower forms is not. *Edwards v. Aguillard.* 482 U.S. 578, 107 S.Ct. 2573, 96 L.Ed.2d 510 (1987) (holding unconstitutional, under Establishment Clause, Louisiana's "Balanced Treatment for Creation-Science and Evolution-Science in Public School Instruction Act").

Peloza would have us accept his definition of "evolution" and "evolutionism" and impose his definition on the school district as its own, a definition that cannot be found in the dictionary, in the Supreme Court cases, or anywhere in the common understanding of the words. Only if we define "evolution" and "evolutionism" as does Peloza as a concept that embraces the belief that the universe came into existence without a Creator might he make out a claim. This we need not do. To say red is green or black is white does not make it so. Nor need we for the purposes of a

12(b)(6) motion accept a made-up definition of "evolution." Nowhere does Peloza point to anything that conceivably suggests that the school district accepts anything other than the common definition of "evolution" and "evolutionism." It simply required him as a biology teacher in the public schools of California to teach "evolution." Peloza nowhere says it required more.

The district court dismissed his claim, stating:

Since the evolutionist theory is not a religion, to require an instructor to teach this theory is not a violation of the Establishment Clause. . . . Evolution is a scientific theory based on the gathering and studying of data, and modification of new data. It is an established scientific theory which is used as the basis for many areas of science. As scientific methods advance and become more accurate, the scientific community will revise the accepted theory to a more accurate explanation of life's origins. Plaintiffs assertions that the teaching of evolution would be a violation of the Establishment Clause is unfounded.

Id. at 12–13. We agree.

B. Free Speech

[4] Peloza alleges the school district ordered him to refrain from discussing his religious beliefs with students during "instructional time," and to tell any students who attempted to initiate such conversations with him to consult their parents or clergy. He claims the school district, in the following official reprimand, defined "instructional time" as any time the students are on campus, including lunch break and the time before, between, and after classes:

You are hereby directed to refrain from any attempt to convert students to Christianity or initiating conversations about your religious beliefs during instructional time, which the District believes includes any time students are required to be on campus as well as the time students immediately arrive for the purposes of attending school for instruction, lunch time, and the time immediately prior to students' departure after the instructional day. . . .

While at the high school, whether he is in the classroom or outside of it during contract time, Peloza is not just any ordinary citizen. He is a teacher. He is one of those especially respected persons chosen to teach in the high school's classroom. He is clothed with the mantle of one who imparts knowledge and wisdom. His expressions of opinion are all the more believable because he is a teacher. The likelihood of high school students equating his views with those of the school is substantial. To permit him to discuss his religious beliefs with students during school time on school grounds would violate the Establishment Clause of the First Amendment. Such speech would not have a secular purpose, would have the primary effect of advancing religion, and would entangle the school with religion. In sum, it would flunk all three parts of the test articulated in *Lemon V. Kurtzman,*–403 U.S. 602, 91 S.Ct. 2105, 29 L.Ed.2d 745 (1971). See *Roberts V. Madigan*, 921 F.2d 1047, 1056–58 (10th Cir.1990) (teacher could be prohibited from reading Bible during silent reading period, and from stocking two books on Christianity on shelves, because these things could leave students with the impression that Christianity was officially sanctioned), cert. denied, -U.S. -, 112 S.Ct. 3025,120 L.Ed.2d 896 (1992).

The district court did not err in dismissing the part of Peloza's section 1983 claim that was predicated on an alleged violation of his right to free speech under the First Amendment. . . .

II. The Section 1985(3) Claim

In support of his claim under 42 U.S.C. §1985(3), Peloza alleges in his complaint that the defendants conspired to deprive him of equal protection of the laws under the Fourteenth Amendment; free speech under the First and Fourteenth Amendments; life, liberty or property without due process of law under the Fifth and Fourteenth Amendments; and the free exercise of his religious beliefs under the First and Fourteenth Amendments. In addition, he alleges the defendants violated his rights under the Establishment Clause of the First and Fourteenth Amendments. He alleges that the defendants engaged in this conspiracy pursuant to their class-based animus against practicing Christians.*(7)*

As we stated previously, Peloza's allegations are insufficient to support a claim based on a violation of his constitutional rights of free speech and due process. Accordingly, his allegations of a conspiracy to violate these constitutional rights do not state a claim. See *Great American Fed. S & L Ass'n V. Novotny*, 442 U.S. 366, 372, 99 S.Ct. 2345, 2349, 60 L.Ed.2d 957 (1979) ("Section 1985(3) provides no substantive rights itself; it merely provides a remedy for violation of the rights it designates").

Because Peloza failed to allege a conspiracy to do something that would violate his free speech or due process rights, or his rights under the Establishment Clause, his section 1985(3) claim predicated on a violation of these rights falls. We do not decide whether free speech, due process rights, or Establishment Clause rights, fall within the protection of section 1985(3).*(8)*

III. State Law Claims

Peloza's state law claims were pendent to his federal claims and were dismissed for lack of jurisdiction when the district court dismissed all the federal claims. We affirm their dismissal. . . .

V. CONCLUSION

The district court correctly dismissed Peloza's section 1983 claim based on allegations of a violation of his constitutional rights under the Establishment Clause and his rights to free speech and due process. He failed to allege sufficient facts to state a violation of these rights. The district court also correctly dismissed Peloza's claim under 42 U.S.C. § 1985(3), because he failed to allege facts sufficient to state a violation of those rights; assuming, without deciding, that they fall within the protection of section 1985(3).

We affirm the dismissal of the complaint. We reverse the district court's award of attorney fees to the defendants.

The parties shall bear their own costs on appeal.

AFFIRMED IN PART; REVERSED IN PART.

FREILER V. TANGIPAHOA PARISH BOARD OF EDUCATION

Freiler v. Tangipahoa Parish Board of Education *began in 1994 when the Tangipahoa [Louisiana] Parish Board of Education passed a resolution requiring teachers who discuss evolution in their classes to preface their comments with an oral dis-claimer stating that evolution is not intended to influence students' thinking about the biblical version of creationism. A few months later, parents of some of the school's children challenged the law as being unconstitutional. In 2000, the case reached the U.S. Supreme Court, which let an earlier court's decision stand. That decision dis-cusses oral disclaimers, "intelligent design," and "creation science."*

REVISED—AUGUST 19, 1999
IN THE UNITED STATES COURT OF APPEALS
FOR THE FIFTH CIRCUIT
No. 97–30879 & No. 98–30132

HERB FREILER; SAM SMITH, Individually and in his capacity as Adminis-trator of the Estate of his minor child Steven Smith; JOHN JONES,

Plaintiffs-Appellees, v. TANGIPAHOA PARISH BOARD OF EDUCATION; E. F. BAILEY; ROBERT CAVES; MAXINE DIXON; LEROY HART; RUTH WATSON; DONNIE WILLIAMS, SR.; ART ZIESKE, Individually and in their capacities as members of the School Board; TED CA-SON, Individually and in his capacity as Superintendent of Schools,

Defendants-Appellants.

Appeal from the United States District Court for the Eastern District of Louisiana

August 13, 1999

Before KING, Chief Judge, and POLITZ and BENAVIDES, Circuit Judges.

BENAVIDES, Circuit Judge:

Parents of children in the Tangipahoa Parish Public Schools brought this suit to enjoin their school board from mandating that a disclaimer be read immediately before the teaching of evolution in all elementary and secondary classes. The district court held that the disclaimer constituted an establishment of religion in violation of the First Amendment. We affirm.

I.

The teaching of evolution has created controversy for many years in the Tangi-pahoa Parish Public Schools ("TPPS"). Following a failed attempt to introduce cre-ation science into the Tangipahoa curriculum as a legitimate scientific alternative to evolution, the Tangipahoa Parish Board of Education ("School Board" or "Board") adopted a resolution disclaiming the endorsement of evolution.(1) The resolution, which passed by a 5–4 vote of the School Board on April 19, 1994, reads:

Whenever, in classes of elementary or high school, the scientific theory of evolu-tion is to be presented, whether from textbook, workbook, pamphlet, other written material, or oral presentation, the following statement shall be quoted immediately before the unit of study begins as a disclaimer from endorsement of such theory.

It is hereby recognized by the Tangipahoa Board of Education, that the lesson to be presented, regarding the origin of life and matter, is known as the Scientific Theory of Evolution and should be presented to inform students of the scientific concept and not intended to influence or dissuade the Biblical version of Creation or any other concept.

It is further recognized by the Board of Education that it is the basic right and privilege of each student to form his/her own opinion and maintain beliefs taught by parents on this very important matter of the origin of life and matter. Students are urged to exercise critical thinking and gather all information possible and closely examine each alternative toward forming an opinion.

Preceding the adoption of the resolution, School Board members and parents who were present at the April 19, 1994, meeting discussed the language of the disclaimer. In particular, debate centered on the inclusion of the phrase "Biblical version of Creation." A School Board member, Logan Guess, voiced concerns that the reference to the Bible excluded non-Christian viewpoints from the disclaimer. He argued that, even though the disclaimer also included the phrase "or any other concept," School Board members were concerned only with declining to endorse evolution because of its inconsistency with the Biblical version of creation. Bailey, the board member who proposed the disclaimer, justified including the phrase, arguing that because "there are two basic concepts out there" (presumably creation science and evolution), and because he believed that "perhaps 95 percent" of the community "fall into the category of believing [in] divine creation," the Board should not "shy away, or hide away from saying that this is not to dissuade from the Biblical version." In his closing remarks immediately before the Board voted to adopt the disclaimer, Bailey further suggested that evolution theory as taught in science class should not be confused with fact and that the School Board should explicitly decline to endorse evolution theory because of its inconsistency with the faith of the larger community.

On November 7, 1994, approximately seven months after the resolution passed, several parents of children in the TPPS brought suit in the U.S. District Court for the Eastern District of Louisiana, challenging the validity of the disclaimer under provisions in the United States and Louisiana constitutions barring laws "respecting an establishment of religion."(2) U.S. Const. amends., I, XIV; La. Const. art. I, sec. 8. The district court concluded that the resolution was devoid of secular purpose and therefore ran afoul of the first prong of the three-part test of *Lemon v. Kurtzman*, 403 U.S. 602, 612–13 (1971). In reaching this conclusion, the district court discredited the School Board's assertion that its secular purpose in adopting the disclaimer was to promote critical thinking and information gathering by students on the subject of the origin of life. The court noted that School Board members did not mention this purported purpose during the adoption debate and that the Tangipahoa Parish Public Schools already encouraged students to think critically about all issues before the adoption of the disclaimer. The district court found that the statements made by School Board members both during the adoption debate and while testifying at trial revealed that the disclaimer, in fact, had a religious purpose—i.e., to satisfy the religious concerns of the majority that the teaching of evolution in public school contradicted lessons taught in Sunday school. Accordingly, the court held the resolution invalid under the federal and state constitutions and enjoined the reading of the disclaimer. The School Board and the named individual defendants then brought this appeal.

II.

The sole issue for our resolution is whether the specific disclaimer adopted by the Tangipahoa Parish Board of Education contravenes the First Amendment. We limit our analysis to the precise language of the disclaimer and the context in which it was adopted. We do not confront the broader issue of whether the reading of any disclaimer before the teaching of evolution would amount to an unconstitutional establishment of religion.

States and their duly authorized boards of education have the right to prescribe the academic curricula of their public school systems. Courts therefore must exercise great "care and restraint" when called upon to intervene in the operation of public schools. *Epperson v. Arkansas*, 393 U.S. 97, 104, 89 S. Ct. 266, 270 (1968). Given, however, that the "vigilant protection of constitutional freedoms" is nowhere more vital than in American public education, *id.*, 89 S. Ct. at 270, the right to prescribe public school curriculum must of necessity be limited in scope. States may not require that teaching and learning be tailored to the principles or prohibitions of any religious sect or dogma. *See id.* at 106, 89 S. Ct. at 271. . . .

III.

. . .We find that the contested disclaimer does not further the first articulated objective of encouraging informed freedom of belief or critical thinking by students. Even though the final sentence of the disclaimer urges students "to exercise critical thinking and gather all information possible and closely examine each alternative toward forming an opinion," we find that the disclaimer as a whole furthers a contrary purpose, namely the protection and maintenance of a particular religious viewpoint. In the first paragraph to be read to school children, the Tangipahoa Board of Education declares that the "Scientific Theory of Evolution . . . should be presented to inform students of the scientific concept" but that such teaching is "not intended to influence or dissuade the Biblical version of Creation or any other concept." From this, school children hear that evolution as taught in the classroom need not affect what they already know. Such a message is contrary to an intent to encourage critical thinking, which requires that students approach new concepts with an open mind and a willingness to alter and shift existing viewpoints. This conclusion is even more inescapable when the message of the first paragraph is coupled with the statement in the last that it is "the basic right and privilege of each student to . . . maintain beliefs taught by parents on [the] . . . matter of the origin of life. . . ." We, therefore, find that the disclaimer as a whole does not serve to encourage critical thinking and that the School Board's first articulated purpose is a sham.

We find that the disclaimer does further the second and third purposes articulated by the School Board. The disclaimer explicitly acknowledges the existence of at least one alternative theory for the origin of life, i.e., the Biblical version of creation. Additionally, the disclaimer reminds school children that they can rightly maintain beliefs taught by their parents on the subject of the origin of life. We have no doubt that the disclaimer will further its second and third avowed objectives of disclaiming any orthodoxy of belief that could be implied from the exclusive place of evolution in the public school curriculum and reducing student/parent offense caused by the teaching of evolution. Accordingly, we conclude that these two purposes are sincere. . . .

B.

. . . the School Board argues that the contested disclaimer's primary effect is "to communicate to students that they are free to form their own opinions or maintain beliefs taught by parents concerning the origin of life and matter." According to the School Board, the disclaimer advances freedom of thought, as well as sensitivity to, and tolerance for, diverse beliefs in a pluralistic society. We disagree.

. . . After careful consideration of the oral arguments, the briefs, the record on appeal, and the language of the disclaimer, we conclude that the primary effect of the disclaimer is to protect and maintain a particular religious viewpoint, namely belief in the Biblical version of creation. In reaching this conclusion, we rely on the interplay of three factors: (1) the juxtaposition of the disavowal of endorsement of evolution with an urging that students contemplate alternative theories of the origin of life; (2) the reminder that students have the right to maintain beliefs taught by their parents regarding the origin of life; and (3) the "Biblical version of Creation" as the only alternative theory explicitly referenced in the disclaimer.

We note that the term "disclaimer," as used by the School Board to describe the passage to be read to students before lessons on evolution, is not wholly accurate. Beyond merely "disclaiming" endorsement of evolution, the two paragraph passage urges students to take action—to "exercise critical thinking and gather all information possible and closely examine each alternative" to evolution.*(3)* The disclaimer, taken as a whole, encourages students to read and meditate upon religion in general and the "Biblical version of Creation" in particular.*(4)*

Although it is not per se unconstitutional to introduce religion or religious concepts during school hours, there is a fundamental difference between introducing religion and religious concepts in "an appropriate study of history, civilization, ethics, comparative religion, or the like" and the reading of the School Board-mandated disclaimer now before us. *Stone v. Graham*, 449 U.S. 39, 42, 101 S. Ct. 192, 194 (1980). The TPPS disclaimer*(5)* does not encourage students to think about religion in order to provide context for a political controversy studied in a history class, *see, e.g., Aguillard*, 482 U.S. at 607 n.8, 107 S. Ct. at 2590 n.8 (Powell, J., concurring) ("For example, the political controversies in Northern Ireland, the Middle East, and India cannot be understood properly without reference to the underlying religious beliefs and the conflicts they tend to generate."), or to promote understanding of different religions, *see, e.g., School District of Abington v. Schempp*, 374 U.S. 203, 225, 83 S. Ct. 1560, 1573 (1963) ("[I]t might well be said that one's education is not complete without a study of comparative religion or the history of religion and its relationship to the advancement of civilization."). Instead, the disclaimer—including the directive to "exercise critical thinking" in the second paragraph, together with the explicit reference to the "Biblical version of Creation" in the first paragraph—urges students to think about religious theories of "the origin of life and matter" as an *alternative* to evolution, the State-mandated curriculum. . . .

The benefit to religion conferred by the reading of the Tangipahoa disclaimer is more than indirect, remote, or incidental. As such, we conclude that the disclaimer impermissibly advances religion, thereby violating the second prong of the *Lemon* test as well as the endorsement test.

VI.

For the foregoing reasons, we affirm the district court's ruling that the disclaimer violates the First Amendment and the district court's award of attorneys' fees to Appellee Freiler.

AFFIRMED.

1. The passage of the disclaimer was not the first action by the School Board concerning the teaching of evolution. In December 1993, a member of the School Board proposed a *Policy on the Inclusion of Religious Material and Discussions on Religion in the Curriculum and in Student Activities* ("Policy"). That same member later proposed a *Revised Draft of Policy* ("Revised Policy"). These policies would have allowed the teaching of alternative theories of the origin of mankind, including Creation science. Even though it was defeated in Committee, the Revised Policy was discussed at a March 1994 School Board meeting. During that meeting, the Board rejected two items in the Revised Policy concerning the study of creation science and a graduation ceremony prayer.

The Board passed four other items included in the Revised Policy. Those items provided that (1) no religious belief or non-belief should be promoted or disparaged by the school system; (2) religious materials may be included in secular education (e.g., literature, art, humanities, etc.); (3) artistic expressions (e.g., music, art, etc.) could have religious themes if they were presented objectively; and (4) students could distribute religiously oriented materials as long as students followed the school's rules pertaining to content-neutral time, place, and manner restrictions.

2. The First Amendment of the United States Constitution in relevant part provides: "Congress shall make no law respecting an establishment of religion or prohibiting the free exercise thereof. . . ." This prohibition is applicable to the states through the Fourteenth Amendment. *See Stone v. Graham*, 449 U.S. 39, 41 n. 2, 101 S. Ct. 192, 193 n. 2 (1980); *School District of Abington v. Schempp*, 374 U.S. 203, 215–16, 83 S. Ct. 1560, 1567–68 (1963).

3. In passing on the constitutionality of the contested disclaimer, we consider the disclaimer as a whole. Accordingly, we do not express an opinion as to whether the first paragraph standing alone impermissibly advances religion.

4. The School Board asserts that the reference to the "Biblical version of Creation" is merely illustrative, affording meaning to the phrase "other concepts." The School Board's use of a religious concept as the only illustration of an "other concept[]," however, supports our conclusion that the disclaimer impermissibly advances religion. *Cf. Ingebretsen v. Jackson Public School District*, 88 F.3d 274, 279 (5th Cir. 1996) (explaining that a government measure advances religion when it "gives a preferential, exceptional benefit to religion [or a particular form of religion] that it does not extend to anything else"). We also note that the record does not comport with the School Board's characterization of its reason for including "Biblical version of Creation" in the disclaimer. When the School Board debated the propriety of the proposed disclaimer, a member suggested deleting the reference to the Biblical version of Creation. The Board ultimately rejected that suggestion, apparently not because doing so might confuse students who needed an illustrative reference, but because doing so would, in the words of the disclaimer's sponsor, "gut . . . the basic message of the [disclaimer]."

5. Despite our conclusion that the statement to be read student does more than "disclaim" evolution, we will continue to refer to the entire statement as a disclaimer for purposes of convenience.

Falconer, Hugh, 158
Falwell, Jerry, 63, 77 (n 9), 79, 94
(n 3), **122–123,** 241
Family Life, America, and God
(FLAG), 81, 242, 243
Faubus, Orval, 47, 47 (photo), 50, 60
(n 18), **123**
Ferguson, Miriam A. ("Ma"), 32, 40 (n
37), **123,** 191
Ferguson, W. F., 14, 40 (n 37), **123**
*A Few, and New Observations, Upon
the Book of Genesis* (Lightfoot),
131–132, 152
The Finality of Higher Criticism
(Riley), 169
First Amendment. *See under*
Constitutional issues
*First Lessons in Botany and Vegetable
Physiology* (Gray), 5 (n 1), 125
First Principles (Spencer), 162
Fisher, Larry, 80–81, **123,** 239
Fisher, Ronald A., 118, **123,** 200, 203
FitzRoy, Robert, **123**
FLAG (Family Life, America, and
God), 81, 242, 243
Flood geology, 135, 138–139
Florida, teaching of evolution in, 241.
See also Antievolution legislation;
Balanced treatment argument and
legislation
Footprints in Stone (film), 251
Footprints of God (Brown), 116
Ford, Arch, 48
Ford, John, 65
Fortas, Abe, 56, 61 (n 20), 77 (n 10),
123–124
Foundation for Thought and Ethics,
111 (n 1)
Franklin, Rosalind, 206
Free speech rights, 10, 72, 257, 267
Freiler, Herb, 106, **124,** 261
*Freiler v. Tangipahoa Board of
Education,* 106–107, 124, 261,
264, 265–267
documents, 361–366
Fundamentalism, 2, 109
and defense strategy in Scopes trial,
17
and opposition to evolution theory in
early 1920s, 4–5, 10
origin of term, 5 (n 2), 169
The Fundamentalist (magazine), 172,
191
The Fundamentals (booklets), 145, 169
Fundamentals of Geology (Price), 169
Gabler, Melvin and Norma, 33, **124,**
213, 214, 220–221, 231, 249

Galbreath, Charles, 218
Galileo, 118–119, **124,** 151, 152, 192,
257
Gee, Thomas, 101
Geisler, Norman, 90–91
Genes, Genesis, and Evolution (Klotz),
206–207
Genesis Act (Tennessee), 72–73, 76
(n 5), 229–230, 232, 233–234
*The Genesis Flood: The Biblical Record
and Its Scientific Implications*
(Morris and Whitcomb), 6 (n 3),
73, 139, 147, 206, 208, 211
*The Genetical Theory of Natural
Selection* (R. Fisher), 123, 200
Genetics and the Origin of Species
(Dobzhansky), 121, 150, 201,
202, 204
George (magazine), 264
Georgia, teaching of evolution in, 3,
29, 73, 194, 230, 237, 239. *See
also* Balanced treatment argument
and legislation
Gish, Duane T., 93, 95 (n 11), 97,
124, 124 (photo), 223, 226, 227,
228–229, 236, 259
God or Gorilla (Martin), 15
God's Masterpiece—Man's Body
(Brown), 116
*Good Science, Bad Science: Teaching
Evolution in the States* (Lerner),
268
Gore, John J., 185
Gosse, Philip H., **125**
Gould, Stephen Jay, 122, **125,** 225,
234, 237, 238, 240, 262
*Grand Canyon: Monument to
Catastrophe* (Austin), 95 (n 14)
Graves, Bill, 263
Gray, Asa, 2, 5 (n 1), **125,** 125
(photo), 149, 161, 162, 164,
166
"Great Chain of Being," 114
Greater Little Rock Evangelical
Fellowship, 80, 81, 87, 242
Green, Grafton, 25, 197
Griffith, Fred, 198
Grobman, Arnold B., 221
Grose, Vernon, 65, **125,** 221, 227
Guste, William, 101, 250
Guyot, Arnold, **125–126**

Haeckel, Ernst H., **126**
Haggard, A. P., 184
Haggard, Wallace, 36 (n 8), **126,** 183,
188
Haldane, John B. S., 118, **126,** 203

McKenzie, J. Gordon, 36 (n 8), **134,** 188

McLaughlin, Roy, 244

McLean, Bill, 94 (n 2), **134**

McLean v. Arkansas Board of Education, 79–93, 97, 99, 110, 118, 122, 123, 127, 134, 137, 148, 190, 242, 245–247, 252

  consequences, 92–93, 240, 249

  decision by Judge Overton, 86–92, 239, 246

  documents, 305–323

  media coverage, 85

  plaintiffs' strategy, 91

McPherson, Aimee Semple, 3, **134**

McVey, Frank, 4, **134,** 175

McWherter, Ned Ray, 72, 229, 248–249

The Mechanism of Mendelian Heredity (Morgan), 135, 170

The Menace of Modernism (Riley), 170

Mencken, H. L., 13, 15, 18, 19, 22, 27, 35, 37 (n 14), **134–135,** 187, 188, 207

Mendel, Gregor, **135,** 146, 163, 168

Metcalf, Maynard, 38 (n 19), 187

Methodists, Southern, 31

  opposition to antievolution laws, 29, 196

Methods of Study in Natural History (Agassiz), 165

Metzger, Oren, 190

Michigan, teaching of evolution in, 110. *See also under* Antievolution legislation; Balanced treatment argument and legislation

Middle Tennessee State University, 209

Miller, Stanley, 206

Mills, L. N., 32

Milner, Lucile, 183

Mims, Forrest M., III, 254

Mindy the Monkey, 12

Minnesota, teaching of evolution in, 107–108, 196, 263, 270. *See also under* Antievolution legislation

Minor, Virginia, 47, 48, **135**

Miracles of Science (Brown), 116

"The Missing Link," 10

Mississippi, teaching of evolution in, 28–29, 39 (n 32), 67–68, 86, 180, 193, 194. *See also under* Antievolution legislation

Missouri, equal time for teaching creationism in, 76. *See also under* Antievolution legislation

Mixter, Russell, 208

Modern Biology (Otto and Towle), 47,

55, 60 (n 9)

The Monkey Business: A Scientist Looks at Creationism (Eldredge), 246

"Monkey Trial." *See* Scopes trial

Moody Bible Institute Monthly, 28, 203

Moon, Truman J., 13–14, 40 (n 37), 44, 59 (n 3), 172

Moore, Aubrey, 212

Moore, John N., **135,** 229

Moore, Roy S., 268

Moral Majority, 77 (n 9), 80, 123, 242, 243, 244

Morgan, Harcourt A., 182

Morgan, Howard, **135**

Morgan, Thomas Hunt, 121, **135,** 170, 203

Mormons, 212

Morowitz, Harold, 91

Morris, Henry, 6 (n 4), 63, 67, 70–71, 73, 74, 82, 90, 93, 95–96 (nn 11, 14), **135–136,** 136 (photo), 141, 147, 205, 206, 208, 211, 212, 216–217, 221–222, 226, 228, 230–233, 235, 241, 248, 249–250, 251, 253, 258, 261, 270

Morris, John, 77 (n 9), 254

Morrison, Cameron, 178

Moyer, Wayne, 94 (n 5), 240

Mozert v. Hawkins, 251

Muller, Hermann, 33, 135, 208, 209

Murray, John, 158, 160

Murray, Madeline, 77 (n 10)

NABT. *See* National Association of Biology Teachers

Nashville Banner, 20

Nashville Tennessean, 191

National Academy of Sciences, 64, 95 (n 9), 97, 104 (n 2), 225, 245, 254, 262, 263, 268

National Association of Bible Teachers, 40 (n 36)

National Association of Biology Teachers (NABT), 64, 72, 76 (n 6), 83, 94 (n 2), 225–226, 227, 231, 232, 245

National Center for Science Education, 241, 261

National Defense Education Act, 33

National Education Association, 185, 198, 218

National Heritage Academies, 265

National Research Council, 260, 264

National School Board Association, 270

Protestants, 2. *See also specific denominations*

"The Psychology of the Anti-Evolutionist" (Mather), 195

Public opinion, surveys on evolution and creationism, 2, 84, 240, 241, 255, 260, 261, 262, 266

Public schools. *See* Teaching of creationism; Teaching of evolution

Punctuated equilibrium, 122, 125

Purcell, Joe, 56

Q.E.D.: Or, New Light on the Doctrine of Creation (Price), 170–171

Rach, J. R., 175

Rafferty, Max, 65, 214, 217, 221

Rappleyea, George, 9–10, 11 (photo), 18, 23, 24, 35, 39 (n 25), 40 (n 40), **139,** 183, 184, 187, 194

Raulston, John Tate, 14, 17–18, 20, 20 (photo), 21, 22, 26, 30, 36 (nn 5, 8), 37 (n 12), **139,** 143, 184, 186, 187

Ray, John, **139,** 152

Read Your Bible sign, 12, 21

Reagan, Ronald, 64, 65, 79, 104 (n 6), 221, 222, 238

Reason in the Balance (Johnson), 259

Redi, Francesco, 152

Reece, Raleigh, 40 (n 40), **139**

Reed, Murray O., 50, 52, 53, 54, 60 (n 14), **140,** 217, 219

Rehnquist, William H., 103

Religion and Science Association, 201

Religious right. *See* Fundamentalism

The Remarkable Birth of Planet Earth (Morris), 226, 241

Republican Party, 110, 254, 260

Research Science Bureau, 31, 141, 172

Researches on Fossil Bones (Cuvier), 119

Rhea County Courthouse, 187

Rice, Edward L., **140,** 182, 192

Riddle, Oscar, **140,** 201, 202, 209

Riles, Wilson, 225

Riley, William Bell, 3, 30, **140,** 167–172, 177, 178, 183, 196

Rimmer, Harry, 116, **140–141,** 169, 172

Robertson, Pat, 94 (n 3), 108, **141,** 244, 251, 263

Robinson, Fred E., 9, 19, **141**

Rogers, Will, 35

Rosensohn, Samuel, 24

Rotenberry, Astor L., 44, 59 (n 1), **141,** 195, 197, 198

Rozzell, Forrest, 48, 60 (n 12), **141,** 216

Santorum, Rick, 271

Scalia, Antonin, 101, 104

Schleiden, Mathias, 156–157

Schoenfeld, Nathan, 46, 215

School District of Abington Township v. Schempp, 213, 214

Schwann, Theodor, 157

Science

    as defined in decision in *McLean v. Arkansas Board of Education,* 88–92, 94–95 (n 9)

    promotion of science education during Cold War, 208, 221

    scientific literacy, 252

Science (magazine), 114

"Science and Creation Series" (textbooks), 73

Science and Creationism (National Academy of Sciences), 254

Science League of America, 143, 179, 195

The Science of Power (Kidd), 129, 171

Science, Scripture, and the Young Earth (ICR), 95 (n 14)

Scientific American (magazine), 254, 263

Scientific creationism. *See* Creation science

Scientific Creationism (Morris), 71, 232

Scientific Creationism Handbook #10 (Gabler), 249

The Scientific Framework for California Public Schools, 64–67, 215, 221, 237, 240, 243

Scofield, Cyrus I., **141–142**

The Scofield Reference Bible, 141–142, 169

Scopes, John Thomas, 7, 11 (photo), 43

    and appeal of conviction for teaching evolution, 23, 25

    epitaph, 224

    life after trial and appeal, 33–34, 40–41 (n 41), 57, 58 (photo), 103, 123, 128, 133, 134, 135, 136, **142,** 143, 168, 171, 183, 184, 187, 188 (photo), 190, 194, 210, 212, 215, 220, 223, 224 (photo). *See also* Scopes trial

    on trial for teaching evolution, 14, 15, 16, 17, 18, 19, 20, 22, 27–28, 35 (n 1), 36 (n 6), 37 (nn 11, 13), 38 (n 20)